SIX PLAYS
OF
CLIFFORD
ODETS

SIX PLAYS
OF
CLIFFORD
ODETS

WITH A PREFACE BY
THE AUTHOR

With an Introduction
by Harold Clurman

GROVE PRESS, INC.
NEW YORK

CONTENTS

FOR PEARL GEISINGER,
MY MOTHER

PREFACE

by Clifford Odets

At the ripe age of thirty-three (to the day!) I have the pleasure of writing a few prefatory words to a collection of my first six plays. However, the talent represented in these plays is essentially synthetic, not analytic; and for this reason it is not my intention to do as Oscar Wilde said of a friend, "He has nothing to say and he says it." My belief, in other words, is that the plays will say whatever is to be said; most of them have bones in them and will stand up unsupported.

Notwithstanding, a writer must be permitted to express preferences in terms of his own work. *Paradise Lost,* poorly received as a practical theatre work, remains my favorite play in this group. While not unmindful of its harsh and ungracious form, I must be permitted to say that our modern audiences, critics included, still must have their plays, like salt-water taffy, cut to fit the mouth. *Paradise Lost* shares with *Rocket to the Moon* a depth of perception, a web of sensory impressions and a level of both personal and social experience not allotted to the other plays here. True, at least two of the other remaining four plays are more *immediately useful,* but my choice still stands.

Now, since we are on the subject, much of my concern during the past years has been with fashioning a play immediately and dynamically useful and yet as psychologically profound as my present years and experience will permit. To some extent this pressing problem (pressing since we are living in a time when new art works should shoot bullets) has been most closely approached in a new play not included in this volume, *The Silent Partner.* Rightfully that play belongs in this collection in the place of *Rocket to the Moon,* for of the two it was conceived and written first. Revisions have changed it, but in terms of inner and outer progression it belongs among the first six, part and parcel of a "first-period" group. Theatre exigencies being what they are . . .

When these plays were written it was almost impossible for me to do more or differently with them. Much of them was felt, conceived and written out of a personal need. Now after the fact, after the melancholy facts, the writer is a better craftsman, his horizon lifting wider. That temptation to improve upon these plays is often present. Nevertheless, none has been rewritten in part or whole: let them stand, crudities and all, as a small parade of a young talent discovering and shaping itself. If you have acquired by now the distressing sense that I am situating myself historically, correct! Talent should be respected.

Two more items remain to be mentioned. I have insisted on retaining, in the form of an appendix, the original introductions of these plays. This insistence stems from a conviction that two of these introductions by Harold Clurman, Group Theatre Director and constant good friend, are among the first-class theatre writing of our time.

Lastly, a pair of acknowledgments. Fortunate is the writer in this strange and inimical world who finds a devoted helpful obstetrician for births and beginnings. Harold Clurman and I have stood in this relationship, groaning mortal and devoted Persian surgeon. This is not to forget the Group Theatre actors and actresses, all dear and good friends, who have given such inspired performances of all these plays.

New York,
July 18, 1939

INTRODUCTION

by Harold Clurman

"We cancel our experience. This is an American habit," Leo Gordon in Odets's *Paradise Lost,* ruminates. It is an American habit —nowhere more prevalent than in our theater. Because Odets is categorized as the signal playwright of the thirties, it is fatuously simple to set him down, as some have done, as "dated."

All drama is dated: it is always a product of a particular moment. We know very little about art if we mistake the surface or specific material of a play, novel, or painting for its true subject, its import or essential communication. We do not dismiss Homer's epic because wars are no longer engaged in over a beautiful girl!

The thirties were a million years ago: TV was just a rumor then, and gas cost twenty cents a gallon. It was the time of the Great Depression. In Odets's four 1935 plays, written when he was twenty-eight, there is as much enthusiasm as sadness. It was in many respects a hopeful time (". . . nothing to fear but fear itself."). The lyric afflatus which ends each of these plays is perhaps somewhat forced, an afterthought or wish, but the overall effect is youthfully energetic and rousing.

Waiting for Lefty is undoubtedly "dated" because it is a call for unionization among taxi drivers. The play, which may be said to be a dramatic broadside or poster, ends with a shout, "Strike, Strike, Strike!!!" But the audience which full-heartedly rose to the summons was not composed of taxi drivers nor of folk chiefly concerned with union politics. The strike they looked forward to was the day when life, as Odets puts it in *Awake and Sing!*, wouldn't "be printed on dollar bills."

The play's title springs out of the mouth of the prophet Isaiah, "Awake and sing, ye who dwell in the dust." In so far as Odets's model of a hopeful society in 1935 was the Soviet Union, his earliest plays are dated, but the basic theme, central to most of his work, is phrased, to begin with, in grandfather Jacob's observation in *Awake and Sing!:* "In my day the propaganda was for God. Now it's for success."

"It's trying to be a man," a whole, fully realized person, Odets repeatedly tells us, in a world in which Success—"your name in the papers," "fame and fortune"—is God. Because of it our America suffers "a profound dislocation." It is a perturbation of the soul which arises from the conflict between a native idealism and a worshipful materialism. It is given its most sharply dramatic and simplistically symbolic embodiment in *Golden Boy,* which opposes the fist to the fiddle. The expensive and luxurious auto here becomes an idol. "Those cars," the boy confesses, "are poison in my blood." Such metaphors—the fist and the fiddle, the car, etc.—are all too commonplace, even shabby, to represent the forces to tempt the young man's spirit. But they are conspicuously American, and Odets is indefeasibly American both in his dream of the America of the grade school history book—along with Emerson, Thoreau, Whitman—and in his blood-tie with the average guy in the street. (I remember Odets saying as we walked one Saturday night in 1940 on a dismally raffish thoroughfare, "There's not a person in this crowd in whom I do not find a part of myself.") Odets is literally a popular playwright, one close to the people, the most ordinary people. After the four 1935 plays, that is, after Odets has experienced what Willy Wax, the dance director in *Rocket to the Moon* refers to as the "painless perversion" of Hollywood, his plays turn troubled and somber, even as his skill becomes more assured. (There are suicides in *Golden Boy* and another in the 1949 *Big Knife.*) Still the idealism persists in the desperate yearning and seeking voiced by Lorna in *Golden Boy* and with childhood pathos by little Cleo in *Rocket,* who avows ". . . if there's roads, I'll take them. I'll go up all those roads till I find what I want. . . . Don't you think there's a world of gentle men and women? Must all men live afraid to laugh and sing? Can't we sing at work and love our work? It's too late getting to play at life, I want to *live* it. Something has to feel real to me. . . . I'm looking for a whole full world. . . ." Less innocently perhaps, the young of the fifties and sixties were clamoring for the same things—though they appear to be silent now.

Odets was a headlong romantic. The baldest expression of his romanticism was in *Till the Day I Die,* a play he wrote as a curtain raiser to *Waiting for Lefty* when the Group Theater was to move the latter play "uptown." One of the first anti-Nazi plays to be produced on

Broadway, *Till the Day I Die* with its glamorization of underground conspiratorial struggle on behalf of a righteous cause reminds me that in his boyhood, Odets's favorite book was *Les Misérables,* and I wouldn't be surprised if *The Three Musketeers* had been on the same shelf.

Odets's romanticism at its height gushes with joy; in its decline it turns to an aching melancholy. Both spring from a single source of conviction: "Life should have some dignity." It is the spirit of the romantic Artist raising the standard of his self-appointed mission to redeem humanity. Odets might have echoed Victor Hugo when he declared, "You say the poet is in the sky; so is lightning!" Odets's words ring out.

This brings us to the matter of Odets's writing. It is an ungrammatical jargon—and constantly lyric. It is composed of words heard on the street, in drugstores, bars, sports arenas, and rough restaurants. (Odets used to cut out newspaper photos of faces to help him flesh the characters who might speak his language.) It is the speech of New York; half-educated Jews, Italians, Irish, transformed into something new-minted, individual, and unique. Above all it makes for crackling theater dialogue—ask the actors! His dialogue is moving, even thrilling, and very often hilarious. It is not "English"; in a sense it is not "realistic" at all. It is *"Odets"*; and also incontrovertibly ours in unguarded moments. Listen: "I'm so nervous, look, I weighed myself twice in the subway." "That sort of life [the good life] ain't for the dogs which is us. Christ, Baby! I got like thunder in my chest when we're together. God damnit, it's trying to be a man on the earth." "The Clancy family is growing nuts." "You're so wrong I ain't laughing." "The big-shot money men want us like that . . . highly insulting us—." "I'm piling up a fortune. Why? To be the richest man in the cemetery?" "Ask yourself a pertinent remark." What does "it needs a new world" mean? We know very well what it means; we know with more intimacy than if it were correctly stated.

George Jean Nathan, whose evaluation of Odets shifted back and forth, noted one undeniable excellence. Odets wrote some of the finest love scenes to be found in American drama. An all-enveloping warmth, love in its broadest sense, is a constant in all Odets's writing, the very root of his talent. It is there in tumultuous harangues, in his denunciations and his murmurs. It is by turns hot and tender. Sometimes it sounds in whimpers. It is present as much in the scenes between grandfather and grandson in *Awake* as in those of Joe and

Lorna in *Golden Boy*. It is touchingly wry in *Rocket*. This explains why these scenes are chosen by so many actors for auditions and classwork.

In a peculiarly old-fashioned way, Odets is every inch a theater person: hence his enormous effectiveness. His first experience in the theater was an actor in stock companies, of which such barnstorming chestnuts as *Ten Nights in a Barroom* were a staple of the repertoire. George M. Cohan, who couldn't have sympathized in the slightest degree with Odets's "ideology," immediately warmed to this theatrical facility. *Golden Boy* is not the best of Odets's plays, but it tells its story with so much "punch" that audiences which miss or are indifferent to its point enjoy it thoroughly as a damned good show. And it is to be additionally noted that this play which reveals Odets not only in regard to his central preoccupation but to his personal problem (indeed, it provides an insight into the tragic aspects of his career) is often taken to be a prize fight melodrama just as *Lefty* by the unaware is set down as merely left-wing propaganda.

Odets understood his inner demon, which brought about the struggle of his temperament and conscience. He dramatized it in his last plays, *Clash by Night*, *The Country Girl*, *The Big Knife*, and *The Flowering Peach*. But he is also there in Lorna's description of Joe Bonaparte, the cockeyed golden boy, with his urge to power: "You're a miserable creature. You want your arm in *gelt* up to the elbow. You'll take fame so people won't laugh or scorn your face. You'll give your soul for those things. But every time you turn your back your little soul kicks you in the teeth. It don't give in so easy." Indeed it doesn't: when Joe, in training for a big bout, sees someone carrying a violin case, he turns pale and loses the fight he might easily have won.

His nature is not for fighting. He is a potential artist. "With music I'm never alone when I'm alone," he says. "Playing music . . . that's like saying 'I'm a man. I belong here. How do you do, World— good evening!' When I play music nothing is closed to me. I'm not afraid of people and what they say. There's no war in music. It's not like the streets. But when you leave your room . . . down in the streets it's war! Music can't help me there. . . . You can't get even with people by playing the fiddle. If music shot bullets I'd like it better. Artists and people like that are freaks today. . . ." There we have the bruise, the break in the inner personality. It leads us back to the central theme of which all Odets's plays are subtle variations. What crushes Odets's people—those who allow themselves to be crushed—is not simply the economic situation, the Depression, but the temper of the society as a whole, of which the Depression of the thirties was only an episode, a wounding symptom. It is our humanity which is in constant danger of being destroyed. That has not changed; we are still under mortal pressure of every sort, something we should be sharply reminded of in the present epoch of confusion, lethargy, "affluence," fear and trembling!

Rocket to the Moon is a modern love story. Its focus is slightly askew, because while Stark occupies the center of the stage, it is Cleo, the silly girl, as one critic called her, who is the crucial figure: she is in quest of love, of maturity in a society which devitalizes all but the exceptional person. She does not speak of a new social, economic, political order; hers is a universal plea for a fullness of life which she is too ignorant to define, but whose meaning we understand and whose feeling we share. That the play's "message" is conveyed in the tiny vessel of a "silly" dentist's secretary who speaks a Bronx-Broadway-pop magazine lingo is typical of Odets's entire work in its broadest connotations and individual artistry.

Rocket to the Moon, along with *Paradise Lost,* contains Odets's most brilliant writing. It is thoroughly alive in speech and characterization. Very few American playwrights, if any, have drawn so rich a gallery of portraits in secondary as well as major figures. To name a few: there is the mousey and darling fool, Myron, in *Awake and Sing!,* Sam Feinschreiber, the bamboozled and frightened immigrant in the same play, the mortified cynic, Moe Axelrod (ditto), the heartbroken and terrified racketeer, Kewpie, in *Paradise Lost,* and in the same roster, the morally abcessed Sam Katz. Then there is Siggie, the lovable lout in *Golden Boy.* And then too in *Paradise Lost* we find Gus, the shattered and absurd remnant of a former day, who, while he anticipates the coming war, touchingly recalls, in the manner of an old-time 1912 tune, "How beautiful the summer nights before the Big War." Especially memorable are such creations as the homosexual gunman, Eddie Fuselli, the golden boy's demonic "guardian" (one of the most understanding studies, according to such experts as Tom Dewey and J. Edgar Hoover, of a gangster) and Mister Prince, the majestic "clown" of *Rocket to the Moon,* and the wonderful waif, Cleo.

As late as 1970 Walter Kerr, relatively "conservative" in theater esthetics, was able to write, "There is scarcely a wrong line, a wrong gesture in Mister Odets' plays. Nothing has become transparent or cheaply crafted over the intervening years, because it was all thickness to begin with, writhing tissue, words of impulse. . . . Our heritage is better than we thought." I myself might not have gone so far, but on rereading the plays now, I am convinced that no American playwright since O'Neill has been more greatly gifted than Odets.

WAITING FOR LEFTY

CHARACTERS

FATT

JOE

EDNA

MILLER

FAYETTE

IRV

FLORRIE

SID

CLAYTON

AGATE KELLER

HENCHMAN

REILLY

DR. BARNES

DR. BENJAMIN

A MAN

WAITING FOR LEFTY

As the curtain goes up we see a bare stage. On it are sitting six or seven men in a semi-circle. Lolling against the proscenium down left is a young man chewing a toothpick: a gunman. A fat man of porcine appearance is talking directly to the audience. In other words he is the head of a union and the men ranged behind him are a committee of workers. They are now seated in interesting different attitudes and present a wide diversity of type, as we shall soon see. The fat man is hot and heavy under the collar, near the end of a long talk, but not too hot: he is well fed and confident. His name is HARRY FATT.

FATT: You're so wrong I ain't laughing. Any guy with eyes to read knows it. Look at the textile strike—out like lions and in like lambs. Take the San Francisco tie-up—starvation and broken heads. The steel boys wanted to walk out too, but they changed their minds. It's the trend of the times, that's what it is. All we workers got a good man behind us now. He's top man of the country—looking out for our interests—the man in the White House is the one I'm referrin' to. That's why the times ain't ripe for a strike. He's working day and night—

VOICE *(from the audience):* For who? *(The* GUNMAN *stirs himself.)*

FATT: For you! The records prove it. If this was the Hoover régime, would I say don't go out, boys? Not on your tintype! But things is different now. You read the papers as well as me. You know it. And that's why I'm against the strike. Because we gotta stand behind the man who's standin' behind us! The whole country——

ANOTHER VOICE: Is on the blink! *(The* GUNMAN *looks grave.)*

FATT: Stand up and show yourself, you damn red! Be a man, let's see what you look like! *(Waits in vain.)* Yellow from the word go! Red and yellow makes a dirty color, boys. I got my eyes on four or five of them in the union here. What the hell'll they do for you? Pull you out and run away when trouble starts. Give those birds a chance and they'll have your sisters and wives in the whore houses, like they done in Russia. They'll tear Christ off his bleeding cross. They'll wreck your homes and throw your babies in the river. You think that's bunk? Read the papers! Now listen, we can't stay here all night. I gave you the facts in the case. You boys got hot suppers to go to and——

ANOTHER VOICE: Says you!

GUNMAN: Sit down, Punk!

ANOTHER VOICE: Where's Lefty? *(Now this question is taken up by the others in unison.* FATT *pounds with gavel.)*

FATT: That's what I wanna know. Where's your pal, Lefty? You elected him chairman—where the hell did he disappear?

VOICES: We want Lefty! Lefty! Lefty!

FATT *(pounding):* What the hell is this—a circus? You got the committee here. This bunch of cowboys you elected. *(Pointing to man on extreme right end.)*

MAN: Benjamin.

FATT: Yeah, Doc Benjamin. *(Pointing to other men in circle in seated order):* Benjamin, Miller, Stein, Mitchell, Phillips, Keller. It ain't my fault Lefty took a run-out powder. If you guys—

A GOOD VOICE: What's the committee say?

OTHERS: The committee! Let's hear from the committee! (FATT *tries to quiet the crowd, but one of the seated men suddenly comes to the front. The* GUNMAN *moves over to center stage, but* FATT *says:)*

FATT: Sure, let him talk. Let's hear what the red boys gotta say! *(Various shouts are coming from the audience.* FATT *insolently goes back to his seat in the middle of the circle. He sits on his raised platform and relights his cigar. The* GUNMAN *goes back to his post.* JOE, *the new speaker, raises his hand for quiet. Gets it quickly. He is sore.)*

JOE: You boys know me. I ain't a red boy one bit! Here I'm carryin' a shrapnel that big I picked up in the war. And maybe I don't know it when it rains! Don't tell me red! You know what we are? The black and blue boys! We been kicked around so long we're black and blue from head to toes. But I guess anyone who says straight out he don't like it, he's a red boy to the leaders of the union. What's this crap about goin' home to hot suppers? I'm asking to your faces how many's got hot suppers to go home to? Anyone who's sure of his next meal, raise your hand! A certain gent sitting behind me can raise them both. But not in front here! And that's why we're talking strike—to get a living wage!

VOICE: Where's Lefty?

JOE: I honest to God don't know, but he didn't take no run-out powder. That Wop's got more guts than a slaughter house. Maybe a traffic jam got him, but he'll be here. But don't let this red stuff scare you. Unless fighting for a living scares you. We gotta make up our minds. My wife made up my mind last week, if you want the truth. It's plain as the nose on Sol Feinberg's face we need a strike. There's us comin' home every night—eight, ten hours on the cab. "God," the wife says, "eighty cents ain't money—don't buy beans almost. You're workin' for the company," she says to me, "Joe! you ain't workin' for me or the family no more!" She says to me, "If you don't start . . ."

I. JOE AND EDNA

The lights fade out and a white spot picks out the playing space within the space of seated men. The seated men are very dimly visible in the outer dark, but more prominent is FATT *smoking his cigar and often blowing the smoke in the lighted circle.*

A tired but attractive woman of thirty comes into the room, drying her hands on an apron. She stands there sullenly as JOE *comes in from the other side, home from work. For a moment they stand and look at each other in silence.*

JOE: Where's all the furniture, honey?

EDNA: They took it away. No installments paid.

JOE: When?

EDNA: Three o'clock.

JOE: They can't do that.

EDNA: Can't? They did it.

JOE: Why, the palookas, we paid three-quarters.

EDNA: The man said read the contract.

JOE: We must have signed a phoney. . . .

EDNA: It's a regular contract and you signed it.

JOE: Don't be so sour, Edna. . . . *(Tries to embrace her.)*

EDNA: Do it in the movies, Joe—they pay Clark Gable big money for it.

JOE: This is a helluva house to come home to. Take my word!

EDNA: Take MY word! Whose fault is it?

JOE: Must you start that stuff again?

EDNA: Maybe you'd like to talk about books?

JOE: I'd like to slap you in the mouth!

EDNA: No you won't.

JOE *(sheepishly):* Jeez, Edna, you get me sore some time. . . .

EDNA: But just look at me—I'm laughing all over!

JOE: Don't insult me. Can I help it if times are bad? What the hell do you want me to do, jump off a bridge or something?

EDNA: Don't yell. I just put the kids to bed so they won't know they missed a meal. If I don't have Emmy's shoes soled tomorrow, she can't go to school. In the meantime let her sleep.

JOE: Honey, I rode the wheels off the chariot today. I cruised around five hours without a call. It's conditions.

EDNA: Tell it to the A & P!

JOE: I booked two-twenty on the clock. A lady with a dog was lit . . . she gave me a quarter tip by mistake. If you'd only listen to me— we're rolling in wealth.

EDNA: Yeah? How much?

JOE: I had "coffee and—" in a beanery. *(Hands her silver coins.)* A buck four.

EDNA: The second month's rent is due tomorrow.

JOE: Don't look at me that way, Edna.

EDNA: I'm looking through you, not at you. . . . Everything was gonna be so ducky! A cottage by the waterfall, roses in Picardy. You're a four-star-bust! If you think I'm standing for it much longer, you're crazy as a bedbug.

JOE: I'd get another job if I could. There's no work—you know it.

EDNA: I only know we're at the bottom of the ocean.

JOE: What can I do?

EDNA: Who's the man in the family, you or me?

JOE: That's no answer. Get down to brass tacks. Christ, gimme a break, too! A coffee and java all day. I'm hungry, too, Babe. I'd work my fingers to the bone if—

EDNA: I'll open a can of salmon.

JOE: Not now. Tell me what to do!

EDNA: I'm not God!

JOE: Jeez, I wish I was a kid again and didn't have to think about the next minute.

EDNA: But you're not a kid and you do have to think about the next minute. You got two blondie kids sleeping in the next room. They need food and clothes. I'm not mentioning anything else—But we're stalled like a flivver in the snow. For five years I laid awake at night listening to my heart pound. For God's sake, do something, Joe, get wise. Maybe get your buddies together, maybe go on strike for better money. Poppa did it during the war and they won out. I'm turning into a sour old nag.

JOE (*defending himself*): Strikes don't work!

EDNA: Who told you?

JOE: Besides that means not a nickel a week while we're out. Then when it's over they don't take you back.

EDNA: Suppose they don't! What's to lose?

JOE: Well, we're averaging six-seven dollars a week now.

EDNA: That just pays for the rent.

JOE: That is something, Edna.

EDNA: It isn't. They'll push you down to three and four a week before you know it. Then you'll say, "That's somethin'," too!

JOE: There's too many cabs on the street, that's the whole damn trouble.

EDNA: Let the company worry about that, you big fool! If their cabs didn't make a profit, they'd take them off the streets. Or maybe you think they're in business just to pay Joe Mitchell's rent!

JOE: You don't know a-b-c, Edna.

EDNA: I know this—your boss is making suckers outa you boys every minute. Yes, and suckers out of all the wives and the poor innocent kids who'll grow up with crooked spines and sick bones. Sure, I see it in the papers, how good orange juice is for kids. But damnit our kids get colds one on top of the other. They look like little ghosts. Betty never saw a grapefruit. I took her to the store last week and she pointed to a stack of grapefruits. "What's that!" she said. My God, Joe—the world is supposed to be for all of us.

JOE: You'll wake them up.

EDNA: I don't care, as long as I can maybe wake you up.

JOE: Don't insult me. One man can't make a strike.

EDNA: Who says one? You got hundreds in your rotten union!

JOE: The union ain't rotten.

EDNA: No? Then what are they doing? Collecting dues and patting your back?

JOE: They're making plans.

EDNA: What kind?

JOE: They don't tell us.

EDNA: It's too damn bad about you. They don't tell little Joey what's happening in his bitsie witsie union. What do you think it is—a ping pong game?

JOE: You know they're racketeers. The guys at the top would shoot you for a nickel.

EDNA: Why do you stand for that stuff?

JOE: Don't you wanna see me alive?

EDNA *(after a deep pause):* No . . . I don't think I do, Joe. Not if you can lift a finger to do something about it, and don't. No, I don't care.

JOE: Honey, you don't understand what—

EDNA: And any other hackie that won't fight . . . let them all be ground to hamburger!

JOE: It's one thing to—

EDNA: Take your hand away! Only they don't grind me to little pieces! I got different plans. *(Starts to take off her apron.)*

JOE: Where are you going?

EDNA: None of your business.

JOE: What's up your sleeve?

EDNA: My arm'd be up my sleeve, darling, if I had a sleeve to wear. *(Puts neatly folded apron on back of chair.)*

JOE: Tell me!

EDNA: Tell you what?

JOE: Where are you going?

EDNA: Don't you remember my old boy friend?

JOE: Who?

EDNA: Bud Haas. He still has my picture in his watch. He earns a living.

JOE: What the hell are you talking about?

EDNA: I heard worse than I'm talking about.

JOE: Have you seen Bud since we got married?

EDNA: Maybe.

JOE: If I thought . . . *(He stands looking at her.)*

EDNA: See much? Listen, boy friend, if you think I won't do this it just means you can't see straight.

JOE: Stop talking bull!

EDNA: This isn't five years ago, Joe.

JOE: You mean you'd leave me and the kids?

EDNA: I'd leave *you* like a shot!

JOE: No. . . .

EDNA: Yes! (JOE *turns away, sitting in a chair with his back to her.*

Outside the lighted circle of the playing stage we hear the other seated members of the strike committee. "She will . . . she will . . . it happens that way," etc. This group should be used throughout for various comments, political, emotional and as general chorus. Whispering. . . . The fat boss now blows a heavy cloud of smoke into the scene.)

JOE *(finally):* Well, I guess I ain't got a leg to stand on.

EDNA: No?

JOE *(suddenly mad):* No, you lousy tart, no! Get the hell out of here. Go pick up that bull-thrower on the corner and stop at some cushy hotel downtown. He's probably been coming here every morning and laying you while I hacked my guts out!

EDNA: You're crawling like a worm!

JOE: You'll be crawling in a minute.

EDNA: You don't scare me that much! *(Indicates a half inch on her finger.)*

JOE: This is what I slaved for!

EDNA: Tell it to your boss!

JOE: He don't give a damn for you or me!

EDNA: That's what I say.

JOE: Don't change the subject!

EDNA: This is the subject, the *exact subject!* Your boss makes this subject. I never saw him in my life, but he's putting ideas in my head a mile a minute. He's giving your kids that fancy disease called the rickets. He's making a jelly-fish outa you and putting wrinkles in my face. This is the subject every inch of the way! He's throwing me into Bud Haas' lap. When in hell will you get wise——

JOE: I'm not so dumb as you think! But you are talking like a red.

EDNA: I don't know what that means. But when a man knocks you down you get up and kiss his fist! You gutless piece of boloney.

JOE: One man can't——

EDNA *(with great joy):* I don't say one man! I say a hundred, a thousand, a whole million, I say. But start in your own union. Get those hack boys together! Sweep out those racketeers like a pile of dirt! Stand up like men and fight for the crying kids and wives. Goddamnit! I'm tired of slavery and sleepness nights.

JOE *(with her):* Sure, sure! . . .

EDNA: Yes. Get brass toes on your shoes and know where to kick!

JOE *(suddenly jumping up and kissing his wife full on the mouth):*

Listen, Edna, I'm goin' down to 174th Street to look up Lefty
Costello. Lefty was saying the other day . . . *(He suddenly stops.)*
How about this Haas guy?

EDNA: Get out of here!

JOE: I'll be back! *(Runs out. For a moment* EDNA *stands triumphant.
There is a blackout and when the regular lights come up,* JOE
MITCHELL *is concluding what he has been saying):*

JOE: You guys know this stuff better than me. We gotta walk out!
(Abruptly he turns and goes back to his seat.)

Blackout

II. LAB ASSISTANT EPISODE

Discovered: MILLER, *a lab assistant, looking around; and* FAYETTE,
an industrialist.

FAY: Like it?

MILLER: Very much. I've never seen an office like this outside the
movies.

FAY: Yes, I often wonder if interior decorators and bathroom fixture
people don't get all their ideas from Hollywood. Our country's
extraordinary that way. Soap, cosmetics, electric refrigerators—
just let Mrs. Consumer know they're used by the Crawfords and
Garbos—more volume of sale than one plant can handle!

MILL: I'm afraid it isn't that easy, Mr. Fayette.

FAY: No, you're right—gross exaggeration on my part. Competition is
cutthroat today. Market's up flush against a stone wall. The astron-
omers had better hurry—open Mars to trade expansion.

MILL: Or it will be just too bad!

FAY: Cigar?

MILL: Thank you, don't smoke.

FAY: Drink?

MILL: Ditto, Mr. Fayette.

FAY: I like sobriety in my workers . . . the trained ones, I mean. The
pollacks and niggers, they're better drunk—keeps them out of
mischief. Wondering why I had you come over?

MILL: If you don't mind my saying—very much.

FAY *(patting him on the knee):* I like your work.

MILL: Thanks.

FAY: No reason why a talented young man like yourself shouldn't string along with us—a growing concern. Loyalty is well repaid in our organization. Did you see Siegfried this morning?

MILL: He hasn't been in the laboratory all day.

FAY: I told him yesterday to raise you twenty dollars a month. Starts this week.

MILL: You don't know how happy my wife'll be.

FAY: Oh, I can appreciate it. *(He laughs.)*

MILL: Was that all, Mr. Fayette?

FAY: Yes, except that we're switching you to laboratory A tomorrow. Siegfried knows about it. That's why I had you in. The new work is very important. Siegfried recommended you very highly as a man to trust. You'll work directly under Dr. Brenner. Make you happy?

MILL: Very. He's an important chemist!

FAY *(leaning over seriously):* We think so, Miller. We think so to the extent of asking you to stay within the building throughout the time you work with him.

MILL: You mean sleep and eat in?

FAY: Yes. . . .

MILL: It can be arranged.

FAY: Fine. You'll go far, Miller.

MILL: May I ask the nature of the new work?

FAY *(looking around first):* Poison gas. . . .

MILL: Poison!

FAY: Orders from above. I don't have to tell you from where. New type poison gas for modern warfare.

MILL: I see.

FAY: You didn't know a new war was that close, did you?

MILL: I guess I didn't.

FAY: I don't have to stress the importance of absolute secrecy.

MILL: I understand!

FAY: The world is an armed camp today. One match sets the whole world blazing in forty-eight hours. Uncle Sam won't be caught napping!

MILL *(addressing his pencil):* They say 12 million men were killed in that last one and 20 million more wounded or missing.

FAY: That's not our worry. If big business went sentimental over human life there wouldn't be big business of any sort!

MILL: My brother and two cousins went in the last one.

FAY: They died in a good cause.

MILL: My mother says "no!"

FAY: She won't worry about you this time. You're too valuable behind the front.

MILL: That's right.

FAY: All right, Miller. See Siegfried for further orders.

MILL: You should have seen my brother—he could ride a bike without hands. . . .

FAY: You'd better move some clothes and shaving tools in tomorrow. Remember what I said—you're with a growing organization.

MILL: He could run the hundred yards in 9:8 flat. . . .

FAY: Who?

MILL: My brother. He's in the Meuse-Argonne Cemetery. Mama went there in 1926. . . .

FAY: Yes, those things stick. How's your handwriting, Miller, fairly legible?

MILL: Fairly so.

FAY: Once a week I'd like a little report from you.

MILL: What sort of report?

FAY: Just a few hundred words once a week on Dr. Brenner's progress.

MILL: Don't you think it might be better coming from the Doctor?

FAY: I didn't ask you that.

MILL: Sorry.

FAY: I want to know what progress he's making, the reports to be purely confidential—between you and me.

MILL: You mean I'm to watch him?

FAY: Yes!

MILL: I guess I can't do that. . . .

FAY: Thirty a month raise . . .

MILL: You said twenty. . . .

FAY: Thirty!

MILL: Guess I'm not built that way.

FAY: Forty. . . .

MILL: Spying's not in my line, Mr. Fayette!

FAY: You use ugly words, Mr. Miller!

MILL: For ugly activity? Yes!

FAY: Think about it, Miller. Your chances are excellent. . . .

MILL: No.

FAY: You're doing something for your country. Assuring the United States that when those goddamn Japs start a ruckus we'll have offensive weapons to back us up! Don't you read your newspapers, Miller?

MILL: Nothing but Andy Gump.

FAY: If you were on the inside you'd know I'm talking cold sober truth! Now, I'm not asking you to make up your mind on the spot. Think about it over your lunch period.

MILL: No.

FAY: Made up your mind already?

MILL: Afraid so.

FAY: You understand the consequences?

MILL: I lose my raise——

Simultaneously: { MILL: And my job!
          FAY: And your job!
          MILL: You misunderstand——

MILL: Rather dig ditches first!

FAY: That's a big job for foreigners.

MILL: But sneaking—and making poison gas—that's for Americans?

FAY: It's up to you.

MILL: My mind's made up.

FAY: No hard feelings?

MILL: Sure hard feelings! I'm not the civilized type, Mr. Fayette. Nothing suave or sophisticated about me. Plenty of hard feelings! Enough to want to bust you and all your kind square in the mouth! (*Does exactly that.*)

Blackout

III. THE YOUNG HACK AND HIS GIRL

Opens with girl and brother. FLORENCE *waiting for* SID *to take her to a dance.*

FLOR: I gotta right to have something out of life. I don't smoke, I don't drink. So if Sid wants to take me to a dance, I'll go. Maybe if you was in love you wouldn't talk so hard.

IRV: I'm saying it for your good.

FLOR: Don't be so good to me.

IRV: Mom's sick in bed and you'll be worryin' her to the grave. She don't want that boy hanging around the house and she don't want you meeting him in Crotona Park.

FLOR: I'll meet him anytime I like!

IRV: If you do, yours truly'll take care of it in his own way. With just one hand, too!

FLOR: Why are you all so set against him?

IRV: Mom told you ten times—it ain't him. It's that he ain't got nothing. Sure, we know he's serious, that he's stuck on you. But that don't cut no ice.

FLOR: Taxi drivers used to make good money.

IRV: Today they're makin' five and six dollars a week. Maybe you wanta raise a family on that. Then you'll be back here living with us again and I'll be supporting two families in one. Well . . . over my dead body.

FLOR: Irv, I don't care—I love him!

IRV: You're a little kid with half-baked ideas!

FLOR: I stand there behind the counter the whole day. I think about him—

IRV: If you thought more about Mom it would be better.

FLOR: Don't I take care of her every night when I come home? Don't I cook supper and iron your shirts and . . . you give me a pain in the neck, too. Don't try to shut me up! I bring a few dollars in the house, too. Don't you see I want something else out of life. Sure, I want romance, love, babies. I want everything in life I can get.

IRV: You take care of Mom and watch your step!

FLOR: And if I don't?

IRV: Yours truly'll watch it for you!

FLOR: You can talk that way to a girl. . . .

IRV: I'll talk that way to your boy friend, too, and it won't be with words! Florrie, if you had a pair of eyes you'd see it's for your own good we're talking. This ain't no time to get married. Maybe later—

FLOR: "Maybe Later" never comes for me, though. Why don't we send Mom to a hospital? She can die in peace there instead of looking at the clock on the mantelpiece all day.

IRV: That needs money. Which we don't have!

FLOR: Money, Money, Money!

IRV: Don't change the subject.

FLOR: This is the subject!

IRV: You gonna stop seeing him? *(She turns away.)* Jesus, kiddie, I remember when you were a baby with curls down your back. Now I gotta stand here yellin' at you like this.

FLOR: I'll talk to him, Irv.

IRV: When?

FLOR: I asked him to come here tonight. We'll talk it over.

IRV: Don't get soft with him. Nowadays is no time to be soft. You gotta be hard as a rock or go under.

FLOR: I found that out. There's the bell. Take the egg off the stove I boiled for Mom. Leave us alone Irv. (SID *comes in—the two men look at each other for a second.* IRV *exits.*)

SID *(enters):* Hello, Florrie.

FLOR: Hello, Honey. You're looking tired.

SID: Naw, I just need a shave.

FLOR: Well, draw your chair up to the fire and I'll ring for brandy and soda . . . like in the movies.

SID: If this was the movies I'd bring a big bunch of roses.

FLOR: How big?

SID: Fifty or sixty dozen—the kind with long, long stems—big as that. . . .

FLOR: You dope. . . .

SID: Your Paris gown is beautiful.

FLOR *(acting grandly):* Yes, Percy, velvet panels are coming back again. Madame La Farge told me today that Queen Marie herself designed it.

SID: Gee . . . !

FLOR: Every princess in the Balkans is wearing one like this. *(Poses grandly.)*

SID: Hold it. *(Does a nose camera—thumbing nose and imitating grinding of camera with other hand. Suddenly she falls out of the posture and swiftly goes to him, to embrace him, to kiss him with love. Finally):*

SID: You look tired, Florrie.

FLOR: Naw, I just need a shave. *(She laughs tremulously.)*

SID: You worried about your mother?

FLOR: No.

SID: What's on your mind?

FLOR: The French and Indian War.

SID: What's on your mind?

FLOR: I got us on my mind, Sid. Night and day, Sid!

SID: I smacked a beer truck today. Did I get hell! I was driving along thinking of US, too. You don't have to say it—I know what's on your mind. I'm rat poison around here.

FLOR: Not to me. . . .

SID: I know to who . . . and I know why. I don't blame them. We're engaged now for three years. . . .

FLOR: That's a long time. . . .

SID: My brother Sam joined the navy this morning—get a break that way. They'll send him down to Cuba with the hootchy-kootchy girls. He don't know from nothing, that dumb basket ball player!

FLOR: Don't you do that.

SID: Don't you worry, I'm not the kind who runs away. But I'm so tired of being a dog, Baby, I could choke. I don't even have to ask what's going on in your mind. I know from the word go, 'cause I'm thinking the same things, too.

FLOR: It's yes or no—nothing in between.

SID: The answer is no—a big electric sign looking down on Broadway!

FLOR: We wanted to have kids. . . .

SID: But that sort of life ain't for the dogs which is us. Christ, Baby! I get like thunder in my chest when we're together. If we went off together I could maybe look the world straight in the face, spit in its eye like a man should do. Goddamnit, it's trying to be a man on the earth. Two in life together.

FLOR: But something wants us to be lonely like that—crawling alone in the dark. Or they want us trapped.

SID: Sure, the big shot money men want us like that.

FLOR: Highly insulting us——

SID: Keeping us in the dark about what is wrong with us in the money sense. They got the power and mean to be damn sure they keep it. They know if they give in just an inch, all the dogs like us will be down on them together—an ocean knocking them to hell and back and each singing cuckoo with stars coming from their nose and ears. I'm not raving, Florrie——

FLOR: I know you're not, I know.

SID: I don't have the words to tell you what I feel. I never finished school. . . .

FLOR: I know. . . .

SID: But it's relative, like the professors say. We worked like hell to send him to college—my kid brother Sam, I mean—and look what he done—joined the navy! The damn fool don't see the cards is stacked for all of us. The money man dealing himself a hot royal flush. Then giving you and me a phony hand like a pair of tens or something. Then keep on losing the pots 'cause the cards is stacked

against you. Then he says, what's the matter you can't win—no
stuff on the ball, he says to you. And kids like my brother believe it
'cause they don't know better. For all their education, they don't
know from nothing. But wait a minute! Don't he come around and
say to you—this millionaire with a jazz band—listen Sam or Sid or
what's-your-name, you're no good, but here's a chance. The whole
world'll know who you are. Yes sir, he says, get up on that ship and
fight those bastards who's making the world a lousy place to live in.
The Japs, the Turks, the Greeks. Take this gun—kill the slobs like a
real hero, he says, a real American. Be a hero! And the guy you're
poking at? A real louse, just like you, 'cause they don't let him
catch more than a pair of tens, too. On that foreign soil he's a guy
like me and Sam, a guy who wants his baby like you and hot sun on
his face! They'll teach Sam to point the guns the wrong way, that
dumb basket ball player!

FLOR: I got a lump in my throat, Honey.

SID: You and me—we never even had a room to sit in somewhere.

FLOR: The park was nice . . .

SID: In winter? The hallways . . . I'm glad we never got together.
This way we don't know what we missed.

FLOR *(in a burst):* Sid, I'll go with you—we'll get a room somewhere.

SID: Naw . . . they're right. If we can't climb higher than this together—we better stay apart.

FLOR: I swear to God I wouldn't care.

SID: You would, you would—in a year, two years, you'd curse the day.
I seen it happen.

FLOR: Oh, Sid. . . .

SID: Sure, I know. We got the blues, Babe—the 1935 blues. I'm talkin'
this way 'cause I love you. If I didn't, I wouldn't care. . . .

FLOR: We'll work together, we'll—

SID: How about the backwash? Your family needs your nine bucks.
My family——

FLOR: I don't care for them!

SID: You're making it up, Florrie. Little Florrie Canary in a cage.

FLOR: Don't make fun of me.

SID: I'm not, Baby.

FLOR: Yes, you're laughing at me.

SID: I'm not. *(They stand looking at each other, unable to speak.
Finally, he turns to a small portable phonograph and plays a
cheap, sad, dance tune. He makes a motion with his hand; she*

comes to him. They begin to dance slowly. They hold each other tightly, almost as though they would merge into each other. The music stops, but the scratching record continues to the end of the scene. They stop dancing. He finally looses her clutch and seats her on the couch, where she sits, tense and expectant.)

SID: Hello, Babe.

FLOR: Hello. *(For a brief time they stand as though in a dream.)*

SID *(finally):* Good-bye, Babe. *(He waits for an answer, but she is silent. They look at each other.)*

SID: Did you ever see my Pat Rooney imitation? *(He whistles Rosy O'Grady and soft-shoes to it. Stops. He asks:)*

SID: Don't you like it?

FLOR *(finally):* No. *(Buries her face in her hands. Suddenly he falls on his knees and buries his face in her lap.)*

Blackout

IV. LABOR SPY EPISODE

FATT: You don't know how we work for you. Shooting off your mouth won't help. Hell, don't you guys ever look at the records like me? Look in your own industry. See what happened when the hacks walked out in Philly three months ago! Where's Philly? A thousand miles away? An hour's ride on the train.

VOICE: Two hours!!

FATT: Two hours . . . what the hell's the difference. Let's hear from someone who's got the practical experience to back him up. Fellers, there's a man here who's seen the whole parade in Philly, walked out with his pals, got knocked down like the rest—and blacklisted after they went back. That's why he's here. He's got a mighty interestin' word to say. *(Announces): Tom Clayton! (As* CLAYTON *starts up from the audience,* FATT *gives him a hand which is sparsely followed in the audience.* CLAYTON *comes forward.)*

Fellers, this is a man with practical strike experience—Tom Clayton from little ole Philly.

CLAYTON *(a thin, modest individual):* Fellers, I don't mind your booing. If I thought it would help us hacks get better living conditions, I'd let you walk all over me, cut me up to little pieces. I'm one of you myself. But what I wanna say is that Harry Fatt's right. I only been working here in the big town five weeks, but I know conditions just like the rest of you. You know how it is—don't take long to feel the sore spots, no matter where you park.

CLEAR VOICE *(from audience):* Sit down!

CLAYTON: But Fatt's right. Our officers is right. The time ain't ripe. Like a fruit don't fall off the tree until it's ripe.

CLEAR VOICE: Sit down, you fruit!

FATT *(on his feet):* Take care of him, boys.

VOICE *(in audience, struggling):* No one takes care of me. *(Struggle in house and finally the owner of the voice runs up on stage, says to speaker):*

SAME VOICE: Where the hell did you pick up that name! Clayton! This rat's name is Clancy, from the old Clancys, way back! Fruit! I almost wet myself listening to that one!

FATT *(gunman with him):* This ain't a barn! What the hell do you think you're doing here!

SAME VOICE: Exposing a rat!

FATT: You can't get away with this. Throw him the hell outa here.

VOICE *(preparing to stand his ground):* Try it yourself. . . . When this bozo throws that slop around. You know who he is? That's a company spy.

FATT: Who the hell are you to make—

VOICE: I paid dues in this union for four years, that's who's me! I gotta right and this pussy-footed rat ain't coming in here with ideas like that. You know his record. Lemme say it out——

FATT: You'll prove all this or I'll bust you in every hack outfit in town!

VOICE: I gotta right. I gotta right. Looka *him,* he don't say boo!

CLAYTON: You're a liar and I never seen you before in my life!

VOICE: Boys, he spent two years in the coal fields breaking up any organization he touched. Fifty guys he put in jail. He's ranged up and down the east coast—shipping, textiles, steel—he's been in everything you can name. Right now——

CLAYTON: That's a lie!

VOICE: Right now he's working for that Bergman outfit on Columbus Circle who furnishes rats for any outfit in the country, before, during, and after strikes. *(The man who is the hero of the next episode goes down to his side with other committee men.)*

CLAYTON: He's trying to break up the meeting, fellers!

VOICE: We won't search you for credentials. . . .

CLAYTON: I got nothing to hide. Your own secretary knows I'm straight.

VOICE: Sure. Boys, you know who this sonovabitch is?

CLAYTON: I never seen you before in my life!!

VOICE: Boys, I slept with him in the same bed sixteen years. HE'S MY OWN LOUSY BROTHER!!

FATT *(after pause):* Is this true? *(No answer from* CLAYTON.*)*

VOICE *(to* CLAYTON*):* Scram, before I break your neck! (CLAYTON *scrams down center aisle,* VOICE *says, watching him):* Remember his map—he can't change that—Clancy! *(Standing in his place says):* Too bad you didn't know about this, Fatt! *(After a pause.)* The Clancy family tree is bearing nuts! *(Standing isolated clear on the stage is the hero of the next episode.)*

Blackout

V. INTERNE EPISODE

Dr. Barnes, an elderly distinguished man, is speaking on the telephone. He wears a white coat.

DR. BARNES: No, I gave you my opinion twice. You outvoted me. You did this to Dr. Benjamin yourself. That is why you can tell him yourself. *(Hangs up phone, angrily. As he is about to pour himself a drink from a bottle on the table, a knock is heard.)*

BARNES: Who is it?

BENJAMIN *(without):* Can I see you a minute, please?

BARNES *(hiding the bottle):* Come in, Dr. Benjamin, come in.

BENJ: It's important—excuse me—they've got Leeds up there in my place—He's operating on Mrs. Lewis—the hysterectomy—it's my job. I washed up, prepared . . . they told me at the last minute. I don't mind being replaced, Doctor, but Leeds is a damn fool! He shouldn't be permitted——

BARNES *(dryly):* Leeds is the nephew of Senator Leeds.

BENJ: He's incompetent as hell.

BARNES *(obviously changing subject, picks up lab. jar):* They're doing splendid work in brain surgery these days. This is a very fine specimen. . . .

BENJ: I'm sorry, I thought you might be interested.

BARNES *(still examining jar):* Well, I am, young man, I am! Only remember it's a charity case!

BENJ: Of course. They wouldn't allow it for a second, otherwise.

BARNES: Her life is in danger?

BENJ: Of course! You know how serious the case is!

BARNES: Turn your gimlet eyes elsewhere, Doctor. Jigging around like a cricket on a hot grill won't help. Doctors don't run these hospitals. He's the Senator's nephew and there he stays.

BENJ: It's too bad.

BARNES: I'm not calling you down either. *(Plopping down jar suddenly.)* Goddamnit, do you think it's my fault?

BENJ *(about to leave):* I know . . . I'm sorry.

BARNES: Just a minute. Sit down.

BENJ: Sorry, I can't sit.

BARNES: Stand then!

BENJ *(sits):* Understand, Dr. Barnes, I don't mind being replaced at the last minute this way, but . . . well, this flagrant bit of class distinction—because she's poor——

BARNES: Be careful of words like that—"class distinction." Don't belong here. Lots of energy, you brilliant young men, but idiots. Discretion! Ever hear that word?

BENJ: Too radical?

BARNES: Precisely. And some day like in Germany, it might cost you your head.

BENJ: Not to mention my job.

BARNES: So they told you?

BENJ: Told me what?

BARNES: They're closing Ward C next month. I don't have to tell you the hospital isn't self-supporting. Until last year that board of trustees met deficits. . . . You can guess the rest. At a board meeting Tuesday, our fine feathered friends discovered they couldn't meet the last quarter's deficit—a neat little sum well over $100,000. If the hospital is to continue at all, its damn——

BENJ: Necessary to close another charity ward!

BARNES: So they say. . . . *(A wait.)*

BENJ: But that's not all?

BARNES *(ashamed):* Have to cut down on staff too. . . .

BENJ: That's too bad. Does it touch me?

BARNES: Afraid it does.

BENJ: But after all I'm top man here. I don't mean I'm better than others, but I've worked harder.

BARNES: And shown more promise. . . .

BENJ: I always supposed they'd cut from the bottom first.

BARNES: Usually.

BENJ: But in this case?

BARNES: Complications.

BENJ: For instance? (BARNES *hesitant.*)

BARNES: I like you, Benjamin. It's one ripping shame.

BENJ: I'm no sensitive plant—what's the answer?

BARNES: An old disease, malignant, tumescent. We need an antitoxin for it.

BENJ: I see.

BARNES: What?

BENJ: I met that disease before—at Harvard first.

BARNES: You have seniority here, Benjamin.

BENJ: But I'm a Jew! (BARNES *nods his head in agreement.* BENJ *stands there a moment and blows his nose.*)

BARNES (*blows his nose*): Microbes!

BENJ: Pressure from above?

BARNES: Don't think Kennedy and I didn't fight for you!

BENJ: Such discrimination, with all those wealthy brother Jews on the board?

BARNES: I've remarked before—doesn't seem to be much difference between wealthy Jews and rich Gentiles. Cut from the same piece!

BENJ: For myself I don't feel sorry. My parents gave up an awful lot to get me this far. They ran a little dry goods shop in the Bronx until their pitiful savings went in the crash last year. Poppa's peddling neckties. . . . Saul Ezra Benjamin—a man who's read Spinoza all his life.

BARNES: Doctors don't run medicine in this country. The men who know their jobs don't run anything here, except the motormen on trolley cars. I've seen medicine change—plenty—anesthesia, sterilization—but not because of rich men—in *spite* of them! In a rich man's country your true self's buried deep. Microbes! Less. . . . Vermin! See this ankle, this delicate sensitive hand? Four hundred years to breed that. Out of a revolutionary background! Spirit of '76! Ancestors froze at Valley Forge! What's it all mean! Slops! The honest workers were sold out then, in '76. The Constitution's for rich men then and now. Slops! (*The phone rings.*)

BARNES *(angrily):* Dr. Barnes. *(Listens a moment, looks at* BENJA-
MIN.) I see. *(Hangs up, turns slowly to the younger Doctor.)* They
lost your patient. (BENJ *stands solid with the shock of this news but
finally hurls his operation gloves to the floor.)*

BARNES: That's right . . . that's right. Young, hot, go and do it! I'm
very ancient, fossil, but life's ahead of you, Dr. Benjamin, and
when you fire the first shot say, "This one's for old Doc Barnes!"
Too much dignity—bullets. Don't shoot vermin! Step on them! If I
didn't have an invalid daughter——

BARNES *(goes back to his seat, blows his nose in silence):* I have said
my piece, Benjamin.

BENJ: Lots of things I wasn't certain of. Many things these radicals say
. . . you don't believe theories until they happen to you.

BARNES: You lost a lot today, but you won a great point.

BENJ: Yes, to know I'm right? To really begin believing in something?
Not to say, "What a world!", but to say, "Change the world!" I
wanted to go to Russia. Last week I was thinking about it—the
wonderful opportunity to do good work in their socialized medicine——

BARNES: Beautiful, beautiful!

BENJ: To be able to work——

BARNES: Why don't you go? I might be able——

BENJ: Nothing's nearer what I'd like to do!

BARNES: Do it!

BENJ: No! Our work's here—America! I'm scared. . . . What future's
ahead, I don't know. Get some job to keep alive—maybe drive a
cab—and study and work and learn my place——

BARNES: And step down hard!

BENJ: Fight! Maybe get killed, but goddamn! We'll go ahead! (BENJA-
MIN *stands with clenched fist raised high.)*

Blackout

AGATE: *Ladies and Gentlemen,* and don't let anyone tell you we ain't
got some ladies in this sea of upturned faces! Only they're wearin'
pants. Well, maybe I don't know a thing; maybe I fell outa the
cradle when I was a kid and ain't been right since—you can't tell!

VOICE: Sit down, cockeye!

AGATE: Who's paying you for those remarks, Buddy?—Moscow Gold?
Maybe I got a *glass eye,* but it come from working in a factory at

the age of eleven. They hooked it out because they didn't have a shield on the works. But I wear it like a medal 'cause it tells the world where I belong—deep down in the working class! We had delegates in the union there—all kinds of secretaries and treasurers . . . walkin' delegates, but not with blisters on their feet! Oh no! On their fat little ass from sitting on cushions and raking in mazuma. (SECRETARY *and* GUNMAN *remonstrate in words and actions here.*) Sit down, boys. I'm just sayin' that about unions in general. I know it ain't true here! Why no, our officers is all aces. Why, I seen our own secretary Fatt walk outa his way not to step on a cockroach. No boys, don't think——

FATT *(breaking in):* You're out of order!

AGATE *(to audience):* Am I outa order?

ALL: No, no. Speak. Go on, etc.

AGATE: Yes, our officers is all aces. But I'm a member here—and no experience in Philly either! Today I couldn't wear my union button. The damnest thing happened. When I take the old coat off the wall, I see she's smoking. I'm a sonovagun if the old union button isn't on fire! Yep, the old celluloid was makin' the most god-awful stink: the landlady come up and give me hell! You know what happened? That old union button just blushed itself to death! Ashamed! Can you beat it?

FATT: Sit down, Keller! Nobody's interested!

AGATE: Yes they are!

GUNMAN: Sit down like he tells you!

AGATE *(continuing to audience):* And when I finish——*(His speech is broken by* FATT *and* GUNMAN *who physically handle him. He breaks away and gets to other side of stage. The two are about to make for him when some of the committee men come forward and get in between the struggling parties.* AGATE'S *shirt has been torn.)*

AGATE *(to audience):* What's the answer, boys? The answer is, if we're reds because we wanna strike, then we take over their salute too! Know how they do it? *(Makes Communist salute.)* What is it? An uppercut! The good old uppercut to the chin! Hell, some of us boys ain't even got a shirt to our backs. What's the boss class tryin' to do —make a nudist colony outa us? *(The audience laughs and suddenly* AGATE *comes to the middle of the stage so that the other cabmen back him up in a strong clump.)*

AGATE: Don't laugh! Nothing's funny! This is your life and mine! It's skull and bones every incha the road! Christ, we're dyin' by inches!

For what? For the debutant-ees to have their sweet comin' out parties in the Ritz! Poppa's got a daughter she's gotta get her picture in the papers. Christ, they make 'em with our blood. Joe said it. Slow death or fight. It's war! *(Throughout this whole speech* AGATE *is backed up by the other six workers, so that from their activity it is plain that the whole group of them are saying these things. Several of them may take alternate lines out of this long last speech.)*

You Edna, God love your mouth! Sid and Florrie, the other boys, old Doc Barnes—fight with us for right! It's war! Working class, unite and fight! Tear down the slaughter house of our old lives! Let freedom really ring.

These slick slobs stand here telling us about bogeymen. That's a new one for the kids—the reds is bogeymen! But the man who got me food in 1932, he called me Comrade! The one who picked me up where I bled—he called me Comrade too! What are we waiting for. . . . Don't wait for Lefty! He might never come. Every minute——*(This is broken into by a man who has dashed up the center aisle from the back of the house. He runs up on stage, says):*

MAN: Boys, they just found Lefty!

OTHERS: What? What? What?

SOME: Shhh. . . . Shhh. . . .

MAN: They found Lefty. . . .

AGATE: Where?

MAN: Behind the car barns with a bullet in his head!

AGATE *(crying):* Hear it, boys, hear it? Hell, listen to me! Coast to coast! HELLO AMERICA! HELLO. WE'RE STORMBIRDS OF THE WORKING-CLASS. WORKERS OF THE WORLD. . . . OUR BONES AND BLOOD! And when we die they'll know what we did to make a new world! Christ, cut us up to little pieces. We'll die for what is right! put fruit trees where our ashes are!

(To audience): Well, what's the answer?

ALL: STRIKE!

AGATE: LOUDER!

ALL: STRIKE!

AGATE and OTHERS on Stage: AGAIN!

ALL: STRIKE, STRIKE, STRIKE!!!

Curtain

AWAKE AND SING

FOR MY FATHER AND MOTHER

Awake and Sing was presented by the Group Theatre at the Belasco Theatre on the evening of February 19th, 1935, with the following members of the Group Theatre Acting Company:

	Played by
MYRON BERGER	*Art Smith*
BESSIE BERGER	*Stella Adler*
JACOB	*Morris Carnovsky*
HENNIE BERGER	*Phoebe Brand*
RALPH BERGER	*Jules Garfield*
SCHLOSSER	*Roman Bohnen*
MOE AXELROD	*Luther Adler*
UNCLE MORTY	*J. E. Bromberg*
SAM FEINSCHREIBER	*Sanford Meisner*

The entire action takes place in an apartment in the Bronx, New York City

The production was directed by HAROLD CLURMAN
The setting was designed by BORIS ARONSON

THE CHARACTERS OF THE PLAY

All of the characters in Awake and Sing! *share a fundamental activity: a struggle for life amidst petty conditions.*

BESSIE BERGER, *as she herself states, is not only the mother in this home but also the father. She is constantly arranging and taking care of her family. She loves life, likes to laugh, has great resourcefulness and enjoys living from day to day. A high degree of energy accounts for her quick exasperation at ineptitude. She is a shrewd judge of realistic qualities in people in the sense of being able to gauge quickly their effectiveness. In her eyes all of the people in the house are equal. She is naïve and quick in emotional response. She is afraid of utter poverty. She is proper according to her own standards, which are fairly close to those of most middle-class families. She knows that when one lives in the jungle one must look out for the wild life.*

MYRON, *her husband, is a born follower. He would like to be a leader. He would like to make a million dollars. He is not sad or ever depressed. Life is an even sweet event to him, but the "old days" were sweeter yet. He has a dignified sense of himself. He likes people. He likes everything. But he is heartbroken without being aware of it.*

HENNIE *is a girl who has had few friends, male or female. She is proud of her body. She won't ask favors. She travels alone. She is fatalistic about being trapped, but will escape if possible. She is self-reliant in the best sense. Till the day she dies she will be faithful to a loved man. She inherits her mother's sense of humor and energy.*

RALPH *is a boy with a clean spirit. He wants to know, wants to learn. He is ardent, he is romantic, he is sensitive. He is naïve too. He is trying to find why so much dirt must be cleared away before it is possible to "get to first base."*

JACOB, *too, is trying to find a right path for himself and the others. He is aware of justice, of dignity. He is an observer of the others, compares their activities with his real and ideal sense of life. This produces a reflective nature. In this home he is a constant boarder. He is a sentimental idealist with no power to turn ideal to action. With physical facts—such as housework—he putters. But as a barber he demonstrates the flair of an artist. He is an old Jew with living eyes in his tired face.*

UNCLE MORTY *is a successful American business man with five good senses. Something sinister comes out of the fact that the lives of others seldom touch him deeply. He holds to his own line of life. When he is generous he wants others to be aware of it. He is pleased by attention—a rich relative to the* BERGER *family. He is a shrewd judge of material values. He will die unmarried. Two and two make four, never five with him. He can blink in the sun for hours, a fat tomcat. Tickle him, he laughs. He lives in a penthouse with a real Japanese butler to serve him. He sleeps with dress models, but not from his own showrooms. He plays cards for hours on end. He smokes expensive cigars. He sees every Mickey Mouse cartoon that appears. He is a 32-degree Mason. He is really deeply intolerant finally.*

MOE AXELROD *lost a leg in the war. He seldom forgets that fact. He has killed two men in extra-martial activity. He is mordant, bitter. Life has taught him a disbelief in everything, but he will fight his way through. He seldom shows his feelings: fights against his own sensitivity. He has been everywhere and seen everything. All he wants is* HENNIE. *He is very proud. He scorns the inability of others to make their way in life, but he likes people for whatever good qualities they possess. His passionate outbursts come from a strong but contained emotional mechanism.*

SAM FEINSCHREIBER *wants to find a home. He is a lonely man, a foreigner in a strange land, hypersensitive about this fact, conditioned by the humiliation of not making his way alone. He has a sense of others laughing at him. At night he gets up and sits alone in the dark. He hears acutely all the small sounds of life. He might have been a poet in another time and place. He approaches his wife as if he were always offering her a delicate flower. Life is a high chill wind weaving itself around his head.*

SCHLOSSER, *the janitor, is an overworked German whose wife ran away with another man and left him with a young daughter who in turn ran away and joined a burlesque show as chorus girl. The man suffers rheumatic pains. He has lost his identity twenty years before.*

THE SCENE

Exposed on the stage are the dining room and adjoining front room of the BERGER *apartment. These two rooms are typically furnished. There is a curtain between them. A small door off the front room leads to* JACOB'S *room. When his door is open one sees a picture of* SACCO *and* VANZETTI *on the wall and several shelves of books. Stage left of this door presents the entrance to the foyer hall of the apartment. The two other bedrooms of the apartment are off this hall, but not necessarily shown.*

Stage left of the dining room presents a swinging door which opens on the kitchen.

Awake and sing, ye that dwell in dust:

ISAIAH—26:19

AWAKE AND SING!

ACT ONE

Time: The present; the family finishing supper.

Place: An apartment in the Bronx, New York City.

RALPH: Where's advancement down the place? Work like crazy! Think they see it? You'd drop dead first.

MYRON: Never mind, son, merit never goes unrewarded. Teddy Roosevelt used to say——

HENNIE: It rewarded you—thirty years a haberdashery clerk! (JACOB *laughs.*)

RALPH: All I want's a chance to get to first base!

HENNIE: That's all?

RALPH: Stuck down in that joint on Fourth Avenue—a stock clerk in a silk house! Just look at Eddie. I'm as good as he is—pulling in two-fifty a week for forty-eight minutes a day. A headliner, his name in all the papers.

JACOB: That's what you want, Ralphie? Your name in the paper?

RALPH: I wanna make up my own mind about things . . . be something! Didn't I want to take up tap dancing, too?

BESSIE: So take lessons. Who stopped you?

RALPH: On what?

BESSIE: On what? Save money.

RALPH: Sure, five dollars a week for expenses and the rest in the house. I can't save even for shoe laces.

BESSIE: You mean we shouldn't have food in the house, but you'll make a jig on the street corner?

RALPH: I mean something.

BESSIE: You also mean something when you studied on the drum, Mr. Smartie!

RALPH: I don't know. . . . Every other day to sit around with the blues and mud in your mouth.

MYRON: That's how it is—life is like that—a cake-walk.

RALPH: What's it get you?

HENNIE: A four-car funeral.

RALPH: What's it for?

JACOB: What's it for? If this life leads to a revolution it's a good life. Otherwise it's for nothing.

BESSIE: Never mind, Pop! Pass me the salt.

RALPH: It's crazy—all my life I want a pair of black and white shoes and can't get them. It's crazy!

BESSIE: In a minute I'll get up from the table. I can't take a bite in my mouth no more.

MYRON *(restraining her):* Now, Momma, just don't excite your-self——

BESSIE: I'm so nervous I can't hold a knife in my hand.

MYRON: Is that a way to talk, Ralphie? Don't Momma work hard enough all day? (BESSIE *allows herself to be reseated.)*

BESSIE: On my feet twenty-four hours?

MYRON: On her feet——

RALPH *(jumps up):* What do I do—go to night-clubs with Greta Garbo? Then when I come home can't even have my own room? Sleep on a day-bed in the front room! *(Choked, he exits to front room.)*

BESSIE: He's starting up that stuff again. *(Shouts to him):* When Hennie here marries you'll have her room—I should only live to see the day.

HENNIE: Me, too. *(They settle down to serious eating.)*

MYRON: This morning the sink was full of ants. Where they come from I just don't know. I thought it was coffee grounds . . . and then they began moving.

BESSIE: You gave the dog eat?

JACOB: I gave the dog eat. (HENNIE *drops a knife and picks it up again.)*

BESSIE: You got dropsy tonight.

HENNIE: Company's coming.

MYRON: You can buy a ticket for fifty cents and win fortunes. A man came in the store—it's the Irish Sweepstakes.

BESSIE: What?

MYRON: Like a raffle, only different. A man came in——

BESSIE: Who spends fifty-cent pieces for Irish raffles? They threw out a family on Dawson Street today. All the furniture on the sidewalk. A fine old woman with gray hair.

JACOB: Come eat, Ralph.

MYRON: A butcher on Beck Street won eighty thousand dollars.

BESSIE: Eighty thousand dollars! You'll excuse my expression, you're bughouse!

MYRON: I seen it in the paper—on one ticket—765 Beck Street.

BESSIE: Impossible!

MYRON: He did . . . yes he did. He says he'll take his old mother to Europe . . . an Austrian——

HENNIE: Europe . . .

MYRON: Six per cent on eighty thousand—forty-eight hundred a year.

BESSIE: I'll give you money. Buy a ticket in Hennie's name. Say, you can't tell—lightning never struck us yet. If they win on Beck Street we could win on Longwood Avenue.

JACOB (ironically): If it rained pearls—who would work?

BESSIE: Another county heard from. (RALPH enters and silently seats himself.)

MYRON: I forgot, Beauty—Sam Feinschreiber sent you a present. Since I brought him for supper he just can't stop talking about you.

HENNIE: What's that "mockie" bothering about? Who needs him?

MYRON: He's a very lonely boy.

HENNIE: So I'll sit down and bust out crying " 'cause he's lonely."

BESSIE (opening candy): He'd marry you one two three.

HENNIE: Too bad about him.

BESSIE (naïvely delighted): Chocolate peanuts.

HENNIE: Loft's week-end special, two for thirty-nine.

BESSIE: You could think about it. It wouldn't hurt.

HENNIE (laughing): To quote Moe Axelrod, "Don't make me laugh."

BESSIE: Never mind laughing. It's time you already had in your head a serious thought. A girl twenty-six don't grow younger. When I was your age it was already a big family with responsibilities.

HENNIE (laughing): Maybe that's what ails you, Mom.

BESSIE: Don't you feel well?

HENNIE: 'Cause I'm laughing? I feel fine. It's just funny—that poor guy sending me presents 'cause he loves me.

BESSIE: I think it's very, very nice.

HENNIE: Sure . . . swell!

BESSIE: Mrs. Marcus' Rose is engaged to a Brooklyn boy, a dentist. He came in his car today. A little dope should get such a boy. (Finished with the meal, BESSIE, MYRON and JACOB rise. Both HENNIE and RALPH sit silently at the table, he eating. Suddenly she rises.)

HENNIE: Tell you what, Mom. I saved for a new dress, but I'll take you and Pop to the Franklin. Don't need a dress. From now on I'm planning to stay in nights. Hold everything!

BESSIE: What's the matter—a bedbug bit you suddenly?

HENNIE: It's a good bill—Belle Baker. Maybe she'll sing "Eli, Eli."

BESSIE: We was going to a movie.

HENNIE: Forget it. Let's go.

MYRON: I see in the papers *(as he picks his teeth)* Sophie Tucker took off twenty-six pounds. Fearful business with Japan.

HENNIE: Write a book, Pop! Come on, we'll go early for good seats.

MYRON: Moe said you had a date with him for tonight.

BESSIE: Axelrod?

HENNIE: I told him no, but he don't believe it. I'll tell him no for the next hundred years, too.

MYRON: Don't break appointments, Beauty, and hurt people's feelings. (BESSIE *exits.*)

HENNIE: His hands got free wheeling. *(She exits.)*

MYRON: I don't know . . . people ain't the same. N-O- The whole world's changing right under our eyes. Presto! No manners. Like the great Italian lover in the movies. What was his name? The Sheik. . . . No one remembers? *(Exits, shaking his head.)*

RALPH *(unmoving at the table)*: Jake . . .

JACOB: Noo?

RALPH: I can't stand it.

JACOB: There's an expression—"strong as iron you must be."

RALPH: It's a cock-eyed world.

JACOB: Boys like you could fix it some day. Look on the world, not on yourself so much. Every country with starving millions, no? In Germany and Poland a Jew couldn't walk in the street. Everybody hates, nobody loves.

RALPH: I don't get all that.

JACOB: For years, I watched you grow up. Wait! You'll graduate from my university. *(The others enter, dressed.)*

MYRON *(lighting)*: Good cigars now for a nickel.

BESSIE *(to JACOB)*: After take Tootsie on the roof. *(To RALPH)*: What'll you do?

RALPH: Don't know.

BESSIE: You'll see the boys around the block?

RALPH: I'll stay home every night!

MYRON: Momma don't mean for you——

RALPH: I'm flying to Hollywood by plane, that's what I'm doing. *(Doorbell rings.* MYRON *answers it.)*

BESSIE: I don't like my boy to be seen with those tramps on the corner.

MYRON *(without):* Schlosser's here, Momma, with the garbage can.

BESSIE: Come in here, Schlosser. *(Sotto voce)* Wait, I'll give him a piece of my mind. (MYRON *ushers in* SCHLOSSER *who carries a garbage can in each hand.)* What's the matter the dumbwaiter's broken again?

SCHLOSSER: Mr. Wimmer sends new ropes next week. I got a sore arm.

BESSIE: He should live so long your Mr. Wimmer. For seven years already he's sending new ropes. No dumbwaiter, no hot water, no steam——In a respectable house, they don't allow such conditions.

SCHLOSSER: In a decent house dogs are not running to make dirty the hallway.

BESSIE: Tootsie's making dirty? Our Tootsie's making dirty in the hall?

SCHLOSSER *(to* JACOB): I tell you yesterday again. You must not leave her——

BESSIE *(indignantly):* Excuse me! Please don't yell on an old man. He's got more brains in his finger than you got—I don't know where. Did you ever see—he should talk to you an old man?

MYRON: Awful.

BESSIE: From now on we don't walk up the stairs no more. You keep it so clean we'll fly in the windows.

SCHLOSSER: I speak to Mr. Wimmer.

BESSIE: Speak! Speak. Tootsie walks behind me like a lady any time, any place. So good-bye . . . good-bye, Mr. Schlosser.

SCHLOSSER: I tell you dot—I verk verry hard here. My arms is. . . . *(Exits in confusion.)*

BESSIE: Tootsie should lay all day in the kitchen maybe. Give him back if he yells on you. What's funny?

JACOB *(laughing):* Nothing.

BESSIE: Come. *(Exits.)*

JACOB: Hennie, take care. . . .

HENNIE: Sure.

JACOB: Bye-bye. (HENNIE *exits.* MYRON *pops head back in door.)*

MYRON: Valentino! That's the one! *(He exits.)*

RALPH: I never in my life even had a birthday party. Every time I went and cried in the toilet when my birthday came.

JACOB *(seeing* RALPH *remove his tie):* You're going to bed?

RALPH: No, I'm putting on a clean shirt.

JACOB: Why?

RALPH: I got a girl. . . . Don't laugh!

JACOB: Who laughs? Since when?

RALPH: Three weeks. She lives in Yorkville with an aunt and uncle. A bunch of relatives, but no parents.

JACOB: An orphan girl—tch, tch.

RALPH: But she's got me! Boy, I'm telling you I could sing! Jake, she's like stars. She's so beautiful you look at her and cry! She's like French words! We went to the park the other night. Heard the last band concert.

JACOB: Music. . . .

RALPH *(stuffing shirt in trousers):* It got cold and I gave her my coat to wear. We just walked along like that, see, without a word, see. I never was so happy in all my life. It got late . . . we just sat there. She looked at me—you know what I mean, how a girl looks at you —right in the eyes? "I love you," she says, "Ralph." I took her home. . . . I wanted to cry. That's how I felt!

JACOB: It's a beautiful feeling.

RALPH: You said a mouthful!

JACOB: Her name is——

RALPH: Blanche.

JACOB: A fine name. Bring her sometimes here.

RALPH: She's scared to meet Mom.

JACOB: Why?

RALPH: You know Mom's not letting my sixteen bucks out of the house if she can help it. She'd take one look at Blanche and insult her in a minute—a kid who's got nothing.

JACOB: Boychick!

RALPH: What's the diff?

JACOB: It's no difference—a plain bourgeois prejudice—but when they find out a poor girl—it ain't so kosher.

RALPH: They don't have to know I've got a girl.

JACOB: What's in the end?

RALPH: Out I go! I don't mean maybe!

JACOB: And then what?

RALPH: Life begins.

JACOB: What life?

RALPH: Life with my girl. Boy, I could sing when I think about it! Her and me together—that's a new life!

JACOB: Don't make a mistake! A new death!

RALPH: What's the idea?

JACOB: Me, I'm the idea! Once I had in *my* heart a dream, a vision, but came marriage and then you forget. Children come and you forget because——

RALPH: Don't worry, Jake.

JACOB: Remember, a woman insults a man's soul like no other thing in the whole world!

RALPH: Why get so excited? No one——

JACOB: Boychick, wake up! Be something! Make your life something good. For the love of an old man who sees in your young days his new life, for such love take the world in your two hands and make it like new. Go out and fight so life shouldn't be printed on dollar bills. A woman waits.

RALPH: Say, I'm no fool!

JACOB: From my heart I hope not. In the meantime——*(Bell rings.)*

RALPH: See who it is, will you? *(Stands off.)* Don't want Mom to catch me with a clean shirt.

JACOB *(calls):* Come in. *(Sotto voce)* Moe Axelrod. (MOE *enters.)*

MOE: Hello girls, how's your whiskers? *(To* RALPH): All dolled up. What's it, the weekly visit to the cat house?

RALPH: Please mind your business.

MOE: Okay, sweetheart.

RALPH *(taking a hidden dollar from a book):* If Mom asks where I went——

JACOB: I know. Enjoy yourself.

RALPH: Bye-bye. *(He exits.)*

JACOB: Bye-bye.

MOE: Who's home?

JACOB: Me.

MOE: Good. I'll stick around a few minutes. Where's Hennie?

JACOB: She went with Bessie and Myron to a show.

MOE: She what?!

JACOB: You had a date?

MOE *(hiding his feelings):* Here—I brought you some halavah.

JACOB: Halavah? Thanks. I'll eat a piece after.

MOE: So Ralph's got a dame? Hot stuff—a kid can't even play a card game.

JACOB: Moe, you're a no-good, a bum of the first water. To your dying day you won't change.

MOE: Where'd you get that stuff, a no-good?

JACOB: But I like you.

MOE: Didn't I go fight in France for democracy? Didn't I get my goddam leg shot off in that war the day before the armistice? Uncle Sam give me the Order of the Purple Heart, didn't he? What'd you mean, a no-good?

JACOB: Excuse me.

MOE: If you got an orange I'll eat an orange.

JACOB: No orange. An apple.

MOE: No oranges, huh?—what a dump!

JACOB: Bessie hears you once talking like this she'll knock your head off.

MOE: Hennie went with, huh? She wantsa see me squirm, only I don't squirm for dames.

JACOB: You came to see her?

MOE: What for? I got a present for our boy friend, Myron. He'll drop dead when I tell him his gentle horse galloped in fifteen to one. He'll die.

JACOB: It really won? The first time I remember.

MOE: Where'd they go?

JACOB: A vaudeville by the Franklin.

MOE: What's special tonight?

JACOB: Someone tells a few jokes . . . and they forget the street is filled with starving beggars.

MOE: What'll they do—start a war?

JACOB: I don't know.

MOE: You oughta know. What the hell you got all the books for?

JACOB: It needs a new world.

MOE: That's why they had the big war—to make a new world, they said—safe for democracy. Sure every big general laying up in a Paris hotel with a half dozen broads pinned on his mustache. Democracy! I learned a lesson.

JACOB: An imperial war. You know what this means?

MOE: Sure, I know everything!

JACOB: By money men the interests must be protected. Who gave you such a rotten haircut? Please *(fishing in his vest pocket),* give me for a cent a cigarette. I didn't have since yesterday——

MOE *(giving one):* Don't make me laugh. *(A cent passes back and forth between them,* MOE *finally throwing it over his shoulder.)* Don't look so tired all the time. You're a wow—always sore about something.

JACOB: And you?

MOE: You got one thing—you can play pinochle. I'll take you over in a game. Then you'll have something to be sore on.

JACOB: Who'll wash dishes? (MOE *takes deck from buffet drawer.)*

MOE: Do 'em after. Ten cents a deal.

JACOB: Who's got ten cents?

MOE: I got ten cents. I'll lend it to you.

JACOB: Commence.

MOE *(shaking cards):* The first time I had my hands on a pack in two days. Lemme shake up these cards. I'll make 'em talk. (JACOB *goes to his room where he puts on a Caruso record.)*

JACOB: You should live so long.

MOE: Ever see oranges grow? I know a certain place——One summer I laid under a tree and let them fall right in my mouth.

JACOB *(off, the music is playing; the card game begins):* From "L'Africana" . . . a big explorer comes on a new land—"O Paradiso." From act four this piece. Caruso stands on the ship and looks on a Utopia. You hear? "Oh paradise! Oh paradise on earth! Oh blue sky, oh fragrant air——"

MOE: Ask him does he see any oranges? (BESSIE, MYRON *and* HENNIE *enter.)*

JACOB: You came back so soon?

BESSIE: Hennie got sick on the way.

MYRON: Hello, Moe. . . . (MOE *puts cards back in pocket.)*

BESSIE: Take off the phonograph, Pop. *(To* HENNIE): Lay down . . . I'll call the doctor. You should see how she got sick on Prospect Avenue. Two weeks already she don't feel right.

MYRON: Moe . . . ?

BESSIE: Go to bed, Hennie.

HENNIE: I'll sit here.

BESSIE: Such a girl I never saw! Now you'll be stubborn?

MYRON: It's for your own good, Beauty. Influenza——

HENNIE: I'll sit here.

BESSIE: You ever seen a girl should say no to everything. She can't stand on her feet, so——

HENNIE: Don't yell in my ears. I hear. Nothing's wrong. I ate tuna fish for lunch.

MYRON: Canned goods. . . .

BESSIE: Last week you also ate tuna fish?

HENNIE: Yeah, I'm funny for tuna fish. Go to the show—have a good time.

BESSIE: I don't understand what I did to God He blessed me with such children. From the whole world——

MOE (coming to aid of HENNIE): For Chris' sake, don't kibitz so much!

BESSIE: You don't like it?

MOE (aping): No, I don't like it.

BESSIE: That's too bad, Axelrod. Maybe it's better by your cigar-store friends. Here we're different people.

MOE: Don't gimme that cigar store line, Bessie. I walked up five flights——

BESSIE: To take out Hennie. But my daughter ain't in your class, Axelrod.

MOE: To see Myron.

MYRON: Did he, did he, Moe?

MOE: Did he what?

MYRON: "Sky Rocket"?

BESSIE: You bet on a horse!

MOE: Paid twelve and a half to one.

MYRON: There! You hear that, Momma? Our horse came in. You see, it happens, and twelve and a half to one. Just look at that!

MOE: What the hell, a sure thing. I told you.

BESSIE: If Moe said a sure thing, you couldn't bet a few dollars instead of fifty cents?

JACOB (laughs): "Aie, aie, aie."

MOE (at his wallet): I'm carrying six hundred "plunks" in big denominations.

BESSIE: A banker!

MOE: Uncle Sam sends me ninety a month.

BESSIE: So you save it?

MOE: Run it up, Run-it-up-Axelrod, that's me.

BESSIE: The police should know how.

MOE (shutting her up): All right, all right——Change twenty, sweetheart.

MYRON: Can you make change?

BESSIE: Don't be crazy.

MOE: I'll meet a guy in Goldman's restaurant. I'll meet 'im and come back with change.

MYRON *(figuring on paper):* You can give it to me tomorrow in the store.

BESSIE *(acquisitive):* He'll come back, he'll come back!

MOE: Lucky I bet some bucks myself. *(In derision to* HENNIE*):* Let's step out tomorrow night, Par-a-dise. *(Thumbs his nose at her, laughs mordantly and exits.)*

MYRON: Oh, that's big percentage. If I picked a winner every day. . . .

BESSIE: Poppa, did you take Tootsie on the roof?

JACOB: All right.

MYRON: Just look at that—a cake walk. We can make——

BESSIE: It's enough talk. I got a splitting headache. Hennie, go in bed. I'll call Dr. Cantor.

HENNIE: I'll sit here . . . and don't call that old Ignatz 'cause I won't see him.

MYRON: If you get sick Momma can't nurse you. You don't want to go to a hospital.

JACOB: She don't look sick, Bessie, it's a fact.

BESSIE: She's got fever. I see in her eyes, so he tells me no. Myron, call Dr. Cantor. (MYRON *picks up phone, but* HENNIE *grabs it from him.)*

HENNIE: I don't want any doctor. I ain't sick. Leave me alone.

MYRON: Beauty, it's for your own sake.

HENNIE: Day in and day out pestering. Why are you always right and no one else can say a word?

BESSIE: When you have your own children——

HENNIE: I'm not sick! Hear what I say? I'm not sick! Nothing's the matter with me! I don't want a doctor. (BESSIE *is watching her with slow progressive understanding.)*

BESSIE: What's the matter?

HENNIE: Nothing, I told you!

BESSIE: You told me, but——*(A long pause of examination follows.)*

HENNIE: See much?

BESSIE: Myron, put down the . . . the. . . . *(He slowly puts the phone down.)* Tell me what happened. . . .

HENNIE: Brooklyn Bridge fell down.

BESSIE *(approaching):* I'm asking a question. . . .

MYRON: What's happened, Momma?

BESSIE: Listen to me!

HENNIE: What the hell are you talking?

BESSIE: Poppa—take Tootsie on the roof.

HENNIE *(holding JACOB back):* If he wants he can stay here.

MYRON: What's wrong, Momma?

BESSIE *(her voice quivering slightly):* Myron, your fine Beauty's in trouble. Our society lady. . . .

MYRON: Trouble? I don't under—is it——?

BESSIE: Look in her face. *(He looks, understands and slowly sits in a chair, utterly crushed.)* Who's the man?

HENNIE: The Prince of Wales.

BESSIE: My gall is busting in me. In two seconds——

HENNIE *(in a violent outburst):* Shut up! Shut up! I'll jump out the window in a minute! Shut up! *(Finally she gains control of herself, says in a low, hard voice):* You don't know him.

JACOB: Bessie. . . .

BESSIE: He's a Bronx boy?

HENNIE: From out of town.

BESSIE: What do you mean?

HENNIE: From out of town!!

BESSIE: A long time you know him? You were sleeping by a girl from the office Saturday nights? You slept good, my lovely lady. You'll go to him . . . he'll marry you.

HENNIE: That's what you say.

BESSIE: That's what I say! He'll do it, take MY word he'll do it!

HENNIE: Where? *(To JACOB):* Give her the letter. *(JACOB does so.)*

BESSIE: What? *(Reads.)* "Dear sir: In reply to your request of the 14th inst., we can state that no Mr. Ben Grossman has ever been connected with our organization . . ." You don't know where he is?

HENNIE: No.

BESSIE *(walks back and forth):* Stop crying like a baby, Myron.

MYRON: It's like a play on the stage. . . .

BESSIE: To a mother you couldn't say something before. I'm old-fashioned—like your friends I'm not smart—I don't eat chop suey and run around Coney Island with tramps. *(She walks reflectively to buffet, picks up a box of candy, puts it down, says to MYRON):* Tomorrow night bring Sam Feinschreiber for supper.

HENNIE: I won't do it.

BESSIE: You'll do it, my fine beauty, you'll do it!

HENNIE: I'm not marrying a poor foreigner like him. Can't even speak an English word. Not me! I'll go to my grave without a husband.

BESSIE: You don't say! We'll find for you somewhere a millionaire with a pleasure boat. He's going to night school, Sam. For a boy only three years in the country he speaks very nice. In three years he put enough in the bank, a good living.

JACOB: This is serious?

BESSIE: What then? I'm talking for my health? He'll come tomorrow night for supper. By Saturday they're engaged.

JACOB: Such a thing you can't do.

BESSIE: Who asked your advice?

JACOB: Such a thing——

BESSIE: Never mind!

JACOB: The lowest from the low!

BESSIE: Don't talk! I'm warning you! A man who don't believe in God —with crazy ideas——

JACOB: So bad I never imagined you could be.

BESSIE: Maybe if you didn't talk so much it wouldn't happen like this. You with your ideas—I'm a mother. I raise a family, they should have respect.

JACOB: Respect? *(Spits.)* Respect! For the neighbors' opinion! You insult me, Bessie!

BESSIE: Go in your room, Papa. Every job he ever had he lost because he's got a big mouth. He opens his mouth and the whole Bronx could fall in. Everybody said it——

MYRON: Momma, they'll hear you down the dumbwaiter.

BESSIE: A good barber not to hold a job a week. Maybe you never heard charity starts at home. You never heard it, Pop?

JACOB: All you know, I heard, and more yet. But Ralph you don't make like you. Before you do it, I'll die first. He'll find a girl. He'll go in a fresh world with her. This is a house? Marx said it—abolish such families.

BESSIE: Go in your room, Papa.

JACOB: Ralph you don't make like you!

BESSIE: Go lay in your room with Caruso and the books together.

JACOB: All right!

BESSIE: Go in the room!

JACOB: Some day I'll come out I'll——*(Unable to continue, he turns, looks at* HENNIE, *goes to his door and there says with an attempt at humor):* Bessie, some day you'll talk to me so fresh . . . I'll leave the house for good! *(He exits.)*

BESSIE *(crying):* You ever in your life seen it? He should dare! He should just dare say in the house another word. Your gall could bust from such a man. *(Bell rings,* MYRON *goes.)* Go to sleep now. It won't hurt.

HENNIE: Yeah? (MOE *enters, a box in his hand.* MYRON *follows and sits down.)*

MOE *(looks around first—putting box on table):* Cake. *(About to give* MYRON *the money, he turns instead to* BESSIE): Six fifty, four bits change . . . come on, hand over half a buck. *(She does so. Of* MYRON): Who bit him?

BESSIE: We're soon losing our Hennie, Moe.

MOE: Why? What's the matter?

BESSIE: She made her engagement.

MOE: Zat so?

BESSIE: Today it happened . . . he asked her.

MOE: Did he? Who? Who's the corpse?

BESSIE: It's a secret.

MOE: In the bag, huh?

HENNIE: Yeah. . . .

BESSIE: When a mother gives away an only daughter it's no joke. Wait, when you'll get married you'll know. . . .

MOE *(bitterly):* Don't make me laugh—when I get married! What I think a women? Take 'em all, cut 'em in little pieces like a herring in Greek salad. A guy in France had the right idea—dropped his wife in a bathtub fulla acid. *(Whistles.)* Sss, down the pipe! Pfft— not even a corset button left!

MYRON: Corsets don't have buttons.

MOE *(to* HENNIE): What's the great idea? Gone big time, Paradise? Christ, it's suicide! Sure, kids you'll have, gold teeth, get fat, big in the tangerines——

HENNIE: Shut your face!

MOE: Who's it—some dope pullin' down twenty bucks a week? Cut your throat, sweetheart. Save time.

BESSIE: Never mind your two cents, Axelrod.

MOE: I say what I think—that's me!

HENNIE: That's you—a lousy fourflusher who'd steal the glasses off a blind man.

MOE: Get hot!

HENNIE: My God, do I need it—to listen to this mutt shoot his mouth off?

MYRON: Please. . . .

MOE: Now wait a minute, sweetheart, wait a minute. I don't have to take that from you.

BESSIE: Don't yell at her!

HENNIE: For two cents I'd spit in your eye.

MOE *(throwing coin to table):* Here's two bits. (HENNIE *looks at him and then starts across the room.)*

BESSIE: Where are you going?

HENNIE *(crying):* For my beauty nap, Mussolini. Wake me up when it's apple blossom time in Normandy. *(Exits.)*

MOE: Pretty, pretty—a sweet gal, your Hennie. See the look in her eyes?

BESSIE: She don't feel well. . . .

MYRON: Canned goods. . . .

BESSIE: So don't start with her.

MOE: Like a battleship she's got it. Not like other dames—shove 'em and they lay. Not her. I got a yen for her and I don't mean a Chinee coin.

BESSIE: Listen, Axelrod, in my house you don't talk this way. Either have respect or get out.

MOE: When I think about it . . . maybe I'd marry her myself.

BESSIE *(suddenly aware of* MOE): You could——What do you mean, Moe?

MOE: You ain't sunburnt—you heard me.

BESSIE: Why don't you, Moe? An old friend of the family like you. It would be a blessing on all of us.

MOE: You said she's engaged.

BESSIE: But maybe she don't know her own mind. Say, it's——

MOE: I need a wife like a hole in the head. . . . What's to know about women, I know. Even if I asked her. She won't do it! A guy with one leg—it gives her the heebie-jeebies. I know what she's looking for. An arrow-collar guy, a hero, but with a wad of jack. Only the two don't go together. But I got what it takes . . . plenty, and more where it comes from. . . . *(Breaks off, snorts and rubs his knee. A pause. In his room* JACOB *puts on Caruso singing the lament from "The Pearl Fishers.")*

BESSIE: It's right—she wants a millionaire with a mansion on River-side Drive. So go fight City Hall. Cake?

MOE: Cake.

BESSIE: I'll make tea. But one thing—she's got a fine boy with a business brain. Caruso! *(Exits into the front room and stands in the dark, at the window.)*

MOE: No wet smack . . . a fine girl. . . . She'll burn that guy out in a month. (MOE *retrieves the quarter and spins it on the table.)*

MYRON: I remember that song . . . beautiful. Nora Bayes sang it at the old Proctor's Twenty-third Street—"When It's Apple Blossom Time in Normandy." . . .

MOE: She wantsa see me crawl—my head on a plate she wants! A snowball in hell's got a better chance. *(Out of sheer fury he spins the quarter in his fingers.)*

MYRON *(as his eyes slowly fill with tears):* Beautiful . . .

MOE: Match you for a quarter. Match you for any goddam thing you got. *(Spins the coin viciously.)* What the hell kind of house is this it ain't got an orange!!

Slow Curtain

ACT TWO

SCENE I

One year later, a Sunday afternoon. The front room. JACOB *is giving his son* MORDECAI (UNCLE MORTY) *a haircut, newspapers spread around the base of the chair.* MOE *is reading a newspaper, leg propped on a chair.* RALPH, *in another chair, is spasmodically reading a paper.* UNCLE MORTY *reads colored jokes. Silence, then* BESSIE *enters.*

BESSIE: Dinner's in half an hour, Morty.

MORTY *(still reading jokes):* I got time.

BESSIE: A duck. Don't get hair on the rug, Pop. *(Goes to window and pulls down shade.)* What's the matter the shade's up to the ceiling?

JACOB *(pulling it up again):* Since when do I give a haircut in the dark? *(He mimics her tone.)*

BESSIE: When you're finished, pull it down. I like my house to look respectable. Ralphie, bring up two bottles seltzer from Weiss.

RALPH: I'm reading the paper.

BESSIE: Uncle Morty likes a little seltzer.

RALPH: I'm expecting a phone call.

BESSIE: Noo, if it comes you'll be back. What's the matter? *(Gives him money from apron pocket.)* Take down the old bottles.

RALPH *(to JACOB):* Get that call if it comes. Say I'll be right back. *(JACOB nods assent.)*

MORTY *(giving change from vest):* Get grandpa some cigarettes.

RALPH: Okay. *(Exits.)*

JACOB: What's new in the paper, Moe?

MOE: Still jumping off the high buildings like flies—the big shots who lost all their cocoanuts. Pfft!

JACOB: Suicides?

MOE: Plenty can't take it—good in the break, but can't take the whip in the stretch.

MORTY *(without looking up):* I saw it happen Monday in my building.

My hair stood up how they shoveled him together—like a pancake —a bankrupt manufacturer.

MOE: No brains.

MORTY: Enough . . . all over the sidewalk.

JACOB: If someone said five-ten years ago I couldn't make for myself a living, I wouldn't believe——

MORTY: Duck for dinner?

BESSIE: The best Long Island duck.

MORTY: I like goose.

BESSIE: A duck is just like a goose, only better.

MORTY: I like a goose.

BESSIE: The next time you'll be for Sunday dinner I'll make a goose.

MORTY (*sniffs deeply*): Smells good. I'm a great boy for smells.

BESSIE: Ain't you ashamed? Once in a blue moon he should come to an only sister's house.

MORTY: Bessie, leave me live.

BESSIE: You should be ashamed!

MORTY: Quack quack!

BESSIE: No, better to lay around Mecca Temple playing cards with the Masons.

MORTY (*with good nature*): Bessie, don't you see Pop's giving me a haircut?

BESSIE: You don't need no haircut. Look, two hairs he took off.

MORTY: Pop likes to give me a haircut. If I said no he don't forget for a year, do you, Pop? An old man's like that.

JACOB: I still do an A-1 job.

MORTY (*winking*): Pop cuts hair to fit the face, don't you, Pop?

JACOB: For sure, Morty. To each face a different haircut. Custom built, no ready made. A round face needs special——

BESSIE (*cutting him short*): A graduate from the B.M.T. (*going*): Don't forget the shade. (*The phone rings. She beats* JACOB *to it.*) Hello? Who is it, please? . . . Who is it please? . . . Miss Hirsch? No, he ain't here. . . . No, I couldn't say when. (*Hangs up sharply.*)

JACOB: For Ralph?

BESSIE: A wrong number. (JACOB *looks at her and goes back to his job.*)

JACOB: Excuse me!

BESSIE (*to* MORTY): Ralphie took another cut down the place yester-day.

MORTY: Business is bad. I saw his boss Harry Glicksman Thursday. I bought some velvets . . . they're coming in again.

BESSIE: Do something for Ralphie down there.

MORTY: What can I do? I mentioned it to Glicksman. He told me they squeezed out half the people. . . . (MYRON *enters dressed in apron.*)

BESSIE: What's gonna be the end? Myron's working only three days a week now.

MYRON: It's conditions.

BESSIE: Hennie's married with a baby . . . money just don't come in. I never saw conditions should be so bad.

MORTY: Times'll change.

MOE: The only thing'll change is my underwear.

MORTY: These last few years I got my share of gray hairs. (*Still reading jokes without having looked up once.*) Ha, ha, ha—Popeye the sailor ate spinach and knocked out four bums.

MYRON: I'll tell you the way I see it. The country needs a great man now—a regular Teddy Roosevelt.

MOE: What this country needs is a good five-cent earthquake.

JACOB: So long labor lives it should increase private gain——

BESSIE (*to* JACOB): Listen, Poppa, go talk on the street corner. The government'll give you free board the rest of your life.

MORTY: I'm surprised. Don't I send a five-dollar check for Pop every week?

BESSIE: You could afford a couple more and not miss it.

MORTY: Tell me jokes. Business is so rotten I could just as soon lay all day in the Turkish bath.

MYRON: Why'd I come in here? (*Puzzled, he exits.*)

MORTY (*to* MOE): I hear the bootleggers still do business, Moe.

MOE: Wake up! I kissed bootlegging bye-bye two years back.

MORTY: For a fact? What kind of racket is it now?

MOE: If I told you, you'd know something. (HENNIE *comes from bedroom.*)

HENNIE: Where's Sam?

BESSIE: Sam? In the kitchen.

HENNIE (*calls*): Sam. Come take the diaper.

MORTY: How's the Mickey Louse? Ha, ha, ha. . . .

HENNIE: Sleeping.

MORTY: Ah, that's life to a baby. He sleeps—gets it in the mouth—

sleeps some more. To raise a family nowadays you must be a damn
fool.

BESSIE: Never mind, never mind, a woman who don't raise a family—
a girl—should jump overboard. What's she good for? *(To* MOE—*to
change the subject):* Your leg bothers you bad?

MOE: It's okay, sweetheart.

BESSIE *(to* MORTY): It hurts him every time it's cold out. He's got four
legs in the closet.

MORTY: Four wooden legs?

MOE: Three.

MORTY: What's the big idea?

MOE: Why not? Uncle Sam gives them out free.

MORTY: Say, maybe if Uncle Sam gave out less legs we could balance
the budget.

JACOB: Or not have a war so they wouldn't have to give out legs.

MORTY: Shame on you, Pop. Everybody knows war is necessary.

MOE: Don't make me laugh. Ask me—the first time you pick up a
dead one in the trench—then you learn war ain't so damn necessary.

MORTY: Say, you should kick. The rest of your life Uncle Sam pays you
ninety a month. Look, not a worry in the world.

MOE: Don't make me laugh. Uncle Sam can take his *seventy* bucks
and——*(Finishes with a gesture.)* Nothing good hurts. *(He rubs his
stump.)*

HENNIE: Use a crutch, Axelrod. Give the stump a rest.

MOE: Mind your business, Feinschreiber.

BESSIE: It's a sensible idea.

MOE: Who asked you?

BESSIE: Look, he's ashamed.

MOE: So's your Aunt Fanny.

BESSIE *(naïvely):* Who's got an Aunt Fanny? *(She cleans a rubber
plant's leaves with her apron.)*

MORTY: It's a joke!

MOE: I don't want my paper creased before I read it. I want it fresh.
Fifty times I said that.

BESSIE: Don't get so excited for a five-cent paper—our star boarder.

MOE: And I don't want no one using my razor either. Get it straight.
I'm not buying ten blades a week for the Berger family. *(Furious,
he limps out.)*

BESSIE: Maybe I'm using his razor too.

HENNIE: Proud!

BESSIE: You need luck with plants. I didn't clean off the leaves in a month.

MORTY: You keep the house like a pin and I like your cooking. Any time Myron fires you, come to me, Bessie. I'll let the butler go and you'll be my housekeeper. I don't like Japs so much—sneaky.

BESSIE: Say, you can't tell. Maybe any day I'm coming to stay. (HENNIE *exits.*)

JACOB: Finished.

MORTY: How much, Ed. Pinaud? *(Disengages self from chair.)*

JACOB: Five cents.

MORTY: Still five cents for a haircut to fit the face?

JACOB: Prices don't change by me. *(Takes a dollar.)* I can't change——

MORTY: Keep it. Buy yourself a Packard. Ha, ha, ha.

JACOB *(taking large envelope from pocket):* Please, you'll keep this for me. Put it away.

MORTY: What is it?

JACOB: My insurance policy. I don't like it should lay around where something could happen.

MORTY: What could happen?

JACOB: Who knows, robbers, fire . . . they took next door. Fifty dollars from O'Reilly.

MORTY: Say, lucky a Berger didn't lose it.

JACOB: Put it downtown in the safe. Bessie don't have to know.

MORTY: It's made out to Bessie?

JACOB: No, to Ralph.

MORTY: To Ralph?

JACOB: He don't know. Some day he'll get three thousand.

MORTY: You got good years ahead.

JACOB: Behind. (RALPH *enters.*)

RALPH: Cigarettes. Did a call come?

JACOB: A few minutes. She don't let me answer it.

RALPH: Did Mom say I was coming back?

JACOB: No. (MORTY *is back at new jokes.*)

RALPH: She starting that stuff again? (BESSIE *enters.*) A call come for me?

BESSIE *(waters pot from milk bottle):* A wrong number.

JACOB: Don't say a lie, Bessie.

RALPH: Blanche said she'd call me at two—was it her?

BESSIE: I said a wrong number.

RALPH: Please, Mom, if it was her tell me.

BESSIE: You call me a liar next. You got no shame—to start a scene in front of Uncle Morty. Once in a blue moon he comes——

RALPH: What's the shame? If my girl calls I wanna know it.

BESSIE: You made enough mish mosh with her until now.

MORTY: I'm surprised, Bessie. For the love of Mike tell him yes or no.

BESSIE: I didn't tell him? No!

MORTY *(to* RALPH): No! (RALPH *goes to a window and looks out.)*

BESSIE: Morty, I didn't say before—he runs around steady with a girl.

MORTY: Terrible. Should he run around with a foxie-woxie?

BESSIE: A girl with no parents.

MORTY: An orphan?

BESSIE: I could die from shame. A year already he runs around with her. He brought her once for supper. Believe me, she didn't come again, no!

RALPH: Don't think I didn't ask her.

BESSIE: You hear? You raise them and what's in the end for all your trouble?

JACOB: When you'll lay in a grave, no more trouble. *(Exits.)*

MORTY: Quack quack!

BESSIE: A girl like that he wants to marry. A skinny consumptive-looking . . . six months already she's not working—taking charity from an aunt. You should see her. In a year she's dead on his hands.

RALPH: You'd cut her throat if you could.

BESSIE: That's right! Before she'd ruin a nice boy's life I would first go to prison. Miss Nobody should step in the picture and I'll stand by with my mouth shut.

RALPH: Miss Nobody! Who am I? Al Jolson?

BESSIE: Fix your tie!

RALPH: I'll take care of my own life.

BESSIE: You'll take care? Excuse my expression, you can't even wipe your nose yet! He'll take care!

MORTY *(to* BESSIE): I'm surprised. Don't worry so much, Bessie. When it's time to settle down he won't marry a poor girl, will you? In the long run common sense is thicker than love. I'm a great boy for live and let live.

BESSIE: Sure, it's easy to say. In the meantime he eats out my heart. You know I'm not strong.

MORTY: I know . . . a pussy cat . . . ha, ha, ha.

BESSIE: You got money and money talks. But without the dollar who sleeps at night?

RALPH: I been working for years, bringing in money here—putting it in your hand like a kid. All right, I can't get my teeth fixed. All right, that a new suit's like trying to buy the Chrysler Building. You never in your life bought me a pair of skates even—things I died for when I was a kid. I don't care about that stuff, see. Only just remember I pay some of the bills around here, just a few . . . and if my girl calls me on the phone I'll talk to her any time I please. *(He exits.* HENNIE *applauds.)*

BESSIE: Don't be so smart, Miss America! *(To* MORTY*)*: He didn't have skates! But when he got sick, a twelve-year-old boy, who called a big specialist for the last $25 in the house? Skates!

JACOB *(just in. Adjusts window shade):* It looks like snow today.

MORTY: It's about time—winter.

BESSIE: Poppa here could talk like Samuel Webster, too, but it's just talk. He should try to buy a two-cent pickle in the Burland Market without money.

MORTY: I'm getting an appetite.

BESSIE: Right away we'll eat. I made chopped liver for you.

MORTY: My specialty!

BESSIE: Ralph should only be a success like you, Morty. I should only live to see the day when he rides up to the door in a big car with a chauffeur and a radio. I could die happy, believe me.

MORTY: Success she says. She should see how we spend thousands of dollars making up a winter line and winter don't come—summer in January. Can you beat it?

JACOB: Don't live, just make success.

MORTY: Chopped liver—ha!

JACOB: Ha! *(Exits.)*

MORTY: When they start arguing, I don't hear. Suddenly I'm deaf. I'm a great boy for the practical side. *(He looks over to* HENNIE *who sits rubbing her hands with lotion.)*

HENNIE: Hands like a raw potato.

MORTY: What's the matter? You don't look so well . . . no pep.

HENNIE: I'm swell.

MORTY: You used to be such a pretty girl.

HENNIE: Maybe I got the blues. You can't tell.

MORTY: You could stand a new dress.

HENNIE: That's not all I could stand.

MORTY: Come down to the place tomorrow and pick out a couple from the "eleven-eighty" line. Only don't sing me the blues.

HENNIE: Thanks. I need some new clothes.

MORTY: I got two thousand pieces of merchandise waiting in the stock room for winter.

HENNIE: I never had anything from life. Sam don't help.

MORTY: He's crazy about the kid.

HENNIE: Crazy is right. Twenty-one a week he brings in—a nigger don't have it so hard. I wore my fingers off on an Underwood for six years. For what? Now I wash baby diapers. Sure, I'm crazy about the kid too. But half the night the kid's up. Try to sleep. You don't know how it is, Uncle Morty.

MORTY: No, I don't know. I was born yesterday. Ha, ha, ha. Some day I'll leave you a little nest egg. You like eggs? Ha?

HENNIE: When? When I'm dead and buried?

MORTY: No, when *I'm* dead and buried. Ha, ha, ha.

HENNIE: You should know what I'm thinking.

MORTY: Ha, ha, ha, I know. (MYRON *enters.*)

MYRON: I never take a drink. I'm just surprised at myself, I——

MORTY: I got a pain. Maybe I'm hungry.

MYRON: Come inside, Morty. Bessie's got some schnapps.

MORTY: I'll take a drink. Yesterday I missed the Turkish bath.

MYRON: I get so bitter when I take a drink, it just surprises me.

MORTY: Look how fat. Say, you live once. . . . Quack, quack. (*Both exit.* MOE *stands silently in the doorway.*)

SAM (*entering*): I'll make Leon's bottle now!

HENNIE: No, let him sleep, Sam. Take away the diaper. (*He does. Exits.*)

MOE (*advancing into the room*): That your husband?

HENNIE: Don't you know?

MOE: Maybe he's a nurse you hired for the kid—it looks it—how he tends it. A guy comes howling to your old lady every time you look cock-eyed. Does he sleep with you?

HENNIE: Don't be so wise!

MOE (*indicating newspaper*): Here's a dame strangled her hubby with wire. Claimed she didn't like him. Why don't you brain Sam with an axe some night?

HENNIE: Why don't you lay an egg, Axelrod?

MOE: I laid a few in my day, Feinschreiber. Hard-boiled ones too.

HENNIE: Yeah?

MOE: Yeah. You wanna know what I see when I look in your eyes?

HENNIE: No.

MOE: Ted Lewis playing the clarinet—some of those high crazy notes! Christ, you coulda had a guy with some guts instead of a cluck stands around boilin' baby nipples.

HENNIE: Meaning you?

MOE: Meaning me, sweetheart.

HENNIE: Think you're pretty good.

MOE: You'd know if I slept with you again.

HENNIE: I'll smack your face in a minute.

MOE: You do and I'll break your arm. *(Holds up paper.)* Take a look. *(Reads):* "Ten-day luxury cruise to Havana." That's the stuff you coulda had. Put up at ritzy hotels, frenchie soap, champagne. Now you're tied down to "Snake-Eye" here. What for? What's it get you? . . . a 2 x 4 flat on 108th Street . . . a pain in the bustle it gets you.

HENNIE: What's it to you?

MOE: I know you from the old days. How you like to spend it! What I mean! Lizard-skin shoes, perfume behind the ears. . . . You're in a mess, Paradise! Paradise—that's a hot one—yah, crazy to eat a knish at your own wedding.

HENNIE: I get it—you're jealous. You can't get me.

MOE: Don't make me laugh.

HENNIE: Kid Jailbird's been trying to make me for years. You'd give your other leg. I'm hooked? Maybe, but you're in the same boat. Only it's worse for you. I don't give a damn no more, but you gotta yen makes you——

MOE: Don't make me laugh.

HENNIE: Compared to you I'm sittin' on top of the world.

MOE: You're losing your looks. A dame don't stay young forever.

HENNIE: You're a liar. I'm only twenty-four.

MOE: When you comin' home to stay?

HENNIE: Wouldn't you like to know?

MOE: I'll get you again.

HENNIE: Think so?

MOE: Sure, whatever goes up comes down. You're easy—you remember—two for a nickel—a pushover! *(Suddenly she slaps him. They both seem stunned.)* What's the idea?

HENNIE: Go on . . . break my arm.

MOE *(as if saying "I love you")*: Listen, lousy.

HENNIE: Go on, do something!

MOE: Listen——

HENNIE: You're so damn tough!

MOE: You like me. *(He takes her.)*

HENNIE: Take your hand off! *(Pushes him away.)* Come around when it's a flood again and they put you in the ark with the animals. Not even then—if you was the last man!

MOE: Baby, if you had a dog I'd love the dog.

HENNIE: Gorilla! *(Exits.* RALPH *enters.)*

RALPH: Were you here before?

MOE *(sits):* What?

RALPH: When the call came for me?

MOE: What?

RALPH: The call came. (JACOB *enters.)*

MOE *(rubbing his leg):* No.

JACOB: Don't worry, Ralphie, she'll call back.

RALPH: Maybe not. I think somethin's the matter.

JACOB: What?

RALPH: I don't know. I took her home from the movie last night. She asked me what I'd think if she went away.

JACOB: Don't worry, she'll call again.

RALPH: Maybe not, if Mom insulted her. She gets it on both ends, the poor kid. Lived in an orphan asylum most of her life. They shove her around like an empty freight train.

JACOB: After dinner go see her.

RALPH: Twice they kicked me down the stairs.

JACOB: Life should have some dignity.

RALPH: Every time I go near the place I get heart failure. The uncle drives a bus. You oughta see him—like Babe Ruth.

MOE: Use your brains. Stop acting like a kid who still wets the bed. Hire a room somewhere—a club room for two members.

RALPH: Not that kind of proposition, Moe.

MOE: Don't be a bush leaguer all your life.

RALPH: Cut it out!

MOE *(on a sudden upsurge of emotion):* Ever sleep with one? Look at 'im blush.

RALPH: You don't know her.

MOE: I seen her—the kind no one sees undressed till the undertaker works on her.

RALPH: Why give me the needles all the time? What'd I ever do to you?

MOE: Not a thing. You're a nice kid. But grow up! In life there's two kinds—the men that's sure of themselves and the ones who ain't! It's time you quit being a selling-plater and got in the first class.

JACOB: And you, Axelrod?

MOE *(to* JACOB): Scratch your whiskers! *(To* RALPH): Get independent. Get what-it-takes and be yourself. Do what you like.

RALPH: Got a suggestion? (MORTY *enters, eating.)*

MOE: Sure, pick out a racket. Shake down the cocoanuts. See what that does.

MORTY: We know what it does—puts a pudding on your nose! Sing Sing! Easy money's against the law. Against the law don't win. A racket is illegitimate, no?

MOE: It's all a racket—from horse racing down. Marriage, politics, big business—everybody plays cops and robbers. You, you're a racketeer yourself.

MORTY: Who? Me? Personally I manufacture dresses.

MOE: Horse feathers!

MORTY *(seriously):* Don't make such remarks to me without proof. I'm a great one for proof. That's why I made a success in business. Proof—put up or shut up, like a game of cards. I heard this remark before—a rich man's a crook who steals from the poor. Personally, I don't like it. It's a big lie!

MOE: If you don't like it, buy yourself a fife and drum—and go fight your own war.

MORTY: Sweatshop talk. Every Jew and Wop in the shop eats my bread and behind my back says, "a sonofabitch." I started from a poor boy who worked on an ice wagon for two dollars a week. Pop's right here—he'll tell you. I made it honest. In the whole industry nobody's got a better name.

JACOB: It's an exception, such success.

MORTY: Ralph can't do the same thing?

JACOB: No, Morty, I don't think. In a house like this he don't realize even the possibilities of life. Economics comes down like a ton of coal on the head.

MOE: Red rover, red rover, let Jacob come over!

JACOB: In my day the propaganda was for God. Now it's for success. A boy don't turn around without having shoved in him he should make success.

MORTY: Pop, you're a comedian, a regular Charlie Chaplin.

JACOB: He dreams all night of fortunes. Why not? Don't it say in the movies he should have a personal steamship, pyjamas for fifty dollars a pair and a toilet like a monument? But in the morning he wakes up and for ten dollars he can't fix the teeth. And millions more worse off in the mills of the South—starvation wages. The blood from the worker's heart. (MORTY *laughs loud and long.*) Laugh, laugh . . . tomorrow not.

MORTY: A real, a real Boob McNutt you're getting to be.

JACOB: Laugh, my son. . . .

MORTY: Here is the North, Pop.

JACOB: North, south, it's one country.

MORTY: The country's all right. A duck quacks in every pot!

JACOB: You never heard how they shoot down men and women which ask a better wage? Kentucky 1932?

MORTY: That's a pile of chopped liver, Pop. (BESSIE *and others enter.*)

JACOB: Pittsburgh, Passaic, Illinois—slavery—it begins where success begins in a competitive system. (MORTY *howls with delight.*)

MORTY: Oh Pop, what are you bothering? Why? Tell me why? Ha ha ha. I bought you a phonograph . . . stick to Caruso.

BESSIE: He's starting up again.

MORTY: Don't bother with Kentucky. It's full of moonshiners.

JACOB: Sure, sure——

MORTY: You don't know practical affairs. Stay home and cut hair to fit the face.

JACOB: It says in the Bible how the Red Sea opened and the Egyptians went in and the sea rolled over them. *(Quotes two lines of Hebrew.)* In this boy's life a Red Sea will happen again. I see it!

MORTY: I'm getting sore, Pop, with all this sweatshop talk.

BESSIE: He don't stop a minute. The whole day, like a phonograph.

MORTY: I'm surprised. Without a rich man you don't have a roof over your head. You don't know it?

MYRON: Now you can't bite the hand that feeds you.

RALPH: Let him alone—he's right!

BESSIE: Another county heard from.

RALPH: It's the truth. It's——

MORTY: Keep quiet, snotnose!

JACOB: For sure, charity, a bone for an old dog. But in Russia an old man don't take charity so his eyes turn black in his head. In Russia they got Marx.

MORTY (*scoffingly*): Who's Marx?

MOE: An outfielder for the Yanks. (MORTY *howls with delight.*)

MORTY: Ha ha ha, it's better than the jokes. I'm telling you. This is Uncle Sam's country. Put it in your pipe and smoke it.

BESSIE: Russia, he says! Read the papers.

SAM: Here is opportunity.

MYRON: People can't believe in God in Russia. The papers tell the truth, they do.

JACOB: So you believe in God . . . you got something for it? You! You worked for all the capitalists. You harvested the fruit from your labor? You got God! But the past comforts you? The present smiles on you, yes? It promises you the future something? Did you found a piece of earth where you could live like a human being and die with the sun on your face? Tell me, yes, tell me. I would like to know myself. But on these questions, on this theme—the struggle for existence—you can't make an answer. The answer I see in your face . . . the answer is your mouth can't talk. In this dark corner you sit and you die. But abolish private property!

BESSIE (*settling the issue*): Noo, go fight City Hall!

MORTY: He's drunk!

JACOB: I'm studying from books a whole lifetime.

MORTY: That's what it is—he's drunk. What the hell does all that mean?

JACOB: If you don't know, why should I tell you.

MORTY (*triumphant at last*): You see? Hear him? Like all those nuts, don't know what they're saying.

JACOB: I know, I know.

MORTY: Like Boob McNutt you know! Don't go in the park, Pop—the squirrels'll get you. Ha, ha, ha. . . .

BESSIE: Save your appetite, Morty. (*To* MYRON): Don't drop the duck.

MYRON: We're ready to eat, Momma.

MORTY (*to* JACOB): Shame on you. It's your second childhood. (*Now they file out.* MYRON *first with the duck, the others behind him.*)

BESSIE: Come eat. We had enough for one day. (*Exits.*)

MORTY: Ha, ha, ha. Quack, quack. (*Exits.*)

(JACOB *sits there trembling and deeply humiliated.* MOE *approaches him and thumbs the old man's nose in the direction of the dining room.*)

MOE: Give 'em five. (*Takes his hand away.*) They got you pasted on the wall like a picture, Jake. *(He limps out to seat himself at the table in the next room.)*

JACOB: Go eat, boychick. (RALPH *comes to him.)* He gives me eat, so I'll climb in a needle. One time I saw an old horse in summer . . . he wore a straw hat . . . the ears stuck out on top. An old horse for hire. Give me back my young days . . . give me fresh blood . . . arms . . . give me——*(The telephone rings. Quickly* RALPH *goes to it.* JACOB *pulls the curtains and stands there, a sentry on guard.)*

RALPH: Hello? . . . Yeah, I went to the store and came right back, right after you called. *(Looks at* JACOB.)

JACOB: Speak, speak. Don't be afraid they'll hear.

RALPH: I'm sorry if Mom said something. You know how excitable Mom is . . . Sure! What? . . . Sure, I'm listening. . . . Put on the radio, Jake. (JACOB *does so. Music comes in and up, a tango, grating with an insistent nostalgic pulse. Under the cover of the music* RALPH *speaks more freely.)* Yes . . . yes . . . What's the matter? Why're you crying? What happened? *(To* JACOB:) She's putting her uncle on. Yes? . . . Listen, Mr. Hirsch, what're you trying to do? What's the big idea? Honest to God. I'm in no mood for joking! Lemme talk to her! Gimme Blanche! *(Waits.)* Blanche? What's this? Is this a joke? Is that true? I'm coming right down! I know, but——You wanna do that? . . . I know, but——I'm coming down . . . tonight! Nine o'clock . . . sure . . . sure . . . sure. . . . *(Hangs up.)*

JACOB: What happened?

MORTY *(enters):* Listen, Pop. I'm surprised you didn't—— *(He howls, shakes his head in mock despair, exits.)*

JACOB: Boychick, what?

RALPH: I don't get it straight. *(To* JACOB): She's leaving. . . .

JACOB: Where?

RALPH: Out West——To Cleveland.

JACOB: Cleveland?

RALPH: . . . In a week or two. Can you picture it? It's a put-up job. But they can't get away with that.

JACOB: We'll find something.

RALPH: Sure, the angels of heaven'll come down on her uncle's cab and whisper in his ear.

JACOB: Come eat. . . . We'll find something.

RALPH: I'm meeting her tonight, but I know——(BESSIE *throws open the curtain between the two rooms and enters.*)

BESSIE: Maybe we'll serve for you a special blue plate supper in the garden?

JACOB: All right, all right. (BESSIE *goes over to the window, levels the shade and on her way out, clicks off the radio.*)

MORTY (*within*): Leave the music, Bessie. (*She clicks it on again, looks at them, exits.*)

RALPH: I know . . .

JACOB: Don't cry, boychick. (*Goes over to* RALPH.) Why should you make like this? Tell me why you should cry, just tell me. . . . (JACOB *takes* RALPH *in his arms and both, trying to keep back the tears, trying fearfully not to be heard by the others in the dining room, begin crying.*) You mustn't cry. . . .

(*The tango twists on. Inside the clatter of dishes and the clash of cutlery sound.* MORTY *begins to howl with laughter.*)

Curtain

SCENE II

That night. The dark dining room.

AT RISE JACOB *is heard in his lighted room, reading from a sheet, declaiming aloud as if to an audience.*

JACOB: They are there to remind us of the horrors—under those crosses lie hundreds of thousands of workers and farmers who murdered each other in uniform for the greater glory of capitalism. (*Comes out of his room.*) The new imperialist war will send millions to their death, will bring prosperity to the pockets of the capitalist—aie, Morty—and will bring only greater hunger and misery to the masses of workers and farmers. The memories of the last world slaughter are still vivid in our minds. (*Hearing a noise he quickly retreats to his room.* RALPH *comes in from the street. He sits with hat and coat on.* JACOB *tentatively opens door and asks*): Ralphie?

RALPH: It's getting pretty cold out.

JACOB (*enters room fully, cleaning hair clippers*): We should have steam till twelve instead of ten. Go complain to the Board of Health.

RALPH: It might snow.

JACOB: It don't hurt . . . extra work for men.

RALPH: When I was a kid I laid awake at nights and heard the sounds of trains . . . far-away lonesome sounds . . . boats going up and down the river. I used to think of all kinds of things I wanted to do. What was it, Jake? Just a bunch of noise in my head?

JACOB *(waiting for news of the girl):* You wanted to make for yourself a certain kind of world.

RALPH: I guess I didn't. I'm feeling pretty, pretty low.

JACOB: You're a young boy and for you life is all in front like a big mountain. You got feet to climb.

RALPH: I don't know how.

JACOB: So you'll find out. Never a young man had such opportunity like today. He could make history.

RALPH: Ten P.M. and all is well. Where's everybody?

JACOB: They went.

RALPH: Uncle Morty too?

JACOB: Hennie and Sam he drove down.

RALPH: I saw her.

JACOB *(alert and eager):* Yes, yes, tell me.

RALPH: I waited in Mount Morris Park till she came out. So cold I did a buck'n wing to keep warm. She's scared to death.

JACOB: They made her?

RALPH: Sure. She wants to go. They keep yelling at her—they want her to marry a millionaire, too.

JACOB: You told her you love her?

RALPH: Sure. "Marry me," I said. "Marry me tomorrow." On sixteen bucks a week. On top of that I had to admit Mom'd have Uncle Morty get me fired in a second. . . . Two can starve as cheap as one!

JACOB: So what happened?

RALPH: I made her promise to meet me tomorrow.

JACOB: Now she'll go in the West?

RALPH: I'd fight the whole goddam world with her, but not her. No guts. The hell with her. If she wantsa go—all right—I'll get along.

JACOB: For sure, there's more important things than girls. . . .

RALPH: You said a mouthful . . . and maybe I don't see it. She'll see what I can do. No one stops me when I get going. . . . *(Near to tears, he has to stop.* JACOB *examines his clippers very closely.)*

JACOB: Electric clippers never do a job like by hand.

RALPH: Why won't Mom let us live here?

JACOB: Why? Why? Because in a society like this today people don't love. Hate!

RALPH: Gee, I'm no bum who hangs around pool parlors. I got the stuff to go ahead. I don't know what to do.

JACOB: Look on me and learn what to do, boychick. Here sits an old man polishing tools. You think maybe I'll use them again! Look on this failure and see for seventy years he talked, with good ideas, but only in the head. It's enough for me now I should see your happiness. This is why I tell you—DO! Do what is in your heart and you carry in yourself a revolution. But you should act. Not like me. A man who had golden opportunities but drank instead a glass tea. No. . . . *(A pause of silence.)*

RALPH *(listening):* Hear it? The Boston air mail plane. Ten minutes late. I get a kick the way it cuts across the Bronx every night. *(The bell rings:* SAM, *excited, disheveled, enters.)*

JACOB: You came back so soon?

SAM: Where's Mom?

JACOB: Mom? Look on the chandelier.

SAM: Nobody's home?

JACOB: Sit down. Right away they're coming. You went in the street without a tie?

SAM: Maybe it's a crime.

JACOB: Excuse me.

RALPH: You had a fight with Hennie again?

SAM: She'll fight once . . . some day. . . . *(Lapses into silence.)*

JACOB: In my day the daughter came home. Now comes the son-in-law.

SAM: Once too often she'll fight with me, Hennie. I mean it. I mean it like anything. I'm a person with a bad heart. I sit quiet, but inside I got a——

RALPH: What happened?

SAM: I'll talk to Mom. I'll see Mom.

JACOB: Take an apple.

SAM: Please . . . he tells me apples.

RALPH: Why hop around like a billiard ball?

SAM: Even in a joke she should dare say it.

JACOB: My grandchild said something?

SAM: To my father in the old country they did a joke . . . I'll tell you:

One day in Odessa he talked to another Jew on the street. They didn't like it, they jumped on him like a wild wolf.

RALPH: Who?

SAM: Cossacks. They cut off his beard. A Jew without a beard! He came home—I remember like yesterday how he came home and went in bed for two days. He put like this the cover on his face. No one should see. The third morning he died.

RALPH: From what?

SAM: From a broken heart. . . . Some people are like this. Me too. I could die like this from shame.

JACOB: Hennie told you something?

SAM: Straight out she said it—like a lightning from the sky. The baby ain't mine. She said it.

RALPH: Don't be a dope.

JACOB: For sure, a joke.

RALPH: She's kidding you.

SAM: She should kid a policeman, not Sam Feinschreiber. Please . . . you don't know her like me. I wake up in the nighttime and she sits watching me like I don't know what. I make a nice living from the store. But it's no use—she looks for a star in the sky. I'm afraid like anything. You could go crazy from less even. What I shall do I'll ask Mom.

JACOB: "Go home and sleep," she'll say. "It's a bad dream."

SAM: It don't satisfy me more, such remarks, when Hennie could kill in the bed. (JACOB *laughs.*) Don't laugh. I'm so nervous—look, two times I weighed myself on the subway station. *(Throws small cards to table.)*

JACOB *(examining one):* One hundred and thirty-eight—also a fortune. *(Turns it and reads):* "You are inclined to deep thinking, and have a high admiration for intellectual excellence and inclined to be very exclusive in the selection of friends." Correct! I think maybe you got mixed up in the wrong family, Sam. (MYRON *and* BESSIE *now enter.)*

BESSIE: Look, a guest! What's the matter? Something wrong with the baby? *(Waits.)*

SAM: No.

BESSIE: Noo?

SAM *(in a burst):* I wash my hands from everything.

BESSIE: Take off your coat and hat. Have a seat. Excitement don't help. Myron, make tea. You'll have a glass tea. We'll talk like civilized people. (MYRON *goes.*) What is it, Ralph, you're all dressed up for a party? *(He looks at her silently and exits. To* SAM): We saw a very good movie, with Wallace Beery. He acts like life, very good.

MYRON *(within):* Polly Moran too.

BESSIE: Polly Moran too—a woman with a nose from here to Hunts Point, but a fine player. Poppa, take away the tools and the books.

JACOB: All right. *(Exits to his room.)*

BESSIE: Noo, Sam, why do you look like a funeral?

SAM: I can't stand it. . . .

BESSIE: Wait. *(Yells):* You took up Tootsie on the roof.

JACOB *(within):* In a minute.

BESSIE: What can't you stand?

SAM: She said I'm a second fiddle in my own house.

BESSIE: Who?

SAM: Hennie. In the second place, it ain't my baby, she said.

BESSIE: What? What are you talking? (MYRON *enters with dishes.*)

SAM: From her own mouth. It went like a knife in my heart.

BESSIE: Sam, what're you saying?

SAM: Please, I'm making a story? I fell in the chair like a dead.

BESSIE: Such a story you believe?

SAM: I don't know.

BESSIE: How you don't know?

SAM: She told me even the man.

BESSIE: Impossible!

SAM: I can't believe myself. But she said it. I'm a second fiddle, she said. She made such a yell everybody heard for ten miles.

BESSIE: Such a thing Hennie should say—impossible!

SAM: What should I do? With my bad heart such a remark kills.

MYRON: Hennie don't feel well, Sam. You see, she——

BESSIE: What then?—a sick girl. Believe me, a mother knows. Nerves. Our Hennie's got a bad temper. You'll let her she says anything. She takes after me—nervous. *(To* MYRON): You ever heard such a remark in all your life? She should make such a statement! Bughouse.

MYRON: The little one's been sick all these months. Hennie needs a rest. No doubt.

BESSIE: Sam don't think she means it——

MYRON: Oh, I know he don't, of course——

BESSIE: I'll say the truth, Sam. We didn't half the time understand her ourselves. A girl with her own mind. When she makes it up, wild horses wouldn't change her.

SAM: She don't love me.

BESSIE: This is sensible, Sam?

SAM: Not for a nickel.

BESSIE: What do you think? She married you for your money? For your looks? You ain't no John Barrymore, Sam. No, she liked you.

SAM: Please, not for a nickel. (JACOB *stands in the doorway.*)

BESSIE: We stood right here the first time she said it. "Sam Feinschreiber's a nice boy," she said it, "a boy he's got good common sense, with a business head." Right here she said it, in this room. You sent her two boxes of candy together, you remember?

MYRON: Loft's candy.

BESSIE: This is when she said it. What do you think?

MYRON: You were just the only boy she cared for.

BESSIE: So she married you. Such a world . . . plenty of boy friends she had, believe me!

JACOB: A popular girl. . . .

MYRON: Y-e-s.

BESSIE: I'll say it plain out—Moe Axelrod offered her plenty—a servant, a house . . . she don't have to pick up a hand.

MYRON: Oh, Moe? Just wild about her. . . .

SAM: Moe Axelrod? He wanted to——

BESSIE: But she didn't care. A girl like Hennie you don't buy, should never live to see another day if I'm telling a lie.

SAM: She was kidding me.

BESSIE: What then? You shouldn't be foolish.

SAM: The baby looks like my family. He's got Feinschreiber eyes.

BESSIE: A blind man could see it.

JACOB: Sure . . . sure. . . .

SAM: The baby looks like me. Yes. . . .

BESSIE: You could believe me.

JACOB: Any day. . . .

SAM: But she tells me the man. She made up his name too?

BESSIE: Sam, Sam, look in the phone book—a million names.

MYRON: Tom, Dick and Harry. (JACOB *laughs quietly, soberly.*)

BESSIE: Don't stand around, Poppa. Take Tootsie on the roof. And you don't let her go under the water tank.

JACOB: Schmah Yisroeal. Behold! (*Quietly laughing he goes back into his room, closing the door behind him.*)

SAM: I won't stand he should make insults. A man eats out his——

BESSIE: No, no, he's an old man—a second childhood. Myron, bring in the tea. Open a jar of raspberry jelly. (MYRON *exits.*)

SAM: Mom, you think——?

BESSIE: I'll talk to Hennie. It's all right.

SAM: Tomorrow, I'll take her by the doctor. (RALPH *enters.*)

BESSIE: Stay for a little tea.

SAM: No, I'll go home. I'm tired. Already I caught a cold in such weather. *(Blows his nose.)*

MYRON *(entering with stuffs):* Going home?

SAM: I'll go in bed. I caught a cold.

MYRON: Teddy Roosevelt used to say, "When you have a problem, sleep on it."

BESSIE: My Sam is no problem.

MYRON: I don't mean . . . I mean he said——

BESSIE: Call me tomorrow, Sam.

SAM: I'll phone supper time. Sometime I think there's something funny about me. (MYRON *sees him out. In the following pause Caruso is heard singing within.)*

BESSIE: A bargain! Second fiddle. By me he don't even play in the orchestra—a man like a mouse. Maybe she'll lay down and die 'cause he makes a living?

RALPH: Can I talk to you about something?

BESSIE: What's the matter—I'm biting you?

RALPH: It's something about Blanche.

BESSIE: Don't tell me.

RALPH: Listen now——

BESSIE: I don't wanna know.

RALPH: She's got no place to go.

BESSIE: I don't want to know.

RALPH: Mom, I love this girl. . . .

BESSIE: So go knock your head against the wall.

RALPH: I want her to come here. Listen, Mom, I want you to let her live here for a while.

BESSIE: You got funny ideas, my son.

RALPH: I'm as good as anyone else. Don't I have some rights in the world? Listen, Mom, if I don't do something, she's going away. Why don't you do it? Why don't you let her stay here for a few weeks? Things'll pick up. Then we can——

BESSIE: Sure, sure. I'll keep her fresh on ice for a wedding day. That's what you want?

RALPH: No, I mean you should——

BESSIE: Or maybe you'll sleep here in the same bed without marriage. (JACOB *stands in his doorway, dressed.*)

RALPH: Don't say that, Mom. I only mean. . . .

BESSIE: What you mean, I know . . . and what I mean I also know. Make up your mind. For your own good, Ralphie. If she dropped in the ocean I don't lift a finger.

RALPH: That's all, I suppose.

BESSIE: With me it's one thing—a boy should have respect for his own future. Go to sleep, you look tired. In the morning you'll forget.

JACOB: "Awake and sing, ye that dwell in dust, and the earth shall cast out the dead." It's cold out?

MYRON: Oh, yes.

JACOB: I'll take up Tootsie now.

MYRON (*eating bread and jam*): He come on us like the wild man of Borneo, Sam. I don't think Hennie was fool enough to tell him the truth like that.

BESSIE: Myron! (*A deep pause.*)

RALPH: What did he say?

BESSIE: Never mind.

RALPH: I heard him. I heard him. You don't needa tell me.

BESSIE: Never mind.

RALPH: You trapped that guy.

BESSIE: Don't say another word.

RALPH: Just have respect? That's the idea?

BESSIE: Don't say another word. I'm boiling over ten times inside.

RALPH: You won't let Blanche here, huh. I'm not sure I want her. You put one over on that little shrimp. The cat's whiskers, Mom?

BESSIE: I'm telling you something!

RALPH: I got the whole idea. I get it so quick my head's swimming. Boy, what a laugh! I suppose you know about this, Jake?

JACOB: Yes.

RALPH: Why didn't you do something?

JACOB: I'm an old man.

RALPH: What's that got to do with the price of bonds? Sits around and lets a thing like that happen! You make me sick too.

MYRON (*after a pause*): Let me say something, son.

RALPH: Take your hand away! Sit in a corner and wag your tail. Keep on boasting you went to law school for two years.

MYRON: I want to tell you——

RALPH: You never in your life had a thing to tell me.

BESSIE *(bitterly):* Don't say a word. Let him, let him run and tell Sam. Publish in the papers, give a broadcast on the radio. To him it don't matter nothing his family sits with tears pouring from the eyes. *(To* JACOB): What are you waiting for? I didn't tell you twice already about the dog? You'll stand around with Caruso and make a bughouse. It ain't enough all day long. Fifty times I told you I'll break every record in the house. *(She brushes past him, breaks the records, comes out.)* The next time I say something you'll maybe believe it. Now maybe you learned a lesson. *(Pause.)*

JACOB *(quietly):* Bessie, new lessons . . . not for an old dog. (MOE *enters.)*

MYRON: You didn't have to do it, Momma.

BESSIE: Talk better to your son, Mr. Berger! Me, I don't lay down and die for him and Poppa no more. I'll work like a nigger? For what? Wait, the day comes when you'll be punished. When it's too late you'll remember how you sucked away a mother's life. Talk to him, tell him how I don't sleep at night. *(Bursts into tears and exits.)*

MOE *(sings):* "Good-by to all your sorrows. You never hear them talk about the war, in the land of Yama Yama. . . ."

MYRON: Yes, Momma's a sick woman, Ralphie.

RALPH: Yeah?

MOE: We'll be out of the trenches by Christmas. Putt, putt, putt . . . here, stinker. . . . *(Picks up Tootsie, a small, white poodle that just then enters from the hall.)* If there's reincarnation in the next life I wanna be a dog and lay in a fat lady's lap. Barrage over? How 'bout a little pinochle, Pop?

JACOB: Nnno.

RALPH *(taking dog):* I'll take her up. *(Conciliatory.)*

JACOB: No, I'll do it. *(Takes dog.)*

RALPH *(ashamed):* It's cold out.

JACOB: I was cold before in my life. A man sixty-seven. . . . *(Strokes the dog.)* Tootsie is my favorite lady in the house. *(He slowly passes across the room and exits. A settling pause.)*

MYRON: She cried all last night—Tootsie—I heard her in the kitchen ·like a young girl.

MOE: Tonight I could do something. I got a yen . . . I don't know.

MYRON *(rubbing his head):* My scalp is impoverished.

RALPH: Mom bust all his records.

MYRON: She didn't have to do it.

MOE: Tough tit! Now I can sleep in the morning. Who the hell wantsa hear a wop air his tonsils all day long!

RALPH *(handling the fragment of a record):* "O Paradiso!"

MOE *(gets cards):* It's snowing out, girls.

MYRON: There's no more big snows like in the old days. I think the whole world's changing. I see it, right under our very eyes. No one hardly remembers any more when we used to have gaslight and all the dishes had little fishes on them.

MOE: It's the system, girls.

MYRON: I was a little boy when it happened—the Great Blizzard. It snowed three days without a stop that time. Yes, and the horse cars stopped. A silence of death was on the city and little babies got no milk . . . they say a lot of people died that year.

MOE *(singing as he deals himself cards):*
"Lights are blinking while you're drinking.
That's the place where the good fellows go.
Good-by to all your sorrows,
You never hear them talk about the war,
In the land of Yama Yama
Funicalee, funicala, funicalo. . . ."

MYRON: What can I say to you, Big Boy?

RALPH: Not a damn word.

MOE *(goes "ta ra ta ra" throughout.)*

MYRON: I know how you feel about all those things, I know.

RALPH: Forget it.

MYRON: And your girl. . . .

RALPH: Don't soft soap me all of a sudden.

MYRON: I'm not foreign born. I'm an American, and yet I never got close to you. It's an American father's duty to be his son's friend.

RALPH: Who said that—Teddy R.?

MOE *(dealing cards):* You're breaking his heart, "Litvak."

MYRON: It just happened the other day. The moment I began losing my hair I just knew I was destined to be a failure in life . . . and when I grew bald I was. Now isn't that funny, Big Boy?

MOE: It's a pisscutter!

MYRON: I believe in Destiny.

MOE: You get what-it-takes. Then they don't catch you with your pants down. *(Sings out):* Eight of clubs. . . .

MYRON: I really don't know. I sold jewelry on the road before I married. It's one thing to——Now here's a thing the druggist gave me. *(Reads):* "The Marvel Cosmetic Girl of Hollywood is going on the air. Give this charming little radio singer a name and win five thousand dollars. If you will send——"

MOE: Your old man still believes in Santy Claus.

MYRON: Someone's got to win. The government isn't gonna allow everything to be a fake.

MOE: It's a fake. There ain't no prizes. It's a fake.

MYRON: It says——

RALPH *(snatching it):* For Christ's sake, Pop, forget it. Grow up. Jake's right—everybody's crazy. It's like a zoo in this house. I'm going to bed.

MOE: In the land of Yama Yama. . . . *(Goes on with ta ra.)*

MYRON: Don't think life's easy with Momma. No, but she means for your good all the time. I tell you she does, she——

RALPH: Maybe, but I'm going to bed. *(Downstairs doorbell rings violently.)*

MOE *(ring):* Enemy barrage begins on sector eight seventy-five.

RALPH: That's downstairs.

MYRON: We ain't expecting anyone this hour of the night.

MOE: "Lights are blinking while you're drinking, that's the place where the good fellows go. Good-by to ta ra tara ra," etc.

RALPH: I better see who it is.

MYRON: I'll tick the button. *(As he starts, the apartment doorbell begins ringing, followed by large knocking.* MYRON *goes out.)*

RALPH: Who's ever ringing means it. *(A loud excited voice outside.)*

MOE: "In the land of Yama Yama, Funicalee, funicalo, funic——" *(*MYRON *enters followed by* SCHLOSSER *the janitor.* BESSIE *cuts in from the other side.)*

BESSIE: Who's ringing like a lunatic?

RALPH: What's the matter?

MYRON: Momma. . . .

BESSIE: Noo, what's the matter? *(Downstairs bell continues.)*

RALPH: What's the matter?

BESSIE: Well, well . . . ?

MYRON: Poppa. . . .

BESSIE: What happened?

SCHLOSSER: He shlipped maybe in de snow.

RALPH: Who?

SCHLOSSER *(to* BESSIE): Your fadder fall off de roof. . . . Ja. *(A dead pause.* RALPH *then runs out.)*

BESSIE *(dazed):* Myron. . . . Call Morty on the phone . . . call him. (MYRON *starts for phone.)* No. I'll do it myself. I'll . . . do it. (MYRON *exits.)*

SCHLOSSER *(standing stupidly):* Since I was in dis country . . . I was pudding out de ash can . . . The snow is vet. . . .

MOE *(to* SCHLOSSER): Scram. (SCHLOSSER *exits.)*

(BESSIE *goes blindly to the phone, fumbles and gets it.* MOE *sits quietly, slowly turning cards over, but watching her.)*

BESSIE: He slipped. . . .

MOE *(deeply moved):* Slipped?

BESSIE: I can't see the numbers. Make it, Moe, make it. . . .

MOE: Make it yourself. *(He looks at her and slowly goes back to his game of cards with shaking hands.)*

BESSIE: Riverside 7— . . . *(Unable to talk she dials slowly. The dial whizzes on.)*

MOE: Don't . . . make me laugh. . . . *(He turns over cards.)*

Curtain

ACT THREE

A week later in the dining room. MORTY, BESSIE *and* MYRON *eating. Sitting in the front room is* MOE *marking a "dope sheet," but really listening to the others.*

BESSIE: You're sure he'll come tonight—the insurance man?

MORTY: Why not? I shtupped him a ten-dollar bill. Everything's hot delicatessen.

BESSIE: Why must he come so soon?

MORTY: Because you had a big expense. You'll settle once and for all. I'm a great boy for making hay while the sun shines.

BESSIE: Stay till he'll come, Morty. . . .

MORTY: No, I got a strike downtown. Business don't stop for personal life. Two times already in the past week those bastards threw stink bombs in the showroom. Wait! We'll give them strikes—in the kishkas we'll give them. . . .

BESSIE: I'm a woman. I don't know about policies. Stay till he comes.

MORTY: Bessie—sweetheart, leave me live.

BESSIE: I'm afraid, Morty.

MORTY: Be practical. They made an investigation. Everybody knows Pop had an accident. Now we'll collect.

MYRON: Ralphie don't know Papa left the insurance in his name.

MORTY: It's not his business. And I'll tell him.

BESSIE: The way he feels. *(Enter* RALPH *into front room.)* He'll do something crazy. He thinks Poppa jumped off the roof.

MORTY: Be practical, Bessie. Ralphie will sign when I tell him. Everything is peaches and cream.

BESSIE: Wait for a few minutes. . . .

MORTY: Look, I'll show you in black on white what the policy says. *For God's sake, leave me live! (Angrily exits to kitchen. In parlor,* MOE *speaks to* RALPH *who is reading a letter.)*

MOE: What's the letter say?

RALPH: Blanche won't see me no more, she says. I couldn't care very much, she says. If I didn't come like I said. . . . She'll phone before she leaves.

MOE: She don't know about Pop?

RALPH: She won't ever forget me she says. Look what she sends me
. . . a little locket on a chain . . . if she calls I'm out.

MOE: You mean it?

RALPH: For a week I'm trying to go in his room. I guess he'd like me
to have it, but I can't. . . .

MOE: Wait a minute! *(Crosses over.)* They're trying to rook you—a
freeze-out.

RALPH: Who?

MOE: That bunch stuffin' their gut with hot pastrami. Morty in particular. Jake left the insurance—three thousand dollars—for you.

RALPH: For me?

MOE: Now you got wings, kid. Pop figured you could use it. That's
why. . . .

RALPH: That's why what?

MOE: It ain't the only reason he done it.

RALPH: He done it?

MOE: You think a breeze blew him off? (HENNIE *enters and sits.*)

RALPH: I'm not sure what I think.

MOE: The insurance guy's coming tonight. Morty "shtupped" him.

RALPH: Yeah?

MOE: I'll back you up. You're dead on your feet. Grab a sleep for
yourself.

RALPH: No!

MOE: Go on! *(Pushes boy into room.)*

SAM *(whom* MORTY *has sent in for the paper):* Morty wants the paper.

HENNIE: So?

SAM: You're sitting on it. *(Gets paper.)* We could go home now, Hennie! Leon is alone by Mrs. Strasberg a whole day.

HENNIE: Go on home if you're so anxious. A full tub of diapers is
waiting.

SAM: Why should you act this way?

HENNIE: 'Cause there's no bones in ice cream. Don't touch me.

SAM: Please, what's the matter. . . .

MOE: She don't like you. Plain as the face on your nose. . . .

SAM: To me, my friend, you talk a foreign language.

MOE: A quarter you're lousy. (SAM *exits.*) Gimme a buck, I'll run it up
to ten.

HENNIE: Don't do me no favors.

MOE: Take a chance. *(Stopping her as she crosses to doorway.)*

HENNIE: I'm a pushover.

MOE: I say lotsa things. You don't know me.

HENNIE: I know you—when you knock 'em down you're through.

MOE *(sadly):* You still don't know me.

HENNIE: I know what goes in your wise-guy head.

MOE: Don't run away. . . . I ain't got hydrophobia. Wait. I want to tell you. . . . I'm leaving.

HENNIE: Leaving?

MOE: Tonight. Already packed.

HENNIE: Where?

MORTY *(as he enters followed by the others):* My car goes through snow like a dose of salts.

BESSIE: Hennie, go eat. . . .

MORTY: Where's Ralphie?

MOE: In his new room. *(Moves into dining room.)*

MORTY: I didn't have a piece of hot pastrami in my mouth for years.

BESSIE: Take a sandwich, Hennie. You didn't eat all day. . . . *(At window):* A whole week it rained cats and dogs.

MYRON: Rain, rain, go away. Come again some other day. *(Puts shawl on her.)*

MORTY: Where's my gloves?

SAM *(sits on stool):* I'm sorry the old man lays in the rain.

MORTY: Personally, Pop was a fine man. But I'm a great boy for an honest opinion. He had enough crazy ideas for a regiment.

MYRON: Poppa never had a doctor in his whole life. . . . *(Enter RALPH.)*

MORTY: He had Caruso. Who's got more from life?

BESSIE: Who's got more? . . .

MYRON: And Marx he had.

(MYRON *and* BESSIE *sit on sofa.)*

MORTY: Marx! Some say Marx is the new God today. Maybe I'm wrong. Ha ha ha. . . . Personally I counted my ten million last night. . . . I'm sixteen cents short. So tomorrow I'll go to Union Square and yell no equality in the country! Ah, it's a new generation.

RALPH: You said it!

MORTY: What's the matter, Ralphie? What are you looking funny?

RALPH: I hear I'm left insurance and the man's coming tonight.

MORTY: Poppa didn't leave no insurance for you.

RALPH: What?

MORTY: In your name he left it—but not for you.

RALPH: It's my name on the paper.

MORTY: Who said so?

RALPH *(to his mother):* The insurance man's coming tonight?

MORTY: What's the matter?

RALPH: I'm not talking to you. *(To his mother):* Why?

BESSIE: I don't know why.

RALPH: He don't come in this house tonight.

MORTY: That's what *you* say.

RALPH: I'm not talking to you, Uncle Morty, but I'll tell you, too, he don't come here tonight when there's still mud on a grave. *(To his mother):* Couldn't you give the house a chance to cool off?

MORTY: Is this a way to talk to your mother?

RALPH: Was that a way to talk to your father?

MORTY: Don't be so smart with me, Mr. Ralph Berger!

RALPH: Don't be so smart with *me.*

MORTY: What'll you do? I say he's coming tonight. Who says no?

MOE *(suddenly, from the background):* Me.

MORTY: Take a back seat, Axelrod. When you're in the family——

MOE: I got a little document here. *(Produces paper.)* I found it under his pillow that night. A guy who slips off a roof don't leave a note before he does it.

MORTY *(starting for MOE after a horrified silence):* Let me see this note.

BESSIE: Morty, don't touch it!

MOE: Not if you crawled.

MORTY: It's a fake. Poppa wouldn't——

MOE: Get the insurance guy here and we'll see how——*(The bell rings.)* Speak of the devil. . . . Answer it, see what happens. (MORTY *starts for the ticker.)*

BESSIE: Morty, don't!

MORTY *(stopping):* Be practical, Bessie.

MOE: Sometimes you don't collect on suicides if they know about it.

MORTY: You should let. . . . You should let him. . . . *(A pause in which* ALL *seem dazed. Bell rings insistently.)*

MOE: Well, we're waiting.

MORTY: Give me the note.

MOE: I'll give you the head off your shoulders.

MORTY: Bessie, you'll stand for this? *(Points to* RALPH.) Pull down his pants and give him with a strap.

RALPH (*as bell rings again*): How about it?

BESSIE: Don't be crazy. It's not my fault. Morty said he should come tonight. It's not nice so soon. I didn't——

MORTY: I said it? Me?

BESSIE: Who then?

MORTY: You didn't sing a song in my ear a whole week to settle quick?

BESSIE: I'm surprised. Morty, you're a big liar.

MYRON: Momma's telling the truth, she is!

MORTY: Lissen. In two shakes of a lamb's tail, we'll start a real fight and then nobody won't like nobody. Where's my fur gloves? I'm going downtown. (*To* SAM): You coming? I'll drive you down.

HENNIE (*to* SAM, *who looks questioningly at her*): Don't look at me. Go home if you want.

SAM: If you're coming soon, I'll wait.

HENNIE: Don't do me any favors. Night and day he pesters me.

MORTY: You made a cushion——sleep!

SAM: I'll go home. I know . . . to my worst enemy I don't wish such a life——

HENNIE: Sam, keep quiet.

SAM (*quietly; sadly*): No more free speech in America? (*Gets his hat and coat.*) I'm a lonely person. Nobody likes me.

MYRON: I like you, Sam.

HENNIE (*going to him gently; sensing the end*): Please go home, Sam. I'll sleep here. . . . I'm tired and nervous. Tomorrow I'll come home. I love you . . . I mean it. (*She kisses him with real feeling.*)

SAM: I would die for you. . . . (SAM *looks at her. Tries to say something, but his voice chokes up with a mingled feeling. He turns and leaves the room.*)

MORTY: A bird in the hand is worth two in the bush. Remember I said it. Good night. (*Exits after* SAM.) (HENNIE *sits depressed.* BESSIE *goes up and looks at the picture calendar again.* MYRON *finally breaks the silence.*)

MYRON: Yesterday a man wanted to sell me a saxophone with pearl buttons. But I——

BESSIE: It's a beautiful picture. In this land, nobody works. . . . Nobody worries. . . . Come to bed, Myron. (*Stops at the door, and says to* RALPH): Please don't have foolish ideas about the money.

RALPH: Let's call it a day.

BESSIE: It belongs for the whole family. You'll get your teeth fixed——

RALPH: And a pair of black and white shoes?

BESSIE: Hennie needs a vacation. She'll take two weeks in the mountains and I'll mind the baby.

RALPH: I'll take care of my own affairs.

BESSIE: A family needs for a rainy day. Times is getting worse. Prospect Avenue, Dawson, Beck Street—every day furniture's on the sidewalk.

RALPH: Forget it, Mom.

BESSIE: Ralphie, I worked too hard all my years to be treated like dirt. It's no law we should be stuck together like Siamese twins. Summer shoes you didn't have, skates you never had, but I bought a new dress every week. A lover I kept—Mr. Gigolo! Did I ever play a game of cards like Mrs. Marcus? Or was Bessie Berger's children always the cleanest on the block?! Here I'm not only the mother, but also the father. The first two years I worked in a stocking factory for six dollars while Myron Berger went to law school. If I didn't worry about the family who would? On the calendar it's a different place, but here without a dollar you don't look the world in the eye. Talk from now to next year—this is life in America.

RALPH: Then it's wrong. It don't make sense. If life made you this way, then it's wrong!

BESSIE: Maybe you wanted me to give up twenty years ago. Where would you be now? You'll excuse my expression—a bum in the park!

RALPH: I'm not blaming you, Mom. Sink or swim—I see it. But it can't stay like this.

BESSIE: My foolish boy. . . .

RALPH: No, I see every house lousy with lies and hate. He said it, Grandpa—Brooklyn hates the Bronx. Smacked on the nose twice a day. But boys and girls can get ahead like that, Mom. We don't want life printed on dollar bills, Mom!

BESSIE: So go out and change the world if you don't like it.

RALPH: I will! And why? 'Cause life's different in my head. Gimme the earth in two hands. I'm strong. There . . . hear him? The air mail off to Boston. Day or night, he flies away, a job to do. That's us and it's no time to die. *(The airplane sound fades off as* MYRON *gives alarm clock to* BESSIE *which she begins to wind.)*

BESSIE: "Mom, what does she know? She's old-fashioned!" But I'll tell you a big secret: My whole life I wanted to go away too, but with children a woman stays home. A fire burned in *my* heart too, but now it's too late. I'm no spring chicken. The clock goes and Bessie goes. Only my machinery can't be fixed. *(She lifts a button: the alarm rings on the clock; she stops it, says "Good night" and exits.)*

MYRON: I guess I'm no prize bag. . . .

BESSIE *(from within):* Come to bed, Myron.

MYRON *(tears page off calendar):* Hmmm. . . . *(Exits to her.)*

RALPH: Look at him, draggin' after her like an old shoe.

MOE: Punch drunk. *(Phone rings.)* That's for me. *(At phone.)* Yeah? . . . Just a minute. *(To* RALPH*):* Your girl . . .

RALPH: Jeez, I don't know what to say to her.

MOE: Hang up? (RALPH *slowly takes phone.)*

RALPH: Hello. . . . Blanche, I wish. . . . I don't know what to say. . . . Yes . . . Hello? . . . *(Puts phone down.)* She hung up on me . . .

MOE: Sorry?

RALPH: No girl means anything to me until. . . .

MOE: Till when?

RALPH: Till I can take care of her. Till we don't look out on an airshaft. Till we can take the world in two hands and polish off the dirt.

MOE: That's a big order.

RALPH: Once upon a time I thought I'd drown to death in bolts of silk and velour. But I grew up these last few weeks. Jake said a lot.

MOE: Your memory's okay?

RALPH: But take a look at this. *(Brings armful of books from* JACOB'S *room—dumps them on table.)* His books, I got them too—the pages ain't cut in half of them.

MOE: Perfect.

RALPH: Does it prove something? Damn tootin'! A ten-cent nail-file cuts them. Uptown, downtown, I'll read them on the way. Get a big lamp over the bed. *(Picks up one.)* My eyes are good. *(Puts book in pocket.)* Sure, inventory tomorrow. Coletti to Driscoll to Berger—that's how we work. It's a team down the warehouse. Driscoll's a show-off, a wiseguy, and Joe talks pigeons day and night. But they're like me, looking for a chance to get to first base too. Joe razzed me about my girl. But he don't know why. I'll tell him. Hell, he might tell me something I don't know. Get teams together all over. Spit on your hands and get to work. And with enough teams together maybe we'll get steam in the warehouse so our fingers don't freeze off. Maybe we'll fix it so life won't be printed on dollar bills.

MOE: Graduation Day.

RALPH *(starts for door of his room, stops):* Can I have . . . Grandpa's note?

MOE: Sure you want it?

RALPH: Please—(MOE *gives it.*) It's blank!

MOE *(taking note back and tearing it up):* That's right.

RALPH: Thanks! *(Exits.)*

MOE: The kid's a fighter! *(To* HENNIE): Why are you crying?

HENNIE: I never cried in my life. *(She is now.)*

MOE *(starts for door. Stops):* You told Sam you love him. . . .

HENNIE: If I'm sore on life, why take it out on him?

MOE: You won't forget me to your dyin' day—I was the first guy. Part of your insides. You won't forget. I wrote my name on you— indelible ink!

HENNIE: One thing I won't forget—how you left me crying on the bed like I was two for a cent!

MOE: Listen, do you think——

HENNIE: Sure. Waits till the family goes to the open air movie. He brings me perfume. . . . He grabs my arms——

MOE: You won't forget me!

HENNIE: How you left the next week?

MOE: So I made a mistake. For Chris' sake, don't act like the Queen of Roumania!

HENNIE: Don't make me laugh!

MOE: What the hell do you want, my head on a plate?! Was my life so happy? Chris', my old man was a bum. I supported the whole damn family—five kids and Mom. When they grew up they beat it the hell away like rabbits. Mom died. I went to the war; got clapped down like a bedbug; woke up in a room without a leg. What the hell do you think, anyone's got it better than you? I never had a home either. I'm lookin' too!

HENNIE: So what?!

MOE: So you're it—you're home for me, a place to live! That's the whole parade, sickness, eating out your heart! Sometimes you meet a girl—she stops it—that's love. . . . So take a chance! Be with me, Paradise. What's to lose?

HENNIE: My pride!

MOE *(grabbing her):* What do you want? Say the word—I'll tango on a dime. Don't gimme ice when your heart's on fire!

HENNIE: Let me go! *(He stops her.)*

MOE: WHERE?!!

HENNIE: What do you want, Moe, what do you want?

MOE: You!

HENNIE: You'll be sorry you ever started——

MOE: You!

HENNIE: Moe, lemme go——*(Trying to leave):* I'm getting up early— lemme go.

MOE: No! . . . I got enough fever to blow the whole damn town to hell. *(He suddenly releases her and half stumbles backwards. Forces himself to quiet down.)* You wanna go back to him? Say the word. I'll know what to do. . . .

HENNIE *(helplessly):* Moe, I don't know what to say.

MOE: Listen to me.

HENNIE: What?

MOE: Come away. A certain place where it's moonlight and roses. We'll lay down, count stars. Hear the big ocean making noise. You lay under the trees. Champagne flows like——*(Phone rings.* MOE *finally answers the telephone):* Hello? . . . Just a minute. *(Looks at* HENNIE.*)*

HENNIE: Who is it?

MOE: Sam.

HENNIE *(starts for phone, but changes her mind):* I'm sleeping. . . .

MOE *(in phone):* She's sleeping. . . . *(Hangs up. Watches* HENNIE *who slowly sits.)* He wants you to know he got home O.K. . . . What's on your mind?

HENNIE: Nothing.

MOE: Sam?

HENNIE: They say it's a palace on those Havana boats.

MOE: What's on your mind?

HENNIE *(trying to escape):* Moe, I don't care for Sam—I never loved him——

MOE: But your kid—?

HENNIE: All my life I waited for this minute.

MOE *(holding her):* Me too. Made believe I was talkin' just bedroom golf, but you and me forever was what I meant! Christ, baby, there's one life to live! Live it!

HENNIE: Leave the baby?

MOE: Yeah!

HENNIE: I can't. . . .

MOE: You can!

HENNIE: No. . . .

MOE: But you're not sure!

HENNIE: I don't know.

MOE: Make a break or spend the rest of your life in a coffin.

HENNIE: Oh God, I don't know where I stand.

MOE: Don't look up there. Paradise, you're on a big boat headed south. No more pins and needles in your heart, no snake juice squirted in your arm. The whole world's green grass and when you cry it's because you're happy.

HENNIE: Moe, I don't know. . . .

MOE: Nobody knows, but you do it and find out. When you're scared the answer's zero.

HENNIE: You're hurting my arm.

MOE: The doctor said it—cut off your leg to save your life! And they done it—one thing to get another. *(Enter* RALPH.)

RALPH: I didn't hear a word, but do it, Hennie, do it!

MOE: Mom can mind the kid. She'll go on forever, Mom. We'll send money back, and Easter eggs.

RALPH: I'll be here.

MOE: Get your coat . . . get it.

HENNIE: Moe!

MOE: I know . . . but get your coat and hat and kiss the house good-by.

HENNIE: The man I love. . . . (MYRON *entering.)* I left my coat in Mom's room. *(Exits.)*

MYRON: Don't wake her up, Beauty. Momma fell asleep as soon as her head hit the pillow. I can't sleep. It was a long day. Hmmm. *(Examines his tongue in buffet mirror):* I was reading the other day a person with a thick tongue is feeble-minded. I can do anything with my tongue. Make it thick, flat. No fruit in the house lately. Just a lone apple. *(He gets apple and paring knife and starts paring.)* Must be something wrong with me—I say I won't eat but I eat. (HENNIE *enters dressed to go out.)* Where you going, little Red Riding Hood?

HENNIE: Nobody knows, Peter Rabbit.

MYRON: You're looking very pretty tonight. You were a beautiful baby too. 1910, that was the year you was born. The same year Teddy Roosevelt come back from Africa.

HENNIE: Gee, Pop; you're such a funny guy.

MYRON: He was a boisterous man, Teddy. Good night. *(He exits, paring apple.)*

RALPH: When I look at him, I'm sad. Let me die like a dog, if I can't get more from life.

HENNIE: Where?

RALPH: Right here in the house! My days won't be for nothng. Let Mom have the dough. I'm twenty-two and kickin'! I'll get along. Did Jake die for us to fight about nickels? No! "Awake and sing," he said. Right here he stood and said it. The night he died, I saw it like a thunderbolt! I saw he was dead and I was born! I swear to God, I'm one week old! I want the whole city to hear it—fresh blood, arms. We got 'em. We're glad we're living.

MOE: I wouldn't trade you for two pitchers and an outfielder. Hold the fort!

RALPH: So long.

MOE: So long.

(They go and RALPH *stands full and strong in the doorway seeing them off as the curtain slowly falls.)*

Curtain

TILL THE DAY I DIE

Till the Day I Die was suggested by "a letter" appearing in
Those Who Are Stronger by F. C. Weiskopf.

Till the Day I Die was first presented by the Group Theatre at the Longacre Theatre on the evening of March 26th, 1935, with the following members of the Group Theatre Acting Company:

	Played by
CARL TAUSIG	*Walter Coy*
BAUM	*Elia Kazan*
ERNST TAUSIG	*Alexander Kirkland*
TILLY	*Margaret Barker*
ZELDA	*Eunice Stoddard*
DETECTIVE POPPER	*Lee J. Cobb*
MARTIN, AN ORDERLY	*Bob Lewis*
ANOTHER ORDERLY	*Harry Stone*
CAPTAIN SCHLEGEL	*Lewis Leverett*
ADOLPH	*Herbert Ratner*
ZELTNER	*David Kortchmar*
SCHLUPP	*Russell Collins*
EDSEL PELTZ	*William Challee*
1ST STORM TROOPER	*Samuel Roland*
2ND STORM TROOPER	*Harry Stone*
3RD STORM TROOPER	*Gerrit Kraber*
4TH STORM TROOPER	*Abner Biberman*
BOY	*Wendell Keith Phillips*
OLD MAN	*George Heller*
OTHER PRISONERS	*Elia Kazan, David Kortchmar, Paul Morrison*
MAJOR DUHRING	*Roman Bohnen*
FRAU DUHRING	*Dorothy Patten*
1ST DETECTIVE	*Gerrit Kraber*
2ND DETECTIVE	*David Kortchmar*
SECRETARY	*George Heller*
ARNO	*Samuel Roland*
STIEGLITZ	*Lee Martin*
JULIUS	*Bernard Zanville*
WOMEN	*Ruth Nelson, Paula Miller*

The action takes place in Berlin in 1935.

SCENE 1—*An underground room.*
SCENE 2—*Office room in the Columbia Brown House.*
SCENE 3—*Barracks room, Brown House.*
SCENE 4—*Office room.*
SCENE 5—*Tilly's room.*
SCENE 6—*An underground meeting room.*
SCENE 7—*Carl's room.*

Till the Day I Die *was suggested by a letter from Germany printed in* The New Masses.

The production was directed by CHERYL CRAWFORD
The scenery was designed by ALEXANDER CHERTOFF *from suggestions by* PAUL MORRISON.

TILL THE DAY I DIE

SCENE I

A small room underground in Berlin, 1935.

A small man with a rueful face, named BAUM, *is silently operating a hectograph machine. Watching him are the two brothers* ERNST *and* CARL TAUSIG. *Downstage at a long littered table sits an alert girl who is concentrated on work before her. Her name is* TILLY WESTERMANN. *The two brothers watch the operating machine for quite some time.* CARL *finally picks up a leaflet which has just come from the machine. Scans it, replaces it finally.*

CARL: How long will this stencil hold out?

BAUM *(singing out the answer):* Another hundred.

ERNST: That's plenty. This particular leaflet's going to make some of our Nazi friends perspire once it gets into the workers' hands. Workers might like to know the American embargo on German goods has increased 50% in the last six months. They might like to know wages are down one-third and vital foods are up seventy-five per cent.

TILLY *(without looking up):* Stop loafing, comrades.

ERNST *(humor ugly):* She says that to a man who hasn't slept for thirty hours.

CARL: Listen, Dodo, you better take care. Just out of a sick bed, and——

ERNST: Good as new. I could swing you around my finger.

CARL *(laughing):* Try it. *(They spar with good nature.)*

TILLY: Comrades! Stop loafing!

CARL: That's right. *(Picks up leaflets.)* How many of these do I take?

ERNST: Two hundred. Get them to Zeltner. He'll take care of distribution.

CARL: Listen, Ernst, I hate to say it, I don't trust Zeltner. (TILLY *suddenly looks up,* BAUM *turns his head.)*

ERNST: Why don't you trust Zeltner?

CARL: He is too damn brave, too damn willing to die for what he calls "The Cause," too damn downright curious.

ERNST: In the last analysis maybe just romantic.

CARL: He wanted to know this address. Is that romantic?

ERNST: He asked?

CARL: This morning. I told him Berlin's a big city.

TILLY: Did he press the point?

CARL: No, but his knuckles went white around the pencil.

ERNST: We are prepared to move on a moment's notice. Baum's removing the machine as soon as he is finished. In the meantime deliver this package to Zeltner.

CARL: Why take a chance?

ERNST: When we see what he does with this package we'll know where we stand.

CARL (seriously): I see.

BAUM: I used to be a peaceful man who planted tulips.

ERNST: Get going, Carl, the back streets.

TILLY (not looking up): All Comrades to be referred to by first names. Please remember to spread the word.

BAUM (sings): "Oh Tannenbaum."

CARL: I don't suppose you and Tilly could come to Frieda's to hear some Bach tonight.

ERNST: With all this work?

CARL: Do you know the trio hasn't met for five months?

BAUM (sings): My father hated music.

ERNST: My fingers are stiff as boards.

BAUM: The day he died a six-piece band accompanied him right to the cemetery.

ERNST: Not to have touched a violin for six months? Incredible!

CARL: See you tomorrow.

ERNST (stopping him): Wait a minute, Carl. I know what's on your mind. Every time we say good-bye we both think, "When will we meet again? . . . What will tomorrow bring? . . . Is this the last time together?"

CARL (trying to jest): Look, a mind-reader.

ERNST: You must be careful, Carl.

CARL: I know how you feel.

ERNST: You've got an awful hot head. You mustn't ever lose your temper when you find yourself in a jam.

CARL (laughing): Don't worry about your little brother, he is slippery as an eel.

BAUM: Did you ever eat a pickled eel?

ERNST: Be careful.

CARL: Sure. *(The brothers grip hands and look at each other.)* Know what I do? When I walk in the streets I sing. That makes them say "He's above board, he can't be doing underground work." But they don't know I'm singing because I know where we'll be some day. When I sing——

TILLY: You sing yourself right out of here, comrade. Right this minute.

CARL *(laughing):* Correctmente, as the Spaniards say. Adios.

ERNST: Adios.

TILLY: And pull the door tight.

BAUM: Don't take no wooden money. (CARL *exits.)*

ERNST: I wouldn't like to see him in a detention camp. Emil went yesterday. *(Walks up to BAUM):* Will the rest take long?

BAUM: Yes. *(Counts deliberate turn of crank.)* One, two, three. That's the whole run. *(Stops.)*

ERNST: Good.

BAUM: Oh, I'm a fast worker.

TILLY: Learn it from your father?

BAUM *(beginning to clean and pack up machine as ERNST takes printed sheets down to table and packs them):* My father? You should have seen him. A dead ringer for Von Hindenburg. A Corporal of 1870. What would happen if he lived today? Some Nazi would say "A war hero," tickle him under the arm—presto! The next day he would be wearing a brown shirt and killing workers a mile a minute. A real smoke.

ERNST: What's the time?

BAUM *(looking at watch):* Time for supper. Seven o'clock.

ERNST: Where's Zelda?

TILLY: Said she would be here at six.

ERNST: She is usually on time. Here is the last package to go.

TILLY: I hope Zelda won't crack. She hasn't heard from Hugo for three months.

BAUM *(seriously):* Hugo? He might be dead by now. Like the report on Schlagel yesterday. Trying to escape, they said. To fill a man's back full of lead like that. *(Puts on a ragged coat.)*

ERNST: Take some money for your supper. *(Puts coins on table.)* This much to spare.

BAUM *(shy as a young girl):* I don't like to take it, Ernst.

ERNST: Well, we're even—I don't like to give it. *(Indicates machine in box.)* Mark it "glass."

BAUM: I used to be crazy on tulip bulbs. For years I spent my weekly salary on them.

TILLY: "Glass" in big letters!

BAUM *(doing so):* Do you spell glass with one "s" or two?

ERNST: Two.

TILLY *(laughing):* That's one your father didn't teach you.

BAUM: It's no joke. I'm getting dehydrated, that's what I am. Yep, the juices is going right outa me. *(Picks up package.)* Well, don't take no wooden money. *(Exits.)*

TILLY: I like him.

ERNST: He's a good worker. *(Suddenly shows faintness.)*

TILLY *(up and to him):* What's the matter, Ernst?

ERNST *(sitting):* I guess I'm tired. Maybe the body doesn't throw off disease bugs as easy as I think.

TILLY: If I say you need a month's rest, you'll say "Who does my work?" Is that right?

ERNST: Right!

TILLY: Dammit, I'll do your work.

ERNST: Alone?

TILLY: Why not?

ERNST: Tempting, but improbable.

TILLY: You and your male chauvinism!

ERNST *(with smiling protest):* No, Tilly, no.

TILLY: Today I'm particularly concerned with you.

ERNST: You want to know a secret? There is something altogether lovely and birdlike about you. *(Knock on the door.)* Zelda?

TILLY *(softly):* I'll see. *(She goes, and for a brief moment, ERNST allows his real weariness to show, but straightens up as TILLY enters with ZELDA.)*

ERNST *(overbrightly):* Late, Zelda?

ZELDA: Yes, I—I——*(Suddenly begins to cry, head in arms on table.)*

ERNST: Dear Zelda, what happened?

TILLY *(framing name with lips):* Hugo. (ERNST *goes behind* ZELDA *as if to say some comforting thing but realizes better. Looks at* TILLY *and shakes his head pityingly.* ZELDA *finally straightens up and dries her eyes.)*

ZELDA: I got the news this morning. They say he jumped out the window. Hugo would do that! They sent the body to his mother. I'll spend the night with her. Is it all right?

ERNST: Sure it is.

ZELDA: I'll deliver the leaflets first. This package? (ERNST *nods. She takes it.*) Tell the comrades to stay away from the funeral. They'll be watching. (ERNST *embraces her, she exits.*)

ERNST *(in a burst):* Hell! I'd like to go and sit in a park somewhere!

TILLY: They met in the park. She told me once. He was feeding pigeons. You I met on the subway three years ago. Today is an anniversary for us.

ERNST: Really?

TILLY: Zelda took the wind out of my lungs. I wanted to propose. . . .

ERNST: Something nice?

TILLY: A walk in the park—a small supper—then we would walk home slowly, quietly. You'd let me hold your hand. . . . Poor Zelda.

ERNST: My present dream of the world—I ask for happy laughing people everywhere. I ask for hope in eyes: for wonderful baby boys and girls I ask, growing up strong and prepared for a new world. I won't ever forget the first time we visited the nursery in Moscow. Such faces on those children! Future engineers, doctors; when I saw them I understood most deeply what the revolution meant.

TILLY: Maybe we could have one like that, a baby I mean.

ERNST: When the day comes that we don't have to live like rats in sewers——Did I thank you for nursing me the past three weeks?

TILLY: Not a word came out of that stingy mouth. *(He kisses her in thanks.)* Did I thank you for the birthday card?

ERNST: Not a word came out of that stingy mouth. *(She kisses him in thanks.)* Did I thank you for the woolen socks?

TILLY: Ingratitude! *(Kisses her again.)* And you Comrade Tausig, I never thanked you just for living!

ERNST: Ahhh . . . *(Kisses her fully this time. She finally breaks away.)*

TILLY: Stop loafing on my mouth, comrade. *(Looking at papers on table.)* We have to finish this.

ERNST: Getting tough again?

TILLY: Seriously, I decoded the milk bill. There are nine names and addresses of party officials to be memorized by your most excellent brain.

ERNST: Berlin?

TILLY: Look it over. The rest of the room's as clean as a plucked chicken. Not a suspicious word.

ERNST: Who's Spitzer? *(Examines list.)*

TILLY: Rosenfeld, I think.

ERNST: And Strasser?

TILLY: My brother, Hans.

ERNST: Chris' sake, when did you see him last?

TILLY: Four months ago.

ERNST: I think we——*(A low knock on the door stops him. Both freeze into position. From now on they whisper.)* Did someone knock?

TILLY *(listening)*: Just a minute. *(Knock is louder.)*

ERNST: Don't answer. *(Tears name list in half.)* Memorize those. Quick!

VOICE *(outside)*: Open the door!

ERNST: Sisst! *(Both stand there memorizing.)*

VOICE *(as knocking increases)*: Open the door—Secret Police.

TILLY: The Gestapo!

ERNST: That bastard, Zeltner! *(Saying address aloud: 783-783-783. . . . Finally the knocking stops.)* Don't stop. *(Her lips move rapidly and silently.)* All right?

TILLY: All right. *(But she goes on. Knocking comes again and "Secret Police." ERNST lights end of his paper. Watches her while paper burns. Finally she nods her head and he touches lighted paper to hers. Both burn down and are stamped to dust on the floor.)*

ERNST *(all in whispers)*: You and I were here on the couch. *(Puts coat and vest on back of chair.)*

TILLY: An affair?

ERNST: You're in the business. Your room. *(Points to himself.)* Your customer. Push your hair around. *(She does so.)*

TILLY: All ready. *(Musses up couch.)*

VOICE *(outside)*: Open the door! This is the Secret Police.

Slow Fadeout

In the dark between this scene and the next the shrill sounds of a half dozen whistles, variously pitched, slowing with hysterical intensity.
This device to be carried throughout.

SCENE II

Office in a Nazi Brown House. A fat detective in a trench coat and brown derby at telephone on desk which also holds typewriter. His name is POPPER. *Two* ORDERLIES *in Nazi uniform at the side sitting on a bench. They are counting from a list. To one side of the desk stands* ERNST TAUSIG, *a prisoner.*

POPPER *(excited and angry on phone):* I'm waiting for you. *(Waits, drums fingers, spits.)* I'm waiting for you, I said. Mommer God! You think I've got all day.

ORDERLY *(begins to count aloud):* Thirty-seven, thirty-eight, thirty-nine——

POPPER *(yelling at them):* Dumbbells, can't you see I'm trying to work here. Mommer God, it's full of crazy people, the whole house. Hello! The one I mean is the Communist Ernst Tausig. Find the rest of the report and bring it to me on the third floor immediately. Captain Schlegel is waiting for the report. What? No, Schlegel, S as in Samuel. *(Hastily corrects himself.)* No, I mean S as in Storm Trooper. Also you made a mistake on the first part of the report. Don't give me back talk, Dumbbell, the report is in front of my eyes here. His girl friend was released. A plain out and out whore. What? No, not war, whore. *(Turns to* ORDERLY, *in desperation.)* You tell him.

ORDERLY 1 *(immediately at phone):* W-h-o-r-e. *(Retires primly.)*

POPPER *(back at phone):* We brought him in yesterday. So look in the top file right away. *(Hangs up.)* Imagine, that nobody tells me it's my fault, I'll poke my finger through his eye. Such confusion!

ORDERLY 1 *(sympathetically):* Terrible!

POPPER: The country is running over with those red ants. Such confusion.

ORDERLY 2: Terrible!

POPPER: Take the typewriter.

ORDERLY 2: Me?

POPPER: You.

ORDERLY 2: Yes, sir. *(Comes over to desk, a pleasant type.)* Where will I take it?

POPPER: What's the matter with you? To type, to type.

ORDERLY 2: I can't type.

POPPER: You can't type?

ORDERLY 2: No, sir.

POPPER: Dumbbell.

ORDERLY 1: Terrible!

POPPER *to* ORDERLY 1: Can you type?

ORDERLY 1: No, sir.

POPPER: So shut up. Such disorder, such confusion. Every Brown house I was connected with in the past six months is like this. Mommer God, they'll say I'm inefficient, they'll kill me. *(Suddenly turning on* ERNST): You! You make trouble for Captain Schlegel and I'll—I don't know what I'll do to you. You know where you are?

ERNST: Yes.

POPPER: You know what happens in the Columbia Brown House to Communists?

ERNST: Yes.

POPPER: Why did you say you never lived in Linden Street?

ERNST: I never did.

POPPER *to* ORDERLIES: Did you hear that? He said he never lived there. *(To* ERNST): Never in possession of certain illegal materials in connection with the underground work?

ERNST: No.

POPPER *(shaking finger under* ERNST'S *nose):* Listen, stinker, I—— *(Controls himself, goes back to behind desk.)* Write down the liar's answer. *(Writes it down himself.)* You were last employed by the Musical Instrument Company, Eberhard?

ERNST: Yes.

POPPER: Write down he was last employed by that company. *(Writes it down himself. Trooper passes through, whispers "Courage" to* ERNST.) You know we have here enough information to burn you in hell. For three weeks we watched you, you red fox. Do you—— *(Suddenly stops as* CAPTAIN SCHLEGEL *enters, followed by an* ORDERLY *named* ADOLPH. POPPER *continues, fawningly):* Good morning, Captain Schlegel.

SCHLEGEL *(a man like Goering):* Is this him?

POPPER: Yes, sir, this is the one, Captain Schlegel.

SCHLEGEL: Any illegal papers found on him?

POPPER: He got rid of them before the arrest, Captain.

SCHLEGEL: Red fighter?

POPPER: Without a doubt, Captain.

SCHLEGEL: Writer?

POPPER: Former editor of a unit paper, Captain.

SCHLEGEL *(to* ERNST *as he examines report from desk):* That so?

ERNST: Formerly so.

POPPER: Flat as the rug when you catch them. Otherwise burning Reichstags twice a day.

SCHLEGEL: Never mind. Where's the rest of the report?

POPPER: Begging your pardon, Captain, they can't find it downstairs.

SCHLEGEL: You'd better be careful, Popper. Such inefficiency will not be tolerated.

POPPER *(whining):* I do the best I can, Captain.

SCHLEGEL: Never mind, never mind. *(To* ERNST): How long have you belonged to the Communist Party?

ERNST: Since 1923.

SCHLEGEL: You deny belonging to the underground party at the present time?

ERNST: I do.

SCHLEGEL: You are on friendly terms with foreigners?

ERNST: No.

SCHLEGEL: You are not familiar with certain Bulgarian incendiaries?

ERNST: No.

SCHLEGEL: Married?

ERNST: No.

SCHLEGEL: Any children?

ERNST *(smiling):* No.

SCHLEGEL: What's funny?

ERNST: Nothing.

SCHLEGEL *(taking* ERNST *by his coat lapels):* Wipe off the smile. *(Releases* ERNST *and dusts off hands as if contaminated).* What unit did you work with?

ERNST: Unit Number Twenty-fifteen.

SCHLEGEL: Who was the unit organizer?

ERNST: A man named Hess.

SCHLEGEL: Where is he now?

ERNST: I saw him last one year ago.

POPPER *(until now holding back his eagerness):* Where does he live, huh? *(*CAPTAIN *gives* POPPER *a superior look.* POPPER *fades apologetically.)*

SCHLEGEL: You had charge of a secret printing press on Hartsheim Street?

ERNST: No.

SCHLEGEL: You insist you did not help organize the underground press in Berlin.

ERNST: I did not.

SCHLEGEL: No illegal leaflets?

ERNST: No.

SCHLEGEL *(goes over and takes rifle from* ORDERLY. *Taps twice on floor with butt of rifle, hands it back to* ORDERLY *and returns to* ERNST *at the same time taking the report up from desk):* This report—all a tissue of lies you say?

ERNST: I cannot say. (A MAN *enters—wears mask—limps.)*

SCHLEGEL *(turning to the man):* What's his name?

MAN: Ernst Tausig.

SCHLEGEL: His work?

MAN: The underground press.

SCHLEGEL: You may go, Zerrago. (MAN *goes.)*

ERNST: We knew the rat as Zeltner. (CAPTAIN *suddenly slaps him in the face.)*

SCHLEGEL: Control your tongue. When you are asked you will speak, concerning three matters. A, identification of prisoners; B, names; C, addresses. Until then keep quiet. *(Turns from him, walks directly away, but suddenly turns and throws the whole sheaf of paper in* ERNST'S *face.)*

POPPER: He thinks he's in kindergarten.

SCHLEGEL: You'll be in kindergarten, if you don't keep your face shut. *(Approaches* ERNST, *examines him from all sides.)* I hear you're a musician of sorts.

ERNST: Yes.

SCHLEGEL: Play an instrument?

ERNST: Formerly the violin.

SCHLEGEL: Such sensitive hands. Hold them up. (ERNST *does so.)* So filthy. Put them on the desk. (ERNST *does so.)* So, a scraper of catgut. Now, what I have against the communists is—*(holding and turning* ERNST'S *jaw in his hand)*—the snout-like narrowness of their non-Nordic jaws. The nostrils display sensual and voluptuous self-indulgence, talking with the aid of hands and feet; non-Nordic characteristics. *(Walking away from* ERNST, *wipes his hands on a handkerchief.)*

ADOLPH: For every S. A. man killed in Berlin, Brandenburg, three communists will have to answer with their lives.

SCHLEGEL: A violin is an eloquent instrument. Perhaps you are familiar with Beethoven's Opus sixty-one, the violin concerto. Answer yes or no.

ERNST: Yes.

SCHLEGEL: In the key of D? *(Having taken rifle from* ORDERLY'S *hand, he suddenly brings down the butt of it on* ERNST'S *fingers, smashing them. Roars):* With the Joachim Cadenza? (ERNST, *writhing with pain, puts his smashed right hand under his left armpit and almost faints.* CAPTAIN SCHLEGEL *now roars the rest):* And if you think that's the end, let me tell you by tomorrow you'll find your neck half broken instead of three lousy fingers!!! Stand up straight! Do you hear me? (ERNST *straightens up.)* Put your hand down. Put it down!!! (ERNST *slowly does so.)* In ten minutes your old slut of a mother won't know you. *(Suddenly, softly):* Unless you answer my questions. *(Waits.)* You refuse . . . ?

ERNST *(finally, controlling his pain):* I have nothing to say.

SCHLEGEL: Take him to the barrack rooms. Take him out of my sight.

ORDERLY 2: Yes, sir.

SCHLEGEL *(to* ORDERLY 1): Get out.

ORDERLY 1: Yes, sir. *(Exits quickly with* ERNST.)

SCHLEGEL: We've been too easy with that one.

POPPER: Yes, sir, he's a fresh guy.

SCHLEGEL: What the hell are they saving him for?

POPPER: I can't say. I seen the order myself signed by Major Duhring. Handle him with kid gloves, it says. He was in a position to know a big pile of names and addresses. Major Duhring is expected next week to personally question him.

SCHLEGEL *(bitterly):* Duhring? Duhring?

POPPER: He's soft as butter but he knows how to make them talk.

SCHLEGEL: Oh, I see. He can make them talk, but I can't.

POPPER: No, Captain, I only meant——

SCHLEGEL: Get out. You make me vomit.

POPPER: Yes, Captain. *(Bows his way out backwards and bumps into chair. Exits.)*

SCHLEGEL *(turning around the room in anger):* I think that Popper one must have Jewish blood. He hasn't the brains of a trained flea. What strikes you as being funny, Adolph?

ADOLPH: How that fat slob bowed his way out.

SCHLEGEL: I have seen you in a few peculiar positions at times. In fact, it might be much better for both of us if you weren't so graceful with those expressive hands of yours. Flitting around here like a soulful antelope. I'm lonely, I've got no one in the whole world.

ADOLPH: You've got me, Eric.

SCHLEGEL: Hitler is lonely too. So is God.

ADOLPH: I know.

SCHLEGEL: I lost my temper and smashed him against orders.

ADOLPH: You need a rest. You're nervous.

SCHLEGEL: Say it—nervous as a woman—say it! Yes, that's the third one in a week I haven't been able to get a word out of. All I need is for them to find out about us and I am through for good. My God, you don't know who to trust.

ADOLPH: Trust me.

SCHLEGEL (examining ADOLPH'S *face between his hands*): You? You're as fickle as a girl. You know that song by Hugo Wolf, I wish all your charm was painted. It's written for you and me. Last night I heard a lieder concert. There weren't fifty people in the audience. The country is gripped by fear. Houses are locked by day and night.

ADOLPH: Please . . . I'm very fond of you.

SCHLEGEL: Fond? You probably carry tales. . . . I know, you love the Captain's uniform, not the man.

ADOLPH: You're hurting me.

SCHLEGEL: What does a child like you know?

ADOLPH: Please, I mean. . . . (Suddenly begins to cry.)

SCHLEGEL: Sisst! You'll drive me crazy. Where do you think you are? Go out and wash your face. (Looks at papers on desk.) Who's crazy, they or me? Saving a communist because they think he'll spill the beans. I thought I told you to go.

ADOLPH: Please.

SCHLEGEL: Get out of here, don't you hear me? Get out!

ADOLPH: Yes, sir. (Hurries out.)

SCHLEGEL (looks at papers, scatters them around): My God! My God! What's the world coming to? Where's it going? My God!

Blackout

Whistles in the dark

SCENE III

The barracks room. TROOPERS *playing pinochle. Drink beer. Guns and blackjacks on table.* FIVE PRISONERS *lined up against wall, backs to audience.* YOUNG TROOPER *marching back and forth behind them.* PELTZ *and* WEINER, *two troopers, having a hot argument downstage.*

PELTZ: I'm always for the practical side of the thing.

WEINER: Was you ever in a school, if I'm not getting too personal?

PELTZ: I went to school.

WEINER: Where, if I'm not getting too personal?

PELTZ: Right here in Berlin. We learned all that stuff in school. Napoleon an' all that stuff, but it didn't help in business. Adages an' all that. They're for the idlers. When I was in business we didn't talk about Napoleon. We talked about how much.

WEINER: You are absolutely without doubt the most ignorant man I ever met.

PELTZ: I know, I know, we just don't agree.

WEINER: What made Von Hindenburg a great general?

PELTZ: There was other great generals besides him.

WEINER: There never was a greater one.

PELTZ: How about the few others who was great? Don't you know every generation must have its magnet? You don't see that!

WEINER: What's the use of arguing. It's like religion. Some say—

PELTZ: You got that student stuff, artistic. Me, I'm more for the practical side. But you are a good scholar. Yes, I can see that, Weiner. Was you always that way? More on the student side.

WEINER: What? What the hell are you talking about?

PELTZ: Now you know——

WEINER: You're so dumb! *(Walks away.* PELTZ *shrugs his shoulders, goes back to newspaper.)*

YOUNG TROOPER *(to Elderly Man):* Can't you stand still when you're told to stand still!! *(Kicks him strongly;* MAN *falls; trooper picks him up.)* You weren't too old to be a Social-Democrat, were you!! *(Shoves him back in line.* ANOTHER *brings in* TWO MORE PRISONERS—*One feebly attempts a Nazi salute, says,)* "Heil Hitler," *(but is shoved in line.)*

TROOPER 1 *(at table):* The bastards think they'll save their skin like that! (TROOPER 2 *squirts beer from mouth at prisoner.)*

YOUNG TROOPER: The old one wanted a good day's rest on the floor.

TROOPER 2: Which one? *(Goes to him with bottle.)*

YOUNG TROOPER: This one. (TROOPER 2 *fills mouth with beer, squirts it in* OLD MAN'S *face.* ALL *roar with laughter.)*

TROOPER 1 *(coming over):* Dammit! I know this one. You know where you are?

BOY: Yes sir.

TROOPER 1 *(points to boy):* You was here before, wasn't you?

BOY: Yes sir.

TROOPER 1: What was you arrested for that time?

BOY: I was accused of distributing pamphlets.

TROOPER 1: And what now?

TROOPER 5: Riding on a truck load of illegal literature.

TROOPER 1: Jesus, Mary and Joseph!

BOY: He came up to me—the man. I was standing on the corner and he offered me five marks to help drive the load.

TROOPER 2: You didn't know what was in the boxes?

BOY: No, he didn't tell me that and I didn't ask questions.

TROOPER 1: This little one is telling fairy tales.

BOY: I was glad to earn the five marks.

TROOPER 3 *(at the table):* What did you do it for? They won't believe you now.

BOY: I didn't work since I left school. The labor camps won't accept me because I'm a Communist. What can I do?

TROOPER 1: What you can do? Eat floor wax! *(Hits him; the* BOY *falls.)* Good appetite!

TROOPER 3 *(coming forward):* Leave the boy alone, Max!

TROOPER 5: Look at these remarks. *(Reads from pamphlets.)* "The Brutal Slaughter of Red Front Comrades by Hitler's Brown Murder-Hordes——"

TROOPER 1: Jesus, Mary and Joseph! *(Kicks the fallen boy.)*

TROOPER 3: Leave the boy alone, Max. *(Sorry for him.)*

TROOPER 1: I'll leave him alone!

TROOPER 4 *(still at the table with handful of cards):* If you're playing cards, play.

TROOPER 3: Play cards, Max!

TROOPER 1: All right, Professor. *(The game begins and presently* POPPER *walks in with* ERNST.*)*

POPPER: Over there. (ERNST *goes into line.* POPPER *watches fallen boy get up into line.)* What happened with him?

TROOPER 5: The thunderbolt made a visit. *(Indicates* TROOPER 1.*)*

TROOPER 1 *(jumping up):* You are just too damn smart, Hassel!

POPPER: Silence! (POPPER *goes to them, whispers.* THEY *nod heads as they furtively look* ERNST *over.* POPPER *says, "Don't forget" and exits.* TROOPER 2 *marches around* ERNST *and examines him insolently. Goes back to seat and says to others:)*

TROOPER 2: Not a blemish on the lily!

TROOPER 4: Are we playing cards or not?

TROOPER 1: I will say three fifty in spades.

TROOPER 2: You pay double if you lose.

TROOPER 1: Don't put no evil eye on me, Hassel!

TROOPER 2: Don't you act so mean, Herr Thunderbolt!

TROOPER 1: You wanna make something of it?

TROOPER 2: To me you can't talk like to your snotnose friends!

TROOPER 1: You must think——

TROOPER 3: Boys! Is this the trust the Leader puts in you—to start fights in the barracks with Jews and Bolsheviks watching you.

TROOPER 2: That's right!

TROOPER 5: Heil Hitler. (ALL *salute as if toasting and all sit. Card improvisation.* TROOPER *scene.* WEINER *edges his way over to* PELTZ.)

WEINER: What kind of education can you get from the newspapers?

PELTZ: I see how it is. You like to lay around in those cafés with all the Bohemians. See them lying around with frocks on—dreamers. They can't come to the front—just dreamers.

WEINER: Did you read what Thyssen said?

PELTZ: A big man, a big man.

WEINER: Success is ninety per cent luck, five per cent work, he said.

PELTZ: Exactly, exactly, an' don't any intelligent man say the same? The same thing, he says, the same.

WEINER: What?

PELTZ: That means something, don't it? *(Improvisation on pinochle game goes on in loud voices. The* OLD MAN *who has been swaying now falls again. The* YOUNG TROOPER *looking over a shoulder at the game finally turns and sees the fallen man.)*

YOUNG TROOPER: Look at him—can't stand no more. *(Examines him.)* He's bleeding from the mouth.

TROOPER 3: Take him to the hospital. My trick.

TROOPER 1: He's been standing seven hours.

OLD MAN: Don't hit me, please don't hit me.

YOUNG TROOPER: No, just dusting you off. *(Hits hard.)*

OLD MAN: Please don't hit me. I was in the war. I was decorated for bravery. Von Macksen decorated me for merit.

YOUNG TROOPER: *General* Von Macksen.

OLD MAN: I swear. Don't hit me again. I swear I—Yes, I was—*(Now laughs and goes very hysterical. . . .)* Please, please. . . . *(The THUNDERBOLT runs over—hits the OLD MAN who crumples silently.)*

TROOPER 1: These Social-Democrats is a noisy bunch. *(Has retained hand of cards. Starts back to table and on way says: "The ace of diamonds," puts it on table, says to YOUNG TROOPER):* Court-plaster on his head, Fritz! *(The YOUNG TROOPER drags the OLD MAN out like a sack of sawdust.)*

TROOPER 4 *(as they play cards):* Your muscle's better than his.

TROOPER 1: Whose?

TROOPER 4: Tauchner in 120. He bets anything he can knock a man out in one blow—nine out of ten. Why, yesterday he won fifteen marks and a smoking pipe.

TROOPER 2: That's scientific. Just how you hit them . . . like tearing telephone books.

TROOPER 1: I guess you can do it too!

TROOPER 2: If I want . . .

TROOPER 1: Only you don't want?

TROOPER 2: Maybe I'll show you and maybe I won't.

TROOPER 1: How about a bet—the pack of cards against my belt?

TROOPER 2: With the silver buckle? *(A scream heard from below.)*

TROOPER 1: Yeah.

TROOPER 2: You go first.

TROOPER 1: Then you go and if I don't do it, you go again.

TROOPER 2: That's right.

TROOPER 4: Hand over the bets. *(They do so.)* Try the one Popper brought in. He's the biggest and freshest. *(Calls to ERNST.)* Hey, Blackhead! Fall out of line! *(Pulls him out by coat tail.)* Stand there, pig. *(ERNST stands in place. TROOPER 3 stays at table. The OTHERS approach.)*

TROOPER 2: Who takes this one?

TROOPER 1: You're his size. I'll take that boy. Hey—! *(Pulls out BOY.)*

TROOPER 4: I count three. You both hit together. Ready.

TROOPER 2 *(preparing for blow with the other):* Yes, ready . . .

TROOPER 4: Gentlemen, one . . . (TROOPER 1 *spits on his fist.* TROOPER 2 *stands motionless. The BOY at the count of two will cover his face with his hands.)*

TROOPER 2: Remember, only in the head!

TROOPER 4: Gentlemen—two!

BOY *(covering face):* No.

TROOPER 1: Put your hands down, stinker! (BOY *refuses.)* Put them down, bastard!! (BOY *does so.)*

TROOPER 4: Gentlemen—two and a half. . . .

TROOPER 2: Just a minute.

TROOPER 1: What's the matter——

TROOPER 2: Yours is half fainting—a pushover——

TROOPER 1: Well, I'll take him. You! *(Pulls another out—pushes* BOY *who falls sitting and cries monotonously.)*

TROOPER 4: Now—1—2—3——! (BOTH MEN *let blows fly. The victim of No. 1 goes down in a heap.* ERNST *stands stunned. In disgust* TROOPER 2 *goes back to seat.*

TROOPER 1 *(delighted):* Well, who is the big scientist now?

TROOPER 2: That was a pushover.

TROOPER 4: Max won the bet. *(Hands over the prizes to* TROOPER 1.)

TROOPER 1: You wasn't so smart. *(Suddenly* TROOPER 2 *in a fury lets fly at* ERNST *who slowly crumples to his knees.)*

TROOPER 2: Get back in the line, you louse! *(Stalks back to table and sits moodily with chin on fist.* ERNST *slowly crawls back into line and rises painfully.)*

TROOPER 3: Fritzie, get a bucket of water for the kid. *(He laughs triumphantly.)*

TROOPER 1: Ha, ha, Professor! *(Laughs.)* (PELTZ *and* WEINER *have been arguing throughout this last scene.)*

PELTZ: Oh, there's no question, no question. Then what's the use of cursing the world and blaming it on a handful of rich men?

WEINER *(disgusted completely):* I'm not cursing the world!

PELTZ: Now you was pretty strong there. Tell the truth, wasn't you, Weiner?

WEINER: All I said was——

PELTZ: I don't care what this one or that one says about the rich men. It really don't interest me. Or taxes or socialism. I don't listen to them artists. But just because there's a depression I wouldn't say, "Oh, the goddam rich men."

WEINER: I didn't say the goddam rich men.

PELTZ: Absolutely, absolutely . . .

WEINER: My God, you're dumb! If I'm not getting too personal.

PELTZ: I know, Weiner, I know. Naturally people ain't of the same temper-a-ment. Naturally . . . the practical side—like Herr Doctor Goebbels says here in the paper. *(Reads.)* "The head of a prominent Jew must be displayed on every telegraph pole from Munich to Berlin." No dreamy stuff, Weiner. That's practical. . . . *(A scream heard from below.)*

Fadeout

SCENE IV

The same as 3. Nazi swastika flag as background. ORDERLIES 1 *and* 2 *rediscovered, respectively* EDSEL *and* MARTIN.

EDSEL: "What's the world comin' to," he says to poppa. Poppa began cryin'. My uncle said, "Don't cry 'cause it won't help nothin'." After all he didn't work for three years.

MARTIN: The leader has promised a job to every German.

EDSEL: Don't you think I said that? "Read the papers," I told him. "Plenty of work in Munich." So he laughs and says that he just came from Munich and not a job to be had there. But their papers say plenty of jobs in Berlin.

MARTIN: That sounds to me like red propaganda. Why didn't you arrest him?

EDSEL: My own uncle?

MARTIN: He told a lie, didn't he?

EDSEL: I don't know.

MARTIN: The Leader says there's jobs for everyone.

EDSEL: I know. . . .

MARTIN: Government work on the roads.

EDSEL: Two and a half marks a week. Can a mouse live on it?

MARTIN: Is that a nice thing to say?

EDSEL: Well, can a mouse live on it?

MARTIN: I don't know. Dr. Goebbels spoke on the radio last night. He says we must be prepared for a war with them any day.

EDSEL: Momma said some Jews was very nice people.

MARTIN *(jumps up and goes away):* Say, you better be careful—saying things like that. I don't wanna even know you.

EDSEL: Oh, she says it. Of course I don't agree.

MARTIN: You better be careful. They're hot as hornets around here today. This morning they found the zoölogical garden plastered with red propaganda. They can't find out who done it. They cleaned them all away on one side and when they turned around it was all plastered up on the other side.

EDSEL: They will lose their heads, all them Communists.

MARTIN: Of course. . . .

EDSEL: If they catch them.

MARTIN: The Major brought in some of the leaflets for examination. Right there on the desk. (EDSEL *backs away from desk as if stung.*)

EDSEL: Those things there?

MARTIN: The tissue paper—they print it on tissue papers so the wind blows them all over. A certain lady on Friedrichstrasse, one flew right on her face and when she seen what it was she fainted dead away.

EDSEL *(craning his neck for a look at the desk):* Can you see what they say? Read what it says.

MARTIN: Say, read it yourself.

EDSEL: You're closer to the desk than me.

MARTIN *(they are whispering now):* It don't prove nothing 'cause I'm closer to the desk. *(Slowly edges over. Looks around. Finally whispers):* "Workers of Germany!" *(Springs away, amazed at his own audacity.)*

EDSEL *(whispering):* What?

MARTIN: That's what it says. . . .

EDSEL *(both whispering):* Read some more, Martin, shh. *(Tiptoes to right side and watches out.)*

MARTIN *(looks around and tiptoes to desk. Picks up slip nervously, clears throat, reads):* "The Krupp armament works ran at a loss until Hitler came into power. Now it announces a 6% dividend——" *(Breaks off nervously.)* Watch out, Edsel.

EDSEL: I'm watching. *(Looks off left.)*

MARTIN *(looks left, continues nervously, in a whisper):* "While five and a half million workers are unemployed, which, with their families, constitutes one-third of the German working class, increased military forces are the basis of the Hitler economic . . ." *(Paper drops out of his nervous hands.)*

EDSEL: Pick it up.

MARTIN: I can't.

EDSEL *(comes over):* What are you so nervous for?

MARTIN *(chattering):* Who's nervous?

EDSEL *(himself shaking):* You're sweating.

MARTIN: It's a hot day.

EDSEL: Stand at the door. (MARTIN *does so.* EDSEL *looks around, then picks up paper; reads):* "In the meantime there is no bread, no milk. The Hitler-controlled newspapers print lies. The——"

MARTIN *(suddenly panic-struck):* The Major! (EDSEL *runs around not knowing where to put the slip. Tries to find a place. Suddenly puts it in his mouth and chews violently. As* MAJOR DUHRING *enters, ceases chewing and with* MARTIN *comes rigidly to attention.* MAJOR *walks in, notices* EDSEL.)

MAJOR: What's wrong?

MARTIN: Beg pardon, sir?

MAJOR *(pointing to* EDSEL *who has a mouthful):* You! *(Waits.)* Can't talk? (EDSEL *finally swallows strongly.)*

EDSEL: Yes, sir?

MAJOR: Why are you men loafing around here?

EDSEL: Beg pardon, sir, we were assigned to this room.

MAJOR: What room?

EDSEL: To the examination room.

MAJOR: Now boys, does this look like an examination room? Clear out before I lose my temper. *(They scramble out with heels clicking and salutes.)* All right, all right, get out. *(Laughs when they exit, a tired civilized man. Calls one back.)* You!

MARTIN *(badly scared):* Yes, sir, this is not the examination room.

MAJOR: Here, don't stand there like a whipped dog. I'm not calling you down. Inform them on the floor below to send up the Communist, Ernst Tausig.

BOTH *(bowing and scraping):* Yes, sir. *(Try to get out of door together and comic mixup, finally out.)*

MAJOR *(shakes head with pity):* Hmmm. . . . *(Picks up red leaflet.)* "Workers of Germany. . . ." *(Puts down slip, shakes his head again. Goes up to Nazi insignia, examines it reflectively, with bitterness.* ERNST *is brought in. His back still turned, says to* ORDERLY):* Leave us alone. (ORDERLY *clicks heels, salutes.* MAJOR *with back turned):* Sit down, Tausig. (ERNST, *wearied, mistrustful, does not move.* MAJOR *slowly turns, handkerchief at lower portion of face.)*

MAJOR: What? Another whipped and frightened dog? You may be seated. . . . (ERNST *looks at him a long time and finally sits.)* Cigarette? . . . (ERNST *takes one,* MAJOR *putting it in his mouth and lighting it. Waits to see what* MAJOR *has up his sleeve.)* You look different, Tausig, than when I saw you last—a meeting—in Charlottenburg.

ERNST: I remember you—Duhring.

MAJOR: What happened to your hand?

ERNST: What happened to your "social ideals?"

MAJOR: Why I am in a Nazi uniform happens to be unimportant. A realistic necessity. I am married into one of the finest old German families, Nordic from the year one. The work I do for the National Socialists harms no foe of the Nazi state; in fact I am inclined to believe that if the truth were known, my work may often be interpreted as a positive hindrance. *(Laughs, and then adds soberly.)* Not for publication. Perhaps I don't care. . . . That's nearer the truth. I will not deny the justness of the scorn in your eyes. This may cost me my head. . . . I'm not sure I care. *(Turns around room and comes back.)* I want to warn you. . . . They'll get what they want out of you. Trust me to——

ERNST *(bitterly):* A man tortured by his conscience?

MAJOR: Call it what you will. Here they use——*(Voices heard without.* MAJOR, *harshly, tearing cigarette from* ERNST'S *mouth.)* Stand up! When these three questions are answered——*(Breaks off to greet a blonde* WOMAN *escorted by* CAPTAIN SCHLEGEL.) Good afternoon, dear.

HEDVIG *(his wife, vacuous but energetic):* Ruppert, the handsome captain showed me the way. I had to ask your advice about an important matter.

MAJOR *(ironically to* CAPTAIN): Thank you, Captain.

SCHLEGEL *(with ironic courtesy himself):* You're welcome, Major. Your wife and I chatted pleasantly for ten minutes on the lower floor before I realized her identity.

HEDVIG: Yes, the place is full of nasty-mannered men. They kept me waiting ten minutes. *(Suddenly aware of* ERNST.) Who is this?

MAJOR *(with ironic intent):* A Communist, Hedvig. . . .

HEDVIG *(shrinking away to other side of desk, now protected by* CAPTAIN): Oh!

MAJOR *(smiling in spite of himself):* They don't bite.

SCHLEGEL: Only in the dark.

HEDVIG: Such dirty beasts. Don't they ever wash?

MAJOR: When they have the facilities.

HEDVIG: And these were the ones who were supposed to be masters of the coming new world. *(Slaps him with glove.* ERNST *stands unflinchingly. She drops her glove.* CAPTAIN *picks it up and prof-*

fers it to her.) Oh, no, I couldn't wear it again. (CAPTAIN *puts it on desk.* MAJOR *takes it up.)*

MAJOR *(ironic):* They're expensive gloves. What was on your mind, Hedvig?

HEDVIG: About my broadcast speech. *(Takes it from purse.)*

MAJOR: Did you write it yourself, Hedvig?

HEDVIG: No, Poppa's secretary wrote it, but of course I believe every word of it myself, so it's the same thing, isn't it?

MAJOR: I should think so, Hedvig. *(With ironic seriousness.)*

HEDVIG: I wanted you to hear it before I broadcasted. I don't have to tell you that at least a half million German housewives——

MAJOR: Will put down their housework to listen to Hedvig von Barbossa explain their reason for existence.

HEDVIG: Oh, you! Always anticipating my next word!

MAJOR: A perfect husband. Don't you think so, Captain Schlegel?

CAPTAIN *(ironic. A constant fight goes on between the two men):* By all means.

MAJOR: Hedvig, we are having a very heavy day here.

SCHLEGEL *(ironic):* Oh, very heavy. (MAJOR *gives him a penetrating look—a slight duel goes on between their eyes.)*

MAJOR: So I must ask you to merely give me the gist of the speech, dear. Suppose we say, merely the summation.

HEDVIG: Oh, you! You just aren't interested in my intellectual development.

SCHLEGEL *(ironic):* Your husband is really the busiest officer in our section.

MAJOR: That answers you, my dear. So merely the gist.

HEDVIG: Well . . . I thought I would conclude as follows. *(Reads speech):* "Women must understand their part in this moral renaissance of the German people. Well has it been said by our great leader, 'In eternal warfare mankind will become great. In eternal peace mankind would be ruined.' Yes, my dear friends, war alone puts the stamp of greatness on a people! Let women tend the home! Let women breed warriors! Let women forget the pursuit of culture! Germany must expand! Germany must push her frontiers east and west! Women of Germany, give your lives for this cause!" Is that all right, Ruppert?

MAJOR: Splendid—The whole theory of the fascist state in a paragraph. You might be one of our leading theoreticians one of these days.

HEDVIG: I told Poppa's secretary what to write, I truly did.

MAJOR: Yes, now you must run along, Hedvig. Leave us to our work. Good-bye.

HEDVIG: And remember dinner at the Hauptmann's tonight.

MAJOR: I won't forget. Captain, please see my wife safely out.

SCHLEGEL: Yes, sir. *(Goes with her.)*

MAJOR *to* ERNST: You see the sort of convenient marriages one can sometimes be forced to make.

ERNST: The captain is not your friend.

MAJOR: Nor yours. *(Indicating wife's glove in his hand):* The captain suspects me of leniency to prisoners. My lineage. *(In a sudden emotional outburst):* I tell you a civilized human can't stand it! A great sermon requiem is being played. It's a nightmare! *(Gets himself in control.)* He holds his knowledge over my head like a sword—the captain, I mean. In turn I have collected certain data concerning the captain's private life and loves—enough to have him purged to a blood stain on the wall! We will duel ourselves to death, we too! This amuses you?

ERNST: Yes.

MAJOR: I can understand. Briefly, here is some information. *(Business-like, now)* You can take it or leave it, Tausig. Our side wants information from you. Addresses and names of party officials.

ERNST: Don't have them!

MAJOR: I'm not asking. They're sure you can identify prisoners. They mean to make you do it. You've been here three weeks. Until now they've been comparatively mild. They'll beat you to within an inch of death. You won't want to live. Then they'll nurse you back to health. This will happen several times.

ERNST: I will remember my proletarian task.

MAJOR: It's possible you may forget your proletarian task. Don't smile. A man's made of flesh and bone. They'll inform your comrades through subversive means that you've turned stool pigeon. Before you know it your own unit papers will be passing the word along. In a few months—no friends. No home. Only the new clothes and money in the pocket this side will furnish to keep up the fraud. You still smile? But suppose they put you next to the driver when they make raids? Suppose you are stood outside the courtroom where your comrades will be tried for treason? Will they understand the truth of your position? That's right—screw up your face. . . .

ERNST: My hand hurts.

MAJOR: Get medical attention on the way out. I'll sign an order.

ERNST: On the way out?

MAJOR: On the way out! That's the first step. We're releasing you. You're expected to make contacts with other party members. You'll be followed every minute of the day and night. If you don't prove valuable—*(hands over signed medical order)*—back you come . . . and then begins the breaking-down process. *(Stops.)* Listen, take my advice. There is an easier way out. . . .

ERNST: What is that?

MAJOR: Shoot yourself. There is peace and quiet in the grave. *(Quotes):* "So I returned and considered all the oppressions that are done under the sun . . . wherefore I praised the dead." (SCHLEGEL *enters.)* Very good.

SCHLEGEL: The compliments of General Goering and staff, who will pay us a visit this afternoon.

MAJOR *(wary):* Very good. You saw my wife safely to the door?

SCHLEGEL: To her car.

MAJOR: Very good.

SCHLEGEL: Our prisoner displays a most fraternal attitude. *(Nods towards seated* ERNST.)

MAJOR: Judging from the success of the prisoner's political party in distributing illegal literature, it might be well to fraternize with them in order to learn the secrets of that success.

SCHLEGEL: I resent such remarks before a prisoner. Stand up, you! (ERNST *stands.)*

MAJOR: With both of us in one room I give orders. Remain seated. (ERNST *sits.)*

SCHLEGEL: Major, I regret to inform you as house captain that it is my duty to make various reports concerning——

MAJOR: Silence! *(Furious.)*

SCHLEGEL: Aside from your shoulder straps I am——

MAJOR: Goddamit! Silence!

SCHLEGEL *(turns and walks to door, white with inner rage. Stops, turns):* Jew!

MAJOR: What?

SCHLEGEL: You didn't think I knew that?

MAJOR: Come here. *(Other slowly approaches.)*

SCHLEGEL *(coolly):* What's on your mind? *(They look at each other eye to eye.)*

MAJOR *(finally):* What do you mean?

SCHLEGEL: Does your wife know that?

MAJOR: Know what?

SCHLEGEL: Obviously staff headquarters has never made a close examination of the Duhring family tree.

MAJOR: If I hear one more word out of your mouth——*(Catches and twists his tunic.)*

SCHLEGEL: You'll do that?

MAJOR: With my own hands.

SCHLEGEL *(with smiling insolence):* By gun or sword? Here is one of .38 caliber. *(Insolently hands over gun from his own holster.)* The first instinct of the Jew is to run. *(At this close range the* MAJOR *suddenly pulls the gun trigger. The* CAPTAIN *gets the whole automatic charge in the belly. Grabs himself with both hands. Slowly crumples in a soft pile. Gets to desk—falls behind it.* MAJOR *finally speaks in a soft voice.)*

MAJOR: I didn't want to do it. He asked for it——(ADOLPH *runs in.)* Wait outside. You will escort this prisoner to the street when he leaves the room.

ADOLPH *(seeing body):* Very good. *(Exits smartly.)*

ERNST *(finally):* You're in trouble.

MAJOR: It need not concern you. *(Eyes still on body.)* One thing: see your girl if you like. She reported as a prostitute, not a party worker—which she is.

ERNST: You're mistaken.

MAJOR: I'm telling you! Not asking! See her—it's all right, she won't be molested. And for God's sake give some good girl a kiss for me. I am so slimed over with rottenness. . . . "Red Front" I can't say to you. . . . But "United Front"—I say that. In every capitalist country in the world this day let them work for the united front.

ERNST: I know.

MAJOR: Have the hand fixed. You have the pass. Good luck. . . . Just a second—cigarettes——*(Gives pack.)* Say I am not despised. Please say it.

ERNST: No—really, you are not despised.

MAJOR: You are talking to a dying man.

ERNST: With so much work to do?

MAJOR: I did the work—like an embezzling bank teller—I destroyed three files of valuable information against your comrades this morning. With this murder on my hands, what is to be expected.

You see, the contradictions of my own nature have backed up on me. Get out!

ERNST: Thanks. *(He slowly goes.* MAJOR *stands there. Looks at dead body. Goes back to desk. Sits jauntily on it. Whistles a snatch. Examines and twirls his own gun, thinks about and touches various vulnerable spots of his physiognomy, finally concentrates on one spot, places handkerchief over gun hand—stops. Suddenly puts gun on desk, looks at uniform, removes coat or Nazi arm band. Tears flag off wall. . . . Picks up gun—puts muzzle in mouth. Simultaneously with* BLACKOUT *there is a shot fired. Whistles in the dark.)*

SCENE V

In the dark, under the whistles we pick up on radio music, full and classical. With the lights fading up we see TILLY'S *small room. A rough cot. One window looking out on a world of clear light. A small bureau, wash basin and pitcher of water on it. A door.* TILLY *in an old bathrobe. Music coming from her little radio.* TILLY *dips a corner of a towel in the water, slowly wipes her face clean with it. She finishes. Turns down cot covers. Goes to window, raises shade. Blue night light comes in. She turns down lamp. Turns off radio, but puts it on again. Sits on bed and just as she bends to remove slippers there is a tap on her door. She stays in her bent position for a second, finally when a second knock comes—she slithers to the door. Listens. The knock again.*

TILLY *(in a faint whisper):* Who is it?

VOICE: Ernst. . . .

TILLY *(does not believe it. Comes to center of room. Listens, looks around, finally in a full impulse goes to door. Throws it open.* ERNST *is there. She is away from door. He slowly comes in, closes door, stands against it. For a long time they look at each other silently; finally):* Ernst!

ERNST *(and they are in each other's arms):* Tilly!

TILLY: Alive!

ERNST: Alive!

TILLY: Please, sit here on the bed. *(She escorts him to the bed. He sits. She lowers shade. Turns on lamp. Turns and looks at him; is shocked by his appearance.)* Dear. . . . *(She throws herself at his*

feet, on her knees, holds him as a mother might do with a child.)
You're hurt. . . .

ERNST: Not as much as I might be. Only my back is raw . . . the shirt is stuck to it.

TILLY: Here, I'll fix it. *(Goes to wet towel.)*

ERNST: No, darling, if you touch me there I'll faint.

TILLY: Are you hungry?

ERNST: No, dear, no. Here, someone gave me cigarettes. We'll smoke and talk. Don't be excited. I want news. Here——*(They light cigarettes. She gets a little ashtray—they sit together on cot.)*

TILLY: News, what news? You've been released.

ERNST: They held me in the Columbia House since the arrest. I counted the days when I could remember—twenty-two. . . .

TILLY: Twenty-three, Ernst.

ERNST: You counted too.

TILLY: What then?

ERNST: You don't know what happens, you don't know. No one knows until he walks through that hell. . . .

TILLY: Why have they released you?

ERNST: I am being followed. I'm expected to make party contacts. Don't look out the window. Two of them in the grocery doorway. . . . I couldn't give them the slip. Maybe I shouldn't have come.

TILLY: A man must have some place.

ERNST: It won't harm. We fooled them about your identity. Where's Carl?

TILLY: Safe at work in the suburbs.

ERNST: Good.

TILLY: Were you afraid there?

ERNST: A man who knows that the world contains millions of brothers and sisters can't be afraid. Don't think I haven't screamed with pain—they have ways of arousing every corpuscle to pain—but you keep your mouth shut.

TILLY: Your hand. . . .

ERNST *(wincing):* Don't touch it. *(Gets up. Walks away.)*

TILLY: Sit down again. Don't be afraid of softness, of sorrow.

ERNST *(holds back his emotional impulse to cry on her shoulder. Finally):* What news of the others?

TILLY: Raff is dead.

ERNST *(deeply touched):* How?

TILLY: The report they gave out was that he jumped from a window. And Hans Mathieson. . . .

ERNST: The same?

TILLY: The same.

ERNST: Those brave fighters. . . .

TILLY: I'm glad you're living, Ernst.

ERNST (*suddenly crying out in protest*): Tilly, I must tell you. Tilly, for a week I have been chewing my heart to pieces. All the time I was in the Brown House they were offering me bribes, any inducements to turn informer. First a session of endearment. Then a session of torture. The human body is a tower of strength. After a while comes numbness, but the mind begins to wander. I'm afraid, Tilly—do you hear that, afraid! Something might happen. There is no rest, no possible contact with party members permitted. They will seize me again, return me to the same program. I'm afraid of what might happen. I ask for one hour of peace.

TILLY: Peace in this war?

ERNST: Yes, peace! In the cell there—I know I stayed alive because I knew my comrades were with me in the same pain and chaos. Yes, I know that till the day I die there is no peace for an honest worker in the whole world.

TILLY: Till the day we die there is steady work to do. Let us hope we will both live to see strange and wonderful things. Perhaps we will die before then. Our children will see it then. Ours!

ERNST (*bitterly*): Our children!

TILLY: I'm going to have a baby, Ernst. . . .

ERNST: Who is?

TILLY: I am.

ERNST: You mean it?

TILLY: Your baby. (*Dawn—where even the teakettle sings from happiness.*)

ERNST (*finally, after looking at her and not knowing what to say*): Please, allow me to change the subject. . . . Overgaard, I met him three streets away from here. I made signals with my eyes. He understood. Passed by like a stranger. (*Finally*): A baby?

TILLY: Yes.

ERNST (*walks to window*): It's almost morning. . . .

TILLY (*joining him*): Ernst, the tenderness I feel for you. . . . I don't know how to say. . . . Part of my deepest life came back to me when you walked in the door here. You keep coming up in my eyes like the sense of tears. . . .

ERNST: I understand.

TILLY: It is true our work comes before our personal happiness. But we must try to wrest some joy from life.

ERNST: How can that be when presently I shall be a decoy to trap other wild ducks?

TILLY: We'll manage. Escape is possible one way or another. Now I want you to undress and sleep.

ERNST: Sleep?

TILLY: Under the warm blankets.

ERNST: Sleep in your little bed? My sister, comrade . . . my wife. . . . *(Sits on bed. She takes off his shoes. His coat. He winces as he stretches out.)*

TILLY: It hurts?

ERNST: Yes.

TILLY: Tomorrow we'll fix all these things. Sleep, Ernst, sleep. Tomorrow you can read the full report on the united front. *L'Humanité* came through, several copies.

ERNST *(suddenly sitting up):* What united front?

TILLY: The united front in France.

ERNST: It has happened?

TILLY: I thought you knew?

ERNST: In France they have joined to make a solid front against the fascists?

TILLY: Please don't get so excited, Ernst. *(Tries to calm him.)*

ERNST:Our work is bearing fruit? In that beautiful classic country. The united front? Oh, Tilly, oh, Tilly!! *(And suddenly he is crying in the pillow for all his pains and for the joy of this news.* TILLY *soothes him with understanding.)*

TILLY: Yes, cry, cry. . . . *(She strokes him until the sobs become more quiet. Suddenly there is a knock on the door.* TILLY *whispers):* Quiet! You're sleeping. Don't move. *(He lies still. She stealthily goes to the door).* Who is it?

VOICE *(also whispering):* Open the door. . . .

TILLY: Who is it?

VOICE: Carl! (TILLY *looks around at* ERNST *who raises himself on his hands.* TILLY *quickly opens the door, admits* CARL, *quickly closes door.)*

TILLY: You're spotted! Get out quick!

CARL: Where?

TILLY: They must be right behind you. Watching the house. (CARL *quickly goes over to the cot, touches* ERNST. *Starts for door again where* TILLY *has been listening.)*

TILLY: They're coming! *(Suddenly in a loud voice which* CARL *immediately takes up):* I'm telling you to get out. What's the matter— can't a respectable girl entertain her boy friend.

CARL: You made a date with me. *(Simulates a drunkard.)*

TILLY: You're a liar. Now get out before I call the police.

CARL: Didn't you say it! In the Park didn't you tell me to come tonight? Why, for two marks——*(Door is pushed open: two detectives in trench coats stand there.)*

TILLY: My God! What's this, more customers?

DICK 1: Who's this?

TILLY: A fresh guy who pushed his way in. There's my boy friend, dead tired on the bed, fresh from the jug, and this garbage can won't let him rest.

CARL: Never mind that stuff! When I met her in the Kunzterplatz Tuesday she tells me to come up tonight. "I love you," she tells me.

TILLY: Yah, yah, yah!

DICK *(comes in and looks around. Assistant blocks the door.)* Is this your boy friend?

TILLY: Yeah. He's dead tired. He was——

DICK: All right, all right! *(To* CARL): What do you wanna start up with this alley cat for. You know they do it for anyone.

CARL: Sure. . . . But the next time I meet you in that same place at lunch time——

TILLY: Yah, yah, yah, yah. . . . Thanks, officer—a real man! (DICK *pushes out protesting* CARL *and looks superciliously at* TILLY *as he closes door.* TILLY *stands in her place for a second, listens, then turns down to* ERNST.)

ERNST: Did he get away?

TILLY: They believed every word. *(Suddenly door pushed open.* DICK *stands there again.)* What do you want? . . .

DICK *(advancing into room. Finally):* I forgot my glove, cutie. *(Picks it up from table, goes back to door.)* You wanna be careful. Better girls than you are in the jails.

TILLY: All right.

DICK: Lemme know if anyone makes trouble. . . .

TILLY: All right.

DICK: Or if you're lonely some night.

TILLY: All right.

DICK *(winking. Taps his chest)*: A real man, me. . . .

TILLY *(first locking door)*: Sleep, Ernst, sleep. . . . *(But he is already asleep. She sits herself in window light in profile as daylight comes fuller in the window.*

Blackout. Whistles

SCENE VI

Comrades Scene.

About a dozen party members seated in a small locked room. The SECRETARY *of the unit is finishing a report.* CARL *sits downstage with back to audience.* TILLY *is there. Also little* BAUM *of the first scene. Sitting with a woman holding his hand is a man with a fine-looking head, a famous theoretician, a shawl over his shoulders, gray-haired—*STIEGLITZ. GUARD *at door.*

SECRETARY *(reading)*: Three new theatre-of-action groups have been formed in the last week. They are now functioning regularly throughout the city. Three thousand cheap jazz records have been distributed since the 10th. These each end in one of our speeches. Since the first——*(Stops to admonish a small man named* JULIUS, *who is wending his way through some seated comrades.)* Will the comrades kindly remain seated until the reports are concluded.

JULIUS *(who is revealed to be wearing only one shoe)*: I left my shoe in the corner. My foot is cold.

SECRETARY *(continues)*: Since the first we have spent on Hitler joke books and leaflets the sum of two hundred and ten marks. *(Puts down report.)* I suggest that since we are all agreed on the accuracy of the report that we do not waste time but go ahead to other business. Will someone ask the question?

VARIOUS: The question, etc.

SECRETARY: All in favor will please assent in the usual manner.

ARNO: Just a minute. This seems to me to be in a way like a little steam rolling.

SECRETARY: Does the comrade have any suggestions in reference——

ARNO: No, but it seems——

OTHERS: Sit down, Arno.

ARNO: What about Comrade Tausig?

SECRETARY: Next.

ARNO: How was I supposed to know——

SECRETARY: All in favor. *(The suggestion is passed. There is a slight respite. Improvisation.)* We will now read the roll of honor.

COMRADE *(gets up and reads):* "Unit 2026—Killed in carrying out their proletarian duties, on the 3rd, Friedrich Meyers, Elsa Schorr. On the 12th, George Pfitzner. *(In the background a woman suddenly sobs. She is comforted by another and soon stops.)* Imprisoned or captured during this month, Paul Schnitzler, Ernst Tausig." *(Sits.)*

SECRETARY: This is not time for sentiment, but it would not be wrong to stop for one minute to remark upon the fine qualities of those valiant fighters who are now lost to our cause, some forever. In the case of our slain fighters their merits are known to all of us. In the case of Ernst Tausig we must pause for serious consideration. It has been proposed by the unit functionaries that his name be added to the blacklist. But in accordance with usual procedure we have brought this matter to your attention in the hope of arriving at a wider understanding of the case. Comrade Tilly Westermann.

TILLY *(rises, wipes hands with small handkerchief):* Since the reports on Ernst Tausig come from reliable sources we must give them strong credence. Briefly he was first arrested in March. Three weeks later he was released. (CARL *turns around and looks into the face of the audience.)* At that time he knew he was being followed. They were hoping he would contact party members. This he positively did not do. Four days later he was picked up again. I saw him once after that in the hospital with his brother. *(Lapsing for one line into a less official, less impersonal attitude):* I didn't recognize him. He held my hand. . . . We wanted—— *(Breaks off, stops for a minute, resumes the impersonal tone):* It's no secret to most of you that I am bearing his child. This fact will seem to make for strong partiality on my part. But I protest that because Ernst Tausig was in a room when others identified prisoners is no reason to assume that he has turned informer. This is not the Tausig whom most of us have known and worked with in the last four years or more.

BAUM: Right!

ARNO: How about when Mickle saw him with the police in the

Herfheim Street raid? Maybe he was just knitting a muffler while he was sitting there next to the driver!

SECRETARY: The comrades will please ask permission for the floor. (ARNO *raises his hand.*) Comrade Arno?

ARNO *(on his feet):* Personally, I'm sorry for Tausig. But who can take a chance nowadays? Even if he is not guilty, who can take a chance when the secret police have any connection with him?

SECRETARY: Please be more specific.

ARNO: I mean he must go on the blacklist. Every unit paper in the country must carry his name and description. For our purposes he is deadly, dangerous.

SECRETARY *(recognizing* TILLY): Comrade Westermann?

TILLY: I can't disagree with what has just been said——

ARNO: I should say not!

TILLY: But will the chair permit me to read a small note I received from Ernst last week?

SECRETARY: Please read the note.

TILLY *(reads):* "They are taking my life by the inch. Day and night they press me for an answer—identify prisoners or be killed. I cannot last much longer. The terrible truth is they do not kill me. I am enclosing money which they handed over to me yesterday after forcing me to sit beside their chauffeur when they made a street raid. You may be sure I have kept my mouth shut. Love to Carl and you." *(The man with one shoe comes over and looks at the note.)*

SECRETARY: Before we decide the action in this case would any other comrade care to say something?

GIRL: Perhaps Comrade Stieglitz.

SECRETARY *(looking in his direction):* I don't think. . . . *(Companion of* STIEGLITZ *whispers to him. He nods.)*

ZELDA: He says he will say a few words about the case.

SECRETARY: Comrade Stieglitz has just come back to us from three months in the Sonnenberg detention camp. *(Pointedly.)* I will ask you to listen carefully—to these few remarks from one of our leading theoreticians. *(Small bandage on* STIEGLITZ'S *head. All wait. The imposing-looking man gets up quietly and takes his place at the other side of the room, next to the* SECRETARY. *He looks around him gently, smiles softly at* TILLY.)

STIEGLITZ: Always in such rare cases where there is a doubt as to the accused one's guilt it is the custom to be careful in consideration of the known facts. But a different face is placed on the matter in times of stress and danger. Often. . . . *(He stops, thinks, continues.)* Often the class struggle . . . it seems to me . . . it seems to me . . . *(He stops, a little puzzled, plays with fringe of shawl.)* I was saying . . . *(Looks around helplessly. Walks over to his female companion.)* Where are we, Zelda?

ZELDA: With friends, Benno.

STIEGLITZ: What was I saying?

ZELDA: Please sit down, Benno.

STIEGLITZ: Take me home, Zelda. . . . *(Looks around helplessly.)* Zelda. . . .

SECRETARY *(into the breach):* I think it would be best if he were home.

ZELDA: Yes. We're going, Benno. I have your hat.

STIEGLITZ: I'll hold your hand. Good-bye, my friends, good-bye. You must come to my house for breakfast. We have the sunniest breakfast room. . . . Yes. . . . *(She leads him out. The door is locked behind him. She has been admonished first to be careful.* BAUM *blows his nose vigorously.)*

BAUM: So have the devils broken that noble mind!!

SECRETARY: Comrades, now is no time for sentiment. This is the hour of steel, when——No sentiment! *(But he himself has to hide his tear-filled eyes. Presently controls himself.)*

JULIUS: It's a pretty kettle of fish, I must say.

CARL *(suddenly up):* I would like to say something in reference to my brother.

SECRETARY: Take the floor. *(Piano and violin duo begin downstairs.)*

CARL: Comrades, you are wondering where the music comes from. This is the very same house in which my brother and myself were born and raised. My uncle and his old friend Seligmann are playing. The war, the revolution, the banishing of Jews from Germany have turned their poor old hearts to water. These days you will find them forever—the two of them playing their Mozart and Beethoven sonatas. The music they are playing now is Mozart, the andante of the C Major Sonata—C Major, my dear comrades, is a very wholesome beautiful key. You must excuse what may seem an irrelevant excursion into sentiment. But this is the first piece of Mozart my brother and I ever played together. When we came from school—I am surprised how fresh this dead life is in my memory—nineteen years back—but that's another story. *(Now suddenly turning hard):* But Mozart—is there time for music to-day? What are we fighting for? I need not answer the question. Yes, it is brother against brother. Many a comrade has found with deep realization that he has no home, no brother—even no mothers or fathers! What must we do here? Is this what you asked me? We must expose this one brother wherever he is met. Whosoever looks in his face is to point the finger. Children will jeer him in the darkest streets of his life! Yes, the brother, the erstwhile comrade cast out! There is no brother, no family, no deeper mother than the working class. Long live the struggle for true democracy! *(He sits now. The music finishes before anyone speaks. The vote is called for. All raise their hands in assent except* TILLY. *She looks around at the others. One of the men is eating small nuts loudly. Her hand slowly comes up.)*

Fadeout

SCENE VII

CARL'S *room. Small. Only a door set up in center. In darkness we hear two typewriters. When lights fade up we see* CARL *and* TILLY *each at a typewriter. Typing.* TILLY *finally stops.*

TILLY: A few mistakes.

CARL *(older):* No matter.

TILLY: My heart hurts. Hurt me all day.

CARL: Take care. Lie down before we go.

TILLY: I can't rest. *(Comes down to him.)*

TILLY: Carl, I want to ask you—are you ever afraid?

CARL: Sometimes.

TILLY: Now? Tell the truth.

CARL: Yes, if you want it. The place we're going to is swarming with S.S. men. We might never come out alive. I'm not so masculine that I won't admit I'm scared.

TILLY: All day I had this pain under the heart.

CARL: When will the baby be coming?

TILLY: A long time yet.

CARL *(in a low voice):* What will you call him?

TILLY: If it's a girl, I don't know. If it's a boy. . . .

CARL: Not *his* name.

TILLY (*suddenly clutching him*): Tell me, how do you know? What makes you so sure?

CARL: There's proof—plenty!

TILLY: You believe it?

CARL: In the beginning I didn't. Maybe the brown shirts spread the tales themselves.

TILLY: They've done it before.

CARL: I don't say no. That's why I didn't believe a word I heard at first.

TILLY: Now you believe it.

CARL: Yes. Too many reliable comrades have checked on his activity.

TILLY: Maybe he's drugged. Maybe he walks in his sleep. You know—yes, you know—he would have found some way to do away with himself before he was forced to act as a spy. You know that! You know you do!

CARL: Don't tear my shirt. (*Trying to jest.*)

TILLY (*persistently*): Answer the question!

CARL (*finally, in a burst*): Goddamit, I say he's guilty!

TILLY: If he came here, broken in mind and body, would you refuse to see him? Can you stand there and tell me you wouldn't even listen to what he had to say?

CARL: To me he has nothing to say!

TILLY: He's your brother.

CARL: That won't sell a postage stamp!

TILLY: Suppose he knocks on the door this minute!

CARL: You're in love.

TILLY: Answer what I ask!

CARL: What makes you think you're the only one? Maybe I slept better at night the last two months. Maybe I cried myself to sleep some nights. This big blustering idiot wept like a girl. (*Walks around.*) Yes, yes, the whole thing funnels up in me like fever. My head'll bust a vein!

TILLY (*catching herself*): We're talking too loud.

CARL (*whispering, but with same intense flow*): Seeing him at the hospital the last time—the picture follows me like a dog. I'm sick, I tell you I'm sick of the whole damn affair! (*Sitting.*) Perhaps we ought to change—do our work apart. This way, this is a secret eating thing between us. Each reminds the other.

TILLY: We'll talk about it tomorrow. I want to find a glass of milk before we start to work.

CARL: We'll get some on the corner.

TILLY: The baby has to eat. . . . *(He gets her coat. Smiles at its shabbiness.)*

CARL: Nothing is too good for the proletariat.

TILLY: I had a nice coat once. I had a mother. I had a father. I was a little girl with pigtails and her face scrubbed every morning. I was a good child. I believed in God. In summer I ate mulberries from our own tree. In late summer the ground was rotten where they fell. *(Knock at the door.)* Open the door. Don't ask who it is. It's Ernst, I know it is.

CARL *(looks at her, puzzled.* TILLY *goes to open door. He stops her. Whispering):* Are you crazy?

TILLY: I know it's him.

CARL: Let the door alone.

VOICE *(outside):* Carl. . . .

CARL *(covers door):* You can't let him in.

TILLY: You can't keep him out. *(Waits.)* He's waiting. . . .

CARL: He'll go away.

TILLY: Maybe he's sick.

CARL: And the others in detention camps, they're not sick?

TILLY: You might be wrong.

CARL: Then better one mistake like this than a thousand arrests and murders.

VOICE *(knocks without):* Carl. . . .

TILLY: He won't leave. *(After another knock.)* Give me the key, Carl. (CARL *looks at her. Puts key on table. Walks away. She opens door with it. Opens wide the door. There stands* ERNST. *Looks terrible. Wears a large velour hat, black, making his face look small. This man, sick, broken, alone, desperate, humble, something of amusement in him too. Has a handful of coins he plays with. Clothes are too big on him. Looks like a ghost.)*

ERNST: Tilly. . . .

TILLY: Come in, Ernst.

ERNST: May I . . . ?

TILLY: Come in . . . *(He does so.* CARL *on side, back turned.* TILLY *locks door. Retains key. She takes off his overcoat. He is revealed in a soiled shirt, tails out on one side. Takes off his hat while he plays with coins and looks at floor. His hair is streaked with white. He seems abstracted. Finally, becomes aware of room when coins drop out of his hand. He doesn't notice the coins.)*

ERNST: Tilly. . . . Let me. . . . *(He slowly walks over to her, falls on his knees, kisses her hand. She draws her hand away.)*

CARL *(turning):* Stand up. (ERNST *does so.*) What do you want?

ERNST: I came——

CARL: To tell us lies.

TILLY: Let him talk. There are enough executioners in Germany without——

CARL: For the present I'm not used to one in my own room. For the present I——

ERNST *(in a violent burst):* No. Stop it. No!

CARL: What is "no"? Mickle saw you with the police. Arno saw you in the court. You give the secret police information!

TILLY: They'll hear you in the street!

ERNST: Listen to me——(CARL *makes move for door.* ERNST *blocks it.*) I came to have a talk.

CARL: Get out of my way.

ERNST: No! (CARL *pushes him away, throws him to floor. Finds door locked. Turns to* TILLY. *She puts the table between them):* Give me the key.

TILLY: No. (CARL *looks at* ERNST. *Picks him up from floor. Sits aside.*)

ERNST: It's all right—I understand—you don't want to listen. It's all right—I'll talk to myself. It's a habit now. I talk to myself on the street, frighten children—frighten myself. Don't listen to me. I'll talk to the chair. Here——*(Turns chair around, addresses it as to a person.)* Mr. Chair! First, we understand the situation. Second, the charges are listed in our minds. (TILLY, *out of pity and terror, removes the chair which he has been addressing very earnestly. Finally* ERNST *continues in a low, intense voice):* Now we must examine the living witness: what do you know of what happened? Who told you?

CARL *(jumping up fiercely):* I won't listen to you.

ERNST *(jumping up the same):* What am I asking of you? Pity? No! You must *know,* Tilly must know the accusations against me are untrue. I want you both to stand clear and proud in the world—not to think your brother and husband turned.

CARL: I don't care for the personal issues.

ERNST: Then I care! For my son I care. He need never be ashamed to bear my name.

CARL: Every unit paper in the country screams out you're a rat.

ERNST: And they know?

CARL: You're damn right they know.

ERNST: When I was released from the barracks in General Pape street—did they know then?

CARL: That's four months back.

ERNST: They left me free that time.

CARL: Because you were supposed to lead them to the comrades.

ERNST: But I didn't.

CARL: Because you couldn't walk.

ERNST: So far so good, no?

TILLY: Yes. . . .

ERNST: Then they picked me up again. The whole thing started fresh —questioned day and night. No let-up. Swollen, bleeding, the hospital again. What good was I to them dead? Suddenly you fall— a bucket of water—they stand you up—the lash—dig your nails into the wall to remain standing.

CARL: When did you make up your mind to tell?

ERNST: Not yet!

TILLY: Not yet?

ERNST: They tie your feet, seat you with the driver on the roundups. This makes you seem a guide for them.

CARL: But you never sent a message, not a warning.

ERNST: Two dozen. Intercepted. You don't believe it?

CARL: No.

ERNST: You're made to stand outside the courtroom door where comrades pass.

CARL: We know all about it.

ERNST: Inside they say, "Don't made denials. Your former comrade told us everything." Some comrades believed that.

CARL: That explains the new clothes, money in your pocket?

ERNST: They dressed me up. That was the plan, to look like a paid stool pigeon. Then the first leaflet appears: "Ernst Tausig is a paid stool pigeon." Who printed them? Comrades? No, the Nazis. The comrades keep away. Out of the crowd some one hits me—it happens often. I turn around. Children hoot me on the street. All day and night the rank injustice freezes my heart to ice.

CARL: Why tell us, why——?

ERNST: They have a detective taking me home at nights. I live in his house. I can't understand. They did something to me. Sulphur is running in my veins. At night I wake up perspiring. My tongue is thick, my eyes won't open.

TILLY: Ernst, what can we do?

ERNST: Nothing, nothing. Only I want you to believe me. I must have some one believing me. I'm not a traitor. I'm not so far gone I don't understand the position I'm in. I see what you must do to me. Warn all party members against me. You can't know the truth. Yes, what is one person like me against the whole enslaved German working class? I know I must be cast away. But you two can believe me. Yes, officially you need not believe—but yourselves. Carl, don't look at me that way!

CARL: What is that?

ERNST: What?

CARL: Perfume? You're using perfume? Lady-fingers and whipped cream for breakfast.

ERNST: No, you see how it was. They gave me money. It falls out of my hands. My mind wanders like smoke. I passed the store the other day and it was in the window. Perfumed soap. I bought some. A man must have something. It smells like flowers. *(Sits with abstracted quality. Finally says, after* CARL *removes leaflets on table from his sight):* Five weeks ago—I think it was the 8th of last month—I don't remember—the day we had the thunder shower —the hand was badly infected—it seems I knocked it against the wall or something—the 9th or 10th—they amputated it. We had that fine surgeon, D. B. Kellner. *(There is a luminous full pause. Yes, his hand has been removed and all this time he kept the stump in a pocket. Does not take it out now either.* TILLY, *unbearably moved, comes to him. He refuses her touch. Jumps up.)* Don't touch me. No, it isn't so easy. Three months—it's not so easy. That's why I'm telling you. *You must know everything!* Last night I sat in my room and it came to me. I was thinking that when I went there the next day I would tell them everything. *(Laughs and changes voice to a whisper.)* Do you know what you must do? I brought the whole thing with me. A gun, cleaned, oiled. This morning I did it. With one hand it isn't easy. Kill me!

CARL: What?

ERNST: Take the gun. Carl, you loved me once. Kill me. One day more and I'll stand there like an idiot identifying prisoners for them. I know so many. In all honor and courage you must pull the little trigger. I brought the money. Put it in the fighting fund. Maybe tell a few comrades the truth.

CARL: It is the truth?

ERNST: Yes.

TILLY: There must be no talk of dying.

ERNST: For me there's one thing, Tilly—nothing is left to do. Carl——?

CARL: They've killed you already.

ERNST: That's right. But you're alive. Other comrades are working. The day is coming and I'll be in the final result. That right can't be denied me. In that dizzy dazzling structure some part of me is built. You must understand. Take the gun, Carl.

CARL (*drawing hand away*): I won't do it.

ERNST: I couldn't do it myself. There isn't enough strength left. . . . Tilly, no tears! (*Smiles wearily.*) Such bourgeois traits in a worker . . . What is your answer, Carl?

CARL: That is what you must do. Do it yourself. Before you turn idiot. When you do that the world will know you were innocent. They'll see you came voluntarily, that. . . . (*Suddenly*): Who am I to sit in judgment?

ERNST: These guns are complicated pieces of machinery. (*Has picked it up.*) Our Germans make them like works of art. (*Weighs the gun in his hand.*) Tilly, Carl, our agony is real. But we live in the joy of a great coming people! The animal kingdom is past. Day must follow the night. Now we are ready: we have been steeled in a terrible fire, but soon all the desolate places of the world must flourish with human genius. Brothers will live in the soviets of the world! Yes, a world of security and freedom is waiting for all mankind! (*Looks at them both deeply. Walks to door to room L.*) Do your work, comrades. (*Exits.*)

TILLY (*for a moment stands still. Then starts for room.* CARL *stops her*): Carl, stop him, stop him. (CARL *holds her back.*)

CARL: Let him die. . . .

TILLY: Carl. . . . (*Shot heard within.*)

CARL: Let him live. . . .

Slow Curtain

PARADISE LOST

FOR MY DEAD MOTHER

Paradise Lost was first presented by the Group Theatre at the Longacre Theatre on the evening of December 9th, 1935, with the following members of the Group Theatre Acting Company:

LEO GORDON	Morris Carnovsky
CLARA, *his wife*	Stella Adler
BEN, *their son*	Walter Coy
JULIE, *their younger son*	Sanford Meisner
PEARL, *their daughter*	Joan Madison
GUS MICHAELS, *a family friend*	Roman Bohnen
LIBBY MICHAELS, *his daughter*	Blanche Gladstone
SAM KATZ, *Leo's partner*	Luther Adler
BERTHA, *his wife*	Frieda Altman
KEWPIE	Elia Kazan
MR. PIKE, *the furnace man*	Grover Burgess
MR. MAY	Bob Lewis
SCHNABEL	Louis G. Latzer
ROGO *a shop delegation*	Vincent Sherman
LUCY	Julie Laurence
FELIX	Herbert Ratner
PHIL FOLEY	Lewis Leverett
MILTON	Paul Morrison
NEWSPAPER MEN	Bernard Kisner
	Jacob Sandler
TWO HOMELESS MEN	Russell Collins
	William Challee
DETECTIVES	George Pembroke
	Jack Carr

Staged by HAROLD CLURMAN
Setting by BORIS ARONSON

TIME: The present
PLACE: An American city; the Gordon home.

PARADISE LOST

ACT ONE

Evening. Discovered: PEARL GORDON *on the telephone.*

PEARL: I don't want to talk on the phone. You come over. I'll wait. *(Listens)* I was practising. . . . No, I have no place to go, Felix. Where would I go? . . . I'll wait for you, Felix. *(She hangs up. Stands there thoughtfully a minute.* GUS MICHAELS *enters from stage left; a small, alert man with hair combed down to cover his baldness.)*

GUS: Want your piano tuned? I brought the instruments.

PEARL: No.

GUS: I'm A-1.

PEARL: No.

GUS: I was listenin' before—it needs it.

PEARL: Pretend you're an expert about everything, but keep away from my piano.

GUS: Why, Pearlie, I'm dumbfounded to——

PEARL: If you lay a finger on it, I'll kill you.

GUS: I know I'm an ordinary person, but——*(Enter* CLARA GORDON, *a bird-cage in hand;* MRS. KATZ *behind her.)*

CLARA: What's the matter in *here?*

GUS: Why, I really don't know, Mrs. G. She give me——

PEARL *(crying as she rushes out):* I don't want him to touch my piano!

GUS: She's a high-strung girl—no logic.

CLARA *(with slight sarcasm):* She takes after her father. (LEO GORDON *now enters and sits with a newspaper he pretends to read.)*

CLARA *(with mock scorn):* Look at him! Did you ever hear of a crazier proposition in all your born days?

LEO *(indicating newspaper):* My dear—on every page——

CLARA: He'll take revenge on a plain canary bird.

LEO: I don't want anything German in the house. I must insist on it, Clara.

CLARA: He's a bird we've had four years, lunatic!

GUS: Before Hitler ever come in power.

MRS. KATZ: It's only a bird, Mr. Gordon.

GUS: *I* come from the German people.

CLARA: Look, his nose gets white when he makes up his mind.

LEO *(shamed, but firm):* Give the bird away.

MRS. KATZ: She sings beautiful.

CLARA *(handing over cage to* MRS. KATZ): So take him.

MRS. KATZ: You mean it?

CLARA: If Leo says no, it's no.

MRS. KATZ *(very pleased):* I'll take care of her like a baby.

LEO: Mrs. Katz, please ask Sam to come down after supper.

MRS. KATZ: He's finished in ten minutes. Good-bye. *(At the door)* Thank you. Excuse me. *(Exits.)*

GUS: Now the civil war's over, I'll get back on this radio. *(He goes to radio he's been fixing.* CLARA *starts piling dishes.)*

LEO *(conciliatorily):* Darling, why did you let the maid go?

CLARA: Nowadays twelve dollars a week for a colored girl. Twice a week's plenty.

GUS *(at the radio):* The song appealin' to me most—is the Song of India.

LEO: Business isn't *so* bad.

CLARA: Give it a chance, Leo.

LEO: I'm sorry about the bird, Clara.

CLARA *(laughing):* I found out many years ago I married a fool, but I love him. *(As she is about to exit with a pile of dishes, enter left* JULIE GORDON, *a young man dressed in slippers and bathrobe)* What's the matter, Julie?

JULIE: Why?

CLARA: You look funny.

JULIE: I'm fine—don't worry.

CLARA: I never worried a day in my life. Here today—gone tomorrow! Take a piece of fruit, Gus. *(Exits.)*

GUS *(to* JULIE): You know anything about the big secret television movement in Wall Street?

JULIE: Mr. Pike come yet?

LEO: Not yet.

GUS: You don't know anything about it?

JULIE: No. Where's Ben?

GUS: I seen him in the barber shop.

JULIE: The house feels empty. *(Sits with newspaper.)*

LEO: You can't read a paper nowadays without worry. The world has a profound dislocation.

GUS: Yes, profound, but no logic; no percentage.

LEO: Persecuted people—it doesn't matter what religion.

GUS: Well, if someone told me five, ten years ago I'd be tinkering with a thing called radio, I'd 'a said crazy. It's progress, yes.

LEO: Progress!

GUS (*as* CLARA *enters*): I was thinkin' . . . tryin' to put in a complete line of radios. I'm tired of bein' a poor man. Last week a certain party in the American Tel and Tel was——

CLARA: A personal friend, Gus?

GUS: He says television's comin' in, sure as death. Yes, Mrs. G., I know some pretty important people. Dealers who's prepared, they'll reap a harvest on this television proposition.

CLARA: We could use a harvest ourself.

GUS: Now, if I can raise a small loan——

CLARA: I smelled it a mile away! Take a piece of fruit, Gus.

GUS: No one takes me serious. How is that? I ask Pearlie to let me tune the piano, and she makes out like I'm an ignoramus on the subject. Why, for eleven years, I tuned every piano in Asbury Park.

LEO: You know how she is about her piano.

GUS: And you, Mrs. G., you know I'm an expert on radios.

CLARA (*archly*): Oh, I know you know.

GUS: I thought if Mr. G. would——

CLARA: Leo's money's tied up in the business.

GUS: Just to endorse——

CLARA: We can't do it.

GUS: Steve Brody took a chance.

CLARA: Gus, he can't do it, Gus.

GUS: All my life I wanted to start a little business insteada flittin' around at odd jobs.

CLARA: Maybe you'd like a few facts. One, we lost every penny in the bank crash. Two, my foolish husband took a mortgage on the house to put in the business.

GUS: Hard times. I ought to find a nice widow with ten—twelve thousand.

CLARA: Take a piece of fruit, Gus. (*She exits with more dishes.*)

GUS: I guess failure's gone to my head. (*Back at the radio*) Now we'll have music. Friends, Romans, countrymen, she's workin' like nobody's business. (*Music*) All the jazz bands and crooners in America singin' one sad song—"Give Me Love, Baby." Well, I never seen that solve no problems.

LEO: Clara was telling our Ben not to marry your Libby until he found some means of support.

GUS (*slapping large bronze statue standing upstage*): Oh, it's different with him. He's got the magnetism. A champeen in every muscle of the body. Did you ever think it, that we'd turn out an Olympic champ in our own neighborhood! (*Slaps statue again as* CLARA *enters*) How like a god, I say.

CLARA: If "God" don't get a job soon——

GUS: Don't worry. He's got the real connections.

CLARA: But he never worked a day in his life. A house full of medals and silver cups, but when the first baby comes——

GUS: Ha, ha! Don't you worry your head about them turtledoves. (*Enter* SAM KATZ *with the bird-cage, his wife behind.*)

SAM: What's the big idea, Leo! Since when am I a Nazi-lover? If the bird's no good for your house, he's no good for my house——

LEO: Why, Sam, your wife thought——

SAM: This is no criterion, what Bertha thought.

CLARA: All right, put it down. I'll give it to the colored girl.

SAM: I'm surprised on you, Leo——

GUS: They don't mean no harm.

SAM: Excuse me please, keep quiet.

GUS: No, I won't, I ain't your servant.

SAM: You got the five dollars you owe me?

GUS: No.

SAM: So keep quiet. (GUS *is cowed.*)

CLARA (*angry*): Don't start a fight about nothing, Katz. Go upstairs.

LEO: Clara.

SAM: To insult a man behind his back is nothing by you?

CLARA: You should be locked up!

LEO: Please, Clara. (*She stops her activity*) We made a mistake, Sam. Please excuse us.

CLARA (*with sarcasm*): Yes, excuse us.

LEO (*gently*): Will you come down when the shop delegation arrives, Sam?

SAM: Maybe I'll go hide in a closet while my partner takes the bread from my mouth! (*He looks around belligerently and begins to eat something which he has carried in his hand.*)

CLARA (*ironic*): Any more complaints?

SAM: Yes. Don't call so many bums in the house to eat and sleep in the cellar. It gives us a black eye in the neighborhood. *(Exits.)*

MRS. KATZ: Excuse me. *(Exits.)*

GUS: He thinks he's better than anyone else.

CLARA: The next time I'll knock out his teeth.

LEO: My dear, he's a very unhappy man.

CLARA: I'll still knock out his teeth!

GUS: Is it true she wears a wig, his wife?

LEO: Yes.

GUS: Extra-ordinary!

LEO: She was very sick.

CLARA: Ten years, they want children. *(To* LEO) Don't sit and let Sam call you fancy names. For a change, stand up for your rights.

LEO: My dear, don't worry.

CLARA: Do yourself a personal favor—listen to me: don't trust him for a nickel.

LEO: What are you talking about?

CLARA: I know you like a book. If your head wasn't pinned on your shoulders, would you find it in the morning? And I know Sam Katz. You sit and design pocketbooks, and he runs the business. He brings a check, and one-two it's signed with no questions asked.

LEO: Clara, I've trusted Sam for twenty-two years.

CLARA: A lunatic can make a mistake.

LEO *(laughing):* She's serious—a man I know intimately for thirty years.

CLARA: Never mind! In business "intimately" don't grow hair on a bald man's head.

GUS: That's right.

CLARA *(convinced of the hopelessness of convincing* LEO): Besides, darling, if you go bankrupt, who'll pay my poker debts? *(Enter* KEWPIE.)

KEWPIE: Where's my pal, Ben?

CLARA: Your pal Ben is around the corner in the barber shop.

KEWPIE: O.K. *(Starts out)* Do me a favor, Gussie.

GUS: Don't call me Gussie.

KEWPIE: I left my cab in front of the house, *Mr. Michaels.* Don't let the kids jump on. (KEWPIE *exits.)*

CLARA: I wouldn't mind keeping him out of the house.

LEO: He doesn't mean any harm.

CLARA: No?

LEO: My dear, don't you trust anyone?

CLARA: My dear, I wasn't born yesterday. *(Exits.)*

GUS *(looking at the bird-cage):* Is goldfish again becoming popular? Goldfish and canary birds. I love to have them things around the house. *(Suddenly he is whistling vigorously like a canary)* I'm a son of a gun how he comes singin' out of me, this little bird!

JULIE *(shakes his head gravely):* The stock market was a lifeless affair today.

GUS: I understand you run up a considerable amount, Julie.

JULIE: Sure I did!

GUS: On paper?

JULIE: But suppose I had a real initial thousand! I'd be fifty-two thousand to the good! There it is——*(Shows sheaf of papers)* Since I could sit up in bed, five weeks' play: over ten thousand a week. I look ahead!

GUS: You oughta talk to some of them big men down your bank.

LEO *(naïvely):* That's what I think . . .

JULIE: They don't listen to me—I'm just a clerk. But they will. They don't look ahead and see world movements, situations. What'll happen in Russia next year. Italy. Diesel engines for new stream-line trains! Chromium!

GUS *(very knowingly):* Millions made on radio——

JULIE: You have to know where to get information. This fellow Staleen gave me an idea: said we'd inflate and go off the gold standard a whole six months before we did. I told Mr. Prince. He laughed at me! That bit of information was worth one million dollars if they used it.

GUS: Myopic!

JULIE: But I'm nobody's fool. When the time comes——*(A knock at the inner door)* Come in. *(Door opens.* LUCAS PIKE *stands in the hallway whiskbrooming himself. Enters.)*

LEO: Good evening, Mr. Pike.

PIKE *(slapping dust off gloves as he enters):* Glad you keep the whiskbroom there, Citizen. One fine amount of dust on me when I get through with the day's work. Better tell your wife about the spiders —cellar's full of them. *(To* JULIE) How you feeling?

JULIE: How's the furnace business?

PIKE: Can't kick. I'm itchin' for some chess.

JULIE: Fine.

PIKE: Just as soon as I put Miller's furnace to bed . . . half hour.

CLARA *(as she enters):* Hello, Pike, take a piece of fruit.

JULIE: I'll set up the board. *(He exits.)*

PIKE *(throws paper on table):* They found another dead man today. Over at the garbage dump. There's what a starved man looks like —made that sketch while they took him away.

GUS: Tsch, tsch, tsch!

CLARA *(looking at sketch):* Did you ever?

LEO: Don't show it to me.

CLARA: It sounds like something that happens only in a *foreign* country!

GUS: Times is terrible.

CLARA: Leo! Don't act like the whole world's trouble's your fault.

PIKE: Thanks for this coat: first one I owned in four years.

CLARA: Say, some are rich and some are poor!

LEO: That's no answer, my dear.

CLARA: Why not? Rich and poor—it's a natural condition!

PIKE: It *is not natural* for men to starve while means to produce food are close at hand.

CLARA: Say, maybe I'm wrong. *(There is a knock at the door.* GUS *answers it.)*

GUS: Hello, Phil . . . (PIKE *waits for* PHIL FOLEY *to come in and then exits. He pulls on gloves and waits listening in outer hallway.* MR. FOLEY *is a local politician and is followed by a small college graduate with a small waxed mustache.)*

FOLEY *(with broad good humor):* Sholom Aleichem, Gus! Looking for your friends, the Gordons.

GUS *(pleased as a little dog):* Here they are.

FOLEY: Meet Phil Foley, Mr. Gordon, and the missis of the house. *(Shakes their hands)* Chairman of the Nemo Democratic Club, in case you didn't know. Just in case—ha, ha, ha! Seriously, nothing like catching the early worm.

LEO: Pleased to meet you, Mr. Foley.

FOLEY *(listening):* Hear you got a daughter plays the piano. Hmm, pretty nice!

LEO: My daughter studied with a pupil of Leschititsky.

FOLEY: You don't say! Like to give *you* a piece of advice, Mrs. Gordon: Lookin' a bit dark under the eyes. What's the remedy? Grapefruit juice! What's the trouble? Too much acids, meats and stuff like that. The normal ratio of the human body . . . what is it, Milton?

MILTON *(who lisps):* Eighty percent alkaline, twenty percent acid.

FOLEY: That's it—eighty-twenty! Instead the ordinary person fills his stomach with twenty-eighty! . . . the other way around, see? This acid robs you of your energy, makes you feel kinda low.

MILTON: Robs you of your gasoline. . . .

FOLEY: That's it! And puts shadows under the eyes. Looka me, I can walk through a brick wall. You'd think I was in training for boxing, but I don't box. *(Belches)* Grapefruit juice—there's your answer—brings you back to normal—*the way the Democrats will bring the whole country back to normal!*

CLARA: Before you say it, I'll say it. You want us to vote Democrat?

FOLEY: Gus, *my old friend* Gus, says there's five votes under this one roof. We want you to come out and vote all the stars Tuesday.

CLARA: I voted Democrat since the beginning, Foley, but my husband don't vote.

FOLEY: Don't vote! You're kiddin' me, Mr. Gordon. Why, Gus here tells me you're a man with a head for philosophy and things.

LEO: In my honest opinion, one side is as bad as the other. That's why I don't vote.

FOLEY: You musta read that in some paper.

LEO *(sincerely):* I make up my own mind, Mr. Foley.

FOLEY: Well, Gus, I see our good friend, Mr. Gordon, don't know us and what we stand for. Be surprised, you might want us . . . a son who's a lawyer. Have him join the club and get somewhere, like Milton here—gonna be a big man some day.

LEO: No one in our family is interested in politics, Mr. Foley. I'm sorry.

FOLEY *(to* GUS): Did you explain to our friend how the voting machines——

LEO: I'm sorry, I do not believe in your kind of government.

FOLEY *(after a dead stop and looking around at all):* What? What's that mean?

PIKE *(coming into the room):* I'll tell you what it means! Wherever there's a swamp you get mosquitoes. And wherever there's a rich government you find grafters.

FOLEY: Meaning which?

PIKE: If the shoe fits . . .

FOLEY: I'm a sonofagun! Hear that, Milton?

MILTON: Ridiculous!

PIKE: This is about the richest city in the world. A person starves to death in it every other day. Not enough alkaline. That's what it means! Hunger and degradation—eighty-twenty. Maybe we ought to take the government over in our own hands and make it something different.

FOLEY *(to* LEO*)*: Those your sentiments?

LEO: I'm sorry . . .

FOLEY: Looks like we walked in on a nest of Reds.

PIKE *(coldly)*: We happen to be Americans.

FOLEY: Hell, that's radical talk. We don't need your kind of votes. Maybe you ain't even citizens!

PIKE: For one generation of Irish you're talking pretty big. I'm what they call one hundred per cent American. My ancestors didn't come over on the Mayflower. They missed that one, but came over on the next ferry. I come stock, lock and barrel out of the Parson family. We fought all your wars, from 1776 up to 1918. Two of my boys . . . my only two *(Shows picture in watch)* . . . you call me a Red and I'll break your goddam neck!

FOLEY: What kind of language is that to use in front of a lady! *(Choked up,* PIKE *turns away)* Gus, I'm pretty sorry to see you mixed up in this buncha radicals. I certainly never expected it on Shakespeare Place. See me later at the club.

GUS *(in a small voice)*: Fine and dandy, Phil. . . . (FOLEY *strides out; and* MILTON.)

PIKE: Sorry I bust out that way. It happens to be Armistice Day. . . . *(He finishes with a gesture and exits.)*

CLARA: Now we're Reds!

GUS: He meant Mr. P.

CLARA: Do you see shadows under my eyes?

GUS: No. . . .

CLARA *(shrugging her shoulders)*: For a minute I was worried.

GUS *(soberly)*: I always kept Mrs. Michaels' picture in my watch, too. *(Winding watch)* I love when the night time comes, for then I can wind my watch . . . and I love to wind my watch. . . . *(There is a sudden flurry of voices heard outside. Now enter* BEN *with* LIBBY *held under his arm, she kicking and laughing, followed by* KEWPIE *who is angry. All speaking simultaneously:)*

BEN: Lafayette, we are here! Gus, I met our sonofagun baby and brought her back with me. *(Puts her down.)*

LIBBY *(enjoying it)*: Hon, you mussed me all up!

KEWPIE: That Roumanian phony!

BEN: Forget it.

KEWPIE: I'll take his head off his shoulders! You heard him call you a nance!

BEN: Because I was getting a manicure. Forget it.

KEWPIE: Looka the kids hopping on the cab. *(Knocks at window and yells "Hey!")*

BEN: They tear me to pieces every time I step out.

LIBBY: We better hurry if we're stepping out tonight.

BEN: They'll hold the game for Ben Gordon.

CLARA: Lunatic, take off your hat in the house!

BEN: Hear that? Pal o' my cradle days calling me a lunatic! Can't do it, Clara. Got to keep the haircomb in place. *(Shows hair)* Max worked an hour on it. But don't I make a bum out of a hat! *(Puts hat on again)* Got the tickets, Kewpie?

KEWPIE: Two on the north side.

BEN: Swell. Say, Leo, give my man Friday five dollars, will you?

KEWPIE: It's on the house.

CLARA: What's the big idea?

BEN: Four stars!

CLARA: For what?

BEN: Every day's four stars for Mrs. Gordon's little boy Ben!

LIBBY *(defiantly):* Tell them, Ben.

BEN *(drawing himself up grandly):* We did it!

CLARA AND GUS: What?

BEN *(executes a tap dance):* Bells on our fingers, rings on our toes! Married!

LIBBY: Yes, we got married this afternoon at City Hall.

CLARA: Honest to God!

BEN *(sings):* Cross my heart and hope to die. . . .

GUS: I'm dumbfound! Just dumbfound!

LEO: Congratulations. . . .

CLARA: Lunatic, couldn't you wait?

LIBBY: I expected some crack like that from you!

BEN *(preventing an argument):* Why wait, Mom? The world's at our doorstep! *(To* KEWPIE*)* Did you phone Post?

KEWPIE: He's coming up with a cameraman.

BEN: Libby baby, you'll see your rosebud face in every paper in the country this week. The news-reel man oughta be along any minute with his sound truck!

CLARA *(doorbell rings a tattoo;* KEWPIE *goes):* Tell Pearlie to come down, Leo. (LEO *knocks on a radiator pipe in the corner; piano playing stops upstairs.* KEWPIE *brings on* POST *and* CAMERAMAN.)

BEN: Hell-o, Post!

POST (*a dark man with a dead face*): Hitched up, I hear. I used to think you'd get married in an airplane.

BEN: Meet the frau, Post . . . the rest of the Gordon tribe.

GUS: I'm the bride's father.

POST (*saturnine*): Greetings.

BEN: Gus Michaels—owns the best motorcycle in town. Bring it in, Gus.

CLARA: Lunatic! Keep it in the hall. (CAMERAMAN *is unfolding instrument.*)

BEN: No, ma'am. We'll take a picture on it! Me and Libby. How's that, Dave?

POST: Marvel-lousy!

GUS (*going for cycle*): She's a beautiful machine.

POST (*looking* LIBBY *over*): Yeah, wonderful.

BEN: Hold everything: he's getting the little birdie ready!

POST: What'll I tell our three million circulation?

BEN (*picking up raccoon tail off handlebar of highly decorated cycle and putting it to his chin*): Tell them the champ miler of the world is growing old, Maggie, and is soon putting away his spikes for lobster, champagne and a big berth in Wall Street. (PEARL *enters and stands at doorway*) Private connections made while crossing the Atlantic and Pacific——

CAMERAMAN: Want the motorcycle, Dave?

POST: Sure. Hop up, Ben. Put Greta Garbo on the handlebars.

BEN (*after it is done*): How's that?

POST: Wonderful.

BEN (*as they pose*): Tweet tweet.

CAMERAMAN: Hold it . . . oke . . . again, don't move . . . oke!

POST: One with the family . . . in front of the statue. (*Reads*) "Representative American youth . . ."

LEO: This is our daughter, Mr. Post.

POST: Greetings.

CLARA (*just as* JULIE *enters*): Ben and Libby got married today. (*Simultaneously*)

JULIE: Congratulations.

GUS (*to* POST): My daughter was a seven months' baby.

BEN: Thanks. Get in the picture.

GUS: He wants the family to pose.

PEARL: Don't want my picture.

BEN: Don't spoil the party.

PEARL: No. *(Draws away.)*

POST *(wearily):* Let's go. . . .

BEN: Bashful; runs in the family. (CAMERAMAN *steadies them and gets two snaps)* And while you're at it, tell the readers I owe it all to my mother. She thinks I'm nuts. Maybe I am, but she fed me cod liver oil, shredded wheat——

GUS: Vitamins!

BEN: And that's how I came to be the champ.

CLARA: It's no joke, Post. I raised my whole family on Grade A milk.

BEN: Let's make it a real field day while we're at it. Here's my father —been shelling out since I started running. Paid every cent without a murmur. And this shy member of the tribe—*(Indicates* PEARL)—who takes after my father—is a very fine pianist. She——

PEARL: Mind your business!

BEN: Can't get a break with the concert managers because that needs real money.

PEARL: I don't think you're funny one bit.

BEN: I'm not being funny.

PEARL: To a nitwit life is one laugh after another.

LIBBY: You keep quiet!

PEARL: I'm talking to my brother . . . who thinks he owns the world because he won some medals. The great genius who never earned a nickel in his whole life. You've got some nerve—daring to get married. *(Exits.)*

LIBBY: I'm just as proud as she is and——

BEN: Libby, don't——

LIBBY: She had no right to say a thing like that!

BEN: It's true, my sweet. You married a curly-headed bozo with an electric sparkle in his eyes and a mouth and ten fingers to kiss you all over. But nothing else except promises—excuse us for getting so personal in front of company. *(Suddenly very depressed, he goes to sit at window.)*

JULIE *(to* POST): A drink of wine?

POST: Why not? *(He and* JULIE *and* OTHERS *drink)* Sappy days!

GUS: Yes, to the bride and groom. She was a seven months' baby. Just imagine, we never thought she'd live.

POST *(waving farewell):* Carbolic, Ben.

BEN: Thanks, Dave. So long.

GUS *(to* POST): Say it's my motorcycle.

POST: Invite me for a good home-cooked meal.

CLARA: Sure, any time.

POST: Carbolic! *(Goes, with his assistant.)*

GUS: "To have and to hold from this day forward—till death do us part." *(Finishes his wine, blows his nose, vigorously, and wheels out his motorcycle.)*

LIBBY: Hon, let's get to the hockey game.

BEN: I don't feel like it.

LIBBY: I swear to God I don't understand you half the time.

BEN: Ben Gordon's up and he's down. That's how he is—moods. (GUS *re-enters)* Listen, family, we got married today. I have a good idea what you think—it's gonna be an economic tragedy. We all know I can't run no more——

GUS: What?

BEN: Sure, my heart. I told Libby yesterday. The doctor says I'm through! But I saw Alfred Bond yesterday—the big A.A.U. official—he says not to worry, a swell berth waiting for me in Wall Street. Will we make money! All the books you can read, Leo. A concert career for Pearlie—that—dope! And Gus can have a better stamp collection than the King of England! Just be patient.

LEO: Who said anything to you, Ben?

BEN: I'll make good!

GUS: You certainly got that magnetism, Ben.

LIBBY: My Ben can be anything he wants.

CLARA: Your Ben!

LIBBY: He might even go in the movies. (PEARL'S *piano begins again upstairs—"Für Elise")* I want fun out of life!

CLARA *(as she exits):* Fun's in the dictionary!

KEWPIE *(silently sullen until now):* The cab's waiting.

BEN *(laughing with returned good spirits):* Two minutes till I change my suit. *(He kisses* LIBBY *and exits.)*

GUS: The King of England . . . he's a man I feel sorry for—a wax figgerhead. I'll help Mrs. G. with the dishes. *(Exits.)*

JULIE: Good luck, Libby.

LIBBY: Thanks. (JULIE *exits.)*

LEO *(timidly):* I hope you will be very happy.

LIBBY *(indifferently):* Thanks. . . .

LEO: Ben's a good boy. . . .

LIBBY: I oughta know.

LEO: Yes. . . . *(Hesitant and not knowing what to say, he exits with newspaper.)*

KEWPIE *(alone with* LIBBY *at last):* But he's no money man!

LIBBY: I married a man with a big future.

KEWPIE: Good in the receiving department, but lousy in the shipping.

LIBBY: Don't pick on me!

KEWPIE: You and that soft juicy body, like a mushmelon.

LIBBY: You're a hundred miles away.

KEWPIE: Suppose I tell him what happened when he went to Europe?

LIBBY: He don't believe such things about me. He'd throw you around for saying it.

KEWPIE: Don't you know he's yellow in his heart? Get wise to that skyrocket: *starts* with a bang!

LIBBY: Ben's the most handsome man I know.

KEWPIE: A burnt out spark plug?

LIBBY: Stop pickin' on me!

KEWPIE: You're a little squab, and you laid right down in the sand with me, under the boardwalk.

LIBBY: So what?

KEWPIE: Purely horizontal.

LIBBY: Did I say I was ice, with Ben running races the whole summer in Europe? It happened like that—down "the island," the summer, the night and all that. I'm not sorry for a thing I done! Telling me— a cheap cab driver with a dozen phony side lines. You don't drive no gold chariot, Kewpie.

KEWPIE: I do, only you don't see it, Mabel!

LIBBY: Don't call me Mabel. You're sore because he tells me poems. You act like his best friend, but you're the worst enemy——

KEWPIE: Who said——?

LIBBY: You'll knife him in the back!

KEWPIE: Who said——?

LIBBY: Well, I'm telling you so you won't start up again. For me Ben's a home run with the bases full.

KEWPIE: He got everything I ever laid my hands on first.

LIBBY: Don't tell me!

KEWPIE *(holding her):* A sleeping clam at the bottom of the ocean, but I'll wake you up. I'm through with the little wars; no more hacking, making a pound in a good day. Like old man Pike says, every man for himself nowadays, and when you're in a jungle you look out for the wild life. I put on my Chinese good luck ring and I'm out to get mine. You're the first stop!

LIBBY: Goof!

KEWPIE: I start with Joe the Shark next week. You could string along with me. You——

LIBBY: Stop foaming at the mouth.

KEWPIE *(out of control):* You knew I had a fever for you. You did it to spite me! (LEO *enters; sees them together this way.)*

LEO: What's wrong?

LIBBY *(breaking away):* Kewpie's telling my fortune.

LEO: Libby . . . I love my sons better than life. I know . . . I know you're inclined to be a little wild. . . .

LIBBY: Where do you get that stuff?

LEO *(painfully):* I know you'll make a good wife, but married life brings new responsibilities and . . .

LIBBY: You got your nerve!

LEO: Excuse me for . . . *(He exits.)*

KEWPIE: Your shell's lined with pearls.

LIBBY: Shut your face!

BEN *(as he enters):* Hey, you look swell in that new coat. *(Embracing her.)* Who loves Ben?

LIBBY *(throughout aware of the effect on* KEWPIE*)*: Libby. Who loves Libby?

BEN *(jokingly):* Kewpie! Hey, I love your rocks and rills, darling. How your shoulders move when you walk—I love that too.

LIBBY: Hon, you're mussing me up again.

BEN: Happy?

LIBBY: Sure, every day's Saturday.

BEN *(to* KEWPIE*)*: What do you think of her?

KEWPIE *(in a low controlled voice):* She's a juicy baby, all right.

BEN *(laughing):* Four stars!

KEWPIE *(suddenly):* But dumb—nothing between the acts!

LIBBY: I'll smack his face in a minute! He's always making a pass for me, Ben. You shoulda heard him just now.

BEN: What did he say? *(She won't answer.)*

KEWPIE: Tell him. . . .

LIBBY: That's your worst enemy!

BEN *(amused):* Kewpie?

LIBBY: Yeah, a carbon copy who hates your guts.

BEN: I wish . . . I could make you out, Kewpie . . . you're changing.

KEWPIE: Don't talk soda water. Only take my word—I'm a better friend than she is.

LIBBY: How do you get that way?

KEWPIE: All my life you got a square deal. Always in front smackin' them down left and right when they got in your way. Now she says ten words—you're ready to throw me over!

BEN: Christ, life goes like the river; why get excited?

KEWPIE: What did she ever do for you? Did she tell you about Bill Crawford? Eddie Meyers?

LIBBY: If you listen to him I'll walk right out!

BEN: Listen, Kewpie, we intend to stay married! Sore 'cause I took Libby away from you?

KEWPIE: In case you'd like to know, I'm sore on my whole damn life.

BEN: Why take it out on us?

LIBBY: He even said you couldn't make a living for me!

BEN *(to* KEWPIE*)*: I never expected to hear that from you. A—The future's all mapped out. B—Anything I owe you you get back. And about Libby—X Y Z—if I stepped on your toes, I'm sorry. We fell in love. The best man won.

KEWPIE *(finally)*: Okay. . . .

LIBBY: I notice you're not so wise when Ben's around.

KEWPIE: Shut up or I'll poke you one!

BEN *(laughing it off)*: Coast to coast . . .

LIBBY: You think he don't mean it? *I'll* ride downtown in his cab?!

KEWPIE: Crawl for all I care.

BEN: Say . . . what the hell is this?

KEWPIE: I'm outa control, Ben. Take your hand away. You know I got a temper. Whata you let her kid me for? You know you're aces with me. Only don't let her give me the needles! (BEN *turns and looks at* LIBBY.)

LIBBY: Now it's *my* fault!

BEN: You know he's got a quick temper.

LIBBY: Sure, little Barney Google! (KEWPIE *quickly walks over to* LIBBY *and slaps her smartly across the mouth. As quickly* BEN *gets between them and swings a punch to* KEWPIE *who in turn swings over two, the second of which knocks* BEN *down and out for a few seconds.)*

KEWPIE: I'll take on a regiment!

BEN *(dazed and slowly sitting up):* You want . . .

LIBBY: Make him black and blue, Ben! (BEN *slowly gets up.*) Gonna let him get away with that?

BEN *(as* KEWPIE *backs off):* Some day I'll get sore at you.

KEWPIE: Did I hurt you, Ben?

BEN: I didn't feel it.

KEWPIE *(ashamed):* You know how I am—in there boppin' away before I know it. I don't work with my head, Ben.

BEN: Sure . . .

KEWPIE: Smack me in the mouth, Ben. Hit me . . .

BEN: Don't be a kid!

LIBBY: What's this, a love duet?

KEWPIE: If you're ready, the cab's waiting . . .

BEN: We won't go downtown.

KEWPIE: What about the tickets?

BEN: You know what you can do with them.

KEWPIE: Don't be sore, Ben.

BEN *(blowing up):* I'm not, I'm not! I'm just goddam sick in my heart! Get the hell out!

KEWPIE: I know I'm a pro-anti, but——

BEN: Get out . . . (CLARA *enters with cigarette in mouth.*)

CLARA: What's the matter?

BEN: Not a thing, Clara.

KEWPIE *(at the door):* See you tomorrow? *(No answer.)* See you tomorrow. *(Exits.)*

CLARA: What happened?

BEN: Nothing, I said. *(To* LIBBY): Was that true?

LIBBY: What?

BEN: What he said about Crawford?

LIBBY: For cryin' out loud, how can . . .

BEN *(harshly):* I just asked. I'll get my coat. *(Takes cigarette from his mother's mouth and exits smoking it.)*

CLARA: What happened?

LIBBY: Kewpie hit him. (GUS *enters with stamp album; sits at table.*)

CLARA: I'll break his hands, that bandit!

LIBBY: Ben didn't hit him back . . .

CLARA: He'll end in the electric chair.

BEN *(enters):* Let's go.

LIBBY: Where to?

BEN: Empire. We'll see Marlene Dietrich.

GUS: Marlene—she's the intellect and artistic type.

BEN: Is Leo around?

CLARA: You want some money?

BEN *(reluctantly):* Yes . . . *(She gives him some dollar bills from pocket.* GUS *wets stamp hinges with his tongue.)*

CLARA: Don't worry—I marked it on the ice. Enjoy yourself. (BEN *slaps his statue as he passes it and exits.)*

LIBBY: See you in the funny papers, Pop! *(Gives* CLARA *a malicious look, exits.)*

GUS *(engrossed):* Good-bye . . .

CLARA: My whole family's crazy, except Julie. He takes after me.

GUS: Marlene, I got her in the harem of my head.

CLARA: And so are you!

GUS *(coming out of reverie):* What?

CLARA: Crazy!

GUS: I have my troubles, Mrs. G. Be surprised how often I think about it—takin' my life by my own hand.

CLARA *(dressing in street clothes):* ! ! !

GUS: But I turn the radio on instead of the gas . . . Ha, ha, ha. (JULIE *enters.)*

JULIE: Mom . . .

CLARA: What?

JULIE: Are you going out tonight?

CLARA: To a card game with the girls. What's the matter, Julie?

JULIE: The house feels empty . . .

CLARA: Play a chess game after.

JULIE: Yes . . .

CLARA: What's the matter, big boy?

JULIE: Momma, I don't know . . .

CLARA: You're acting very funny.

JULIE: I'm frightened.

CLARA: Of what?

JULIE: No upward trend. I feel like a weak market.

CLARA: Dope! You were sick in bed for two months! You expect to fly like an eagle the first week?

JULIE: I won't get better.

CLARA: Dr. Clurman says you'll be back in the bank in a week.

JULIE: I don't believe it! In high school we had a kid named Gilbert.

He had sleeping sickness, too. When he came back to school he began to get old. In two years . . . he died.

CLARA: What's that got to do with Julie Gordon? *(Piano plays upstairs.)*

JULIE: Doctors can't fix it . . .

CLARA: My beautiful boy, don't bother your head. Do yourself a favor, listen to me: You'll have your own children. In our whole family you alone will be a success.

JULIE: Don't close your door at night.

CLARA: I won't play cards. *(Begins to take off street clothes.)*

JULIE: Go . . .

CLARA: It's not so terrible to miss a game.

JULIE: Don't worry about me.

CLARA: Julie. . . .

JULIE *(kissing her):* Go to the card game.

CLARA *(going):* Take a piece of fruit. *(Bundled up, she stops at the door.)*

JULIE: Have a good time.

CLARA *(kissing him):* Good night.

GUS: Good night . . .

CLARA: Baby needs a pair of shoes! *(Exits.)*

GUS: I have confidence in your mother.

JULIE: Yes, that's a lady I like. (JULIE *sits at other end of table and eats an apple.)*

GUS: People don't rest enough. The heart don't rest enough, except between beats. Figger it out—76 times a minute . . . 4500 times an hour . . .

JULIE: The night is full of sounds if we listen . . .

GUS *(self-absorbed):* Uh-huh . . .

JULIE: Taxis running down the streets. . . .

GUS: I used to be a photography fiend in the old days. Yes, it was some craze—Eastman, Velox an' all that.

JULIE: Do you like open-air cars in the summer?

GUS *(starts for the door; stops mysteriously):* No, I don't like open-air cars. Mrs. Michaels was killed like that. She was a very nervous woman and put her head out. . . . Did your mother say there was coffee on the stove? (JULIE *nods his head.)* I'll take a cup. *(Stops at the door.)* My wife had one blue eye and one grey eye—there's no use denyin' it, Julie . . . and if you want the whole truth, she was cockeyed; but I loved her very much. *(He exits to kitchen. A knock on inner door.)*

JULIE: Come! (FELIX *enters.*) Hello, Felix.

FELIX: How's the boy?

JULIE: All right. Looking for Pearl?

FELIX: It was on my mind.

JULIE: Go up.

FELIX: I'll wait down here.

JULIE *(going to pipe):* Call her?

FELIX: Please. (JULIE *knocks on pipe.*) It's a nice warm house here. *(Piano stops.)*

JULIE: The leading coal producers are operating in the red.

FELIX: I'm thinking about going to Chicago.

JULIE *(surprised):* Why?

FELIX *(he laughs):* Foolish question number 624.

JULIE: Does Pearl know?

FELIX: Not yet . . .

JULIE: She won't like it.

FELIX: I can't help myself. (PEARL *enters.* JULIE *looks at them both as if silently introducing them; exits.)*

PEARL: Did you eat?

FELIX: Yes. *(He slowly and strongly embraces her and they kiss deeply.)*

PEARL *(finally):* Felix, what happened . . . ?

FELIX: No.

PEARL: He said . . . ?

FELIX: The director. "We got all the fiddlers we need," he said. Firsts and seconds like hair in your head.

PEARL: And?

FELIX: So I gave him a dirty look and walked out.

PEARL *(finally):* What ugly hands I have.

FELIX: Now you know it all.

PEARL: Yes.

FELIX: We could take a chance.

PEARL: Ben got married today.

FELIX: Congratulations . . . but like I said—if we got married, could I back it up? I get up in the morning and play the Bach Chaconne, but that won't make breakfast.

PEARL: Money . . .

FELIX: You don't like to talk about money——

PEARL: I don't.

FELIX: Your mother's right: people can't get married without it.

PEARL: It's two years now.

FELIX: What?

PEARL: We're engaged two years tonight. Armistice Day.

FELIX: The way I see it, Pearlie, the war's still on!

PEARL: Armistice Day . . . I'll go on giving piano lessons. Felix, if I have to go on giving lessons all my life . . .

FELIX: I know.

PEARL: I'd like to run away somewhere. (MRS. KATZ *enters quietly.*)

MRS. KATZ: Excuse me. Where's Momma?

PEARL: I think she went out.

MRS. KATZ: Excuse me. Thank you. *(Exits.)*

FELIX: She sneaks around like a Chinaman in the movies.

PEARL: Mr. Katz hits her sometimes.

FELIX: Listen—I'm a worm in the ground and you're a worm in the ground. Pearlie, I used to think I was a wonderful guy—a musician with a big head of hair. Have a good time—love everybody. Play in the orchestra—play quartets—culture, but without the bucks— who'll get culture? I swear I don't know a girl who can play the piano like you. What's it get you?—Can we get married? Mamma, God rest her soul—she named me Felix after Mendelssohn— Mamma used to say, "Find a rich girl." She didn't know when those little love bugs start creeping, you don't think about that.

PEARL: That's what you think?

FELIX *(bitterly):* The best things in life are free. What lies we believe!

PEARL: I dream at night.

FELIX: And that's what I think——Finished. I'll say good-bye and you'll say good-bye. Find a better man, Pearlie. The kind who *supports* the orchestra.

PEARL: You're going away?

FELIX: Got a better idea?

PEARL: No. *(Pause.)* Where'll you go?

FELIX: Chicago, Detroit, Los Angeles. . . .

PEARL: Write.

FELIX: Well . . . *(Hesitates.)*

PEARL: Don't smoke cigarettes in bed . . .

FELIX *(starting an avowal of love):* Pearlie . . .

PEARL: Please . . .

FELIX: I love you more than my fiddle—more than my life——

PEARL *(repressing her feeling):* Don't be sentimental.

FELIX: Pearlie, if you knew . . .

PEARL: Good-bye. *(She walks away from him.)*

FELIX: You're a funny girl.

PEARL: I know . . . (FELIX *slowly exits.)*

LEO *(enters and sits):* Happiness is not to be found among the material things of life. To do good useful work is the——

PEARL *(in a burst):* Who knows what's good useful work! *(Exits.)* (GUS *enters with coffee.)*

GUS: The German people make the best coffee.

LEO: They have made great trouble in the world today.

GUS: I dare say. (SAM KATZ *enters from above.)*

SAM: You see how much they're worried, the delegation! *(He is followed by his wife, who disappears in a corner of the room.)* Ten o'clock they'll come, when it's time to go in bed!

LEO: They have to come from far downtown, Sam . . .

SAM: It's too bad about them. They raise enough hell in the shop!

LEO: Gerson's wife is having a baby. He can't come.

SAM: Gerson is a dirty piece of humanity! He stands in the shop all day smoking cigarettes. *(Turning on his wife suddenly.)* What's the matter you follow me like a dog, Bertha?

MRS. KATZ *(quietly):* I'll sit here for a few minutes.

SAM *(to the whole room):* She don't let me live. I moved in the next room. Now I sleep in the dining room; can you picture it? Then when I'm first sleeping inside, I can't sleep! Why not? All night she cries!

MRS. KATZ: Nobody cries.

SAM: Some day I'll bust. *(No one answers this but GUS who regally removes himself and stamps from the room. SAM soon continues. Addressing a wide audience.)* A fly spot like Gerson should have a baby! *(The doorbell rings.)* Ah ha! (LEO *goes out in answer.* SAM KATZ *retires to a corner,* LEO *is heard without. As* LEO *brings in three workers—*MR. SCHNABEL, MR. ROGO, *a plump Italian,* LUCY, *a serious intense woman of thirty-two—*SAM KATZ *goes directly up to them and waves a warning finger in their faces.)* Remember! Don't make me no lectures! *(Retires again.)*

ROGO *(cheerfully):* Don't make no lecture, Boss.

LEO: Please make yourself comfortable. *(Indicates chairs.)*

SCHNABEL *(a scholarly-looking man; to* MRS. KATZ): Good evening.

MRS. KATZ: Good evening. *(A hiatus. Discomfort from all.)*

LUCY *(finally):* Gerson can't come.

SAM: We heard it already!

LEO: How is his wife?

LUCY: She is fighting for her life.

LEO: Too bad. *(When this small talk is finished, there is again a pause of intense discomfort.)*

SAM *(finally):* So make your grievance!

LUCY: Mr. Schnabel will speak. *(Defiantly she sits hard.)*

LEO: Yes, please say whatever . . . say what . . .

SCHNABEL: We made some demands, gentlemens, which was not met by you, Mr. Katz. Last week.

LUCY: Concrete demands!

SCHNABEL: Also it was stated at this time it would be necessary to make a new union in the shop. Friday we went to S. Jackson in the Union. On his door it says, "Legal Adviser," gentlemens. But he gives no satisfaction.

ROGO: He don't work for workers!

SCHNABEL: Now we're talking to you, Mr. Gordon. Mr. Katz jumped already several times down my throat.

KATZ: Tisssst!

LEO: What are your demands, Mr. Schnabel?

LUCY: Concrete demands!

SCHNABEL: In the shop the girls work for one dollar a day—nine hours. Forty-five-hour week. Five dollars for girls a week, seven dollars for men. But on pay day Mr. Katz makes us sign statements we get more—thirteen and seventeen. Is this fair, gentlemens? On the wall it reads in the labor code, "Only eight hours' day." Where is it fair?

KATZ: If you don't like it, make a new union.

LUCY: This is an incorrect line!

LEO: Is that true, Sam, what Mr. Schnabel says? They sign two vouchers?

SAM: How else could we keep open the shop?

LEO: But I don't see any reason——

SAM: Either you'll take charge or I'll take charge!

ROGO: We talk to Mr. Gordon.

SAM: Mr. Gordon don't know! I run the business, he sits with artistic designs——

LEO: Please, if I hear——

SAM *(retiring wrathfully):* Finished!

SCHNABEL: Now we ask better wages. Nine dollars for men, seven dollars for girls. Forty-hour week!

LUCY: No exploitation!

ROGO: My girl she is not got money for bloomers in gym.

SAM: Tisssst!

ROGO: Don't make like that—tisssst!

LEO: Go on, Mr. Schnabel . . .

SCHNABEL: Also conditions is very bad in the shop.

LUCY: We keep the lunches under the table where cockroaches run all over it.

ROGO: Only two radiator in this place!

LEO: But we put in gas heaters.

SCHNABEL: It gives everybody headaches.

ROGO: Mr. Katz, he talk fast, walk fast. All our girls is so nervous——

SAM: This is no criterion!

LEO: Don't yell . . .

SAM (yelling): Who's yelling?

SCHNABEL: Yes, it is not important, but our girls are very nervous. Mr. Katz spies on them from behind the curtain.

LEO: I didn't realize conditions were so bad.

SAM: You didn't know it!

LEO: I don't know what to say to you, Mr. Schnabel, but——

SAM: Last week I explained conditions to you. It's impossible to go on otherwise. If they make a strike in the middle of the season we can both lay down in the grave.

SCHNABEL: Gentlemens, we need a living wage.

SAM: If not?

LUCY: Strike!

SAM: Jackson said on the phone no strike!

SCHNABEL: This is true, but we have there a very bad union. For three years we tried to elect good men, but Jake comes to these meetings with gunmen.

LEO (shocked): Gunmen?

ROGO: Oh, you sleep, Boss.

LEO: What is your suggestion?

SCHNABEL: Please meet demands . . .

LEO (after a pause): We'll meet demands.

SAM: We won't meet demands and when a strike comes I'll hire scabs so quick——

LEO: No!

SAM: Yes! Because I got brains and for twenty years I worked to make a little business. For twenty years we sweated blood! Now first a committee comes and says, "My daughter needs bloomers, so hand over the profits!"

LUCY: We'll walk out!

SAM: You hear her? They'll walk out in the middle of the season—the only time in the year we can make a little profit. They'll make a revolution!

LEO (*fervently*): People who support families on five dollars a week have a right to make a revolution!

SAM: If you don't mind too much, leave the business in my hands.

LEO: Sam, we're not rich men—I know it, but the world is so full of misery——

SAM: Who needs radical speeches?

LEO (*to workers*): Please go home. It will all be settled.

LUCY: When?

LEO: In a day or two.

LUCY: Make a promise.

LEO: We'll do something about it—that is my promise. No one will be exploited in the Cameo shop.

SCHNABEL: All right, gentlemens, we hope for the best. Good night.

LEO: Good night.

ROGO: You are good man. Good-bye.

LEO: Good-bye. (*The two men exit.* LUCY *approaches* SAM, *tries to speak. Breaks into tears instead. Exits rapidly.*)

SAM: Tisssst.

LEO: You're right, Sam, I'm no business man.

SAM: Go on designing pocketbooks and don't bother your head.

LEO: But it's wrong. I would not want my life built up on the misery of these people.

SAM: *We* don't have misery!

LEO: Give them the raise.

SAM: Not tomorrow and not next year!

LEO (*after a pause*): Will you think about it, Sam?

SAM: I made up my mind. (*He starts for the door, sees his wife, looks at her balefully.*) Some day they'll find me hanging from a chandelier. (*Exits.* MRS. KATZ *says "Excuse me" and quietly follows him out.* LEO *walks to and fro vigorously.* GUS *enters.*)

LEO: Sam takes advantage of me . . .

GUS: Of your good nature . . . yes.

LEO: Sometimes life is unreal to me. I'm not a practical person. What is to be done?

GUS (portentously): That is the question—"What is to be done?"

LEO: My brain has been sleeping. My mind is made up: our workers must have better conditions! Tomorrow I mean to start fresh. In life we must face certain facts.

GUS: Yes. Only last night I was thinkin' about selling my stamp collection. I figger she's easily worth a few thousand——But I guess I could just never do it . . . Maybe some day though—and go far away to the South Sea Isles and eat coconuts. (PIKE enters after a light knock.)

PIKE: Julie in his room?

LEO: Oh, I forgot—he went to bed. Says to say he was tired. Sit with us, Mr. Pike. Since you left a great thing has happened in our family—our daughter and son were married this afternoon.

PIKE: You don't say!

GUS: A bolt outa the blue!

LEO: Will you have a little drink of wine, Mr. Pike?

PIKE: Glad to, Citizen.

GUS (while LEO gets bottle and glasses): Marriage . . . hmm. I have come to the opinion that the world is on two conflictin' principles —male and female—and some is one and some is the other!

PIKE: Good idea. You oughta tell the President.

GUS (as LEO proceeds to fill three glasses): Gentle as ladyfingers— there she is—the flowin' claret—holy, holy, holy. (With wine up to light.) Now, now, now . . . you drink wine slowly, never fast. Get it in the mouth and around . . . very good!

PIKE: This isn't wine—it's cognac!

LEO: Oh, that's right.

GUS: We are drinkin' to the newly wedded pair, to them scented and anointed on their weddin' night. Music! (Turns on radio. All drink as music comes in and up.)

PIKE: My father used to order sherry by the cask. He exorcised the devils by day, but at night, by George, they crawled all over him! The Lord so loved the world that he gave them missionaries! Yes, you see before your eyes the only missionary's son extant in these States. The old man didn't know enough to spit tobacco over his chin.

GUS: Ha, ha, ha.

LEO: My father was a silent man. His hair was black as coal till the day

he died. A silent man . . . Maybe he knew God intimately. . . . I
loved him like an idol.

GUS: Why, he was a man with fur cuffs! Hair on his arms grew right
down on his wrists—fur cuffs you would say. *(They drink again.)*
My own father—he was dead by that time. How the old women
weep when the husband ain't there to see the only son married.
For you must know that's just what I was—the only son! *(Drinks.)* I
guess my mother was drinkin' champagne before I was born, because as a young man I must say I had expensive tastes. Ha, ha,
that's a joke—I don't mean it! But my old father—not that he was
old, for he died before you could say it of him—he certainly had an
eye for the ladies. *(Drinks.)* Yes, we had a horse and carriage. I
myself believe in inheritance, for it must be admitted I'm sweet on
the ladies myself. Yes, the kinda man who all the time wants a
harem. Ha, ha, ha. *(Drinks.)* Mr. P., what do you think of a woman
who sleeps with cats?

PIKE: Who does?

GUS: *Mrs.* Katz!! Ha, ha, ha, he don't get it!

PIKE *(drinking):* I get it.

GUS: Sam Katz thinks he's better than anyone else.

PIKE *(taking coin from pocket):* See that?——Twenty-five-cent piece.
(Makes an effort with fingers, tosses coin on table.) Bend them in
half sixty a minute.

LEO: You really did it!

GUS: They had a contest in Jersey City last week. A certain party
drank thirty-six bottles of beer in one sittin'! *(Switches radio to
band music.)* Had to pump him out at the hospital for two hours.
(Comes back to another drink.)

LEO: In the last analysis people can make themselves very big fools.

GUS: The way I see it there's two kinda men—there is the true man
and the dream. We're only the dream, yes . . . the dream. That
don't make much sense, don't it?

LEO: Maybe our life is not lived in vain. Maybe each hour is for some
profound purpose . . . we want to hug the world in our arms.

GUS *(staggering slightly to the radio):* The band was playin' on the
mall. . . . *(Switches so that a woman's acidulous voice is heard.)*

RADIO: ". . . them to know if any nation lifted a hand against us in
anger or hate, we, the mothers of America, would not hesitate to
say once more to husbands and sons, 'Your country needs your
fighting strength. Our brave flag must be defended until our last

drop of blood has been given in her defense!' This is what we would say to our men folk."

GUS: Ha, ha, just pumped him dry again!

RADIO: "That is why we celebrate Armistice Day each year. We weep for our fallen dead of the last war. We honor them in word, song and deed. But this day must confirm, must consecrate, I say, our faith to God, our country and our flag! Armistice Day must mean——" (PIKE *suddenly hurls his wine glass at the radio. Snaps off radio. Walks back and forth with great agitation.*)

PIKE: Monkey dust! Gibberish! What do we do when we hear some old bat outa hell say she is ready to give over every fine boy to be blown to hell in another obscene war?! What do we do?!

LEO: Mr. Pike, I think you better not excite yourself.

PIKE: Idiots out prowling the dynamite dumps by night! One struck match and we all blow to hell!

GUS: Better sit. You're lookin' pale around the gills.

PIKE: Who are we, Mr. Gordon? If we remain silent while they make the next war—who then are we with our silence? Accomplices, Citizen! Let me talk out my heart! Don't stop me! Citizens, they have taken our sons and mangled them to death! They have left us lonely in our old age. The bellyrobbers have taken clothes from our backs. We slept in subway toilets here. In Arkansas we picked fruit. I followed the crops north and dreamed of a warmer sun. We lived on and hoped. We lived on garbage dumps. Two of us found canned prunes, ate them and were poisoned for weeks. One died. Now I can't die. But we gave up to despair and life took quiet years. We worked a little. Nights I drank myself insensible. Punched my own mouth. Yes, first American ancestors and me. The circle's complete. Running away, stealing away to stick the ostrich head in sand. Living on a boat as night watchman, tied to shore, not here not there! The American jitters! Idealism! (*Punches himself violently.*) There's for idealism! For those blue-gutted Yankee Doodle bastards are making other wars while we sleep. And if we remain silent while they make this war, we are the guilty ones. For we are the people, and the people is the government, and tear them down from their high places if they dast do what they did in 1914 to '18. (*Slowly sits tremblingly.*)

LEO (*softly*): We cancel our experience. This is an American habit.

GUS: No logic . . .

LEO: But what is to be done?

PIKE: I don't know . . . I mean I don't know . . .

LEO: I will find out how to do as I think.

GUS *(drinking and laughing):* We're decayin', fallin' apart minute by minute.

PIKE: All these years one thing kept me sane: I looked at the telegraph poles. "All those wires are going some place," I told myself. Our country is the biggest and best pig-sty in the world!

GUS: I don't know no better place, Mr. P.

PIKE: I do. All picked out for me: the bottom of the ocean. Very quiet there, the light is soft, food is free . . .

LEO: Without life you cannot help change the world.

PIKE: You have life; do you help change it?

LEO: We do our best . . .

PIKE: Not good enough. I'll put your furnace to bed. *(Exits.)*

GUS: "C'est la guerre!" *(Drinks.)* As a young man I was always figgering in terms of millions. The way I seen it, the one who invented the clothes-pin made a million and why couldn't I? I worked and worked, and finally I got it: a better clothes-pin than anyone ever seen before. But she didn't have no logic, my invention. They cost twelve cents apiece to make. It was about this time I said to myself, "Gus Michaels, what's the use?" So I let my brains fall right back in my head, and I ain't used them since! (PEARL *plays piano upstairs.)* And when the last day comes—by ice or fire—she'll be up there playin' away. Lunes, martes, miercoles, she don't stop. That's how we say Monday, Tuesday, Wednesday in Spanish. You don't hear a word I'm sayin', Mr. G.

LEO: What?

GUS: "And as the Arabs of the desert fold up their tents and steal silently away" . . . *(Tiptoes across the room, saying several times "Shhh-shhh"—salutes* BEN'S *statue; says in drunken admiration "How like a god!" Utters another "Shhh" and quietly tiptoes from the room.* LEO *is completely self-absorbed.)*

Slow Curtain

ACT TWO

The same place. Eighteen months later. Music from above. Cretonne slip covers on most of the furniture.

JULIE *is alone on the stage, dressed in evening clothes. He has changed. A slight tremor runs throughout his body, the face is less plastic, almost mask-like. At present he is looking out the window, arms folded across his chest. When* LEO *enters he watches him intently.* LEO *finally turns and sees he is being watched.*

LEO: Why do you look at me that way, Julie?

JULIE: What way?

LEO: Have I done something to you, Julie?

JULIE: I just look at people . . . *(Picks up newspaper and silently walks out.* LEO *half lowers both shades.* CLARA *enters.)*

CLARA: What's the matter, Leo?

LEO: Nothing.

CLARA: Worried about Gus?

LEO: How long has he lived here?

CLARA: Since they got married . . . hmm . . . a year and a half.

LEO: And in all that time Gus never before stayed away overnight without a word.

CLARA: And in all that time he hasn't worked a week. It's lucky we had Ben's room to give him.

LEO: If he doesn't come by tonight . . .

CLARA: Last night you talked in your sleep. . . .

LEO: What did I say?

CLARA *(not looking at him):* You didn't say, my darling, you cried.

LEO: ? . . .

CLARA: What worries you, Leo? *(Piano starts upstairs.)*

LEO *(after a pause):* Clara, my beautiful dear Clara, what is happening here? Once we were all together and life was good.

CLARA *(shrewdly):* What's on your mind? *(He turns away.)* There's nothing you can't say to me, Leo. Tell me if anything's wrong. If the business fails . . .

LEO: Why should you think of the business?

CLARA: It's bad all over.

LEO: I have to pay the gas and electric . . .

CLARA: Is it the end?

LEO: Not yet. (PIKE *taps on door, enters.*)

PIKE: Any news of Gus?

CLARA: Not yet.

PIKE: He couldn't go nowhere without the ingenious motorcycle.

CLARA: Maybe it's bust. Eat a few nuts.

PIKE: Thanks, but I'll look at your paper first. *(Reads paper.* GUS *enters.)*

CLARA: Look what the cat dragged in!

GUS *(making a face):* Stayed over at one of my yacht clubs last night. . . .

CLARA *(sarcastically):* You coulda phoned from your "yotch" club.

LEO: We were very worried for you, Gus. (GUS *sits wearily.*)

CLARA: Where were you?

GUS: I'm fulla psychical an' toxic poisons.

CLARA: You better eat some supper.

GUS: Yes, that's what I am . . . what they done to me!

PIKE: Where were you?

GUS *(with a sudden burning head):* A man who never broke no law. Not even a ticket for speedin'—no blemish or stain . . . keepin' me there all day and night!

CLARA: Where?

GUS: Prison! Yes, thrust into the cell like that! Shameful! If I called my Tammany friends on the phone . . .

CLARA: Lunatic, what did you go to jail for?

GUS: I protested with that officer—a man who was a drinker—you could smell it on his breath. . . .

CLARA: For what?

GUS *(finally saying it out bravely):* For molestin' a girl in the subway, that is for what! (CLARA *burst into laughter.)* Yes, yes, takin' the word of some tramp girl who was plyin' her trade in the crowded trains. Yes, yes . . . *(Suddenly he is crying.)*

LEO: Please, no one thinks . . .

GUS: No one thinks, no one thinks . . . oh, I know, I know!

CLARA *(soberly):* Did you ever!

GUS *(vehemently):* The judge seen my Masonic pin and he says to this special officer, he says, "Can't you see this man would never do a thing like that?" And when they looked for that woman of the streets, where was she? Nowhere in sight! Flew away for fear of the consequences! Not one scintilla of evidence in their hands!

CLARA: Then don't worry.

GUS: But won't some people believe it? Won't they . . .

LEO: My poor friend . . .

GUS: Yes, yes . . . believe me, the sanctity of human dignity.

CLARA: You'll eat some supper, Gus—pot roast.

GUS: Couldn't eat all day. If I had one nickel to my name I'd sue for libel or somethin'.

CLARA *(as she exits):* Did you ever!? (GUS *sits looking straight ahead.* BEN *enters, carrying large cardboard box; he forces gayness.)*

LEO: Hello, my dear.

BEN *(putting hat on his own statue):* How's business, you liar?! *(Sets down box.)* Where's Clara?

LEO: Getting some supper for Gus. Are you hungry?

BEN: I ate. Posing for animal crackers, Gus? *(Sits.)* Was Libby around?

LEO: How could she leave the baby at night?

GUS *(bitterly, without moving):* Libby can do anything. Livin' three blocks away, she don't come to see her old father once a week!

BEN *(opening box):* Can I sell you a Mickey Mouse Drummer Boy?

LEO: A mechanical toy?

BEN: We buy them for nine cents and sell them for fifteen. Any street corner.

LEO: I think you're tired.

BEN *(bitterly):* The American youth is never tired.

MRS. KATZ *(head in at door):* Where is Mrs. Gordon?

LEO: In the kitchen.

MRS. KATZ *(entering, to* BEN): How's your little baby?

BEN: Four stars! How's yours?

MRS. KATZ: What?

BEN: I say it's lovely weather we're having.

MRS. KATZ: I'll speak to Momma. *(Exits.)*

GUS *(to himself):* Complications . . . *(Piano stops.* PIKE *notates in small book.)*

BEN *(working the drumming toy):* Poor Mickey Mouse! That's it— always the army to join. Or the navy. Leo, if I wasn't afraid of missing Kewpie here, I'd ask a big favor.

LEO: Ask it. . . .

BEN: I'd ask to advance me a buck seventy-five and then go around to

Harry's barber shop and get the whole works—haircut, massage and manicure. Believe you me, I'd like that feeling again.

LEO: Do it.

BEN: No, Kewpie doesn't wait around these days. Says he's got some good work for me . . . good money.

LEO: Something . . . legitimate?

BEN: Who cares?

LEO: Ben, be careful of something dishonest. It doesn't pay.

BEN: Pays *Kewpie* damn well!

LEO: But you're not Kewpie.

BEN: Not that smart.

LEO: You don't mean it.

BEN: Yes, I do.

LEO *(finally):* I don't know what to say.

BEN: Don't say anything! You're an honest man. What's to show for it? Read 'em and weep, that's what!

GUS *(to himself):* Yes, complications . . .

BEN *(to* MRS. KATZ, *passing through):* Mrs. Katz, can I sell you a gross of these drummer boys? A helluva lot of toys for a kid to play with, if you had the kid.

MRS. KATZ: If I had a boy I would buy gold toys. *(Exits.)*

LEO: Why do you hurt her feelings?

BEN: Leo, did you ever see the stuff these guys write on toilet walls? They write because they don't have! Like Kewpie—socking away because that's all he's got.

LEO: Take a job down my shop.

BEN: We went over that before.

LEO: Why not?

BEN: I know you're up to here with business—mortgage still on the house.

LEO: My dear, you're exaggerating.

BEN: *I* know about the 1930's. I'm a child of sorrow. *(Laughing at himself to mask his bitterness.)* A born kick in the pants——"When it's springtime in the Rockies"—sing, dance, hotcha! Aahh— Thanks, Gus, for the money you gave Libby yesterday.

GUS: What?

BEN: The thirty dollars for the rent. Thanks.

GUS: All right. *(Piano begins again.)*

BEN: Flow gently, sweet Afton. (CLARA *enters with food for* GUS.)

CLARA: Hello, Ben! How's business?

BEN: Swimming without my water wings by now.

CLARA: Lunatic, take some fruit.

BEN: Any beer on ice?

CLARA: Three bottles. Kewpie said he'll be late, for you to wait.

BEN *(passing* GUS*)*: Why don't you ask how Libby is?

GUS *(still looking ahead):* How is she?

BEN: Okay. How's your truss? *(Exits.)*

GUS: He don't like me, but it's all right—I don't like myself.

CLARA: I think your Libby makes his life hell.

GUS: I dare say. *(Suddenly slams fist on table.)* God, I would make the world jump if I was a young man again!!

CLARA *(realistically):* Eat before it gets cold. *(Piano stops.* JULIE *enters, followed by* BEN.*)*

JULIE: There's so much noise here.

BEN: Hello America! What's the big idea? *(Of the evening clothes.)*

JULIE: It makes me feel good.

BEN: That's why you're dressed up?

JULIE *(aggressively):* Do you mind?

BEN: No!

CLARA *(replacing beer bottle):* Not on the table. Julie, don't walk around the house so much; sit in one spot for a change.

JULIE *(sitting):* I'm tired of sitting.

CLARA: I'll wash dishes. (PEARL *enters—prowls around.)*

GUS: I'll help.

CLARA: Never mind. Finish eating.

GUS: Complications.

CLARA: My children walk around the house like wild animals. *(Exits.)*

GUS: How happy this pot roast must be if I don't eat her. *(Follows* CLARA *out.* PIKE *is jotting items from newspaper into small book.)*

PIKE: Don't mind me—I'm engaged in a conspiracy of silence.

LEO *(figuring over check book):* How much is 97 and 36?

JULIE: 133.

LEO: The gas bill, I think. . . . *(He wanders out.)*

BEN: What's all that secret writing?

PIKE: Figgers, facts! I look them over when the nights are cold. Keeps me warm. Figgers, facts—I am waiting for a whole world to hang itself. Read any paper, look in any face. Enough rope inchin' up to strangle all of us! In the meantime, look for tough-minded people.

BEN: You never met my wife.

PEARL: I saw your baby in her carriage today.

BEN: Christ, I'm a father! *(To brother and sister.)* Orphans of the storm! We are low enough to crawl under a snake! Julie, Pearl, rise and shine! One of the living heirs must amount to something in this goddam family!

JULIE: Let's shoot some billiards, Ben.

BEN: Sure, why not? Anything to kill time. Tell the world we're down in the cellar pushing balls around. Coast to coast. *(Exits and is followed by JULIE who says:)*

JULIE: The cushions are dead.

PEARL *(after silence):* I'm homesick all the time. For what?

PIKE: No one talks about the depression of the modern man's spirit, of his inability to live a full and human life.

PEARL: What?

PIKE: I'm sayin' the smell of decay may sometimes be a sweet smell. There she is alone in her room with the piano—the white keys banked up like lilies and she suckin' at her own breast.

PEARL: You must be crazy! What are you talking about?

PIKE: You. Your brother——

PEARL: Yes, I know. You think radical ideas will save us all. Just give the world its pound of bread! For my part, I discovered long ago the comic aspects of this so-called class war.

PIKE: Yes, sixteen million unemployed in America is a pretty comic situation.

PEARL: Who cares about sixteen million? I'm interested in myself!

PIKE: Let's *take* yourself. Where's your boy friend?

PEARL: Mind your business!

PIKE: You liar and traitor to your own heart's story! *(Suddenly whirling on PEARL, and gripping her by the arms.)* You! Lay awake dreamin' at night. Don't you know it ain't comin', that land of your dreams, unless you work for it?

PEARL *(pulling away):* I'm not sex starved, do you hear? I'm not! *(The door is pushed open by KEWPIE.)*

PIKE: And this bantam rooster showin' another side of the picture.

KEWPIE: What makes you go?

PIKE: Takin' care of furnaces, Citizen! *(Exits.)*

KEWPIE: He swallowed a load of carpet tacks. (PEARL *moves away in evident disdain.)* You're afraid of me, Mabel.

PEARL: You're afraid of yourself. (PEARL *exits as* GUS *enters with a crumb scraper.)*

KEWPIE: P. S., how's Libby, Gus?

GUS *(very dignified):* Don't you know?

KEWPIE: Come again? *(No answer.)* Libby says your spark plug's falling apart. Maybe you could use a few bucks to fix it?

GUS: Don't want a wooden nickel off you, Mr. Kewpie!

KEWPIE: A few bucks should look like the promised land to you—take 'em!

GUS *(not looking around):* What for?

KEWPIE: Don't gimme no kibitz. Take it!

GUS *(suddenly facing him fully and lowering his voice):* Yes, we know why you're givin' me money. Here, I want you to keep away from my daughter's house when he's out lookin' for work in the morning!

KEWPIE: P. S., you're nuts!

GUS *(bravely):* Yes, I know what I am—a very ordinary person. But you hear what I say? You hear? Do you?

KEWPIE *(scornfully):* Your nose is bleeding!

GUS: Just you keep away from there and don't gimme no money. Don't buy me!

KEWPIE *(taking hold of* GUS, *who shakes him off):* Button up your funny mouth, Gussie!

GUS: I try to speak to her, but she don't listen. All I'm good for is to mind my grandchild while she takes in a movie. You're a small-time character, that's what it is, the whole thing! *(Begins to cry.)*

KEWPIE: Why the gush?

GUS: The whole world's fallin' to pieces, right under our eyes.

KEWPIE *(disgusted):* Where's Ben?

GUS *(fresh at the attack again):* No money! Hear that? No buyin' honor!

KEWPIE: Aaah . . . *(Exits in disgust to kitchen.* GUS *wipes his eyes and blows his nose as* BEN *enters with cue stick in hand.)*

GUS: I'm always gettin' smoke in my eyes something terrible.

BEN: You look damn pessimistic these days, Gus.

GUS: I dare say——

BEN: Kewpie come yet?

GUS: In the kitchen. (BEN *starts out.)* Ben . . . ?

BEN: Yes?

GUS *(nervously, hesitant):* You said before . . . What thirty dollars?

BEN *(turning slowly):* What?

GUS: What thirty dollars?

BEN: For the rent. You didn't give Libby . . . ?

GUS: No . . .

BEN: Where did she get it?

GUS: Ben, I don't know.

BEN: Yes, you do!

GUS: Ben . . . *(Tries to put the table between them.)*

BEN *(with realization):* Kewpie?

GUS: You'll tear my sleeve.

BEN: Where?

GUS *(very lame):* I really don't . . . No, I don't. . . . *(Laughs nervously as* BEN *releases him.)* I'll go brush my teeth. Missed it last night. *(Trying to make a joke.)* See that? Just a slave to habit! Ha! *(Painfully exits.* BEN *stands unaware, but now turns.)*

BEN: Do you think she . . . *(Sees* GUS *is gone.* JULIE *enters.)*

JULIE: When I make a good run, no one sees it. Twelve. Kewpie come yet? *(For answer* KEWPIE *enters.)*

KEWPIE: Get a load of the dress-up!

JULIE: Makes me feel good.

KEWPIE: Lost your shirt in the market?

JULIE: First time in almost two years I wore it. Got any new card tricks?

KEWPIE: No new ones. *(To* BEN, *until now only side-glanced.)* Chase the boy scout out.

BEN *(to* JULIE): We want to talk over some business. Do you mind?

JULIE: No, I don't mind.

KEWPIE: Got any tips on the market?

JULIE: Sure, try "poison on the curb"! *(He starts out one exit, but changes his mind and goes the other way. It doesn't quite matter where he goes is the intention here.)*

KEWPIE: He looks terrible.

BEN *(with a loaded heart):* Yeah . . .

KEWPIE: They can't fix him up? . . .

BEN: No . . .

KEWPIE: Slow death.

BEN: Yeah . . .

KEWPIE: Does he know?

BEN: No, he doesn't.

KEWPIE: Too bad—all dressed up and no place to go. . . . What the hell you looking?

BEN: Why?

KEWPIE: Why? Aunt Tessie's eye! What the hell you always putting on an act?

BEN: I make you uncomfortable?

KEWPIE: Who the hell are you to make me uncomfortable?

BEN: I'm the guy who slept with Mrs. God!

KEWPIE *(searching)*: What?

BEN *(looking at his friend a long time before he speaks)*: We're still under the ice, you and me—we never escaped! Christ, Kewpie! Are we the same kids who used to go up to Whitey Aimer's roof and watch the pigeons fly? You and me and Danny? There's one old pal we know what happened to, where he is. The three of us under the ice with our skates on and not being able to get him out. Then sticking him dead in the box. Dressed in a blue serge suit and a stiff white collar . . . Christ, Kewpie, tell me, tell me—who died there —me or you or him or what?

KEWPIE: What the hell you talking about!

BEN: Is Danny wearing wings in paradise? Or is he a cheap cluck like you and me, trying to make a living, trying to be a man and look the world in the face in some other hell?

KEWPIE *(really touched)*: Nobody's a cheap cluck.

BEN: He ducked out in time.

KEWPIE *(hiding his feelings)*: Always doing a song and dance.

BEN: Last night I couldn't sleep. All the way over to the new bridge, I walked. Stood there for a long time looking in the water. Then I began to run, down the street. I used to like to be out in front. When I fell in that rhythm and knew my reserve—the steady driving forward—I sang inside when I ran. Yeah, sang like an airplane, powerful motors humming in oil. I wanted to run till my heart exploded . . . a funny way to die. . . .

KEWPIE: What's it make me?

BEN: What did I want? To be a great man? Get my picture on a postage stamp? *(Finally tacking.)* Were you over my house this morning after I left?

KEWPIE: No.

BEN: Libby lays there. Wears silk nightgowns and her belly's soft. When I leave she's warm and sleepy.

KEWPIE *(wary)*: What's the idea?

BEN: You never go there in the morning?

KEWPIE: I said no!

BEN: You gave her thirty dollars.

KEWPIE: Who said?

BEN: Maybe you forgot. (*A pause.*) She's my wife. . . .

KEWPIE: Sure.

BEN: You give her money, just like that?

KEWPIE (*finally admitting something*): She needed some dough for the house.

BEN: And the other stuff you've been buying her for months—the pink and black underwear? She needs that to run the house too?

KEWPIE (*after an intense second*): We're that way for each other.

BEN: Which way?

KEWPIE: *That* way!

BEN: You're a liar!

KEWPIE: Libby don't care for you three cents. You're sand in her shoes. I buy her clothes, keep your house running. The new fancy carriage for the kid? My dough! The money in your pocket? Mine! *I'm in you like a tape worm.*

BEN: You pushed me out of bed. . . .

KEWPIE: You're out—I'm in!

BEN: Better than me? You want to be better than me? You picked a lousy model to beat! What an honor to be a better guy than Ben Gordon!

KEWPIE: I am.

BEN: "Did we die there?" I keep asking myself, "or are we living?" The world is flat, like a table—Columbus was wrong—we're being pushed over the edge. (*Suddenly puts down cue. Starts for door, but* KEWPIE *blocks his way.*)

KEWPIE: Where you going?

BEN: To the corner, turn left, three blocks west as the crow flies. If she's still home——

KEWPIE: You got a job now.

BEN: The hell with that!

KEWPIE: No, you do it and like it!

BEN (*a terrible vibrant flare-up*): Who the hell are you talking to?

KEWPIE: Hold your guts a minute!

BEN (*bitterly*): P. S., a gorilla!

KEWPIE: You wanna kill me? Who gives a good goddam! Here! (*Draws gun and shoves it in* BEN'S *hand.*)

BEN: My hand might slip. . . .

KEWPIE: Let it . . . (*They look at each other.* BEN *finally lowers his hand.)* Joe says for you to handle it. We're leaving any minute. The car's on Whitman Avenue.

BEN: Where do we go?

KEWPIE: To Lincoln Avenue.

BEN: Danger?

KEWPIE: Plenty! (JULIE *enters.* BEN *puts the gun away.)*

BEN: Julie, will you take the cue down after?

JULIE: . . . Was that a gun?

BEN: The English sparrow is a pest, Julie. The Gordon exterminating service means to shoot the works!

KEWPIE: It takes ten minutes to get to Lincoln Avenue.

BEN *(to his statue):* Ben, I used to think it meant something: the sweet taking on and off of clothes—the silent tremble of love—the proud possession! *(He laughs and thumbs his nose at the statue.)*

KEWPIE *(giving* BEN *small packet):* Here, I took them outa hock. Libby gave me the tickets.

BEN: Medals? Kewpie, if you were a boy scout your day's work would be done. *(Tosses packet to* JULIE.) A present for your thirteenth birthday.

KEWPIE: We better go.

BEN: Lincoln Avenue or bust? *(To* JULIE): Say good-bye to Pearlie for me.

JULIE: Take care of yourself.

BEN: Sure. . . . *(He looks at his statue for a few seconds, suddenly spits violently in its face and exits.* KEWPIE *goes to statue, carefully wipes off the face with a silk handkerchief. Exits.* LEO *enters with envelopes he is sealing.)*

JULIE *(intent on statue):* Who was it had the wooden horse, Poppa? The Trojans?

LEO: The Greeks. They made a beautiful civilization. Where's Ben?

JULIE: Went with Kewpie.

LEO: Kewpie promised him a job.

JULIE: He left some medals. That day he ran the Finn at the Garden —this gold one.

LEO: Where did I put the checks?

JULIE: Maybe in the envelopes.

LEO: Yes. . . . I forgot. Go for a nice walk, Julie. You stay in the house too much. (PIKE *enters and goes to kitchen, dusting himself off.)* If you go out, mail the letters for me. Checks for the electric and telephone. For most people life is one bill after another. Under the roar of Niagara can a man live a normal life?

JULIE *(getting hat and coat):* The proud possession. . . .

LEO: What?

JULIE: Nothing. (JULIE *takes the several letters.)*

LEO: Yes, take a nice walk. (JULIE *exits.)* Walk down by the convent on Parish Street. There it's very quiet. I stood there one time for an hour. Very quiet and the bells ring. . . . *(Stops when he sees he is talking to himself.* PIKE *enters.)*

PIKE: Can't have a glass of water cold enough for me.

LEO: What is to be done? The convent, the maids of God? Drunkards . . . ? Stamps . . . ? What is to be done?

PIKE *(in direct answer):* Well, Gus is out there taking a shave.

LEO: Two and three in the morning sometimes I find him shaving in front of the mirror.

PIKE: He wants to look good.

LEO: But three in the morning? For whom?

PIKE: Man has to have something.

LEO: Tell me, my friend. You went around the country many times. You saw many kinds of people. Deep down in their cellars—— (PIKE *starts eating and cracking nuts from bowl at elbow.)*

GUS *(entering):* I shave and it come right out again.

LEO: I keep asking myself questions. Never in my forty-seven years have I met a happy man. What is wrong?

PIKE *(cracks nuts with ferocity and lets pieces dribble to table):* This *system!* Breeds wars like a bitch breeds pups! Breeds poverty, degrades men to sentimental gibberin' idiots, mentioning no names. *(Looks sideways at* GUS.) There's your children, you, Sam Katz—a big hand got itself around you, squeezin' like all hell gone on! Uuuh! *(Squeezes another nut and lets its pieces drop.)* Gets you all down to the margin. Dispossessed like me, like another sixteen million in a walking death: unemployed! Then what?

GUS: A new administration!

PIKE: Don't be no medium-sized rabbit, Gus. *(Exits.)*

GUS: No one ever called me that before!

PIKE *(poking head in at door):* Citizens: the fearful heart starin' from your eyes. Directly descended from stake burners. I admit it! Good night. *(Goes.)*

GUS: Bats! All this radical stuff is like marrying the colored maid. But these radicals, they got the artistic freedom . . . and that's what I like. *(He is picking his teeth.)*

LEO: God gives us patience to endure. *(Phone rings.* GUS *answers.)*

GUS: The Gordons' . . . Yes, left with Kewpie. . . . No, Libby, I got my things to attend—there's no place for the motorcycle and I can't leave her in the streets . . . what? . . . Well, it's pretty dark under them stairs, Libby. . . . All right, Libby. *(Hangs up.)* Libby. Going to a picture; wants me to mind the baby.

LEO: *She* likes the movies.

GUS *(after a pause):* I can't explain it to you, Mr. G., how I'm forever hungerin' for the past. It's like a disease in me, eatin' away . . . some nights I have cried myself to sleep—for the old Asbury Park days; the shore dinners at old Sheepshead Bay. *(Begins to dress.)* In those days every house had its little dog—we was no exception, as you well remember, with our Spotty, the fire dog—it was a common sight to see them out walkin' of a summer night, big ones and little ones. How beautiful the summer nights before the Big War! We would sit out there . . . and the streets fulla laughin' playin' children. I had Mrs. Michaels with me in those days. Oh, yes, the pleasant laughin' talk, when we went around to Schoemacher's Ice Cream Parlor. Oh, it was so beautiful in those days! Wasn't it, Mr. G.?

LEO: It was . . .

GUS: Yes. *(Puts on a dirty white aviator's helmet.)* In those days God was in the heavens. It's fierce today, somethin' fierce! Hear them screamin' all around me. What'll happen, Mr. G., what'll happen when those barbarian hordes come sweepin' down on us? *(Taps walls.)* Would these walls stand up under gun shot? That's what I wanna know—would they?

LEO *(amused by the idea):* Who can tell?

GUS: Yes, who can tell? *(Pulling on gloves.)* I'll sleep over there. What a terrible world! They say the birth rate is going down somethin' awful! *(As* GUS *is about to wheel his motorcycle out of the inner hall, down the stairs comes* SAM KATZ, *behind him a small man wearing oxford frame glasses on a ribbon, a brown derby, a black finger guard. Carries rolled up umbrella and brief case.)*

SAM: You got the five dollars you owe me?

GUS: No. *(Begins to move out.)*

SAM: When he sees me, he runs.

GUS: Sam Katz, you irk me! *(Exits with motorcycle.* SAM *comes in, the* STRANGER *behind him.)*

SAM *(closing door):* You'll say hello to Mr. May, Leo. This is my partner, May.

MAY: How do. *(Has a faint Swedish accent.)*

LEO: Good evening.

MAY: Werry nice little house you got here, I was sayin'.

LEO: Yes.

SAM: He had it for fourteen years already. (SAM *closes door leading to kitchen.* MAY *examines statue.)*

MAY: You don't say!—And what's this interestin' piece of art we got here?

SAM: It's his son—a big runner in the Olympic games.

MAY: A real fine wital figure!

SAM: Yesterday Mr. May came . . .

MAY *(breaking in):* Let me tell you how it came to me. I was looking at the floor and quick as a flash it came to me what a good slogan would do for a business. I said to myself, "Why shouldn't my friend Katz have it?" "Katz leather bags has nine lives!" *(Watches for the effect on* LEO.)

SAM: He made up a slogan for our company.

LEO *(puzzled):* It's very nice . . .

SAM: The slogan—"Nine lives"! The business itself should have such life!

LEO: Business could be better. . . .

SAM: If it don't improve soon . . .

MAY *(listening):* Is that in your family? The piano playing?

SAM *(flattering* LEO): His daughter, a big talent.

LEO: She studied with a pupil of Lechititsky.

MAY *(very knowingly):* Hmmm! . . . Many talented personalities dwellin' inside the walls of this city. *(The conversation dies.)*

LEO: What's on your mind, Sam?

SAM: On my mind? Why?

MAY *(to the rescue):* You're wondering what I'm doing here.

LEO: To be frank, yes. But I don't mean——

MAY *(hastily):* Of course not! A man of the world is not one to take umbrage——

SAM: I brought May on a little business.

MAY: There you got it in a nutshell, Mr. Gordon. Assimilated business!

LEO: What kind of business?

MAY (MAY *has the quality of apricot cordial):* Well, there is a historical perspective in these things. Delicate!

LEO: What?

SAM: Delicate!

MAY: For these last three years I handled upward of fifty-three cases. Some of them will pay as triflin' a fee as two hundred dollars. These are cheap jobs—adulterated, what we call. *(Hastily adds):* But don't misunderstand, no prices now. The recommendation is purely suggestive, what we call. *(Leans back with satisfaction.* SAM *waits with bated breath.* LEO *does not understand a word of the speech.)*

LEO *(finally):* I see, but what is your business?

MAY *(leaning forward):* You don't ever know who's listening, do you?

LEO: Listening to what?

MAY: Mr. Gordon. Tell the truth—you're a puzzled gent.

LEO: If you don't mind my saying . . .

MAY: Business with us is what we call purely a state of mind. You take the average small manufacturer. He pays his bills on the first of the month. Right? *(Answers himself.)* Right! *(Again lowers voice.)* Suppose when the first comes, he can't pay. What then?

LEO *(after waiting for the answer):* Yes . . . ?

MAY: Won't it make a state of mind?

LEO: Without doubt.

MAY: "Without doubt!" The manufacturer will not sleep! Won't eat! Irritation in the business and at home. The wife who is so often a thing of beauty, he hits her! In this condition the respected citizen make a werry foolish mistake. Some charlatan will sell him headache pills.

SAM *(in an outburst):* But a smart man—!

MAY *(chiding* SAM *gently before continuing to* LEO): Mr. Katz! . . . But the man of sensitivity, does he leave unturned the rare gold and silver of experience? Does he? No! Six feet away stands the safe. A certain drawer within those swinging doors. Therein he finds what we call "insurance policy." Protection against theft . . . against fire, Mr. Gordon . . . *(Leans back again.)*

LEO: Fire . . . ?

MAY: Purely suggestive. . . . *(Waits for* LEO, *who first looks to* SAM, *and then begins to scrape crumbs with his fingers.)* Yes, you guessed it: Should the respected citizen take aspirins? (LEO *contin-*

*ues to shovel nut shells together. The two watch him closely. Fi-
nally* LEO *says):*

LEO: Your profession is making fires.

MAY: Incorrect! No! *(Suddenly throws orange from table to* LEO.) See
how quick you catched it? Not a thought in your head and you
catched it! Fires happen like that.

LEO: In the last three years you made fifty fires—*happen?*

MAY: Fifty-three.

LEO: Human life is not important?

MAY *(with flashing pride):* Nobody was burned—*ever!!* (LEO *slowly
replaces the orange.)* Don't be afraid, Mr. Gordon. In every
case——

LEO *(quietly; trembling):* Please leave my house.

SAM: Don't be in such a hurry, Leo.

MAY: Everything has a first time, my friend. The respected citizen . . .

LEO: Please leave!

MAY: Don't take umbrage, my friend. Tomorrow's another day.
Here's my card—Edgar F. May. *(Places card on table.)* Purely
suggestive . . .

LEO *(shouting now):* Get out of here!!

SAM: Don't insult humanity with your ignorance!!

MAY: No, he's right. It's his prerogative in his own house. *(Puts his
glasses in their case now.)*

SAM *(bitterly):* Any day now he won't have a house!

MAY *(at the door):* Remember . . . May—between April and June—
May. Good night. *(He exits and is followed by* SAM *who quickly
returns after a slamming door is heard.)*

SAM: Why should you insult humanity?! In the second place—excuse
me—you're crazy! I'm surprised a man shouldn't have more regard
for his family. (JULIE *enters up back, unseen by them)* He don't see
in front two feet.

LEO: I see, I see!

SAM: Like a blind horse you see! He's got a son dying on his feet! So
the last few comforts he takes from the boy's mouth! Your Julie——

LEO *(seeing* JULIE): Keep quiet!

SAM: Your Julie is dying!

LEO: Sam! Silence! (SAM *sees where* LEO *is looking and discovers* JULIE
for himself. JULIE *slowly advances into the room. After a long
pause):* Julie . . . did you mail the letters?

JULIE *(smiling queerly):* . . . .

SAM *(finally):* I made up a story, Julie. (JULIE *picks up* BEN'S *cue and slowly drags himself out.)*

LEO: Sam, Sam . . .

SAM: I get excited. . . . *(Goes to door and stops as he is about to exit.)* Leo, what's left for us?

LEO *(heartsick):* I don't care.

SAM: I'm sorry you don't care, but you raised the pay-roll last year. So now worry how to meet the pay-roll Saturday!

LEO: Take the money from the bank.

SAM: Who told you there's money?

LEO *(with sudden turning awareness):* Who told me?!

SAM: The man in the moon?

LEO: You made collections last month.

SAM *(disparagingly):* Twenty-two hundred.

LEO: *Thirty*-two hundred!

SAM: Thirty-two—so?

LEO: And the money for the Palm Beach line?

SAM: Six hundred.

LEO: *Nine* hundred! That's . . . *(Tries to figure.)* How much?

SAM: You expected it to last forever?

LEO: Forty-one hundred dollars.

SAM *(finally):* We had big expense.

LEO: What expense?

SAM: I paid fire insurance Tuesday. Glazed kid, cardboard, benzine. . . . Twenty dollars for the burglar alarm . . . *(Stops.)*

LEO: What else?

SAM *(trapped):* What else? I don't remember what else! If you're so anxious, look in the books!

LEO: No new stock came in, Sam! Please! (MRS. KATZ *comes in.* SAM *turns on her savagely, escaping.)*

SAM: She's always looking for bargains, my fine wife. Did you ever see, a man like me should wear seconds in everything? Socks, shirts, everything is seconds! Where does she find it?

LEO: Sam, explain this, please!

SAM: A man like me wants to stand on a mountain. So instead he lays in a grave with dirt on his face. Twenty-four hours a day he eats gall!

LEO: Sam!! (CLARA *enters.)*

CLARA: Who closed the door?

SAM: In the circus they got a bearded lady——

LEO: Sammm!

SAM: And in my house I got a baldy woman!

CLARA *(alarmed at* LEO'S *appearance):* What's the matter?

LEO: Get a handkerchief, Clara.

CLARA: What happened?

LEO: Get a handkerchief. *(She hurries out. He sits with head tilted back: nosebleed.)*

SAM *(telling the world):* You Bertha—you'll find me hanging from a chandelier! Why should I live with her? I'm a man like an ox! With one hand I lifted a stamping press. But children I can't have. Look, she sits without expression—a woman with a mixup inside. To *me* it had to happen! Yes, I'm crazy—sick and nervous! Do I ever sleep, do I ever eat? In the winter I freeze; in the summer I sit by the window and eat hot corns! For what should I live? A girl told me I remind her of her father, a general in the Austrian army! Believe me, I had enough girls. You hear me, Bertha? But a man like an ox can't have a son. (CLARA *returns with large handkerchief.* LEO *takes it silently, the attack almost gone;* SAM *prowls back and forth, a bitter lion.)*

CLARA: What happened, Leo?

SAM: Why are you crying, Bertha? Did I hit you? *(To* CLARA): Better first I fell down the stairs and broke my neck!

BERTHA: No.

SAM: Better my eyes fell out from my head before I married you!

BERTHA: No.

SAM: Me, I was in a hurry. A boy went for a row in the Park Sunday. A lonely boy should meet a girl like her and get married! Can you picture it?

CLARA: What happened here?

SAM *(sitting at table opposite* LEO): Me, I took the money, Leo. From an old friend I took his money, from a man like an angel. I died so far back . . . *(Weeps.)*

CLARA: What money?!

BERTHA: From the business.

CLARA: ? ? ? ? ! !

LEO: Yes . . .

SAM: Home is a prison. Sing Sing, my house—it's not different. Eighteen cigars I smoked yesterday. I don't care. . . . *(He puts his face in his hands and shudders.)*

CLARA (*finally, judicially hard and calm*): How much?

LEO: Everything . . .

CLARA: When did you find out?

LEO: Now.

CLARA (*to* SAM): What did you do with the money? (*No answer but a shudder. To* LEO): What did he do with it?

LEO: I don't know.

CLARA (*to* SAM): You played cards?

SAM: Put me in prison!

CLARA: Don't worry!

SAM: Break my bones!

CLARA: If I was a man, you wouldn't have to ask me twice! Give an account, you black-hearted bastard! For years he talked and now not a word! Answer what I asked!! . . . Did you ever? What's next, Leo?

LEO: Voluntary bankruptcy.

BERTHA (*coming forward*): Please, if——

CLARA: Don't say please! A man ruins a business and she says please! You know what bankruptcy means?

BERTHA: Please, he'll make good.

CLARA: With what—chiclets?

BERTHA: You don't understand Sam——

SAM: Never mind.

BERTHA: He's a sick man.

SAM: Don't listen to her one word!

BERTHA: When you understand——

SAM: I'm warning you, Bertha!

BERTHA: For many years I listened to you without a word, Sam. Now it's my turn and you take a back seat. (SAM *now tries physically to dissuade his wife from speaking, tries to push her out of the room.* CLARA *steps in.*)

CLARA: Me your eyes don't frighten. You keep quiet! You sit in the corner. (*She slaps him.*)

LEO: Clara!

BERTHA: Don't hit him, a sick man. God put a mark on his face!

SAM: Don't listen to her, don't listen!

BERTHA: I understand him like a doctor.

SAM: Oh Momma, Momma. . . .

BERTHA: Momma, he says. In the night he cried to God and no answer came. In my arms he cried, and no answer came.

CLARA: Nobody needs a story now.

BERTHA: First understand a person. We'll try to fix it up. I saved some money. But from Sam it's big talk without meaning. All right, we can't have children.

SAM: Tell everybody, tell the world!

BERTHA: He didn't go out with girls. I never worried about that.

SAM: No, no, no. . . . *(Falls on his knees in the outer hall and writhes in prayer on the lower step.)*

BERTHA: We have upstairs a closet full of pills, medicine, electric machines. *For seven years Sam Katz didn't sleep with a girl.*

SAM *(moaning outside):* Bertha, Bertha. . . .

BERTHA: Yes, my old friends, life in the Katz family is a funny proposition. I don't know figures, Mr. Gordon. About nine hundred dollars is laying in the bank. You'll get it tomorrow. More I can't do. We'll go upstairs, Sam.

CLARA: He hasn't consideration for two cents, your Sam.

BERTHA: He's a good boy——*(Goes up to* SAM. *Helps him up from lower step. Wipes his face with handkerchief.)* We'll go home, Sam.

CLARA: I'm sorry I slapped you.

SAM: Excuse me I ever lived. *(They exit together.)*

LEO *(after a silence):* There is no failure. We'll learn to make it right, but we must see the whole thing.

CLARA: How did you find out?

LEO: He brought a man to make a fire in the shop.

CLARA: For the insurance?

LEO: Yes.

CLARA: A wolf!

LEO: Don't be angry with a poor man.

CLARA: But you're a poor man too! All we have in the whole world is the roof over our head. *(Piano starts upstairs.)*

LEO *(sitting heavily):* We will live, my darling Clara, we will live to see strange and wonderful events.

CLARA: I don't intend to live so long.

LEO: In fifty years.

CLARA: In fifty years we will lay in the rain. "Who's this?" they'll say. "A couple of old fools!"

LEO: This can't happen forever! Nothing stands still in life! Pike is right! Backwards or forwards, and even backwards is going ahead.

CLARA: For God's sake, do yourself a personal favor and listen to me! What will *we* do, *now?*

LEO: We'll go on living.

CLARA: Oh, I married a fool. *(Prowls and picks up article. Puts it down.)* I married a fool. *(Picks up another article; replaces it.)* Yes, a fool.

LEO: Yes . . .

CLARA *(picks up card left by* MAY): What is this?

LEO: He left a card.

CLARA: Who?

LEO: The man to make the fire. (CLARA *reads card. Puts it down, walks to fix windows for the night; goes back to card.)*

CLARA: Beaumont? Where is that?

LEO: What?

CLARA: Beaumont 6922——

LEO: Across the river. *(Upstairs* PEARL *begins to range over the keyboard in light fleet exercises.)*

CLARA: What kind of name is that, May?

LEO: I don't know.

CLARA *(putting down card):* Tomorrow you'll go over the books?

LEO: The accountant.

CLARA *(after arranging another detail, at other end of room. Goes back and re-peruses card. Finally brings it forward to* LEO *whose back is to her):* What did you say to him?

LEO: To who?

CLARA: To him. . . .

LEO *(in a low voice):* I said no.

CLARA: Leo, we live once. . . .

LEO: What do you want?

CLARA: Think of tomorrow.

LEO: I am. . . .

CLARA: Leo . . .

LEO: Please . . .

CLARA: If you think . . . (LEO *jumps up.)*

LEO: Don't say that!

CLARA: Where will we go?

LEO: No!

CLARA: Where?!

LEO: Please!

CLARA: Julie needs——

LEO: What do you want me to do?

CLARA: Think, think!

LEO: Tear up the card!

CLARA: No!

LEO: Give it to me!

CLARA: No!

LEO: Clara!

CLARA: You can't tear our life to pieces. No, we worked too many years to——(JULIE *enters.*)

JULIE *(deliberately interrupting):* Momma! . . . Pike banked the fire for the night. . . . (LEO *and* CLARA *stand looking at each other. Finally she tears the card and drops the pieces on the table, but as she exits she is crying.)* What's the matter?

LEO: I make a prayer for inner and outer peace, Julie. For all of us.

JULIE: Leo, don't tell Momma I know. She won't ever sleep if she knows. *(They look at each other in silence.* JULIE *breaks away as* CLARA *enters.)*

CLARA: It's time for bed. Sit down, Julie, don't keep walking around like a wild animal. *(Phone rings.* LEO *answers.)*

LEO: Hello . . . Yes . . . What? . . . Hello, hello! *(Hangs up.)* It was Kewpie. He sounded in a hurry.

JULIE *(standing with newspaper in hand.* PEARL *begins a movement of Beethoven):* What did Kewpie say?

LEO: He was in such a hurry I couldn't make out. Ben got something on Lincoln Avenue, he said.

JULIE: Ben got something——

CLARA: A job?—night work?

LEO: Maybe. Kewpie promised him some work.

CLARA: Ben needs a job. (JULIE *begins his newspaper again, very intently, hiding himself.)*

LEO: What's the matter, Julie?

JULIE: Nothing.

LEO: Don't stay up late—you look tired.

JULIE *(without looking up):* Yes. (CLARA *turns out all lights except lamp where* JULIE *is standing.)*

CLARA: Good night.

JULIE: Good night.

CLARA: Don't forget, Julie—please go to bed soon.

JULIE *(still intent on paper):* Yes.

CLARA: The lock on the back door's broken again.

LEO: Have it fixed.

CLARA *(as they exit):* Tomorrow . . . (JULIE *stands rigid for a min-*

ute. Drops the paper, walks over to BEN'S *statue and hugs it to keep himself from breaking up.* PEARL *passes into a furious section of the sonata as the curtain slowly falls.)*

Curtain

ACT THREE

The same room, but stripped bare, except for a couch, two kitchen chairs, a crate full of books and the statue of BEN. *It is a year and some months later. Against the wall is* GUS'S *motorcycle, a wheel missing. The shades are drawn to full depth.*

JULIE, *sitting in a wheel chair, turned from sight. Only a drooping arm, his hand holding a handkerchief, can be seen.* CLARA *at present is patiently paring his toe nails as she finishes a legend.* PEARL *upstairs is finishing a piece of music.*

CLARA: The voice of the trumpet made wonderful music. Mount Sinai was on fire and an earthquake come out of the ground. Then God called up Moses on the mountain. He gave him the commandments! Keep the Sabbath day, never steal, love your parents—— (JULIE *makes a motion with his drooping hand.* GUS *enters, perusing a small book):* What, Julie? *(She listens closely: his voice is very weak.)* You're right. I heard him. She leaves the police dog in the back yard and he barked all night.

GUS *(absorbed in his book):* They're outa style now, police dogs . . .

CLARA *(resuming her story):* Well, Moses stayed on the mountain forty days and forty nights. They got frightened at the bottom. Everybody was very nervous. "Where's Moses?" Nobody knew what happened. What did those fools do? They put all the gold pieces together, all the jewelry, and melted them, and made a baby cow of gold. Well, believe me, when God saw that he was very, very mad. Moses ran down the hill so fast . . . "What's the big idea!" he said. "Can't I leave you alone for two minutes?" He took that cow and broke it into a thousand pieces. Some people agreed, but the ones who didn't! Finished! God blotted them out of the book. Here today, gone tomorrow! *(Finished, she stands up.)*

GUS *(closing book):* I wonder where Mr. Pike is.

CLARA: Down the cellar. Keep an eye on Julie a minute.

GUS: Sure *(Nods at* JULIE.) Is it all settled, Mrs. G.?

CLARA: Yes.

GUS: When are they comin', Mrs. G.?

CLARA *(playing with scissors):* To take him to the hospital? Tonight. *(Exits.* PEARL *stops playing.)*

GUS *(not quite knowing what to do. Finally approaching* JULIE*):* You want something, Julie? *(No answer. Tries to be cheerful.)* Cushing's Manual of Parliamentary Procedure! *(Holds up the small book.)* Always the chairman in the old days. Motions, agendas——! I had them in my hands like firecrackers! *(Now holds up opera glasses in a strapped case.)* And these opera glasses! My, what a time—Aïda in the Hippodrome. Carmen and all those. *(Tries to cheer up* JULIE *by whistling the Toreador Song from Carmen, going through elaborate play of killing the bull. At this point* PIKE *enters from upstage.* GUS *stops his playing, embarrassed.* PIKE *sets down a tub of assorted junk, an old axe, rubber garden hose, etc.)*

PIKE: All this junk left down the cellar, old tools and stuff.

GUS: Excuse me, Julie. *(Walks over to Pike.)* Did you get it?

PIKE *(dusting off his hands):* Yes. *(Brings envelope out of pocket and gives it to* GUS.*)*

GUS: How much?

PIKE: Two hundred and fifty dollars even. *(A pause.* CLARA *enters and proceeds to put on socks she has brought in for* JULIE. GUS *seats himself on the end of the couch in sad reflection. There is a long sad pause.)* I notice those spiders was never cleaned out. *(Silence again.)*

CLARA *(finally):* I wonder why Leo's so late.

PIKE: Home loans are visible . . . under a microscope.

CLARA: I wanted to go for the loan myself. But Leo said it's a man's job. Why did we wait so long? Why, why . . . ? *(Stands up.)* Is it hot or am I just hot?

PIKE: May first tomorrow—Spring! Flowers buddin', birds twitterin' —south wind—and only Man is vile!

GUS *(walking across to window):* Want the shades all the way down?

CLARA: I don't want people looking in. They see enough when they see the furniture on the sidewalk.

GUS *(peering out from behind blind):* Plentya people out there. Be a mob by eight. Block party! Prosperity block party! Boy scouts' band —fife and drums. American Legion. Big men comin' to speak. State senator. . . . Dr. Norman, whose brother manufactures the chocolate cherries, he's comin'.

PIKE *(with a short hard laugh):* Prosperity block party . . . !

GUS *(suddenly):* There *he* goes!

PIKE: Who?

GUS: Phil Foley marchin' down the street . . . Sponsored the whole thing. (PEARL *enters with portfolio.*)

PEARL: Poppa come yet?

CLARA: No. *(Now* LEO *enters. He looks very tired. Forgets to take off his hat. Goes immediately over to* JULIE.)

LEO *(to* JULIE): How are you feeling, my dear? *(Looks searchingly at* JULIE, *then sits in a chair and holds* JULIE's *hand. Silence.)*

CLARA *(finally):* You're so late. . . .

LEO: *I was not the only person there.*

CLARA: What did they say?

LEO: "No" . . . Forty-eight thousand loans pending in this one state alone.

CLARA: No more loans. . . .

LEO: In the distant future . . .

CLARA: Why did we wait so long to know? *(A pause during which* LEO *notices* PEARL *who has been watching him intently. He crosses over to her.)*

LEO: I'm sorry about the piano, Pearl.

PEARL: When are they coming?

LEO: Tomorrow. I'm very sorry, my dear. *(He cannot look her in the eyes and finally turns to* GUS.) Your friend Foley stopped me on the corner. . . . They want the furniture taken in off the sidewalk.

CLARA: They *what?!*

LEO: Until the party is over.

CLARA: Over my dead body!

LEO: Mr. Foley is not a pleasant man. A big crowd gathered on the corner. Some homeless men joined in. *(He smiles.)* I insisted on our rights.

PIKE: What rights, Citizen?

LEO: The right to leave evicted furniture on the street! *(Suddenly.)* All day I have been seized with an intense desire to escape the country. I feel at any moment——*(Suddenly* PEARL *in her corner slams down the portfolio and bolts from the room.)* Pearlie . . . ! (LEO *hurries out after her.)*

CLARA: The piano's her whole life—like your stamps.

GUS: I suppose. An old friend of mine, Harry Meyers, he used to be in the piano business. A fine and dandy man, but slow in the head. Then he went out on the ocean—April 1912. *There* was a marine disaster! The sinking of the *Titanic*. . . . How history passes. . . .

(Now KEWPIE *suddenly appears in the doorway. He is dressed very prosperously: light gray hat, a smart coat with a velvet collar, gloves, etc. Silence; finally* GUS): You got the wrong house.

KEWPIE: Mind your business, Gussie. *(Advances inward. Silence.)* I hear you're dispossessed . . .

PIKE: No, that furniture's out there for fumigation.

CLARA: Who invited you here?

KEWPIE: Maybe I can help . . .

CLARA: We don't need your help.

KEWPIE: I see I'm still rat poison here. Why not forget it?

CLARA: The day I die I'll forget. Not before. When we die we'll forget everything. Just now we remember!

KEWPIE: So it's a cosmic frame-up, only don't——

CLARA: Get out before my husband—*(She stops as* LEO *enters. A pause.* KEWPIE *fills it by approaching* JULIE.)

KEWPIE: How you feeling, kiddo? *(Listens. Lights a cigarette.)* Don't know what to do with my money these days, so I'm smoking Turkish. *(To* LEO.) Have one . . . *(Emotionally balked.)* Don't be so goddam ritzy, Mr. Gordon. I supported Ben's family for two years!

LEO *(up to him):* You killed my son.

KEWPIE: You're a liar! He wanted to die.

GUS: And we know why.

KEWPIE: He stood there like a rock——

LEO: Get out!

KEWPIE: He stood there soaking up cops' bullets like a sponge—A guy with fifty medals for running. Ben Gordon wanted to die!

GUS: Now you get out, you low life, before I call a cop!

KEWPIE *(furiously, in defense of his entire life):* You gimme worms, the whole bunch! A pack of tramps making believe they own the world because they read a book! I don't read, see! But I saw the handwriting on the wall. I don't stop to say it ain't my cake. I cut a piece without asking! I done something to help myself. You don't! Well, take a lesson from little Kewpie—if you don't like the Constitution, make it over! Christ, then it's my fault 'cause Ben killed himself. That's what he did. He dug his own grave. He was a little kid in a man's world . . . you made him like that. He couldn't earn a living, and he was ashamed.

GUS: Mr. Kewpie, you're so small you ain't visible to the naked eye!

KEWPIE: Don't think I'll ever forget my friend Ben. I carry him around like a medal. He wanted to show he was better than me—

that's why he killed himself. He *was* better. You can have all this money——*(Draws out handful of bills.)* Every goddam nickel!

GUS *(an outraged rooster):* Get out, get out—get off these premises!

KEWPIE: Who wants the cash?

GUS: Get out!

KEWPIE *(after looking at the money, looking at them, suddenly hurls the bills in* GUS'S *face):* P.S., and plenty more where it came from! *(No one moves.* KEWPIE *can hardly catch his breath. It seems for a moment he will burst into tears. He finally stops, picks up all the bills, puts them on top of a box, says):* I wouldn't mind right now if you beat my brains out. *(Walks up to door, stops. He exits. In the following silence* CLARA *strokes* JULIE'S *hair.)*

GUS *(finally):* We have struck him off the agenda forever. (PEARL *begins to play.)*

LEO: He is a lonely boy crying in a wilderness.

CLARA *(to* JULIE): What, darling?

PIKE: What's he say?

CLARA: "United aircraft"—it's an active stock, he says.

LEO: . . . So in the end nothing is real. Nothing is left but our memory of life. Not as it is . . . as it *might* have been. Oh, Clara, your husband is a mixed-up man.

CLARA: That was news in 1912.

PIKE *(indicating money left by* KEWPIE): Must be fifty dollars here.

LEO: It's not ours.

PIKE: He give it to you, Citizen. Don't be impractical about hard cash.

LEO: That's right. Then be practical. Give it back to the ones it belongs to—the homeless men down the corner.

PIKE: A charmin' conceit, I must say. Will I call them in?

LEO: Please. (PIKE *shakes his head and exits.)* Everything is my fault. Clara, tell me what to do . . . *(She turns her back on him with a shrug of her shoulders.* LEO *puts his face in his hands.)*

GUS *(suddenly breaking the silence):* Here's Phil Foley. (FOLEY *enters drunk. Behind him* MILTON. *Both wear official arm bands.)*

FOLEY: Make up your mind?

LEO: I told you before.

FOLEY: Listen, Mr. Gordon——

CLARA: Listen, *Mr. Foley!* In one minute I'll give you a piece of my mind——

FOLEY: It's a big affair——

CLARA: —you won't forget to your dying day!

FOLEY: We don't want no dampers on the party. Straight from the shoulder. We want you to cooperate with us in takin' the stuff off the sidewalk. I feel pretty sorry about——

CLARA: Get out before I push in your red face, Mr. Foley!

FOLEY: You don't understand; this is a *prosperity* block party and——

CLARA: We understand it so well even *you'd* be surprised!

FOLEY *(red faced and earnest)*: We try to help people like you. We really do! What I mean—look—we got a little purse together——

CLARA: The answer is "no" before you finish! It stays on the sidewalk!

FOLEY: Just the principle of the thing with you?

CLARA: No! Principles and ideals don't interest me. But if you're a cat, I'm a tiger! You use a gun, I use a cannon! Get out!

FOLEY *(helpless before her fury)*: I'd like to give you this money.

GUS *(coming out in front suddenly)*: Don't need your help, Phil. Thank God others got the means this time.

FOLEY: Not you.

GUS: Yes! *(Takes money from envelope.)* All this money's theirs.

FOLEY: You owe me plenty.

GUS: Sue me!

FOLEY *(balked properly)*: We'll get every goddam stick in—before the party begins! Why, you think you can get away with something like that on *me?!*

CLARA: Do yourself a personal favor—go home!

FOLEY *(goes to door and stops there. With finality)*: You won't cooperate? *(Waits.)* You won't? . . . we'll see if you won't! *(Addressing persons off stage.)* All right, boys, come on in. *(Two* DETECTIVES *enter insolently; the first flashing a badge.)*

FIRST DETECTIVE *(pointing to* GUS): This the one?

FOLEY *(at* LEO): No, him. He won't cooperate.

FIRST DETECTIVE: Your stuff on the sidewalk?

LEO: Yes. *(Holding back the aggressive* CLARA.) I'll speak to the gentlemen, Clara.

FOLEY *(who is very drunk and worried)*: Don't make no fuss, boys. We're starting any minute.

FIRST DETECTIVE: Why don't you cooperate like this gentleman says?

CLARA *(getting between* LEO *and the* FIRST DETECTIVE): Why, he's so drunk he can't stand!

FOLEY: They talk that way to me . . . work for the underdogs.

CLARA: I'm warning everyone! Take this man out before I murder him!

LEO: Clara! *(Then to* DETECTIVE.) We have owned this house seventeen years——A *sheriff* has put that furniture on the street. But *we* insist it stay there!

FIRST DETECTIVE *(to* POLICEMAN *in hall):* Eddie, trot down the corner. Round up a few boys to give a hand moving that stuff in.

POLICEMAN: Okey-dokey. *(Goes.* PEARL *plays piano upstairs.)*

FIRST DETECTIVE: All right, Mr. Foley—you can start your block party. (FOLEY *exits with a smirk.)* Now remember!—If you care about your health——*(Exits insolently.)*

CLARA *(in a burst of rage):* If we could *do* something! If only our hands weren't tied!

LEO *(slowly):* Gus . . . where did you get the money?

GUS: The money? This money? *(Makes a feeble joke.)* Well, I guess I found my widow.

LEO *(taking* GUS *by the shoulders):* Gus . . .

GUS *(drawing away):* There's an even two fifty here.

LEO *(ignoring the proffered money):* You did . . .

GUS: Settled an old debt.

LEO: You sold them.

GUS: We don't have to fight about some money, do we?

LEO *(finally):* He sold his stamps . . .

CLARA: Oh . . . *(Both look at* GUS, *who stands there like a criminal.)*

GUS *(finally):* Take it, Mr. G.

LEO: This is a very painful moment for all of us.

GUS *(cheerfully, putting envelope in* LEO'S *pocket):* Last of the Mohiggins! *(With a sudden burst.)* Leo, Clara, we had so much sorrow outa life, and now we want a good time! Sky rockets bustin' in the house! Ventriloquism! Beasts and birds! *(Suddenly he is gloriously trilling like a bird. But the whistle ends in defeat. He seats himself on the couch.* PIKE *now enters with two typical homeless* MEN *behind him. Very poorly dressed. The smaller of the two, by name,* PAUL, *stays in the background—seems impressed by books in the crate; rummages through several. Glances around him critically. The other, tall and thin, most of his teeth gone, comes forward.)*

PIKE *(to the* MEN): Come on in, boys. *(They do so.)* His name is Williams. *(To* PAUL.) What's your name?

PAUL: Paul.

PIKE *(to* LEO): Told the boys you mean to give them something.

LEO *(embarrassed):* Yes, my friends . . . I would like you to divide this money.

WILLIAMS (*as* PAUL *looks in a book*): That's a ten dollar bill.

LEO: Yes, it is.

WILLIAMS (*finally*): You think I was born yesterday to let you kid the bib off me like this?

LEO: I'm in no mood for jokes, my friend. People like me are responsible for your condition.

WILLIAMS (*puzzled*): What?

LEO: If it were within my power I would restore to you a whole world which is rightfully yours.

WILLIAMS (*incredulous*): What?

LEO (*holding out the money*): These few dollars belong to you, not me. (WILLIAMS *hesitantly looks around. Then slowly reaches out for the money. Sees it is all in good faith. Slowly moves to the door.* PAUL *grabs him. Takes the money.*)

PAUL: Excuse my dust. (*Comes down to* CLARA.) Lady, he your husband?

CLARA: I think so . . .

PAUL: You better hold this cash. Excuse my dust. Let's go, Williams. (*Herds him to the door, but stops, goes down to* LEO.) Who the hell are *you* to give away money?! Louder and funnier! (*Starts out with finality, but stops again.*) You think you're better off than me and Williams? You're worse! We can take it!

WILLIAMS: Think of the——

PAUL (*silencing him*): Keep quiet, you ignorant man!

WILLIAMS (*of* PAUL, *to the others; grinning*): Ain't he a scream?

PAUL (*waiting impressively for silence, then*): Didn't they just throw you outa your house?

CLARA: Yes.

PAUL: Excuse my pointing! The slight difference in our social standing is you got a whole pair of pants. Also you still believe all this book stuff. (*Picks up book, reads cover.*) Emerson . . . democracy, equality . . .

LEO: Emerson was a great man. He promised men they would walk the earth like gods.

PAUL: Then he was a goddam liar! Why, you're sleeping! All over the country people sleeping. Don't argue! Like Napoleon, I been on that battle field. All over millions dreaming of democracy and liberty which don't exist. That's how it comes out on my knitting machine. Boy, I like your nerve—handing over that cash! Who the hell do you think you are?

CLARA: Tell him, tell him!

PAUL: I look at you and see myself seven years back. I been there. This kind of dream paralyzes the will—confuses the mind. Courage goes. Daring goes . . . and in the nights there is sighing. I had my house in these United States. Like you. Did you have a business?

LEO: Yes.

PAUL: Like me. You had a sorta little paradise here. Now you lost the paradise. That should teach you something. But no! You ain't awake yet. Listen, the whole world is a league of notions today——

WILLIAMS: League of *nations,* you mean.

PAUL: Oh, hush! *(Continues to* LEO.) Everyone's got notions—why, millions are homeless and unhappy in America today. Some say the machines. This ignorant person—*(Points to* WILLIAMS) he's got a whole routine about its glands.

WILLIAMS: Adrenalin juices. Some got 'em and some ain't.

PAUL: As one comic character to another—your blood is piss. *(Apologizing for* WILLIAMS.) Life's way over his head—an airplane.

WILLIAMS *(grinning):* Ain't he a scream?

PAUL *(to* LEO): Why, the house where I lived—the janitor used to get fifteen hundred a year! But don't be fooled by the good old days. That's through for ever. You have been took like a bulldog takes a pussy cat! Finished!

LEO: Finished . . . ?

PAUL: They left you the dust of the road. (PAUL *slowly moves to the door.)*

WILLIAMS: All quiet on the Potomac.

PAUL: Excuse my pointing. *(Both slowly exit: Silence.)*

CLARA: He was right. *(Attracted by* JULIE.) What, Julie? The dog. . . .

GUS *(still sitting sadly on the couch):* He's got the dog on his mind. (LEO *begins to walk back and forth across the room.)*

LEO *(suddenly stops):* No!

CLARA *(attentive only to* JULIE): Yes, Julie . . . Yes, yes . . . *(She is near tears.)*

LEO: No! There is more to life than this! Everything he said is true, but there is more. That was the past, but there is a future. Now we know. We dare to understand. Truly, truly, the past was a dream. But this is real! To know from this that something must be done. That is real. We searched; we were confused! But we searched, and now the search is ended. For the truth has found us. For the first time in our lives—for the first time our house has a real foundation.

Clara, those people outside are afraid. Those people at the block party whisper and point. They're afraid. Let them look in our house. We're not ashamed. Let them look in. Clara, my darling, *listen to me.* Everywhere now men are rising from their sleep. Men, men are understanding the bitter black total of their lives. Their whispers are growing to shouts! They become an ocean of understanding! *No man fights alone.* Oh, if you could only see with me the greatness of men. I tremble like a bride to see the time when they'll use it. My darling, we must have only one regret— that life is so short! That we must die so soon. (CLARA *slowly has turned from* JULIE *and is listening now to her husband.*) Yes, I want to see that new world. I want to kiss all those future men and women. What is this talk of bankrupts, failures, hatred . . . they won't know what that means. Oh, yes, I tell you the whole world is for men to possess. Heartbreak and terror are not the heritage of mankind! The world is beautiful. No fruit tree wears a lock and key. Men will sing at their work, men will love. Ohhh, darling, the world is in its morning . . . and *no man fights alone!* (CLARA *slowly comes down to her husband and kisses him. With real feeling. Every one in the room,* LEO *included, is deeply moved by this vision of the future.* LEO *says):* Let us have air . . . Open the windows. *(As he crosses to the windows a short fanfare is heard without.)*

The curtain slowly descends.

GOLDEN BOY

FOR LUISE

Golden Boy was first presented by the Group Theatre at the Belasco
Theatre on the evening of November 4th, 1937, with the following
members of the Group Theatre Acting Company:

(In order of speech)

TOM MOODY	*Roman Bohnen*
LORNA MOON	*Frances Farmer*
JOE BONAPARTE	*Luther Adler*
TOKIO	*Art Smith*
MR. CARP	*Lee J. Cobb*
SIGGIE	*Jules Garfield*
MR. BONAPARTE	*Morris Carnovsky*
ANNA	*Phoebe Brand*
FRANK BONAPARTE	*John O'Malley*
ROXY GOTTLIEB	*Robert Lewis*
EDDIE FUSELI	*Elia Kazan*
PEPPER WHITE	*Harry Bratsburg*
MICKEY	*Michael Gordon*
CALL BOY	*Bert Conway*
SAM	*Martin Ritt*
LEWIS	*Charles Crisp*
DRAKE	*Howard Da Silva*
DRISCOLL	*Charles Niemeyer*
BARKER	*Karl Malden*

Direction by HAROLD CLURMAN
Settings by MORDECAI GORELIK

SCENES

ACT ONE

SCENE 1. The office of Tom Moody.
SCENE 2. The Bonaparte home. That night.
SCENE 3. The office. Two months later.
SCENE 4. A park bench. A few nights later.
SCENE 5. The Bonaparte home. Midnight, six weeks later.

ACT TWO

SCENE 1. A gymnasium. Five months later.
SCENE 2. The park bench. A few nights later.
SCENE 3. The office. The following day.
SCENE 4. A dressing room in the Arena. Six weeks later.

ACT THREE

SCENE 1. The office. Six months later.
SCENE 2. The dressing room. The following night.
SCENE 3. The Bonaparte home. Several hours later.

GOLDEN BOY

ACT ONE

SCENE I

The small Broadway office of TOM MOODY, *the fight manager.*

The office is scantily furnished, contains desk, chairs, telephone and couch. With MOODY *at present is his girl,* LORNA MOON. *There is a certain quiet glitter about this girl, and if she is sometimes hard, it is more from necessity than choice. Her eyes often hold a soft, sad glance. Likewise,* MOODY'S *explosiveness covers a soft, boyish quality, and at the same time he possesses a certain vulnerable quality which women find very attractive.*

The time is eighteen months ago.

As the lights fade in, we catch these two at the height of one of their frequent fights.

MOODY: Pack up your clothes and go! Go! Who the hell's stopping you?

LORNA: You mean it?

MOODY: You brought up the point yourself.

LORNA: No, I didn't!

MOODY: Didn't you say you had a good mind to leave me?

LORNA: No, I said——

MOODY: You said you were going to pack!

LORNA: I said I feel like a tramp and I don't like it. I want to get married, I want——

MOODY: Go home, Lorna, go home! I ain't got time to discuss it. Gimme some air. It's enough I got my wife on my neck.

LORNA: What does she say?

MOODY: Who?

LORNA: Your wife—your sweet goddam Monica!

MOODY: She wants five thousand dollars to give me the divorce. (LORNA *laughs.*) I don't see that it's funny.

LORNA: Look, Tom, this means as much to me as it does to you. If she's out of the way, we can get married. Otherwise I'm a tramp from Newark. I don't like the feeling.

MOODY: Lorna, for Pete's sake, use your noodle! When I get rid of Monica, we'll marry. Now, do I have to bang you on the nose to make you understand?

LORNA: Go to hell! . . . But come back tonight. (MOODY'S *answer is to look at her, then smile, then walk to her. They kiss.*)

MOODY: If I had the money, I'd buy you something—I don't know what—a big ostrich feather! If Kaplan wins tonight, I'll take you dancing at the Park.

LORNA: He won't win.

MOODY: How do you know? *I* don't know—how do *you* know?

LORNA: Are you crazy? Do you think your Mr. Kaplan can go ten rounds with the Baltimore Chocolate Drop?

MOODY: How do I know?

LORNA: It's the Twentieth Century, Tom—no more miracles. (MOODY'S *face turns worried.* LORNA *smiles.*) You know what I like about you—you take everything so serious.

MOODY: Who will if I don't? I've been off the gold standard for eight years. This used to be a gorgeous town. New York was hot with money. Kaplan gets four hundred bucks tonight. In the old days, that was nothing. Those were the days when I had Marty Welch, the heavyweight contender—Cy Webster who got himself killed in a big, red Stutz. In '27 and 8 you couldn't go to sleep—the town was crawling with attractions.

LORNA: My mother died in '28.

MOODY: I haven't had a break in years. "Carry me back to old Virginny"—that's how I feel. There isn't much of a future. *(Suddenly despondent,* MOODY *goes back to his desk.)*

LORNA: I was fooling.

MOODY: What about?

LORNA: Do you think I'd leave you?

MOODY: Why not? I'm an old man. What can I give you?

LORNA: A bang on the nose for a start. But what can I give you?

MOODY: A boy who can fight. Find me a good black boy and I'll show you a mint.

LORNA: Are good boys so hard to find?

MOODY: Honest to God, you make me sick to my stomach! What do you think I took a trip to Philadelphia? What do you think I went to Chicago? Wasn't I up in Boston for a week? You think good boys are laying around like pop-corn? I'd even take a bantamweight, if I found one.

LORNA: How about a nice lady fighter with a beard——*(Preparing to leave.)* Well, I'll see you tonight, Moody.

MOODY *(thoughtfully):* I'd give me right eye for a good black boy.

LORNA: Let me have your right eye for a minute. *(She kisses his eye.* MOODY *begins to embrace her—she eludes his grasp.)* That's to keep you hot. But if the truth were known—"yours till hell freezes over."

MOODY: I need you, I need you, Lorna—I need you all the time. I'd like to give you everything you want. Push your mouth over. . . . *(LORNA holds her face to his; he kisses her. Suddenly a youth is standing at the office door.* LORNA *sees him and breaks away.)*

BOY *(breathing quickly):* Mr. Moody . . .

MOODY *(spinning around):* Don't you knock when you come in an office?

BOY: Sometimes I knock, sometimes I don't.

MOODY: Say your piece and get the hell out!

BOY: I just ran over from the gym . . .

MOODY: What gym?

BOY: Where Kaplan trains. He just broke his hand. . . . (MOODY *stiffens to attention.)* It's a fact.

MOODY *(grasping the phone):* Is Tokio over there? My trainer?

BOY: He's looking after Kaplan. (MOODY *begins to dial the phone but abruptly changes his mind and replaces the phone.)*

MOODY: You can put me in the bug-house right now. Moody is the name, folks—step right up and wipe your shoes! Ah, that Kaplan! That phonus bolonus! *(He sits at his desk in despair.)* Now I have to call up Roxy Gottlieb and cancel the match. His club's in the red as it is.

BOY: I don't think it's necessary to cancel, Tom.

MOODY *(aware of the* BOY *for the first time):* Oh, you don't? Who the hell are you? And who the hell are you to call me Tom? Are we acquainted?

BOY: I wrote you a couple of letters. I can do that stretch.

MOODY: What stretch?

BOY: Why don't you let me take Kaplan's place tonight?

MOODY *(sarcastically):* Go slow and tell me again . . . what?

BOY *(coolly):* I can take Kaplan's place. . . .

MOODY: You mean you want to fight the Baltimore Chocolate Drop?

You? (The BOY *remains silent.* MOODY *comes out from behind his desk and stands face to face with the* BOY. *With sudden discovery.)* You're cock-eyed too.

BOY *(quietly):* Can't you fix it up with Roxy Gottlieb?

MOODY *(suddenly):* Looka, kid, go home, kid, before I blame Kaplan's glass mitts on *you.* Then you won't like it, and I won't like it, and Miss Moon here, she won't like it.

BOY *(turning to* LORNA): How do you do, Miss Moon. (LORNA *smiles at the* BOY'S *quiet confidence.)* I need a good manager, Mr. Moody. You used to be tops around town—everyone says so. I think you can develop me. I can fight. You don't know it, but I can fight. Kaplan's been through for years. He may be the best fighter in your stable, but he's a stumble-bum for the younger boys growing up. Why don't you give me this chance, Tom?

MOODY: I don't want you calling me Tom! *(He glares at the* BOY *and then returns to the desk and telephone.)*

BOY: I'm waiting for your answer. (MOODY'S *answer is an exasperated glance as he begins to dial the phone. The* BOY *half approaches the desk.)* There are forty-three thousand minutes in a month—can't you give me five?

MOODY: I'll give you this phone in the head in a minute! Who are you? What the hell do you want? Where do you fight?

BOY *(with cool persistence):* We ought to get together, Tom.

MOODY: I don't want you calling me Tom. You're brash, you're fresh, you're callow—and you're cock-eyed! In fact, you're an insult to my whole nature! Now get out! (MOODY *turns back to the phone and begins dialing again. The* BOY *stands there, poised on his toes, not sure of his next move. He turns and looks at* LORNA. *She nods her head and gives him a faint smile of encouragement. On phone.)* This is Tom Moody . . . is Tokio there? . . . *(He hangs up the phone and holds the instrument thoughtfully.)* Tokio's on his way over.

BOY: The Baltimore Chocolate Drop is not as good as you think he is. (MOODY *suddenly whirls around and holds the telephone high over his head in a threatening gesture. The* BOY *steps back lightly and continues.)* I've studied his style for months; I've perfected the exact punch to quench his thirst. Did you ever watch closely? *(Acting it out.)* He likes to pull your lead—he hesitates for a second —he pulls your lead—he slips his face away and then he's in.

Suppose you catch that second when he hesitates—he's open for the punch!

MOODY *(sarcastically):* And what do you do with his left hook?

BOY *(simply):* Avoid it.

MOODY *(lowering the phone):* Looka, you idiot, did you ever hear of Phil Mateo?

BOY: I heard of him.

MOODY: The Chocolate Drop marked him lousy in twelve minutes and ten seconds. Was Kid Peters within your ken? And did you ever hear of Eddie Newton? The Chocolate gave him the blues in two rounds. And Frisco Samuels and Mike Mason . . .

BOY: Did you ever hear of me?

MOODY *(sarcastically):* No, who are you? I would honestly like to know—who are you?

BOY *(quietly):* My name is Bonaparte. (MOODY *howls with laughter, and even* LORNA, *sympathetic to the* BOY, *laughs. The* BOY *continues.)* I don't think it's funny. . . .

MOODY: Didn't that name used to get you a little giggle in school? Tell the truth, Bonaparte. Didn't it?

BOY: Call me Joe.

MOODY *(laughing):* And your eyes . . . Didn't they used to get a little giggle too?

JOE: You don't seem as intelligent as I thought you were.

LORNA *(to the laughing* MOODY, *seeing the* BOY'S *pain):* Stop it, Tom.

MOODY *(laughing):* You can't blame me, Bonaparte. . . . I haven't laughed for years.

JOE: I don't like it. . . . I don't want you to do it. *(Suddenly* JOE *grabs* MOODY *by the coat lapels.* MOODY, *surprised, shakes him off. At the same time a small, quiet man enters the office. He is* TOKIO, MOODY'S *trainer.)* I'm sorry I did that, Tom. We ought to be together, Tom—not apart.

MOODY: Tokio, did you send this kid here?

TOKIO: No.

MOODY: Take him out before I brain him! *(He storms back to his desk.)*

TOKIO *(after looking at the* BOY): You hear about Kaplan?

MOODY: This idiot told me. It's the end of everything! I'm off my top with the whole thing! Kaplan was our meal-ticket. I'm up to the throat in scandal, blackmail, perjury, alimony and all points west!

TOKIO *(turning to* JOE): You oughta be ashamed to show your face in this office.

JOE: If Kaplan's mother fed him milk, he wouldn't have those brittle bones.

MOODY: ? ? ? ?

TOKIO *(to* MOODY): This is the boy who did it to Kaplan.

MOODY: ? ? ?

TOKIO: I went down for an apple and I come back and Kaplan's sparring with this kid—picked him up in the gym. The next thing I know, Kaplan's down on the floor with a busted mitt.

JOE *(modestly):* I took it on the elbow.

MOODY: ! ! *(Silence finally.)*

LORNA: Where do you come from, Bonaparte?

JOE: Here.

LORNA: How old are you?

JOE: Twenty-one—tomorrow.

MOODY *(after a look at* LORNA): Fight much?

JOE: Enough.

MOODY: Where?

JOE *(fabricating):* Albany, Syracuse . . .

LORNA: Does Roxy Gottlieb know you?

JOE: I never fought at his club.

MOODY *(harshly):* Does he know you?

JOE: No. (TOKIO *and* MOODY *look at each other. The phone rings.)*

MOODY *(on the phone):* Hello. . . . "What's this you hear?" . . . You hear the truth, Roxy. . . . He bust his mitt again. . . . I can't help it if you got *fifty* judgments on your club. . . . The same to you. . . . Your mother too! *(Keeping his eyes on* BONAPARTE.) If you tie up your big flabby mouth for a minute, I'll give you some news. I'm in a position to do you a big favor. I got a replacement—*better* than Kaplan . . . Bonaparte. . . . No, Bon-a-parte. *(Holds hand over mouthpiece and asks* BOY) Is that crap?

JOE: No, that's my name.

MOODY *(back at phone):* That's right, like in Napoleon. . . . *(Looks the* BOY *over appraisingly.)* One hundred and thirty.

JOE: Three.

MOODY: Hundred and thirty-three. Your customers'll eat him up. I'll bring him right over . . . you can take my word—the kid's a cock-eyed wonder . . . *your* mother too! *(He hangs up and turns around.* JOE *is the focus of all eyes.)* It's revenge on somebody—maybe God.

JOE *(quietly):* I think you'll be surprised.

MOODY *(sadly):* Do your worst, kid. I've been surprised by experts.

JOE: Don't worry, Tom.

MOODY: Call me Tom again and I'll break your neck!!

Quick Fadeout

SCENE II

Later that night.

The combination dining and front room of the Bonaparte home. A round dining-room table, littered with newspapers, is lighted from directly above like a billiard table. Plaster busts of Mozart and Beethoven are on the sideboard. A cage of love birds at the other side of the room. Sitting at the table are two men: MR. BONA-PARTE, *the father of* JOE, *and a Jewish friend, a* MR. CARP, *who owns the local candy and stationery store.*

As the lights fade in, MR. BONAPARTE *turns his newspaper.* MR. CARP *is slowly pouring beer from a bottle. He begins to sip it as* SIGGIE, MR. BONAPARTE'S *son-in-law, enters from the kitchen. He is bare-footed, dressed in an undershirt, trousers and hung-down suspenders. He brings his own beer and glass, which he begins to fill with an expert's eye. In the silence,* MR. CARP *takes a long, cool sip of beer combined with a murmur of relish.*

CARP *(finally):* I don't take it easy. That's my trouble—if I could only learn to take it easy. . . .

SIGGIE: What do you call it now, what you're doing?

CARP: Say, it's after business hours.

SIGGIE: That's a business? A man who runs a candy store is an outcast of the world. Don't even sell *nickel* candies—*penny* candies!

CARP: And your taxicab business makes you higher in the social scale?

SIGGIE: So I'm an outcast too. Don't change the subject. Like my father-in-law here—he's always changing the subject when I get a little practical on him. *(Putting his beer on the table and scratching himself under the arms like a monkey.)* You—I'm talking about you, Mr. Bonaparte.

MR. BONAPARTE *(suddenly shooting out two words):* Ha ha! *(He then resumes his reading.)*

SIGGIE: Every time I talk money, he gives me that horse laugh. Suppose you bought me a cab—I could pay it off by the week.

MR. BONAPARTE *(who talks with an Italian accent):* I don't go in taxicab business.

SIGGIE: I am married to your daughter and when you do this little thing, you do it for her and me together. A cab in two shifts is a big source of profit. Joe takes the night shift. I'm a married man so you don't expect me to take the night shift. *(ANNA, SIGGIE'S wife, in a night-gown, pokes her head in at the door.)*

ANNA: Come to bed, Siggie. You'll wake up the whole neighborhood. *(ANNA disappears.)*

SIGGIE: See? I'm a married man! You don't expect me to take the night shift.

MR. BONAPARTE *(having heard this talk for months):* No, Siggie . . . no.

SIGGIE: No, what?

MR. BONAPARTE: No taxicab.

SIGGIE: Don't you wanna help your own family, foolish? After all, Joe's your own son—he's a man, no kid no more——

MR. BONAPARTE: Tomorrow's twenty-one.

SIGGIE: If he don't work he'll turn into a real bum. Look how late he's staying out at night.

MR. BONAPARTE: I don't expects for Joe to drive taxi.

SIGGIE: He's got to do something. He can drive like a fire engine. Why not?

MR. BONAPARTE: He gonna do something.

SIGGIE: What? Play his violinsky in the backyards?

ANNA *(looking in at the door again):* Come to bed, Siggie! Poppa, don't talk to him so he'll come to bed! *(ANNA disappears again.)*

SIGGIE *(annoyed):* Women! Always buzzing around. *(MR. BONAPARTE'S only answer is to turn over the newspaper on the table before him.)*

CARP *(reflectively):* Women . . . the less we have to do with women the better. As Schopenhauer says, "Much ado about nothing . . . the comedy of reproduction." *(He wags his head bitterly.)* Women . . . !

SIGGIE: I'm hungry, but I ain't got the heart to go in the kitchen again. It reminds me of how my wife slaves for this family of crazy wops! A fine future for an intelligent woman!

MR. BONAPARTE: She'sa your wife, but also my daughter. She'sa not so intelligent as you say. Also, *you* are not so intelligent!

SIGGIE: You can't insult me, I'm too ignorant! (ANNA *now comes fully into the room. She is buxom, energetic, good-natured and adenoidal.*)

ANNA: Poppa, why don't you let Siggie come to bed? Looka him, walking around barefooted!

MR. BONAPARTE: I don't stop him. . . .

SIGGIE: Sure he stops me—he stops me every night. I'm worried. I don't sleep. It's my Jewish disposition. He don't wanna help me out, your old man. He wants me to drive a company cab and submit to the brutalities of the foremen all my life. I could be in a healthy little enterprise for myself, but your old man don't wanna help me out.

ANNA: Why don't you buy Siggie a cab, Poppa? You got the cash.

SIGGIE: Buy it for Siggie and Joe.

ANNA: For Siggie and Joe—it don't have to be a new one.

SIGGIE (*after giving his wife a stabbing glance*): Sure, even an old one—the way they recondition them now-a-days——

MR. BONAPARTE: Children, gone to bed.

SIGGIE: Don't tell a lie—how much you got in the bank?

MR. BONAPARTE (*with a smile*): Millions.

SIGGIE: Four thousand?

MR. BONAPARTE: No.

SIGGIE: Three? (MR. BONAPARTE *shakes his head.*) Three? . . .

ANNA: What's your business how much he's got?

SIGGIE: Shut up, Duchess! Am I asking for my health? If I wanna take you out of the kitchen, is that the gratitude I get? You and your father, you get my goat! I'm sore!

ANNA: Come to bed, Siggie.

SIGGIE: "Come to bed, come to bed!" What the hell's so special in bed. (ANNA'S *answer is a warm prolonged giggle.*) It's a conspiracy around here to put me to bed. I'm warning one thing: if matters go from worse to worse, don't ever expect me to support this family, I'm warning!

MR. BONAPARTE (*smiling kindly*): We have-a receive the warning. We are in a conspiracy against you—gone to bed. (*He turns back to his newspaper.* SIGGIE *sees he has lost again and now turns on his wife.*)

SIGGIE: Who asked you to stick in your two cents about secondhand cabs? As long as I'm not gonna get it, I'll tell you what I want—a first-class job, fresh from the factory. *(He suddenly swats her on the head with a rolled-up newspaper. She hits him back. He returns her blow.)*

ANNA: Don't be so free with your hands! *(He hits her again. She hits him back.)* You got some nerve, Siggie!

SIGGIE *(hitting her again):* The next time I'll break your neck—I'm super-disgusted with you!

MR. BONAPARTE *(standing up):* Stop this . . .

SIGGIE *(turning to him):* And with you, I'm super-finished! *(Turning back to his wife.)* Sit out here with this Unholy Alliance—I'll sleep alone tonight. *(He starts for the door.* MR. BONAPARTE *puts his arm around* ANNA *who begins to sob.)*

MR. BONAPARTE: Hit your wife in private, not in public!

CARP: A man hits his wife and it is the first step to fascism!

SIGGIE *(to* CARP): What are you talking about, my little prince! I love my wife. You don't stop talking how you hate yours. *(Now to* MR. BONAPARTE.) And as for you, don't make believe you care!—Do I have to fall on my knees to you otherwise? We wanna raise a family —it's a normal instinct. Take your arm off her.

ANNA *(suddenly moving over to* SIGGIE): That's right, poppa. He can hit me any time he likes.

SIGGIE *(his arm around her):* And we don't want you interfering in our affairs unless you do it the right way!

ANNA: That's right, poppa—you mind your g.d. business! (MR. BONAPARTE *repressing a smile, slowly sits.)*

SIGGIE: In the bed, Duchess.

ANNA *(with a giggle):* Good night.

MR. BONAPARTE *and* MR. CARP: Good night. *(She exits. After a belligerent look at the pair at the table,* SIGGIE *follows her.)*

MR. BONAPARTE *(bursting into hushed laughter):* There'sa olda remark—never interfere in the laws of nature and you gonna be happy. Love! Ha ha!

CARP *(gloomily):* Happy? A famous man remarked in the last century, "Pleasure is negative."

MR. BONAPARTE: I feela good. Like-a to have some music! Hey, where'sa my boy, Joe? *(Looks at his watch; is surprised.)* One o'clock . . . don't come home yet. Hey, he make-a me worry!

CARP: You think you got worries? Wait, you're a young man yet. You got a son, Joe. He practised on his fiddle for ten years? He won a gold medal, the best in the city? They gave him a scholarship in the Erickson Institute? Tomorrow he's twenty-one, yeah?

MR. BONAPARTE *(emphatically):* Yeah!

CARP *(leaning forward and dramatically making his point):* Suppose a war comes? Before you know it, he's in the army!

MR. BONAPARTE: Naw, naw! Whata you say! Naw!

CARP *(wagging his head in imitation):* Look in the papers! On every side the clouds of war——

MR. BONAPARTE: My Joe gotta biga talent. Yesterday I buy-a him present! *(With a dramatic flourish he brings a violin case out of the bottom part of the sideboard.)*

CARP *(as the case is opened):* It looks like a coffin for a baby.

MR. BONAPARTE *(looking down at the violin in its case):* His teacher help me to picka him.

CARP *(the connoisseur):* Fine, fine—beautiful, fine! A cultural thing!

MR. BONAPARTE *(touching it fondly):* The mosta golden present for his birthday which I give him tonight.

CARP: How much, if I'm not getting too personal, did such a violin cost you?

MR. BONAPARTE: Twelve hundred dollars.

CARP *(shocked):* What?

MR. BONAPARTE: You're surprised of me? Well, I waita for this moment many years.

CARP *(sitting):* Ask yourself a pertinent remark: could a boy make a living playing this instrument in our competitive civilization today?

MR. BONAPARTE: Why? Don't expect for Joe to be a millionaire. He don't need it, to be millionaire. A good life'sa possible——

CARP: For men like us, yes. But nowadays is it possible for a young man to give himself to the Muses? Could the Muses put bread and butter on the table?

MR. BONAPARTE: No millionaire is necessary. Joe love music. Music is the great cheer-up in the language of all countries. I learn that from Joe. (CARP *sighs as* MR. BONAPARTE *replaces the violin in the buffet.)*

CARP: But in the end, as Schopenhauer says, what's the use to try something? For every wish we get, ten remains unsatisfied. Death is playing with us as a cat and her mouse!

MR. BONAPARTE: You make-a me laugh, Mr. Carp. You say life'sa bad. No, life'sa good. Siggie and Anna fight—good! They love—good!

You say life'sa bad . . . well, is pleasure for you to say so. No? The streets, winter a' summer—trees, cats—I love-a them all. The gooda boys and girls, they who sing and whistle—*(Bursts into a moment of gay whistling)*—very good! The eating and sleeping, drinking wine—very good! I gone around on my wagon and talk to many people—nice! Howa you like the big buildings of the city?

CARP: Buildings? And suppose it falls? A house fell down last week on Staten Island!

MR. BONAPARTE: Ha ha, you make me laugh, ha ha! *(Now enters* FRANK BONAPARTE, *oldest son of the family, simple, intelligent, observant.)*

MR. BONAPARTE: Hello, Frank.

FRANK: Hello, poppa . . . Mr. Carp . . .

CARP *(nodding):* What's new in the world?

FRANK *(dropping newspapers to the table, but keeping one for himself):* Read 'em and weep. March first tomorrow—spring on the way. Flowers soon budding, birds twittering—south wind . . . Cannons, bombs and airplane raids! Where's Joe? Did you give him the fiddle yet?

MR. BONAPARTE: No, not in yet. Siggie and Anna sleep. Hungry?

FRANK *(beginning to undress—putting his coat on the back of a chair):* No, I'm tired. I'll see you in the morning, before I leave.

CARP: Going away again?

FRANK: South. Tex-tiles. There's hell down there in tex-tiles. *(He sits on the other side of the room and looks at a paper.)*

CARP: I don't begin to understand it—tex-tiles! What's it his business if the workers in tex-tiles don't make good wages!

MR. BONAPARTE: Frank, he fight-a for eat, for good life. Why not!

CARP: Foolish!

MR. BONAPARTE: What ever you got ina your nature to do isa not foolish!

CARP *(flipping over the newspaper):* For instance—look: playing baseball isn't foolish?

MR. BONAPARTE: No, if you like-a to do.

CARP: Look! Four or five pages—baseball—tennisball—it gives you an idea what a civilization! You ever seen a baseball game?

MR. BONAPARTE: No.

CARP *(wagging his head):* Hit a ball, catch a ball . . . believe me, my friend—nonsense!

FRANK: Poppa, where did you say Joe was?

MR. BONAPARTE: Don't know——

FRANK: Poppa, you better brace yourself in your chair!

MR. BONAPARTE: What? (FRANK *places the paper before* MR. BONA-PARTE. *He reads aloud.*)

FRANK: Looka this, Joe's had a fight. "Flash: Chocolate Drop fails to K.O. new cock-eyed wonder." Take a look at the picture.

CARP: What?

MR. BONAPARTE: What?

FRANK: It's my little brother Joie, or I don't know a scab from a picket!

MR. BONAPARTE: Had a fight? That is foolish—not possible.

FRANK *(pointing with his finger):* There's his name—Bonaparte.

MR. BONAPARTE *(puzzled):* Musta be some other boy. (FRANK *suddenly flips over the newspaper. The others immediately see the reason:* JOE *stands in the entrance, in the shadows.*)

JOE *(in the shadows):* Gee, you're up late. . . .

MR. BONAPARTE: We waita for you. (JOE *slowly moves into the light. His face is bruised and over one eye is a piece of adhesive tape.*)

JOE *(seeing their looks):* I had a fight—a boy in the park——

MR. BONAPARTE: He hit you?

JOE: I hit him.

MR. BONAPARTE: You hurt?

JOE: No. (MR. BONAPARTE *casts a furtive look in the direction of the other men.*)

MR. BONAPARTE: Whata you fight him for?

JOE: Didn't like what he said to me.

MR. BONAPARTE: What he said?

JOE *(evasively):* It's a long story and I'm tired.

MR. BONAPARTE *(trying to break a pause of embarrassment):* I was say to Mr. Carp tomorrow is your birthday. How you like to be so old?

JOE: I forgot about that! I mean I forgot for the last few hours. Where do you think I was? Do you want the truth?

FRANK: Truth is cheap. We bought it for two cents. (*He turns over the paper and shows* JOE *his own face.* JOE *looks at the picture, likes it. General silence.*)

JOE *(finally, belligerently):* Well, what are you going to do about it?

MR. BONAPARTE *(still puzzled):* Abouta what?

JOE *(challengingly):* Tomorrow's my birthday!

FRANK: What's that got to do with being a gladiator?

JOE *(turning to* FRANK, *with sudden vehemence):* Mind your business! You don't know me—I see you once a year; what do you know about me?

FRANK *(smiling):* You're a dumb kid!

MR. BONAPARTE *(starting to his feet):* Hey, waita one-a minute. What'sa for this excite-a-ment?

JOE *(hotly):* I don't want to be criticized! Nobody takes me serious here! I want to do what I want. I proved it tonight I'm good—I went out to earn some money and I earned! I had a professional fight tonight—maybe I'll have some more.

CARP: You honest to God had a fight?

JOE *(glaring at* CARP): Why not?

FRANK *(to Joe):* No one's criticizin'.

MR. BONAPARTE: That's right.

JOE *(half sheepishly):* I don't know why I got so sore. . . .

FRANK: You're expecting opposition all the time——

MR. BONAPARTE: Sit down, Joe—resta you'self.

JOE: Don't want to sit. Every birthday I ever had I sat around. Now'sa time for standing. Poppa, I have to tell you—I don't like myself, past, present and future. Do you know there are men who have wonderful things from life? Do you think they're better than me? Do you think I like this feeling of no possessions? Of learning about the world from Carp's encyclopaedia? Frank don't know what it means—he travels around, sees the world! *(Turning to* FRANK.) You don't know what it means to sit around here and watch the months go ticking by! Do you think that's a life for a boy my age? Tomorrow's my birthday! I change my life!

MR. BONAPARTE: Justa like that?

JOE: Just like that!

FRANK: And what do you do with music?

JOE: Who says I'm married to music? I take a vacation—the notes won't run away!

FRANK: You're a mysterious kid. Where did you learn the fighting game?

JOE: These past two years, all over the city—in the gyms——

MR. BONAPARTE: Hey, Joe, you sounda like crazy! You no gotta nature for fight. You're musician. Whata you say, heh? Whata you do?

JOE: Let's call it a day.

MR. BONAPARTE: Isa no true whata I say?——

JOE: That's all for tonight. *(His lips tightened, he abruptly exists.)*

MR. BONAPARTE *(calling after him):* Take a gooda sleep, Joe.

FRANK *(smiling):* It looks like the gold bug has visited our house.

CARP *(sadly):* Fortunes! I used to hear it in my youth—the streets of America is paved with gold. Say, you forgot to give him the present.

MR. BONAPARTE *(slowly, puzzled):* I don'ta know . . . he say he gonna fight. . . .

Slow Fadeout

SCENE III

Two months later; MOODY'S *office as seen before.*

MOODY *is pacing back and forth in one of his fuming moods. Those present include* LORNA, *stretched out on the couch, blowing cigarette smoke into the air;* TOKIO *sitting quietly on the window sill; and* ROXY GOTTLIEB, *comfortably spread out in the desk chair, wearing a big white panama hat which he seldom removes.*

ROXY: They don't like him. They seen him in five fights already. He's a clever boy, that Bonaparte, and speedy—but he's first-class lousy in the shipping department! I bought a piece of him, so I got a right to say it: a mosquito gives out better! Did you read what he wrote in his column, that Drake? He writes he's a regular "brain trust."

LORNA: What's wrong with that?

ROXY: I'll tell you in a capsule: the people who'll pay to watch a "brain trust" you could fit in a telephone booth! Roxy Gottlieb is telling you!

MOODY: Roxy's right. Joe pulls his punches. Two months already and he don't throw his hands right and he don't throw them enough.

LORNA: Tom, what do you want the boy to do? You surely know by now he's not a slugger. His main asset is his science—he's a student.

ROXY *(loftily):* Excuse me, Miss Moon. In the prizefight ring the cash customer don't look for stoodents. Einstein lives in a college—a wonderful man in *his* line! Also, while I think of it, a woman's place is in the hay, not in the office!

MOODY *(indignantly):* Where do you come off to make a remark like that?

LORNA *(standing up):* At the moment a woman's place is in the bar—see you later. *(She looks at the others with a peculiar smile and exits.* MOODY *stares at* ROXY *who realizes he has said the wrong thing.)*

MOODY: I'm worried about that boy!

TOKIO: I'd trust him, Tom. Joe knows his own needs, as he says. Don't ask him to change his style. A style is best when it's individual, when it comes out of the inner personality and the lay of the muscles and the set of the bones. That boy stands a chance to make the best lightweight since Benny Simon.

ROXY: On *your* nose!

TOKIO: He's got one of the best defenses I ever seen. And speedy as the wind.

MOODY: But he won't fight!

MOODY: A momma doll gives out better!

TOKIO: He's a peculiar duck—I want him thinking he's the best thing in shoe leather.

MOODY: He thinks so now.

TOKIO: I don't like to contradict you, Tom, but he don't. It's seventy-five percent front. If you want the goods delivered you have to treat him delicate, gentle—like a girl.

ROXY: Like a girl? Why didn't you say so before?

MOODY: No, Roxy, not you—you just treat him like a human being.

TOKIO: I think we can begin the build-up now.

MOODY: A road tour?

TOKIO: I'd like to take him around the Middle West, about fifteen bouts.

ROXY *(answering a look from* MOODY): I didn't say no. But will he cooperate?

TOKIO: As soon as I find the password.

MOODY: What's the password to make this kid go in and slug—that's the problem. *(There is a knock at the door.* MOODY *calls.)* Yes? *(The door opens and* MR. BONAPARTE *stands there hesitantly.)*

MR. BONAPARTE *(timidly):* My name is Joe Bonaparte's father. I come-a to see my son's new friends.

MOODY *(expansively):* Come in, sit down, Mr. Bonaparte.

ROXY *(sitting comfortably):* Take a seat.

MR. BONAPARTE: Am I interrupt?

MOODY: Not at all.

ROXY: What's the matter with your boy?

TOKIO *(to* MR. BONAPARTE): This is Mr. Moody and Mr. Gottlieb.

MR. BONAPARTE *(sitting):* Good afternoon.

MOODY: We were just discussing your son.

MR. BONAPARTE: I please to hear. I like find out froma you how's this boxer business for Joe. Whata good in it for him.

MOODY: Your Joe's a very clever fighter.

ROXY: Can you take it? We want to make your boy famous—a millionaire, but he won't let us—won't cooperate. How do you like it?

MR. BONAPARTE: Why? Whatta he do?

ROXY (going over and facing the old man in a lecturing position): I'll ask *you*. What does he do? What does he do that's right? *Nothing!* We offer him on a gold platter! Wine, women and song, to make a figure of speech. We offer him *magnitudes!* . . .

MR. BONAPARTE (waiting): Yes——?

MOODY: But he won't fight.

MR. BONAPARTE (puzzled): He'sa fighta for you, no?

ROXY: You're right—no! Your boy's got unexplored possibilities— *unexplored!* But you can't make a purse out of somebody's ear.

MOODY (trying to counteract ROXY'S volubility): My colleague is trying to say that Joe keeps holding back in the ring.

MR. BONAPARTE: Holda back?

TOKIO: He nurses his self——

MOODY: He keeps holding back——

TOKIO: His defense is brilliant——

MOODY: Gorgeous——!

ROXY: But where's the offense? You take but you can't give. Figure it out—where would you be in a traffic jam? You know how to reverse—but to shift in second or high?—nothing!

MR. BONAPARTE (quietly to ROXY): Hey, you talka too much—nobody's contradicta you.

ROXY (after a momentary setback): "Everybody'sa contradicta me!" Even you, and I never met you before. (With a reproachful glance he retires to the desk where he sits and sulks.)

MR. BONAPARTE (singling out TOKIO as a man to whom he can speak): Who are you?

TOKIO: Your son's trainer. . . .

MR. BONAPARTE: You interest to helpa my boy?

TOKIO (respectfully): Very much. . . .

MR. BONAPARTE: Me too. Maybe not so as plan by these-a gentleman here. I don't say price fight'sa no good for Joe. Joe like-a to be fame, not feel ashame. . . .

TOKIO: Is Joe afraid of his hands?

MR. BONAPARTE: I don't know. You tella me what'sa what . . . I don't know price fight. His hand coulda get hurt?

MOODY: Every fighter hurts his hands. Sometimes they break——

TOKIO: They heal up in no time.

ROXY *(flaring out):* What's so special about hands? I suppose your kid plays piano!

MR. BONAPARTE: Coulda get hurt? Coulda break?!

ROXY: So what?

MR. BONAPARTE *(up on his feet):* Hey, you! I don't like-a you! You no interest in my boy! *(Proudly.)* My boy'sa besta violin' in New York!

MOODY *(suddenly sickened):* What . . . ?

MR. BONAPARTE: Yes, play the violin!

MOODY: That's it! . . .

ROXY *(anguished by this stupidity):* If I had hair I'd tear it out! Five hundred fiddlers stand on Broadway and 48th Street, on the corner, every day, rain or shine, hot or cold. And your boy dares——! *(Turning to* MOODY.) How do you like it? *(He waves his hands in despair and retires to the desk, where he sits in fuming disgusted silence.)*

MOODY *(repressing a feeling of triumph):* Your boy's afraid of his hands because he fiddles?

MR. BONAPARTE: Yes, musta be!

TOKIO: Why did you come and tell us this?

MR. BONAPARTE: Because I like-a to help my boy. I like-a for him to try himself out. Maybe thisa better business for him. Maybe not. He mus' try to find out, to see whata he want . . . I don't know. Don't help Joe to tell him I come here. Don't say it. *(He slowly walks to the door.)*

MOODY: That means you won't stand in his way?

MR. BONAPARTE: My boy coulda break his hand? Gentleman, I'ma not so happy as you . . . no! *(He slowly exits.)*

MOODY *(joyously):* I'm beginning to see the light! Joe's mind ain't made up that the fist is mightier than the fiddle.

ROXY *(bouncing up and down):* I'll make up his mind. For the money that's involved I'd make Niagara Falls turn around and go back to Canada.

TOKIO: Don't try to bully him into anything.

ROXY: In Roxy Gottlieb he met his match.

MOODY *(explosively):* What the hell's the matter with you, Roxy! Sit down a minute! *(*ROXY *sits.)* As I see it, the job is to handle him gently, to make him see how much we prize him—to kill his doubts with goodness.

ROXY: I got it: the password is honey! . . .

MOODY: Right! The Middle West tour is on! Tokio goes along to build up a real offensive. I take care of the newspapers here. Chris', I thought it was something serious! I'm getting to feel like 1928 again. Call it intuition: I feel like the Resurrection. *(He gets up and begins to stroll about.)* Once we're out of the tunnel, with thirty bouts behind us——

ROXY: If you hear a noise, it's my mouth watering——*(The telephone rings.* MOODY *answers.)*

MOODY: Hello? . . . Yeah . . . I think he'll win——*(Hangs up.)* Who do you think that was? *(Imitating.)* "Fuseli is speaking." Eddie Fuseli!

ROXY: Fuseli? What's he want?

MOODY: Will Joe win against Vincenti Tuesday. Tokio, from now on it's your job.

TOKIO: I got faith in the boy.

MOODY *(to* ROXY): I have to ask one thing—when Joe comes over from the gym let me do the talking.

TOKIO: And don't mention music! (LORNA *enters).*

LORNA: Shh! Here's Joe. (JOE BONAPARTE *enters the office. Immediately* MOODY *and* ROXY *put on their softest kid gloves. Their methods of salesmanship will shortly become so apparent that both* JOE *and* LORNA *become suspicious.)*

MOODY *(slowly circling around):* Glad to see you, Joe. Joe, you remember in reference to what we were speaking about yesterday? Well . . . we had several friends on the long distance phone. We're booking fifteen out of town bouts for you. Tough ones, too.

ROXY: Tonight I'm calling my Chicago connections.

MOODY: We talked it over with Tokio and he says—well, tell him what you said, Tokio—tell him the truth.

TOKIO: I think you got a wonderful future.

MOODY *(to* TOKIO): Name the names, Tokio.

TOKIO: Well, I said Benny Simon—as good as Simon, I said.

MOODY: Tokio's gonna work with you—help you develop a right——

ROXY: And a left! What'sa right without a left?

MOODY: Tokio thinks that when he brings you back you'll be a contender for Number One.

JOE *(a little defensively):* Really? . . .

MOODY: But *you* have to help *us* help *you.*

ROXY: Could Webster say it better?

MOODY *(softly singing a siren song, his arms around* JOE'S *shoulder):* This job needs gorgeous concentration. All your time and thoughts, Joe. No side lines, no side interests——

JOE *(defensively):* I don't go out with girls.

MOODY: You're in the fighting game. It's like being a priest—your work comes first. What would you rather do than fight?

JOE *(defensively):* I don't know what you mean.

MOODY *(carefully picking his words):* Some boys, for instance, like to save their looks. They'd practically throw the fight to keep their nose intact.

JOE *(smiling wryly):* My looks don't interest me. (LORNA *is listening with rapt attention.)*

MOODY *(still singing the siren song):* Then what's holding you back, Joe? You can tell me, Joe. We've set up housekeeping together, Joe, and I want you to tell me if you can't cook a steak—it don't matter. We're married anyway. . . .

JOE *(uneasily):* Who's being put to bed?

MOODY: What do you mean?

JOE: I don't like this seduction scene. *(To* TOKIO.) What are they after?

TOKIO: They think you're afraid of your hands.

MOODY: Are you?

JOE: Half . . .

TOKIO: Why?

ROXY *(bouncing up):* Tell the truth!

JOE: What truth?

MOODY *(holding back* ROXY *with a look):* Are you afraid your hands'll bust, Joe? (JOE *remains silent.)* What's a busted hand to a *fighter?* You can't go in and do your best if you're scared of your mitts . . . can you? You tell me. . . .

JOE: No. . . .

MOODY: Whyn't you give up outside ideas, Joe?

ROXY *(suddenly, in a loud voice to* TOKIO): You shoulda seen that bunch of musicians on 48th Street before. Fiddlers, drummers, cornetists—not a dime in a car-load. Bums in the park! Oh, excuse me, Tom, I was just telling Tokio——(JOE *is now aware that the others know of the violin. Now he is completely closed to them.* MOODY *sees this. He says to* ROXY:)

MOODY (*wrathfully*): What would you like to say, my fine-feathered friend?

ROXY (*simulating bewilderment*): What's the matter? What happened? (*Receiving no answer, he looks around several times and adds, with a shrug:*) I think I'll run across the street and pick up an eight-cylinder lunch.

MOODY: Sprinkle it with arsenic. Do that for me, for me, sweetheart!!

ROXY (*hurt*): That's a fine remark from a friend. (*He haughtily exits.*)

JOE: What do you want, Mr. Moody?

MOODY: At the moment, nothing. I'm puffed out. See you tomorrow over the gym.

JOE: Maybe I won't be there. I might give up fighting as a bad job. I'm not over-convinced it's what I want. I can do other things. . . .

TOKIO: I'll see you tomorrow at the gym, Joe. (JOE *looks at both the men, says nothing, exits.*) That Mr. Gottlieb is a case. See you later.

MOODY (*not looking up*): Okay. (TOKIO *exits.* LORNA *and* MOODY *are alone. She blows cigarette smoke to the ceiling.* MOODY *puts his feet up on the desk and leans back wearily. Snorting through his nostrils*): The password is honey!

LORNA: What was that all about? (*The telephone rings.*)

MOODY (*of the ringing bell*): If that's for me, tear it up. I ain't in, not even for God.

LORNA (*answering*): Hello? . . . (*Putting her hand on the mouthpiece.*) It's Mrs. God—your wife. (MOODY *makes a grimace of distaste but picks up the phone and puts on a sweet voice.*)

MOODY: Yes, Monica darling. . . . Yeah . . . you and your support. . . . You're gonna fifty-buck me to death! . . . Monica, if I had fifty bucks I'd buy myself a big juicy coffin—what?—so throw me in jail. (*He hangs up the phone.*) Bitch! That'll be time number three. She means it too.

LORNA: What was that scene with Bonaparte?

MOODY: Sweetheart, the jig is up! Believe it or not, Bonaparte's a violinist. Maybe he was on the radio. I don't know what the hell he was. His old man came here and told us. His mitts are on his mind. You can't do a thing with a nut like that.

LORNA: Won't he give up the violin?

MOODY: You heard him stalling. This is the end, Lorna. It's our last chance for a decent life, for getting married—we have to make that kid fight! He's *more* than a meal ticket—he's everything we want and need from life! (LORNA *goes over and slaps him on the back.*)

LORNA: Pick up your chin, little man.

MOODY: Don't Brisbane me, Lorna. I'm licked. I'm tired. Find me a mouse hole to crawl in. . . .

LORNA: Why don't you ask me when you want something? You got the brains of a flea. Do you want Bonaparte to fight?

MOODY: Do I wanna see tomorrow?

LORNA: I'll make him fight.

MOODY: How?

LORNA: How? . . . I'm "a tramp from Newark," Tom. . . . I know a dozen ways. . . .

Slow Fadeout

SCENE IV

A few nights later.

JOE *and* LORNA *sit on a bench in the park. It is night. There is carousel music in the distance. Cars ride by in front of the boy and girl in the late spring night. Out of sight a traffic light changes from red to green and back again throughout the scene and casts its colors on the faces of the boy and girl.*

LORNA: Success and fame! Or just a lousy living. You're lucky you won't have to worry about those things. . . .

JOE: Won't I?

LORNA: Unless Tom Moody's a liar.

JOE: You like him, don't you?

LORNA *(after a pause):* I like him.

JOE: I like how you dress. The girls look nice in the summer time. Did you ever stand at the Fifth Avenue Library and watch those girls go by?

LORNA: No, I never did. *(Switching the subject.)* That's the carousel, that music. Did you ever ride on one of those?

JOE: That's for kids.

LORNA: Weren't you ever a kid, for God's sake?

JOE: Not a happy kid.

LORNA: Why?

JOE: Well, I always felt different. Even my name was special—Bonaparte—and my eyes . . .

LORNA: I wouldn't have taken that too serious. . . . *(There is a silent pause.* JOE *looks straight ahead.)*

JOE: Gee, all those cars . . .

LORNA: Lots of horses trot around here. The rich know how to live. You'll be rich. . . .

JOE: My brother Frank is an organizer for the C.I.O.

LORNA: What's that?

JOE: If you worked in a factory you'd know. Did you ever work?

LORNA *(with a smile):* No, when I came out of the cocoon I was a butterfly and butterflies don't work.

JOE: All those cars . . . whizz, whizz. *(Now turning less casual.)* Where's Mr. Moody tonight?

LORNA: He goes up to see his kid on Tuesday nights. It's a sick kid, a girl. His wife leaves it at her mother's house.

JOE: That leaves you free, don't it?

LORNA: What are you hinting at?

JOE: I'm thinking about you and Mr. Moody.

LORNA: Why think about it? I don't. Why should you?

JOE: If you belonged to me I wouldn't think about it.

LORNA: Haven't you got a girl?

JOE: No.

LORNA: Why not?

JOE *(evasively):* Oh . . .

LORNA: Tokio says you're going far in the fighting game.

JOE: Music means more to me. May I tell you something?

LORNA: Of course.

JOE: If you laugh I'll never speak to you again.

LORNA: I'm not the laughing type.

JOE: With music I'm never alone when I'm alone——Playing music . . . that's like saying, "I am man. I belong here. How do you do, World—good evening!" When I play music nothing is closed to me. I'm not afraid of people and what they say. There's no war in music. It's not like the streets. Does this sound funny?

LORNA: No.

JOE: But when you leave your room . . . down in the street . . . it's war! Music can't help me there. Understand?

LORNA: Yes.

JOE: People have hurt my feelings for years. I never forget. You can't get even with people by playing the fiddle. If music shot bullets I'd like it better—artists and people like that are freaks today. The world moves fast and they sit around like forgotten dopes.

LORNA: You're loaded with fireworks. Why don't you fight?

JOE: You have to be what you are——!

LORNA: Fight! see what happens——

JOE: Or end up in the bughouse!

LORNA: God's teeth! Who says you have to be one thing?

JOE: My nature isn't fighting!

LORNA: Don't Tokio know what he's talking about? Don't Tom? Joe, listen: be a fighter! Show the world! If you made your fame and fortune—and you can—you'd be anything you want. Do it! Bang your way to the lightweight crown. Get a bank account. Hire a great doctor with a beard—get your eyes fixed——

JOE: What's the matter with my eyes?

LORNA: Excuse me, I stand corrected. *(After a pause.)* You get mad all the time.

JOE: That's from thinking about myself.

LORNA: How old are you, Joe?

JOE: Twenty-one and a half, and the months are going fast.

LORNA: You're very smart for twenty-one and a half "and the months are going fast."

JOE: Why not? I read every page of the Encyclopaedia Britannica. My father's friend, Mr. Carp, has it. A shrimp with glasses had to do something.

LORNA: I'd like to meet your father. Your mother dead?

JOE: Yes.

LORNA: So is mine.

JOE: Where do you come from? The city is full of girls who look as if they never had parents.

LORNA: I'm a girl from over the river. My father is still alive—shucking oysters and bumming drinks somewhere in the wilds of Jersey. I'll tell you a secret: I don't like you.

JOE *(surprised):* Why?

LORNA: You're too sufficient by yourself . . . too inside yourself.

JOE: You like it or you don't.

LORNA: You're on an island——

JOE: Robinson Crusoe . . .

LORNA: That's right—"me, myself, and I." Why not come out and see the world?

JOE: Does it seem that way?

LORNA: Can't you see yourself?

JOE: No. . . .

LORNA: Take a bird's-eye view; you don't know what's right or wrong. You don't know what to pick, but you won't admit it.

JOE: Do you?

LORNA: Leave me out. This is the anatomy of Joe Bonaparte.

JOE: You're dancing on my nose, huh?

LORNA: Shall I stop?

JOE: No.

LORNA: You're a miserable creature. You want your arm in *gelt* up to the elbow. You'll take fame so people won't laugh or scorn your face. You'd give your soul for those things. But every time you turn your back your little soul kicks you in the teeth. It don't give in so easy.

JOE: And what does your soul do in its perfumed vanity case?

LORNA: Forget about me.

JOE: Don't you want——?

LORNA *(suddenly nasty):* I told you to forget it!

JOE *(quietly):* Moody sent you after me—a decoy! You made a mistake, Lorna, for two reasons. I make up my own mind to fight. Point two, he doesn't know you don't love him——

LORNA: You're a fresh kid.

JOE: In fact he doesn't know anything about you at all.

LORNA *(challengingly):* But you do?

JOE: This is the anatomy of Lorna Moon: she's a lost baby. She doesn't know what's right or wrong. She's a miserable creature who never knew what to pick. But she'd never admit it. And I'll tell you why you picked Moody!

LORNA: You don't know what you're talking about.

JOE: Go home, Lorna. If you stay, I'll know something about you. . . .

LORNA: You don't know anything.

JOE: Now's your chance—go home!

LORNA: Tom loves me.

JOE *(after a long silence, looking ahead):* I'm going to buy a car.

LORNA: They make wonderful cars today. Even the lizzies——

JOE: Gary Cooper's got the kind I want. I saw it in the paper, but it costs too much—fourteen thousand. If I found one second-hand——

LORNA: And if you had the cash——

JOE: I'll get it——

LORNA: Sure, if you'd go in and really fight!

JOE *(in a sudden burst):* Tell your Mr. Moody I'll dazzle the eyes out of his head!

LORNA: You mean it?

JOE *(looking out ahead):* Those cars are poison in my blood. When you sit in a car and speed you're looking down at the world. Speed, speed, everything is speed—nobody gets me!

LORNA: You mean in the ring?

JOE: In or out, nobody gets me! Gee, I like to stroke that gas!

LORNA: You sound like Jack the Ripper.

JOE *(standing up suddenly):* I'll walk you back to your house—your hotel, I mean. (LORNA *stands.* JOE *continues.*) Do you have the same room?

LORNA *(with sneaking admiration):* You're a fresh kid!

JOE: When you're lying in his arms tonight, tell him, for me, that the next World's Champ is feeding in his stable.

LORNA: Did you really read those Britannia books?

JOE: From A to Z.

LORNA: And you're only twenty-one?

JOE: And a half.

LORNA: Something's wrong somewhere.

JOE: I know. . . . *(They slowly walk out as)*

Fadeout

SCENE V

The next week.

It is near midnight in the dining room of the Bonaparte home. An open suitcase rests on the table. SIGGIE *is pouring samples of wine for* LORNA MOON. *He himself drinks appreciatively. To one side sits* MR. BONAPARTE *silently, thoughtfully, watchfully—pretending to read the newspaper.*

SIGGIE: I was fit to be knocked down with a feather when I heard it. I couldn't believe it until I seen him fight over at the Keystone last week. You never know what somebody's got in him—like the man with germs—suddenly he's down in bed with a crisis! (JOE *enters with an armful of clothes which he begins to pack in the suitcase.*)

LORNA: Joe's road tour will do him lots of good. (ANNA *enters and takes off an apron. Silence, in which* SIGGIE *and* LORNA *sip their wine.)*

ANNA: How do you like that wine, Miss Moon? My father makes better wine than any Eyetalian in New York. My father knows everything—don't you, poppa? *(With a faint smile,* MR. BONA-PARTE *shrugs his shoulders.)*

SIGGIE: We're thinking of sending the old man to a leper colony. . . .

ANNA: Don't my husband say funny things? Tell her what you told the janitor Tuesday, Siggie.

SIGGIE: Never mind, never mind.

ANNA: You know how I met Siggie? He was a United Cigar Store clerk and I walked in for a pack of Camels and the first thing you know he said something funny. It was raw, so I can't say it. He had me laughing from the first. Seven years and I haven't stopped laughing yet. *(She laughs loudly, pleasurably.)* This will be the first time Joe ever went traveling. Was you ever out of New York, Miss Moon?

LORNA: Oh, many times.

ANNA: That's nice. Far?

LORNA: California, Detroit, Chicago. I was an airplane hostess for two months.

ANNA: That's nice—it's a real adventure. I'd like to fly.

SIGGIE: Stay on the ground! Fly! What for? Who do you know up there? Eagles?

ANNA: It must be a wonderful way to see life.

LORNA *(drinking):* I've seen life in all its aspects. (MR. BONAPARTE *stands up with a smile.* LORNA'S *eyes follow him as he exits. To* JOE): I think your father left because he don't like me.

JOE: He likes you.

ANNA: My father likes everybody. He's a very deep man. My father has more friends than any man alive. But best of all he likes his horse, Dolly, who drives the fruit wagon. My father can't sit still on Sunday afternoon—he has to go see what that horse is doing. *(Her eyes catch sight of the suitcase.)* Joe, you don't know how to pack. *(She starts over to assist him.)*

SIGGIE *(querulously):* Rest the feet awhile, Duchess.

ANNA *(explaining her move):* He don't know how to pack. *(Beginning to rearrange the suitcase.* MR. BONAPARTE *returns and hands* JOE *a sweater.)*

MR. BONAPARTE: You forget your good sweater.

JOE: Thanks. (MR. BONAPARTE *sits.* JOE *looks at him sideways.*)

ANNA: When you get out to Chicago, buy yourself some new under-wear, Joe. I hear everything's cheaper in Chicago. Is that right, Miss Moon?

LORNA *(after taking another drink):* Chicago? I don't know. I was there only one night—I got news that night my mother died. As a matter of fact, she killed herself.

ANNA: That's very sad.

LORNA: No, my father's an old drunk son-of-a-bitch. Did you ask me about my father?

MR. BONAPARTE *(who has been listening intently):* Yes. . . .

LORNA: Twice a week he kicked my mother's face in. If I let myself go I'd be a drunkard in a year.

ANNA: My father never said one bad word to my mother in her whole lifetime. And she was a big nuisance right up till the day she died. She was more like me, more on the stout side. Take care of your health, Joe, when you're out there. What's better than health?

LORNA *(turning to* MR. BONAPARTE, *with whom she is self-conscious):* The question is, do you like me or do you not?

MR. BONAPARTE *(with a faint smile):* Yes. . . .

LORNA: Your family is very cute——Now do you like me?

MR. BONAPARTE: Yes. . . .

LORNA: Why do you look at me that way?

MR. BONAPARTE: I don't look special. You gonna travel on those train with my son?

LORNA: God's teeth, no! I'm a friend of his manager's, that's all. And a friend of Joe's, too.

MR. BONAPARTE: You are in favor for my son to prizefight? (JOE *looks at his father sideways and exits.*)

LORNA: Certainly. Aren't you?

MR. BONAPARTE: Joe has a dream many year to be superior violin'. Was it boyhood thing? Was it real? Or is this real now? Those are-a my question, Miss Moon. Maybe you are friend to my son. Then I aska you, look out for him. Study him. Help him find what'sa right. Tell me, Miss Moon, when you find out. Help Joe find truthful success. Will you do it for me?

LORNA: I'll be glad to keep my eye on him. (JOE *enters with slippers, which he puts in bag.*)

ANNA *(to* JOE): You could stand some new shirts, too.

SIGGIE: Listen, pop, I'm a natural man and I don't like wise guys. Joe went in the boxing game 'cause he's ashamed to be poor. That's his way to enter a little enterprise. All other remarks are so much alfalfa! (JOE *locks the bag.*)

ANNA *(taking the wine glass from* SIGGIE's *hand):* Drunk as a horse fly!

JOE: It's getting late and the train won't wait.

SIGGIE *(standing up):* My god is success. Need I say more? I'm prouda you, Joe. Come home a champ. Make enough dough to buy your sister's boy friend a new cab. Yes, boys and girls, I'm looking in that old crystal ball and I see strange and wonderful events! Yazoo!

ANNA *(giggling):* Drunk as a horse fly!

JOE *(to* SIGGIE): You can't drive us down to the station in this condition.

SIGGIE: What condition?

ANNA: You're drunk, stupid.

SIGGIE: Shut the face, foolish! Just because I don't hold in my nerves she thinks I'm drunk. If you hold in your nerves you get ulcers. *(To* JOE.) Get your "chapow" and let's go. Or don't you want me to drive you down?

JOE: No.

SIGGIE: I should worry—my cab's in the garage anyway! *(Suddenly he sits.)*

JOE: We'd better start. . . .

LORNA *(to* MR. BONAPARTE): I'd like to have another talk with you some time.

MR. BONAPARTE: Come any time in the evening. You are a very lovely girl. (MR. CARP *stands in the doorway.)* Here is Mr. Carp to say good-bye.

SIGGIE: Come in, my little prince.

CARP *(coming in and shaking hands with* JOE): I wish you good luck in every undertaking.

JOE *(uneasily, because his father is looking at him):* Thanks.

MR. BONAPARTE *(introducing* CARP): Miss Moon, my neighbor, Mr. Carp.

CARP: A pleasure to meet you.

LORNA: Hello. (MR. BONAPARTE *brings the violin case from its hiding place in the buffet.)*

MR. BONAPARTE: Joe, I buy you this some time ago. Don't give cause I don't know whatta you gonna do. Take him with you now. Play for yourself. It gonna remember you your old days of musical life. (JOE *puts down the suitcase and picks up the violin. He plucks the strings, he tightens one of them. In spite of the tension his face turns soft and tender.)*

LORNA: *(watching intently):* We better not miss the train—Tokio's waiting.

MR. BONAPARTE *(of violin):* Take him with you, Joe.

JOE: It's beautiful. . . .

MR. BONAPARTE: Practise on the road. (JOE *abruptly turns and with the violin exits. The others listen, each standing in his place, as rich violin music comes from the other room.* JOE *returns. There is silence as he places the violin on the table in front of his father.)*

JOE *(in a low voice):* Return it, poppa.

ANNA *(hugging* JOE): Have a good trip, Joey.

CARP: Eat in good restaurants. . . . *(There is silence: the* FATHER *and* SON *look at each other. The others in the room sense the drama between the two. Finally:)*

JOE: I have to do this, poppa.

MR. BONAPARTE *(to* JOE): Be careful fora your hands.

JOE: Poppa, give me the word——

MR. BONAPARTE: What word?

JOE: Give me the word to go ahead. You're looking at yesterday—I see tomorrow. Maybe you think I ought to spend my whole life here—you and Carp blowing off steam.

MR. BONAPARTE *(holding himself back):* Oh, Joe, shut your mouth!

JOE: Give me the word to go ahead!

MR. BONAPARTE: Be careful fora your hands!

JOE: I want you to give me the word!

MR. BONAPARTE *(crying out):* No! No word! You gonna fight? All right! Okay! But I don't gonna give no word! No!

JOE: That's how you feel?

MR. BONAPARTE: That'sa how I feel! (MR. BONAPARTE'S *voice breaks and there is nothing for father and son to do but to clutch each other in a hasty embrace. Finally* MR. BONAPARTE *disentangles himself and turns away.* JOE *abruptly grabs up his suitcase and exits.* LORNA *follows, stopping at the door to look back at* MR. BONAPARTE. *In the ensuing silence* ANNA *looks at her father and shakes her head.* SIGGIE *suddenly lumbers to his feet and sounds off like a chime.)*

SIGGIE: Gong gong gong gong!

ANNA: Gee, poppa . . .

SIGGIE: Come to bed, Anna. . . . Anna-banana . . . (SIGGIE *exits.*)

ANNA: Gee, poppa . . . *(She touches her father sympathetically.)*

MR. BONAPARTE *(without turning):* Gone to bed, Anna. . . . (ANNA *slowly exits.* MR. BONAPARTE *now slowly comes back to the table and looks down at the violin.)*

CARP *(seating himself slowly):* Come, my friend . . . we will have a nice talk on a cultural topic. *(Looking at the violin.)* You'll work around a number of years before you make it up, the price of that fiddle. . . . (MR. BONAPARTE *stands looking down at the violin.)*

CARP *(sadly):* Yes, my friend, what is man? As Schopenhauer says, and in the last analysis . . .

Slow Fadeout

ACT TWO

SCENE I

Six months later. Present in the corner of a gymnasium are ROXY, MOODY, LORNA *and* TOKIO. *They are looking off right, watching* JOE BONAPARTE *work out with a partner. From off right come the sounds of typical gym activities: the thud of boxing gloves, the rat-a-tat of the punching bag, and from time to time the general bell which is a signal for rest periods. Tacked on the tin walls are an ad for Everlast boxing equipment, boxing "card" placards, a soiled American flag, some faded exit signs.*

The group watches silently for several seconds after the lights fade in. A BOXER, *wiping his perspiring body with a towel, passes from left to right and looks back at* LORNA'S *legs. As* ROXY *watches, his head moves to and fro in the rhythm of* JOE'S *sparring off stage.* ROXY *nods his head in admiration.*

ROXY: Tokio. I gotta give the devil his dues: in the past six months you done a noble job!

TOKIO *(calling off):* With the left! A long left, Joe! . . .

LORNA *(looking off):* Joe's a very good-looking boy. I never quite noticed it before. *(The general bell sounds; the boxing din off stage stops.)*

MOODY *(rubbing his hands enthusiastically):* "Let it rain, let it pour! It ain't gonna rain where we're headed for!"

ROXY: I'm tickled to death to see the canary birds left his gloves.

TOKIO: He's the king of all he surveys.

MOODY: Boy, oh, boy, how he surprised them in the Bronx last night! . . . But one thing I can't explain—that knockout he took in Philly five weeks ago.

TOKIO: That night he was off his feed, Tom. Where do you see speed like that? That's style, real style—you can't tag him. And he's giving it with both hands.

MOODY: You don't have to sell me his virtues—I'm sold. Nevertheless, he got tagged in Philly.

TOKIO: Here's what happened there: we run into some man when we're leaving the hotel. Joe goes pale. I ask him what it is. "Nothing," he says. But I see for myself—a man with long hair and a violin case. When we turn the corner, he says, "He's after me," he says. As if it's cops and robbers! *(The general bell sounds; the fighting din begins again.)*

ROXY: A kidnapper?

LORNA: Don't be a fool. He was reminded . . .

ROXY: Speak when spoken to, Miss Moon!

MOODY *(moodily):* And when he got in the ring that night, he kept his hands in his pockets?

TOKIO: Yeah. I didn't mention this before—it's not important.

MOODY: But it's still a danger——

TOKIO: No. No.

MOODY: But anyway, we better get him away from his home. We can't afford no more possible bad showings at this stage of the game. No more apparitions, like suddenly a fiddle flies across the room on wings! *(The group again intently watches* JOE *off stage.)*

MOODY: Ooh! Did you see that? He's packing a real Sunday punch in that right. *(Calling off.)* Hit 'im, Joe, hit 'im! *(As an indistinct answer comes back.)* Ha, ha, looka that, hahaha . . . *(Now turning to* TOKIO.) What's your idea of a match with Lombardo?

TOKIO: Can you get it?

MOODY: Maybe.

TOKIO: Get it.

MOODY: Sure?

TOKIO: It's an easy win, on points at least. *(During the last few lines a thin dark man has entered. His dark hair is grayed at the temples, an inarticulate look in his face. He is* EDDIE FUSELI, *a renowned gambler and gunman.)*

EDDIE FUSELI *(approaching the group):* Hello.

ROXY *(nervously):* Hello, Eddie.

MOODY *(turning):* I haven't seen you for a dog's age, Fuseli.

EDDIE *(pointing off left):* You got this certain boy—Bonaparte. I like his looks. American born?

ROXY: Right from here.

EDDIE *(watching* JOE *off):* Like a cat, never off his position. He appeals to me. *(To* MOODY.) They call you the Brown Fox. What's your opinion of this boy?

MOODY *(coolly, on guard):* Possibilities. . . .

EDDIE *(to* TOKIO): What's your idea?

TOKIO: Tom said it.

EDDIE: Could he get on top?

MOODY *(as above):* I can't see that far ahead. I don't read palms.

EDDIE: Could I buy a piece?

MOODY: No.

EDDIE *(coolly):* Could I?

MOODY: No!

EDDIE *(with a certain tenderness):* I like a good fighter. I like to see you after, Tom. *(Of* LORNA.*)* This your girl?

LORNA *(pertly):* I'm my mother's girl.

EDDIE *(with a small mirthless laugh):* Ha ha—that's a hot one. *(He coolly drifts out of the scene on his cat's feet. The general bell sounds. The din ceases.)*

LORNA: What exhaust pipe did he crawl out of?

ROXY: I remember this Eddie Fuseli when he came back from the war with a gun. He's still got the gun and he still gives me goose pimples!

MOODY: That Fuseli's a black mark on my book. Every once in a while he shoots across my quiet existence like a roman candle!

LORNA: Sell or don't sell. But better be careful, that guy's tough. *(A* FIGHTER, *robed, hooded with towel, passes across: A* GAMBLING TYPE *passes in the opposite direction. Both look at* LORNA'S *legs.)*

MOODY: Give a rat like that a finger and you lose a hand before you know it!

TOKIO: Did you know Joe bought a car this morning?

ROXY: What kinda car?

TOKIO: A Deusenberg.

MOODY: One of those fancy speed wagons?

TOKIO *(agreeing):* It cost him five grand, second-hand.

MOODY *(flaring up):* Am I a step-child around here? I'm glad you tell me now, if only outa courtesy!

ROXY *(indignantly):* Whatta you keep a thing like that incognito for?

MOODY: He drives like a maniac! That time we drove to Long Beach? I almost lost my scalp! We can't let him drive around like that! Boy, he's getting a bushel of bad habits! We gotta be careful. *(The general bell sounds again; the fighting din stops.)*

MOODY: Here's the truth: our boy can be the champ in three easy lessons—Lombardo, Fulton, the Chocolate Drop. But we gotta be careful!

LORNA: Here he comes. (JOE *enters in bathrobe, taking off his head-gear, which* TOKIO *takes from him.*)

MOODY *(completely changing his tone):* You looked very good in there, Joe. You're going swell and I like it. I'd work more with that long left if I were you.

JOE: Yes, I was speaking to Tokio about that. I feel my form's improving. I like to work. I'm getting somewhere—I feel it better every day.

LORNA: Happy?

JOE *(looking at her intently):* Every day's Saturday!

ROXY *(officiously):* Say, what's this I hear you bought a Deusenberg?

JOE: What's your objection—I might have some fun?

ROXY: I got my wampum on you. I like to know your habits. Ain't I permitted? (JOE *is about to retort hotly when* MOODY *gently takes his arm in an attempt to soothe him.*)

MOODY: Wait a minute, Joe. After all we have your welfare at heart. And after all a Deusenberg can go one fifty per——(EDDIE FUSELI *appears above, unseen by the others. He listens.*)

JOE: Who'd want to drive that fast?

MOODY: And since we're vitally interested in your future——

JOE *(shaking off* MOODY'S *arm and saying what is really on his mind):* If you're vitally interested in my future, prove it! Get me some fights—fights with contenders, not with dumb-bunny club fighters. Get me some main bouts in the metropolitan area!——

MOODY *(losing his temper):* For a kid who got kayoed five weeks ago, your mouth is pretty big! *(The general bell sounds; the din begins.)*

JOE: That won't happen again! And how about some mention in the press? Twenty-six bouts—no one knows I'm alive. This isn't vacation for me—it's a profession! I'm staying more than a week. Match me up against real talent. You can't go too fast for me. Don't worry about autos!

MOODY: We can go too fast! You're not so good!

JOE *(with a boyish grin):* Look at the records! (JOE *abruptly exits.* TOKIO *follows him, first giving the others a glance.*)

MOODY: Boy, oh, boy, that kid's changing!

ROXY: He goes past my head like a cold wind from the river!

LORNA: But you're gettin' what you want—the contender for the crown!

MOODY: I wish I was sure.

ROXY: Frankenstein! (EDDIE FUSELI *saunters down to the others.*)

EDDIE: I thought it over, Tom. I like to get a piece of that boy.

MOODY (*angrily*): I thought it over, too—not for sale. In fact I had a visitation from Jehovah. He came down on the calm waters and He said, "Let there be unity in the ownership."

EDDIE (*with a dead face*): I had a visit, too. He come down in the bar and He ate a pretzel. And He says, "Eddie Fuseli, I like you to buy a piece!"

MOODY (*trying to delay the inevitable*): Why not see me in my office tomorrow?

EDDIE: It's a cheap office. I get depressed in that office.

MOODY (*finally*): I can't make any guarantees about the boy.

EDDIE: How do you mean it, Tom?

MOODY: I don't know what the hell he'll do in the next six months.

ROXY: Eddie, it's like flap-jacks—up and down—you don't know which side next!

EDDIE (*with his small mirthless laugh*): Ha ha, that's a good one. You oughta be on the radio.

MOODY: No, it's a fact——

ROXY: We had enough headaches already. He's got a father, but how!

EDDIE: Don't want him to fight?

ROXY: His father sits on the kid's head like a bird's nest! (ROXY *puts his hand on* EDDIE'S *arm.*)

EDDIE: Take your hand off. (ROXY *hastily withdraws.*) Let the boy decide. . . .

MOODY: If you buy in?

EDDIE: Let the boy decide.

MOODY: Sure! But if he says no——(*Before* MOODY *can finish* JOE *enters.* EDDIE *whirls around and faces* JOE, *getting his cue from the others. Curiously,* EDDIE *is almost embarrassed before* JOE. *The bell sounds; the din stops.*)

MOODY: Joe, this is Eddie Fuseli. He's a man around town——

EDDIE (*facing* JOE, *his back to the others*): With good connections——

MOODY: He wantsa buy a piece of you——

EDDIE (*whirling around*): I will tell him myself. (*Turning back to* JOE; *with quiet intense dignity.*) I'm Eyetalian too—Eyetalian born, but an American citizen. I like to buy a piece of you. I don't care for no profit. I could turn it back to—*you* could take my share. But I like a good fighter; I like a good boy who could win the crown. It's the in-ter-est of my life. It would be a proud thing for me when Bonaparte could win the crown like I think he can.

MOODY *(confidently)*: It's up to you, Joe, if he buys in.

EDDIE *(wooingly)*: Some managers can't give you what you need——

MOODY: Don't say that!

EDDIE: *Some* managers can't! I'll see you get good bouts . . . also press notices . . . I know how. You're a boy who needs that. You decide . . . *(There is a pause; JOE's eyes flit from LORNA to the others and back to EDDIE.)*

JOE: Not my half.

EDDIE: Not your half.

JOE: As long as Mr. Fuseli doesn't mix in my private life . . . cut it up any way you like. Excuse me, I got a date with Miss Deusenberg. *(The others silently watch JOE exit.)*

EDDIE: A date with who?

MOODY *(snorting)*: Miss Deusenberg!

ROXY: An automobile. It gives you an idea what a boy—"Miss Deusenberg"!

EDDIE: How do you like it, Tom? Big bills or little bills?

MOODY: Don't think you're buying in for an apple and an egg.

EDDIE: Take big bills—they're new, they feel good. See you in that office tomorrow. *(The bell clangs off stage. EDDIE starts off, but abruptly turns and faces ROXY whom he inwardly terrifies.)*

EDDIE: It's a trick you don't know, Roxy: when a bird sits on your head and interferes with the championship, you shoot him off. All kinds of birds. You be surprised how fast they fall on the ground. Which is my intention in this syndicate. *(He smiles thinly and then moves out of the scene like a cat.)*

MOODY: I don't like that!

ROXY: I'm not so happy myself at the present time. How do you like it with our boy for gratitude? He leaves us here standing in our brevities!

LORNA: What makes you think you're worthy of gratitude?

MOODY *(to LORNA)*: For Pete's sake, pipe down! Are you with us or against us?

ROXY *(haughtily, to MOODY)*: Take my advice, Tom. Marry her and the first year give her a baby. Then she'll sit in the corner and get fat and sleepy, and not have such a big mouth! Uncle Roxy's telling you!

LORNA *(to* ROXY): Couldn't you keep quiet about the father to that gunman? Go home and let your wife give *you* a baby!

ROXY: A woman shouldn't interfere——

MOODY: Peace, for chri' sake, peace! Lorna, we're in a bad spot with Joe. He's getting hard to manage and this is the time when everything's gotta be right. I'm seeing Lombardo's manager tomorrow! Now that gunman's on my tail. You have to help me. You and I wanna do it like the story books, "happy ever after"? Then help me.

LORNA: How?

MOODY: Go after the boy. Keep him away from his folks. Get him away from the buggies——

LORNA: How?

MOODY *(impatiently):* You know how.

ROXY: Now you're talking.

LORNA *(pointing to* ROXY): You mean the way I see it on his face?

MOODY: For crying out loud! Where do you come off to make a remark like that?

LORNA: You expect me to sleep with that boy?

MOODY: I could tear your ears off for a remark like that!

ROXY *(discreetly):* I think I'll go grab a corn-beef sandwich. *(He exits.)*

MOODY *(after silence):* Are you mad?

LORNA *(tight-lipped):* No.

MOODY *(seductively):* I'm not a bad guy, Lorna. I don't mean anything bad. . . . All right, I'm crude—sometimes I'm worried and I'm crude. *(The bell clangs; the boxing din stops.)* But what the hell, my heart's in the right place. . . . *(Coming behind her and putting his arms around her as she looks ahead.)* Lorna, don't we both want that sun to come up and shine on us? Don't we? Before you know it the summer'll be here. Then it's the winter again, and it's another year again . . . and we're not married yet. See? . . . See what I mean? . . .

LORNA *(quietly):* Yes. . . .

MOODY *(beaming, but with uncertainty):* That sounds like the girl I used to know.

LORNA: I see what you mean. . . .

MOODY *(worried underneath):* You're not still mad?

LORNA *(briefly):* I'm not mad. *(But she abruptly cuts out of the scene, leaving* MOODY *standing there.)*

MOODY *(shaking his head):* Boy, I still don't know anything about women! . . .

Medium Fadeout

SCENE II

A *few nights later.* LORNA *and* JOE *sit on the same park bench.*

JOE: Some nights I wake up—my heart's beating a mile a minute! Before I open my eyes I know what it is—the feeling that some-one's standing at my bed. Then I open my eyes . . . it's gone—ran away!

LORNA: Maybe it's that old fiddle of yours.

JOE: Lorna, maybe it's you. . . .

LORNA: Don't you ever think of it any more—music?

JOE: What're you trying to remind me of? A kid with a Buster Brown collar and a violin case tucked under his arm? Does that sound appetizing to you?

LORNA: Not when you say it that way. You said it different once. . . .

JOE: What's on your mind, Lorna?

LORNA: What's on yours?

JOE *(simply):* You. . . . You're real for me—the way music was real.

LORNA: You've got your car, your career—what do you want with me?

JOE: I develop the ability to knock down anyone my weight. But what point have I made? Don't you think I know that? I went off to the wars 'cause someone called me a name—because I wanted to be two other guys. Now it's happening. . . . I'm not sure I like it.

LORNA: Moody's against that car of yours.

JOE: I'm against Moody, so we're even.

LORNA: Why don't you like him?

JOE: He's a manager! He treats me like a possession! I'm just a little silver mine for him—he bangs me around with a shovel!

LORNA: He's helped you——

JOE: No, Tokio's helped me. Why don't you give him up? It's terrible to have just a Tuesday-night girl. Why don't you belong to me every night in the week? Why don't you teach me love? . . . Or am I being a fool?

LORNA: You're not a fool, Joe.

JOE: I want you to be my family, my life——Why don't you do it, Lorna, why?

LORNA: He loves me.

JOE: I love you!

LORNA *(treading delicately)*: Well . . . Anyway, the early bird got the worm. Anyway, I can't give him anguish. I . . . I know what it's like. You shouldn't kick Moody around. He's poor compared to you. You're alive, you've got yourself—I can't feel sorry for you!

JOE: But you don't love him!

LORNA: I'm not much interested in myself. But the thing I like best about you . . . you still feel like a flop. It's mysterious, Joe. It makes me put my hand out. *(She gives him her hand and he grasps it.)*

JOE: I feel very close to you, Lorna.

LORNA: I know. . . .

JOE: And you feel close to me. But you're afraid——

LORNA: Of what?

JOE: To take a chance! Lorna darling, you won't let me wake you up! I feel it all the time—you're half dead, and you don't know it!

LORNA *(half smiling)*: Maybe I do. . . .

JOE: Don't smile—don't be hard-boiled!

LORNA *(sincerely)*: I'm not.

JOE: Don't you trust me?

LORNA *(evasively)*: Why start what we can't finish?

JOE *(fiercely)*: Oh, Lorna, deep as my voice will reach—*listen!!* Why can't you leave him? Why?

LORNA: Don't pull my dress off—I hear you.

JOE: Why?

LORNA: Because he needs me and you don't——

JOE: That's not true!

LORNA: Because he's a desperate guy who always starts out with two strikes against him. Because he's a kid at forty-two and you're a man at twenty-two.

JOE: You're sorry for him?

LORNA: What's wrong with that?

JOE: But what do *you* get?

LORNA: I told you before I don't care.

JOE: I don't believe it!

LORNA: I can't help that!

JOE: What did he ever do for you?

LORNA *(with sudden verve):* Would you like to know? He loved me in a world of enemies, of stags and bulls! . . . and I loved him for that. He picked me up in Friskin's hotel on 39th Street. I was nine weeks behind in rent. I hadn't hit the gutter yet, but I was near. He washed my face and combed my hair. He stiffened the space between my shoulder blades. Misery reached out to misery——

JOE: And now you're dead.

LORNA *(lashing out):* I don't know what the hell you're talking about!

JOE: Yes, you do. . . .

LORNA *(withdrawing):* Ho hum. . . . *(There is silence. The soft park music plays in the distance. The traffic lights change. LORNA is trying to appear impassive. JOE begins to whistle softly. Finally LORNA picks up his last note and continues; he stops. He picks up her note, and after he whistles a few phrases she picks him up again. This whistling duet continues for almost a minute. Then the traffic lights change again.)*

LORNA *(beginning in a low voice):* You make me feel too human, Joe. All I want is peace and quiet, not love. I'm a tired old lady, Joe, and I don't mind being what you call "half dead." In fact it's what I like. *(Her voice mounting higher.)* The twice I was in love I took an awful beating and I don't want it again! *(Now half crying.)* I want you to stop it! Don't devil me, Joe. I beg you, don't devil me . . . let me alone. . . . *(She cries softly. JOE reaches out and takes her hand; he gives her a handkerchief which she uses.)*

LORNA *(finally):* That's the third time I cried in my life. . . .

JOE: Now I know you love me.

LORNA *(bitterly):* Well . . .

JOE: I'll tell Moody.

LORNA: Not yet. Maybe he'd kill you if he knew.

JOE: Maybe.

LORNA: Then Fuseli'd kill him. . . . I guess I'd be left to kill myself. I'll tell him. . . .

JOE: When?

LORNA: Not tonight.

JOE: Swiftly, do it swiftly——

LORNA: Not tonight.

JOE: Everything's easy if you do it swiftly.

LORNA: He went up there tonight with six hundred bucks to bribe her into divorce.

JOE: Oh . . .

LORNA (*sadly*): He's a good guy, neat all over—sweet. I'll tell him tomorrow. I'd like a drink.

JOE: Let's drive over the Washington Bridge.

LORNA (*standing*): No, I'd like a drink.

JOE (*standing and facing her*): Lorna, when I talk to you . . . something moves in my heart. Gee, it's the beginning of a wonderful life! A man and his girl! A warm living girl who shares your room. . . .

LORNA: Take me home with you.

JOE: Yes.

LORNA: But how do I know you love me?

JOE: Lorna . . .

LORNA: How do I know it's true? You'll get to be the champ. They'll all want you, all the girls! But I don't care! I've been undersea a long time! When they'd put their hands on me I used to say, "This isn't it! This isn't what I mean!" It's been a mysterious world for me! But, Joe, I think you're it! I don't know why, I think you're it! Take me home with you.

JOE: Lorna!

LORNA: Poor Tom . . .

JOE: Poor Lorna! (*The rest is embrace and kiss and clutching each other.*)

Slow Fadeout

SCENE III

The next day: the office. LORNA *and* MOODY *are present. She has a hangover and is restless.*

MOODY: Boy, you certainly double-scotched yourself last night. What's the idea, you making a career of drinking in your old age? Headache?

LORNA: No.

MOODY: I won't let you walk alone in the park any more, if you do that.

LORNA (*nasty in spite of her best intentions*): Well, if you stayed away from your wife for a change . . .

MOODY: It's pretty late to bring that up, isn't it? Tuesday nights——

LORNA: I can't help it—I feel like a tramp. I've felt like a tramp for years.

MOODY: She was pretty friendly last night.

LORNA: Yeah? Did you sleep with her?

MOODY: What the hell's the matter with you, Lorna? *(He goes to her. She shrugs away from him.)*

LORNA: Keep off the grass! (MOODY *gives her a quizzical look, goes back to his desk and from there gives her another quizzical look.)*

MOODY: Why do you drink like that?

LORNA *(pointing to her chest):* Right here—there's a hard lump and I drink to dissolve it. Do you mind?

MOODY: I don't mind—as long as you keep your health.

LORNA: Aw, Christ!—you and your health talks!

MOODY: You're looking for a fight, dolly-girl!

LORNA: And you'll give it?

MOODY *(with a grin):* No, I'm feeling too good.

LORNA *(sitting wearily):* Who left you a fortune?

MOODY: Better. Monica's seen the light. The truth is she's begun to run around with a retired brewer and now *she* wants the divorce.

LORNA: Good, now she can begin paying *you.*

MOODY: She goes to Reno in a few months.

LORNA *(moodily):* I feel like a tramp. . . .

MOODY: That's what I'm telling you——In a few months we'll be married! *(He laughs with pleasure.)*

LORNA: You still want to marry me? Don't I feel like an old shoe to you?

MOODY *(coming to her):* Honest, you're so dumb!

LORNA *(touched by his boyishness):* You're so sweet. . . .

MOODY: And flash!—I signed Lombardo today! They meet six weeks from tonight.

LORNA: Goody. . . .

MOODY *(disappointed by her flippant reaction, but continuing):* I'm still not sure what he'll show with Lombardo. But my present worry is this: help me get that kid straight. Did you speak to him about the driving last night?

LORNA: I didn't see him. . . .

MOODY: It's very important. A Lombardo win clinches everything. In the fall we ride up to the Chocolate's door and dump him in the gutter! After that . . . I don't like to exaggerate—but the kid's primed! And you and I—Lorna baby, we're set. *(Happily.)* What do you think of that?

LORNA *(evasively):* You draw beautiful pictures. *(A knock sounds on the door.)*

MOODY: Come in. (SIGGIE *enters, dressed in cab driver's garb.)*

SIGGIE: Hello, Miss Moon.

LORNA: Hello. You know Mr. Moody.

SIGGIE *(to* MOODY): Hello.

MOODY: What can we do for you?

SIGGIE: For me you can't do nothing. I'm sore. I'm here against my better instinct. *(Taking a roll of money from his pocket and slapping it on the desk.)* He don't want it—no part of it! My father-in-law don't want it. Joe sent it up—two hundred bucks—enough to choke a horse—but he don't want it!

MOODY: Why?

LORNA: That's nice he remembers his folks.

SIGGIE: Listen, I got a father-in-law nothing's nice to him but feeding his horse and giving a laugh and slicing philosophical salami across the table! He's sore because Joe don't come home half the time. As a matter of fact, ain't he suppose to come to sleep no more? The old man's worried.

MOODY: That's not my concern.

SIGGIE: I can't see what it's such a worry. A boy gets in the higher brackets—what's the worry? He's got enough clothes now to leave three suits home in the closet. *(Turning to* LORNA.) It won't hurt if he sends me a few passes—tell him I said so.

LORNA: How's the wife?

SIGGIE: The Duchess? Still laughing.

LORNA: When you getting that cab?

SIGGIE: Do me a favor, Miss Moon—tell him I could use this wad for the first instalment.

LORNA: I'll tell him. Tell Mr. Bonaparte I saw Joe last night. He's fine.

MOODY: I'll see you get some passes.

SIGGIE: Thanks, thanks to both of you. Adios. *(He exits.)*

LORNA: He and his wife are crazy for each other. Married . . . they throw each other around, but they're like love birds. Marriage is something special. . . . I guess you have to deserve it.

MOODY: I thought you didn't see Joe last night.

LORNA: I didn't, but why worry his father?

MOODY: The hell with his father.

LORNA: The hell with you!

MOODY (*after a brooding pause*): I'll tell you something, Lorna. I'm not overjoyed the way Joe looks at you.

LORNA: How's he look?

MOODY: As if he saw the whole island of Manhattan in your face, and I don't like it.

LORNA: You thought of that too late.

MOODY: Too late for what?

LORNA: To bawl me out.

MOODY: Who's bawling you out?

LORNA: You were about to. Or warn me. I don't need warnings. (*Coasting away from the argument.*) If you saw Joe's father you'd like him.

MOODY: I saw him.

LORNA: If you knew him you'd like him.

MOODY: Who wantsa like him? What do I need him for? I don't like him and I don't like his son! It's a business—Joe does his work, I do mine. Like this telephone—I pay the bill and I use it!

LORNA: He's human. . . .

MOODY: What're we fighting about?

LORNA: We're fighting about love. I'm trying to tell you how cynical I am. Tell the truth, love doesn't last——

MOODY (*suddenly quietly serious*): Everything I said about *Joe*—the opposite goes for you. Love lasts . . . if you want it to. . . . I want it to last. I need it to last. What the hell's all this struggle to make a living for if not for a woman and a home? I don't kid myself. I know what I need. I need you, Lorna.

LORNA: It has to end. . . .

MOODY: What has to end?

LORNA: Everything.

MOODY: What're you talking about?

LORNA: I oughta burn. I'm leaving you. . . .

MOODY (*with a sick smile*): That's what you think.

LORNA (*not looking at him*): I mean it.

MOODY (*as above*): I mean it too.

LORNA (*after looking at him for a moment*): You can't take a joke?

MOODY (*not knowing where he stands*): It all depends. . . . I don't like a joke that pushes the blood down in my feet.

LORNA (*coming to him and putting her arms around his neck*): That's true, you're pale.

MOODY: Who's the man?

LORNA *(heartsick, and unable to tell him the truth):* There's no man, Tom . . . even if there was, I couldn't leave you. *(She looks at him, unable to say more.)*

MOODY *(after a pause):* How about some lunch? I'll buy it. . . .

LORNA *(wearily):* Where would I put it, Tom?

MOODY *(impulsively):* In your hat! *(And suddenly he embraces her roughly and kisses her fully and she allows it.* JOE *walks into the office,* EDDIE FUSELI *behind him. They break apart.)*

JOE: The first time I walked in here that was going on. It's one long duet around here.

MOODY: Hello.

EDDIE *(sardonically):* Hello, Partner. . . . (LORNA *is silent and avoids* JOE'S *looks.)*

JOE: How about that fight with Lombardo?

MOODY: Six weeks from tonight.

JOE: He's gonna be surprised.

MOODY *(coolly):* No one doubts it.

JOE *(sharply):* I didn't say it was doubted!

MOODY: Boy, everyone's off his feed today. It started with the elevator boy—next it's Lorna—now it's you! What are *you* sore about?

LORNA *(trying to turn the conversation; to* JOE*):* Siggie was here looking for you. Your father's worried——

JOE: Not as much as my "manager" worries me.

MOODY: I don't need you to tell me how to run my business. I'll book the matches——

JOE: That doesn't worry me.

MOODY: But you and your speeding worries me! First it's music, then it's motors. Christ, next it'll be girls and booze!

JOE: It's girls already.

LORNA: Joe——

JOE *(bitterly):* Certainly! By the dozens!

EDDIE: Haha—that's a hot one. Don't ask me which is worst—women or spiders.

LORNA: Siggie left this money—your father won't take it. Siggie says buy him a cab——(JOE *takes the money.)*

EDDIE: Your relative? I'll get him a cab. *(To* MOODY*):* How about a flock of bouts for Bonaparte over the summer?

MOODY *(bitterly):* All he wants—practice fights—to make him a better "artiste."

EDDIE: That is what we like. (JOE *is looking at* LORNA.)

MOODY: "We?" Where do *I* come in?

EDDIE: You push the buttons, the *right* buttons. I wanna see Bonaparte with the crown.

MOODY *(sarcastically)*: Your concern touches me deep in my heart!

EDDIE: What's the matter, Tom? You getting tired?

MOODY *(coolly)*: I get tired, don't you?

EDDIE: Don't get tired, Tom . . . not in a crucial time.

MOODY: Get him to give up that Deusenberg.

EDDIE *(after looking at* JOE*)*: That's his fun. . . .

MOODY: His fun might cost your crown.

JOE *(suddenly, to* LORNA*)*: Why did you kiss him?

MOODY *(to* JOE*)*: It's about time you shut your mouth and minded your own goddam business. Also, that you took some orders.

JOE *(suddenly savage)*: Who are you, God?

MOODY: Yes! I'm your maker, you cock-eyed gutter rat! Outa sawdust and spit I made you! I own you—without me you're a blank! Your insolence is gorgeous, but this is the end! I'm a son of a gun! What're you so superior about?

EDDIE: Don't talk so quick, Tom. You don't know . . .

MOODY: I wouldn't take the crap of this last six eight months from the President himself! Cut me up in little pieces, baby—but not me!

EDDIE *(quietly)*: You could get cut up in little pieces.

MOODY *(retiring in disgust)*: Sisst!

EDDIE: You hear me?

MOODY *(from his desk)*: You wanna manage this boy? Help yourself— do it! I'll sell my piece for half of what it's worth. You wanna buy?

EDDIE: You are a funny man.

MOODY: Gimme twenty thousand and lemme out. Ten, I'll take ten. I got my girl. I don't need crowns or jewels. I take my girl and we go sit by the river and it's everything.

JOE: What girl?

MOODY: I'm not on speaking terms with you! *(To* EDDIE*)*: Well?

EDDIE: It would be funny if your arms got broke.

JOE: Wait a minute! Lorna loves me and I love her.

MOODY *(after looking from* JOE *to* LORNA *and back)*: Crazy as a bat! *(He laughs.)*

JOE *(frigidly)*: Is it so impossible?

MOODY: About as possible as hell freezes over. *(He and* JOE *simultaneously turn to* LORNA.*)*

JOE: Tell him. . . .

LORNA *(looking* JOE *in the face):* I love Tom. Tell him what? (JOE *looks at her intently. Silence.* JOE *then turns and quietly exits from the office.* MOODY *shakes his head with a grin.)*

MOODY: Eddie, I take everything back. I was a fool to get sore—that boy's a real nutsy-Fagan! *(He offers his hand.* EDDIE *looks at it and then viciously slaps it down.)*

EDDIE *(repressing a trembling voice):* I don't like no one to laugh at that boy. You call a boy like that a rat? An educated boy? What is your idea to call him cock-eyed? When you do it in front of me, I say, "Tom don't like himself" . . . for Bonaparte is a good friend to me . . . you're a clever manager for him. That's the only reason I take your slop. Do your business, Tom. *(To* LORNA): And that goes for you, too! No tricks, Miss Moon! *(He slowly exits.* MOODY *stands there thoughtfully.* LORNA *moves to the couch.)*

MOODY: I'm a son of a gun!

LORNA: I feel like I'm shot from a cannon.

MOODY: Why?

LORNA: I'm sorry for him.

MOODY: Why? Because he's a queer?

LORNA: I'm not talking of Fuseli. *(Suddenly* LORNA'S *eyes flood with tears.* MOODY *takes her hand, half sensing the truth.)*

MOODY: What's wrong, Lorna? You can tell me. . . .

LORNA: I feel like the wrath of God.

MOODY: You like that boy, don't you?

LORNA: I love him, Tom.

Slow Fadeout

SCENE IV

Six weeks later.

A dressing room before the Lombardo fight. There are a couple of rubbing tables in the room. There are some lockers and a few hooks on which hang pieces of clothing. A door to the left leads to the showers; a door to the right leads to the arena.

As the lights fade in, MR. BONAPARTE *and* SIGGIE *are sitting to one side, on a long wooden bench.* TOKIO *is fussing around in a locker. A fighter,* PEPPER WHITE, *hands already bandaged, is being rubbed down by his trainer-manager,* MICKEY. *Throughout the scene is heard the distant Roar of* THE CROWD *and the clanging of the bell.*

MR. BONAPARTE *(after a silence of intense listening):* What is that noise?

SIGGIE: That's the roar of the crowd.

MR. BONAPARTE: A thousand people?

SIGGIE: Six thousand.

PEPPER WHITE *(turning his head as he lies on his belly):* Nine thousand.

SIGGIE: That's right, nine. You're sitting under nine thousand people. Suppose they fell down on your head? Did you ever think of that? *(The outside door opens;* EDDIE FUSELI *enters. The distant bell clangs.* EDDIE *looks around suspiciously, then asks* TOKIO:)

EDDIE: Where's Bonaparte?

TOKIO: Still with the newspapermen.

EDDIE *(unpleasantly surprised):* He's what?

TOKIO: Tom took him upstairs—some sports writers.

EDDIE: A half hour before a fight? What is Moody trying to do?

TOKIO: Tom's the boss.

EDDIE: Looka, Tokio—in the future you are gonna take your orders from me! *(Pointing to* SIGGIE *and* MR. BONAPARTE): Who is this?

TOKIO: Joe's relatives.

EDDIE *(going over to them):* Is this his father?

MR. BONAPARTE *(somberly):* Yes, thisa his father.

SIGGIE: And this is his brother-in-law. Joe sent passes up the house. We just got here. I thought it was in Coney Island—it's lucky I looked at the tickets. Believe it or not, the old man never seen a fight in his life! Is it human?

EDDIE *(coldly):* Shut your mouth a minute! This is The Arena—— Bonaparte is fighting a good man tonight——

SIGGIE: Ahh, that Lombardo's a bag of oats!

EDDIE: When Bonaparte goes in there I like him to have one thing on his mind—fighting! I hope you understand me. An' I don't like to find you here when I return! I hope you understand that. . . . *(After a full glance at them* EDDIE *gracefully exits.)*

SIGGIE: That's a positive personality!

TOKIO: That's Eddie Fuseli.

SIGGIE: Momma-mia! No wonder I smelled gun powder! *(Turning to* MR. BONAPARTE): Pop, that's a paradox in human behavior: he shoots you for a nickel—then for fifty bucks he sends you flowers!

TOKIO *(referring to the distant bell):* That's the next bout.

SIGGIE *(to* MR. BONAPARTE): Come on, we don't wanna miss the whole show.

MR. BONAPARTE: I waita for Joe.

SIGGIE: You heard what Fuseli said——

MR. BONAPARTE *(with somber stubbornness):* I gonna wait!

SIGGIE: Listen, pop, you——

MR. BONAPARTE *(with sudden force): I say I gonna wait!!*

SIGGIE *(handing* MR. BONAPARTE *a ticket):* Ticket. *(Shrugging.)* Good-bye, you're letting flies in! (SIGGIE *exits jauntily.* MR. BONAPARTE *silently watches* TOKIO *work over the fighter's materials. A* SECOND *comes in, puts a pail under the table where* TOKIO *hovers, and exits.* PEPPER WHITE, *his head turned, watches* MR. BONAPARTE *as he hums a song.)*

PEPPER:

Oh, Sweet Dardanella, I love your harem eyes,

Oh, Sweet Dardanella, I'm a lucky fellow to get such a prize. . . .

(To MR. BONAPARTE): So you're Bonaparte's little boy, Buddy? Why didn't you say so before? Come over here and shake my hand. (MR. BONAPARTE does so.)

PEPPER: Tell Bonaparte I like to fight him.

MR. BONAPARTE: Why?

PEPPER: I like to beat him up.

MR. BONAPARTE *(naïvely, not amused):* Why? You don't like him?

PEPPER: Don't kid me, Buddy! *(A* CALL BOY *looks in at the door.)*

CALL BOY: Pepper White! Ready, Pepper White! (CALL BOY *exits.* PEPPER WHITE *slips off the table and begins to change his shoes.)*

PEPPER *(to* MR. BONAPARTE): When I get back I'll explain you all the ins and outs. *(A* SECOND *enters, takes a pail from* MICKEY *and exits.* LORNA *enters.)*

PEPPER *(indignantly):* Who told girls to come in here?!

LORNA: Modest? Close your eyes. Is Moody . . . ? *(Suddenly seeing* MR. BONAPARTE.) Hello, Mr. Bonaparte!

MR. BONAPARTE *(glad to see a familiar face):* Hello, hello, Missa Moon! Howa you feel?

LORNA: What brings you to this part of the world?

MR. BONAPARTE *(somberly):* I come-a to see Joe. . . .

LORNA: Why, what's wrong?

MR. BONAPARTE *(with a slow shrug):* He don't come-a to see me. . . .

LORNA: Does he know you're here?

MR. BONAPARTE: No. (LORNA *looks at him sympathetically.)*

LORNA *(finally):* It's a three-ring circus, isn't it?

MR. BONAPARTE: How you mean?

LORNA: Oh, I mean you . . . and him . . . and other people . . .

MR. BONAPARTE: I gonna see how he fight.

LORNA: I owe you a report. I wish I had good news for you, but I haven't.

MR. BONAPARTE: Yes, I know . . . he gotta wild wolf inside—eat him up!

LORNA: You could build a city with his ambition to be somebody.

MR. BONAPARTE *(sadly, shaking his head):* No . . . burn down! *(Now the outside door is thrust open—the distant bell clangs. JOE enters, behind him MOODY and ROXY. JOE stops in his tracks when he see LORNA and his father together—the last two persons in the world he wants to see now. His hands are already bandaged, a bathrobe is thrown around his shoulders.)*

JOE: Hello, poppa. . . .

MR. BONAPARTE: Hello, Joe. . . .

JOE *(turning to TOKIO):* Throw out the girls—this isn't a hotel bedroom!

MOODY: That's no way to talk!

JOE *(coolly):* I talk as I please!

MOODY *(angrily):* The future Mrs. Moody——

JOE: I don't want her here!

LORNA: He's right, Tom. Why fight about it? *(She exits.)*

JOE *(to MOODY):* Also, I don't want to see writers again before a fight; it makes me nervous!

ROXY *(softly, for a wonder):* They're very important, Joe——

JOE: *I'm* important! My mind must be clear before I fight. I have to think before I go in. Don't you know that yet?

ROXY *(suddenly):* Yeah, we know—you're a stoodent—you gotta look in your notes.

JOE: What's funny about that? I do, *I do!!*

ROXY *(retreating):* So I said you do! (PEPPER WHITE *comes forward, about to exit; to MOODY.)*

PEPPER: How 'bout a bout with Napoleon?

MOODY: On your way, louse!

PEPPER *(with a grin):* Pickin' setups? (JOE *suddenly turns and starts for PEPPER. TOKIO quickly steps in between the two boys.)*

TOKIO: Save it for the ring! *(The two fighters glare at each other. JOE slowly turns and starts back for the table.)*

PEPPER: You think he'll be the champ? Where'd you ever read about a cock-eye champ? (JOE *spins around, speeds across the room—* PEPPER *is on the floor!* MICKEY *now starts for* JOE. TOKIO *starts for* MICKEY. PEPPER *gets up off the floor and finds himself occupied with* MOODY. *For a moment the fight is general.* EDDIE FUSELI *enters. All see him. The fighting magically stops on the second.*)

EDDIE: What'sa matter? Cowboys and Indians? *(To* PEPPER): Out! (MICKEY *and* PEPPER *sullenly exit.*)

EDDIE *(to* MOODY): I'm lookin' for you! You're a manager and a half! You and your fat friend! *(Meaning* ROXY.) You think this boy is a toy?

JOE: Eddie's the only one here who understands me.

MOODY: Who the hell wantsa understand you! I got one wish—for Lombardo to give you the business! The quicker he taps you off tonight, the better! You gotta be took down a dozen pegs! I'm versus you! Completely versus!

EDDIE *(quietly, to* MOODY): Moody, your brains is in your feet! This is how you handle a coming champ, to give him the jitters before a bout? Go out and take some air! . . . *(Seeing* EDDIE'S *quiet deadlines,* MOODY *swallows his wrath and exits;* ROXY *follows with pursed lips.*)

EDDIE: Lay down, Joe—take it easy. (JOE *sits on a table.*)

EDDIE: Who hurt you, Joe? Someone hurt your feelings?

JOE: Everything's all right.

EDDIE: Tokio, I put fifty bucks on Bonaparte's nose for you. It's my appreciation to you. . . .

TOKIO: Thanks.

EDDIE *(of* MR. BONAPARTE): Whatta you want me to do with him?

JOE: Leave him here.

EDDIE: Tell me if you want something. . . .

JOE: Nothing.

EDDIE: Forget that Miss Moon. Stop lookin' down her dress. Go out there and kill Lombardo! Send him out to Woodlawn! Tear his skull off! . . . as I know Bonaparte can do it! (EDDIE *gives* MR. BONA-PARTE *a sharp look and exits. There is silence intensified by the distant clang of the bell and the muted roar of* THE CROWD. TOKIO *looks over at* MR. BONAPARTE *who has been silently seated on the bench all this time.*)

JOE *(not quite knowing what to say):* How is Anna, poppa?

MR. BONAPARTE: Fine.

JOE: Siggie watching the fights?

MR. BONAPARTE: Yes. . . .

JOE: You look fine. . . .

MR. BONAPARTE: Yes, feela good. . . .

JOE: Why did you send that money back? *(There is no answer.)* Why did you come here? . . . You sit there like my conscience. . . .

MR. BONAPARTE: Why you say so?

JOE: Poppa, I have to fight, no matter what you say or think! This is my profession! I'm out for fame and fortune, not to be different or artistic! I don't intend to be ashamed of my life!

MR. BONAPARTE *(standing up):* Yeah, I understanda you. . . .

JOE: Go out and watch the fights.

MR. BONAPARTE *(somberly):* Yeah . . . you fight. Now I know . . . is'a too late for music. The men musta be free an' happy for music . . . not like-a you. Now I see whatta you are . . . I give-a you every word to fight . . . I sorry for you. . . . *(Silence. The distant roar of* THE CROWD *climbs up and falls down; the bell clangs again.)*

TOKIO *(gently):* I'll have to ask you to leave, Mr. Bonaparte. . . .

MR. BONAPARTE *(holding back his tears):* Joe . . . I hope-a you win every fight. (MR. BONAPARTE *slowly exits. As he opens and closes the door the roar of* THE CROWD *swells up for an instant.)*

TOKIO: Lay down, Joe. There's five minutes left to tune you up.

JOE *(in a low voice):* That's right, tune me up. . . . (JOE *stretches out on his stomach and* TOKIO'S *busy hands start up the back of his legs.)*

TOKIO *(working with steady briskness):* I never worried less about a boy . . . in my life. You're a real sweetheart. . . . *(Suddenly* JOE *begins to cry in his arms.* TOKIO *looks down, momentarily hesitates in his work—then slowly goes ahead with his massaging hands. The* BOY *continues to shake with silent sobs. Again the bell clangs in the distance.)*

TOKIO *(in a soft caressing voice):* You're getting good, honey. Maybe I never told you that before. I seen it happen before. *(Continuing the massaging):* It seems to happen sudden—a fighter gets good. He gets easy and graceful. He learns how to save himself—no energy wasted . . . he slips and slides—he travels with the punch. . . . Oh, sure, I like the way you're shaping up. (TOKIO *continues massaging.* JOE *is silent. His sobbing stops. After a moment* TOKIO *continues):* What was you saying about Lombardo's trick? I understood you to say he's a bull's-eye for a straight shot from the inside. I think you're right, Joe, but that kind of boy is liable to meet you straight-on in a clinch and give you the back of his head under the chin. Watch out for that.

JOE: He needs a straight punch. . . . (JOE *suddenly sits up on the table, his legs dangling.)* Now I'm alone. They're all against me— Moody, the girl . . . you're my family now, Tokio—you and Eddie! I'll show them all—nobody stands in my way! My father's had his hand on me for years. No more. No more for her either—she had her chance! When a bullet sings through the air it has no past —only a future—like me! Nobody, nothing stands in my way! *(In a sudden spurt of feeling* JOE *starts sparring around lightly in a shadow boxing routine.* TOKIO *smiles with satisfaction. Now the roar of* THE CROWD *reaches a frenzied shriek and hangs there. The bell clangs rapidly several times. The roar of* THE CROWD *settles down again.)*

TOKIO: That sounds like the kill. (JOE *draws his bathrobe around him and prances on his toes.)*

JOE: I'm a new boy tonight! I could take two Lombardos! *(Vigorously shaking out his bandaged hands above his head.)* Hallelujah! We're on the Millionaire Express tonight! Nobody gets me! *(The door is thrust open and a* CALL BOY *shouts.)*

CALL BOY: Bonaparte, ready. Bonaparte, ready. (PEPPER WHITE *and* MICKEY *enter as the* CALL BOY *speeds away.* PEPPER *is flushed with victory.)*

PEPPER *(to* JOE): Tell me when you want it; you can have it the way I just give it to Pulaski! (JOE *looks* PEPPER *in the face, flexes his hands several times and suddenly breaks out in laughter, to* PEPPER'S *astonishment.* JOE *and* TOKIO *exit.* PEPPER *throws off his robe and displays his body.)*

PEPPER: Look me over—not a mark. How do you like that for class! I'm in a hurry to grab a cab to Flushing.

MICKEY *(impassively):* Keep away from her.

PEPPER: I don't even hear you.

MICKEY: Keep away from her!

PEPPER: I go for her like a bee and the flower.

MICKEY *(in a droning prophetic voice):* The flower is married. Her husband is an excitable Armenian from the Orient. There will be hell to pay! Keep away from her! *(Now in the distance is heard the indistinct high voice of the announcer.)*

PEPPER: You oughta get me a fight with that cock-eye Napoleon—insteada sticking your nose where it don't belong! I could slaughter him in next to nothing.

MICKEY *(impassively):* If you could make his weight and slaughter him, you'd be the next world's champ. But you can't make his weight, you can't slaughter him, and you can't be the champ. Why the hell don't you take a shower? *(The bell clangs—in the arena,* JOE'S *fight is on.)*

PEPPER *(plaintively, beginning to dress at his locker):* If my girl don't like me without a shower, I'll tell her a thing or two.

MICKEY: If her husband don't tell you first. *(The roar of* THE CROWD *swells up as the door opens and* MR. BONAPARTE *enters. He is unusually agitated. He looks at* PEPPER *and* MICKEY *and sits on a bench. The roar of* THE CROWD *mounts higher than before, then drops.)*

PEPPER *(to* MR. BONAPARTE*):* What's the matter with you?

MR. BONAPARTE *(shaking his head):* Don't like to see . . .

PEPPER *(delighted):* Why? Your boy gettin' smeared?

MR. BONAPARTE: They fighta for money, no?

MICKEY: No, they're fighting for a noble cause——

MR. BONAPARTE: If they wasa fight for cause or for woman, woulda not be so bad.

PEPPER *(still dressing behind the locker door):* I fight for money and I like it. I don't fight for under a thousand bucks. Do I, Mickey?

MICKEY: Nope.

PEPPER *(boasting naïvely):* I didn't fight for under a thousand for five years. Did I, Mickey?

MICKEY *(impassively):* Nope.

PEPPER: I get a thousand bucks tonight, don't I?

MICKEY: Nope.

PEPPER *(up like a shot):* How much? How much tonight?

MICKEY: Twelve hundred bucks.

PEPPER: What? Mickey, I oughta bust you in the nose. How many times do I have to say I don't fight for under one thousand bucks! *(To* MR. BONAPARTE*):* Now you see what I'm up against with this manager!

MICKEY *(impassively):* Okay, you'll get a thousand.

PEPPER: I better, Buddy! That's all I say—I better! *(To* MR. BONA-PARTE*):* I tell him I want to fight your kid and he don't lift a finger. *(The roar of* THE CROWD *crescendos and drops down again.)*

MICKEY: You don't rate no fight with Bonaparte. *(To* MR. BONAPARTE, *of* PEPPER): He's an old man, a fossil!

MR. BONAPARTE: Who?

MICKEY: Him—he's twenty-nine.

MR. BONAPARTE: Old?

MICKEY: In this business, twenty-nine is ancient.

PEPPER: My girl don't think so.

MICKEY: Keep away from her. *(The roar of* THE CROWD *mounts up to a devilish shriek.)*

PEPPER: Wow, is your boy getting schlocked!

MR. BONAPARTE: My boy isa win.

PEPPER: Yeah, and that's why you ran away?

MR. BONAPARTE: Whatta the difference who's-a win? Is terrible to see!

PEPPER *(grinning):* If I wasn't in a hurry, I'd wait around to help pick up your little Joie's head off the floor. *(He draws on a sport shirt.)*

MICKEY *(to* PEPPER): What are you wearing a polo shirt on a winter night for?

PEPPER: For crying out loud, I just bought it! . . . So long, Mr. Bonaparte.

MR. BONAPARTE: I aska you please—whatta happen to a boy's hands when he fight a longa time?

PEPPER *(holding up his fists):* Take a look at mine—I got a good pair. See those knuckles? Flat!

MR. BONAPARTE: Broke?

PEPPER: Not broke, flat!—pushed down!

MR. BONAPARTE: Hurt?

PEPPER: You get used to it.

MR. BONAPARTE: Can you use them?

PEPPER: Go down the hall and look at Pulaski.

MR. BONAPARTE: Can you open thees-a hands?

PEPPER: What for?

MR. BONAPARTE *(gently touching the fists):* So strong, so hard . . .

PEPPER: You said it, Buddy. So long, Buddy. *(To* MICKEY): Take my stuff.

MICKEY: Sam'll take it after. Keep away from her! (PEPPER *looks at* MICKEY *with a sardonic grin and exits followed by* MICKEY.)

MR. BONAPARTE *(to himself):* So strong . . . so useless . . . *(The roar of* THE CROWD *mounts up and calls for a kill.* MR. BONAPARTE *trembles. For a moment he sits quietly on the bench. Then he goes to the door of the shower room and looks around at the boxing paraphernalia. In the distance the bell begins to clang repeatedly.* MR. BONAPARTE *stares in the direction of the arena. He goes to the exit door. The crowd is cheering and howling.* MR. BONAPARTE *hesitates a moment at the door and then rapidly walks back to the bench, where he sits. Head cocked, he listens for a moment. The roar of* THE CROWD *is heated, demanding and hateful. Suddenly* MR. BONAPARTE *jumps to his feet. He is in a murderous mood. He shakes his clenched fist in the direction of the noise—he roars aloud. The roar of* THE CROWD *dies down. The door opens,* PEPPER'S *second,* SAM, *enters, softly whistling to himself. Deftly he begins to sling together* PEPPER'S *paraphernalia.)*

MR. BONAPARTE: What'sa happen in the fight?

SAM: Knockout.

MR. BONAPARTE: Who?

SAM: Lombardo's stiff. (MR. BONAPARTE *slowly sits. Softly whistling,* SAM *exits with the paraphernalia. The outside door is flung open. In come* JOE, TOKIO, MOODY *and* ROXY, *who is elated beyond sanity.* JOE'S *eyes glitter; his face is hard and flushed. He has won by a knockout.)*

ROXY *(almost dancing):* My boy! My darling boy! My dear darling boy! *(Silently* JOE *sits on the edge of the table, ignoring his father after a glance. His robe drops from his shoulders.* ROXY *turns to* MOODY.)

ROXY: How do you like it, Tom? He knocks him out in two rounds!

MOODY *(stiffly, to* JOE): It's good business to call the sports writers in——

ROXY: That's right, give a statement! (MOODY *gives* JOE *a rapid glance and hurriedly exits.)*

ROXY: I'm collecting a bet on you. All my faith and patience is rewarded. *(As he opens the door he almost knocks over* EDDIE FUSELI.) Haha! How do you like it, Eddie? Haha! *(He exits.* EDDIE FUSELI *closes the door and stands with his back to it.* TOKIO *moves up to* JOE *and begins to remove a glove.)*

TOKIO *(gently):* You're a real sweetheart. . . . (TOKIO *removes the sweaty glove and begins to fumble with the lace of the other one.* JOE *carefully moves his glove out of* TOKIO'S *reach, resting it on his opposite arm.)*

JOE *(almost proudly):* Better cut it off. . . . (MR. BONAPARTE *is watching tensely.* EDDIE *watches from the door.)*

TOKIO: . . . Broke? . . .

JOE (*holding the hand out proudly*): Yes, it's broke. . . . (TOKIO *slowly reaches for a knife. He begins carefully to cut the glove.*)

JOE: Hallelujah!! It's the beginning of the world! (MR. BONAPARTE, *lips compressed, slowly turns his head away.* EDDIE *watches with inner excitement and pleasure:* JOE *has become a fighter.* TOKIO *continues with his work.* JOE *begins to laugh loudly, victoriously, exultantly—with a deep thrill of satisfaction.*)

Slow Fadeout

ACT THREE

SCENE I

MOODY'S *office, six months later. Present are* MOODY, *acting the persuasive salesman with two sports writers,* DRAKE *and* LEWIS; ROXY GOTTLIEB *being helpful in his usual manner;* TOKIO, *to one side, characteristically quiet . . . and* JOE BONAPARTE. BONAPARTE *sits on the desk and diffidently swings his legs as he eats a sandwich. His success has added a certain bellicosity to his attitude; it has changed his clothing to silk shirts and custom-made suits.*

MOODY: He's got his own style. He won't rush——

ROXY: Nobody claims our boy's Niagara Falls.

DRAKE *(a newspaperman for twenty years):* Except himself!

MOODY: You newspaper boys are right.

DRAKE: We newspaper boys are always right!

MOODY: He won't take chances tomorrow night if he can help it. He'll study his man, pick out flaws—then shoot at them.

JOE *(casually):* It won't matter a helluva lot if I win late in the bout or near the opening. The main thing with Bonaparte is to win.

DRAKE *(dryly):* Well, what does Bonaparte expect to do tomorrow night?

JOE *(as dryly):* Win.

MOODY: Why shouldn't we have a win from the Chocolate Drop? Look at our record!——

LEWIS *(good-natured and slow):* We just wanna get an impression——

MOODY: Seventeen knockouts? Fulton, Lombardo, Guffey Talbot—?

JOE: Phil Weiner . . .

MOODY: Weiner?

ROXY: That's no powderpuff hitter!

LEWIS: In this fight tomorrow night, can you name the round?

JOE: Which round would you like?

DRAKE: You're either a genius or an idiot!

MOODY: Joe don't mean——

DRAKE *(sharply):* Let him talk for himself.

JOE (*getting off the desk*): Listen, Drake, I'm not the boy I used to be —the honeymoon's over. I don't blush and stammer these days. Bonaparte goes in and slugs with the best. In the bargain his brain is *better* than the best. That's the truth; why deny it?

DRAKE: The last time you met Chocolate you never even touched him!

JOE: It's almost two years since I "never even touched him." Now I know how!

MOODY: What Joe means to say——

DRAKE: He's the genuine and only modest cock-eyed wonder!

JOE: What good is modesty? I'm a fighter! The whole essence of prizefighting is immodesty! "I'm better than you are—I'll prove it by breaking your face in!" What do you expect? A conscience and a meek smile? I don't believe that bull the meek'll inherit the earth!

DRAKE: Oh, so it's the earth you want!

JOE: I know what I want—that's my business! But I don't want your guff!

DRAKE: I have two sons of my own—I like boys. But I'm a son-of-a-bitch if I can stomach your conceit!

MOODY (*trying to save the situation*): They serve a helluva rum Collins across the street——

DRAKE: Bonaparte, I'll watch for Waterloo with more than interest!

MOODY: Why don't we run across for a drink? How 'bout some drinks?

DRAKE: Tom, you can buy me twenty drinks and I still won't change my mind about him. (*He exits.*)

LEWIS (*smiling*): You're all right, Bonaparte.

JOE: Thanks. . . .

LEWIS (*clinching a cigarette at the desk*): How's that big blonde of yours, Tom?

MOODY: Fine.

LEWIS: How does she feel about the wedding bells? Sunday is it? (*This is news to* JOE, *and* MOODY *knows it is.*)

MOODY (*nervously*): Happy, the way I am. Yeah, Sunday.

ROXY: How about the drinks? We'll drink to everybody's health!

LEWIS (*to* JOE): Good luck tomorrow.

JOE: Thanks. . . . (*They exit,* MOODY *throwing a resentful look at* JOE. JOE *and* TOKIO *are left. In the silence* JOE *goes back to the remains of his lunch.*)

TOKIO: That Drake is a case.

JOE (*pushing the food away*): They don't make cheesecake the way they used to when I was a boy. Or maybe I don't like it any more. When are they getting married?

TOKIO: Moody? Sunday.

JOE: Those writers hate me.

TOKIO: You give them too much lip.

JOE (*looking down at his clenched fists*): I'd rather give than take it. That's one reason I became a fighter. When did Moody get his divorce?

TOKIO: Few weeks ago. . . . (*Cannily.*) Why don't you forget Lorna?

JOE (*as if not understanding*): What?

TOKIO: I'll say it again . . . why not forget her? (*No answer comes.*) Joe, you're loaded with love. Find something to give it to. Your heart ain't in fighting . . . your *hate* is. But a man with hate and nothing else . . . he's half a man . . . and half a man . . . is no man. Find something to love, or someone. Am I stepping on your toes?

JOE (*coldly*): I won't be unhappy if you mind your business.

TOKIO: Okay. . . . (TOKIO *goes to the door, stops there.*) Watch your dinner tonight. No girls either.

JOE: Excuse me for saying that——

TOKIO (*with a faint smile*): Okay. (TOKIO *opens the door and* LORNA MOON *enters.* TOKIO *smiles at her and exits. She carries a pack of newspapers under her arm.* JOE *and she do not know what to say to each other—they wish they had not met here.* LORNA *crosses and puts the newspapers on the desk. She begins to bang through the desk drawers, looking for the scissors.*)

JOE: I hear you're making the leap tomorrow. . . .

LORNA: Sunday. . . .

JOE: Sunday. (*Intense silence.*)

LORNA (*to say anything*): I'm looking for the scissors. . . .

JOE: Who're you cutting up today?

LORNA (*bringing out the shears*): Items on Bonaparte, for the press book. (*She turns and begins to unfold and clip a sheet of newspaper.* JOE *is at a loss for words.*)

JOE (*finally*): Congratulations. . . .

LORNA (*without turning*): Thanks. . . . (*In a sudden irresistible surge* JOE *tears the papers out of* LORNA'S *hands and hurls them behind the desk. The two stand facing each other.*)

JOE: When I speak to you, look at me!

LORNA: What would you like to say? *(They stand face to face, straining. Finally:)*

JOE: Marry anyone you like!

LORNA: Thanks for permission!

JOE: Queen Lorna, the tramp of Newark!

LORNA: You haven't spoken to me for months. Why break your silence?

JOE: You're a historical character for me—dead and buried!

LORNA: Then everything's simple; go about your business.

JOE: Moody's right for you—perfect—the mating of zero and zero!

LORNA: I'm not sorry to marry Tom——

JOE *(scornfully):* That's from the etiquette book—page twelve: "When you marry a man say you like it!"

LORNA: I know I could do worse when I look at you. When did you look in the mirror last? Getting to be a killer! You're getting to be like Fuseli! You're not the boy I cared about, not you. You murdered that boy with the generous face—God knows where you hid the body! I don't know you.

JOE: I suppose I never kissed your mouth——

LORNA: What do you want from me? Revenge? Sorry—we're all out of revenge today!

JOE: I wouldn't look at you twice if they hung you naked from a Christmas tree! *(At this moment EDDIE FUSELI enters with a pair of packages. He looks intently at LORNA, then crosses and puts the packages on the desk. He and JOE are dressed almost identically. LORNA exits without a word. EDDIE is aware of what has happened but begins to talk casually about the packages.)*

EDDIE: This one's your new headgear. This is shirts from Jacobs Brothers. He says the neck bands are gonna shrink, so I had him make sixteens—they'll fit you after one washing. *(Holding up a shirt.)* You like that color?

JOE: Thanks.

EDDIE: Your brother-in-law drove me over. Picked him up on 49th. Don't you ever see them no more?

JOE *(sharply):* What for?

EDDIE: What'sa matter?

JOE: Why? You see a crowd around here, Eddie?

EDDIE: No.

JOE: That's right, you don't! But I do! I see a crowd of Eddies all around me, suffocating me, burying me in good times and silk shirts!

EDDIE *(dialing the telephone):* You wanna go to the Scandals tonight? I got tickets. *(Into the telephone):* Charley? Fuseli is speaking. . . . I'm giving four to five on Bonaparte tomorrow. . . . Four G's worth. . . . Yes. *(Hanging up the phone.)* It's gonna be a good fight tomorrow.

JOE *(belligerently).* How do you know?

EDDIE: I know Bonaparte. I got eighteen thousand spread out on him tomorrow night.

JOE: Suppose Bonaparte loses?

EDDIE: I look at the proposition from all sides—I know he'll win.

JOE: What the hell do you think I am? A machine? Maybe I'm lonely, maybe——

EDDIE: You wanna walk in a parade? Everybody's lonely. Get the money and you're not so lonely.

JOE: I want some personal life.

EDDIE: I give Bonaparte a good personal life. I got loyalty to his cause. . . .

JOE: You use me like a gun! Your loyalty's to keep me oiled and polished!

EDDIE: A year ago Bonaparte was a rookie with a two-pants suit. Now he wears the best, eats the best, sleeps the best. He walks down the street respected—the golden boy! They howl their heads off when Bonaparte steps in the ring . . . and I done it for him!

JOE: There are other things. . . .

EDDIE: There's no other things! Don't think so much—it could make you very sick! You're in this up to your neck. You owe me a lot—I don't like you to forget. You better be on your toes when you step in that ring tomorrow night. (EDDIE *turns and begins to dial the telephone.)*

JOE: Your loyalty makes me shiver. (JOE *starts for the door.)*

EDDIE: Take the shirts.

JOE: What do I want them for? I can only wear one at a time. . . . (EDDIE *speaks into the phone.)*

EDDIE: Meyer? . . . Fuseli is speaking. . . . I'm giving four to five on Bonaparte tomorrow. . . . Two? . . . Yeah. . . . *(About to exit,*

JOE *stands at the door and watches* EDDIE *as he calmly begins to dial the phone again.)*

Medium Fadeout

SCENE II

The next night.

The lights fade in on an empty stage. We are in the same dressing room as seen in Act Two. Far in the distance is heard the same roar of THE CROWD. *The distant bell clangs menacingly. The room is shadows and patches of light. The silence here has its own ugly dead quality.*

LORNA MOON *enters. She looks around nervously; she lights a cigarette; this reminds her to rouge her lips; she puffs the cigarette. The distant bell clangs again.* EDDIE FUSELI *enters, pale and tense. He sees* LORNA *and stops short in his tracks. There is an intense silence as they look at each other.*

LORNA: How's the fight?

EDDIE: I like to talk to you.

LORNA: Is Joe still on his feet?

EDDIE: Take a month in the country, Miss Moon.

LORNA: Why?

EDDIE *(repressing a murderous mood):* Give the boy . . . or move away.

LORNA: I get married tomorrow. . . .

EDDIE: You heard my request—give him or go!

LORNA: Don't Moody count?

EDDIE: If not for Bonaparte they'd find you in a barrel long ago—in the river or a bush!

LORNA: I'm not afraid of you. . . . *(The distant bell clangs.)*

EDDIE *(after turning his head and listening):* That's the beginning of the eighth. Bonaparte's unsettled—fighting like a drunken sailor. He can't win no more, unless he knocks the Chocolate out. . . .

LORNA *(at a complete loss):* Don't look at me . . . what'd you . . . I . . .

EDDIE: Get outa town! (THE ROAR *of* THE CROWD *mounts to a demand for a kill.)*

EDDIE *(listening intently):* He's like a bum tonight . . . and a bum done it! You! *(The roar grows fuller.)* I can't watch him get slaughtered. . . .

LORNA: I couldn't watch it myself. . . . *(The bell clangs loudly several times.* THE ROAR *of* THE CROWD *hangs high in the air.)* What's happening now?

EDDIE: Someone's getting murdered. . . .

LORNA: It's me. . . .

EDDIE *(quietly, intensely):* That's right . . . if he lost . . . the trees are ready for your coffin. (THE ROAR *of* THE CROWD *tones down.)* You can go now. I don't wanna make a scandal around his name. . . . I'll find you when I want you. Don't be here when they carry him in.

LORNA *(at a complete loss):* Where do you want me to go?

EDDIE *(suddenly releasing his wrath):* Get outa my sight! You turned down the sweetest boy who ever walked in shoes! You turned him down, the golden boy, that king among the ju-ven-niles! He gave you his hand—you spit in his face! You led him on like Gertie's whoore! You sold him down the river! And now you got the nerve to stand here, to wait and see him bleeding from the mouth!——

LORNA: Fuseli, for God's sake——

EDDIE: Get outa my sight!

LORNA: Fuseli, please——

EDDIE: Outa my sight, you nickel whoore! *(Completely enraged and out of control,* EDDIE *half brings his gun out from under his left armpit.* JOE *appears in the doorway. Behind him are* ROXY, MOODY *and a* SECOND.)

JOE: Eddie! (EDDIE *whirls around. The others enter the room. In the ensuing silence,* MOODY, *sensing what has happened, crosses to* LORNA.)

LORNA *(quietly):* What happened?

ROXY: What happened? *(He darts forward and picks up* JOE'S *arm in the sign of victory. The arm drops back limply.)* The monarch of the masses!

EDDIE *(to the* SECOND): Keep everybody out. Only the newspaper boys. *(The* SECOND *exits and closes the door.* JOE *sits on a table. Physically he is a very tired boy. There is a high puff under one eye; the other is completely closed. His body is stained with angry splotches.)*

TOKIO *(gently):* I have to hand it to you, Joe. . . .

ROXY *(explaining to the frigid* EDDIE, *elaborately):* The beginning of the eighth: first the bell! Next the Chocolate Drop comes out like a waltz clog, confident. Oh, he was so confident! Haha! The next thing I know the Chocolate's on the floor, the referee lifts our arm, we got on our bathrobe and we're here in the dressing room! How do you like it?

EDDIE *(narrowly):* I like it.

TOKIO *(taking off* JOE's *gloves):* I'll have you feelin' better in a minute. *(After which he cuts the tapes.)*

JOE: I feel all right.

EDDIE *(to* TOKIO): Gimme his gloves.

MOODY *(wary of* JOE): That's a bad lump under your eye.

JOE: Not as bad as the Chocolate Drop got when he hit the floor!

ROXY: Darling, how you gave it to him! Not to my enemies!

JOE: 'Twas a straight right—with no trimmings or apologies! Aside from fouling me in the second and fifth——

MOODY: I called them on it——

ROXY: I seen the bastard——

JOE: That second time I nearly went through the floor. I gave him the fury of a lifetime in that final punch! (EDDIE *has taken the soggy boxing gloves for his own property.* TOKIO *is daubing the bruise under* JOE's *eye.)* And did you hear them cheer! *(Bitterly, as if reading a news report.)* Flash! As thousands cheer, that veritable whirlwind Bonaparte—that veritable cock-eye wonder, Bonaparte—he comes from behind in the eighth stanza to slaughter the Chocolate Drop and clinch a bout with the champ! Well, how do you like me, boys? Am I good or am I good?

ROXY: Believe *me!*

TOKIO *(attempting to settle* JOE): You won the right for a crack at the title. You won it fair and clean. Now lay down. . . .

JOE *(in a vehement outburst):* I'd like to go outside my weight and beat up the whole damn world!

MOODY *(coldly):* Well, the world's your oyster now!

TOKIO *(insistently):* Take it easy. Lemme fix that eye, Joe——*(Now a bustling little Irishman,* DRISCOLL, *hustles into the room.)*

DRISCOLL: Who's got the happy boy's gloves?

EDDIE: Here . . . why? (DRISCOLL *rapidly takes the gloves, "breaks" and examines them.)*

TOKIO: What's the matter, "Drisc"?

JOE: What's wrong?

DRISCOLL *(handing the gloves back to* EDDIE): Chocolate's a sick boy.

Your hands are clean. (DRISCOLL *hustles for the door.* JOE *is up and to him.*)

JOE: What happened?

DRISCOLL *(bustling):* It looks like the Pride of Baltimore is out for good. Change your clothes.

JOE: How do you mean?

DRISCOLL: Just like I said—out! (DRISCOLL *pats* JOE'S *shoulder, hustles out, closing the door in* JOE'S *face.* JOE *slowly sits on the nearest bench. Immediately* TOKIO *comes to him, as tender as a mother.*)

TOKIO: You didn't foul him—you're a clean fighter. You're so honest in the ring it's stupid. If something's happened, it's an accident. *(The others stand around stunned, not knowing what to do or say.)*

MOODY *(very worried):* That's right, there's nothing to worry about.

ROXY *(ditto):* That's right. . . .

JOE: Gee. . . . (JOE *stands up, slowly crosses the room and sits on the table, head in his hands, his back to the others. No one knows what to say.*)

EDDIE *(to* MOODY): Go out there and size up the situation. (MOODY, *glad of the opportunity to leave the room, turns to the door which is suddenly violently thrust open.* BARKER, *the* CHOCOLATE DROP'S *manager, pushes* MOODY *into the room with him, leaving the door open. From outside a small group of curious people look in.* BARKER, *bereft of his senses, grabs* MOODY *by the coat lapel.*)

BARKER: Do you know it? Do you know it?

MOODY: Now wait a minute, Barker——(BARKER *runs over to* JOE *and screams:*)

BARKER: You murdered my boy! He's dead! You killed him!

TOKIO *(getting between* JOE *and* BARKER): Just a minute!

BARKER *(literally wringing his hands):* He's dead! Chocolate's dead!

TOKIO: We're very sorry about it. Now pull yourself together. (EDDIE *crosses the room and slams the door shut as* BARKER *points an accusing finger at* JOE *and screams*):

BARKER: This dirty little wop killed my boy!

EDDIE *(coming to* BARKER): Go back in your room.

BARKER: Yes he did!! (EDDIE'S *answer is to shove* BARKER *roughly toward the door, weeping):* Yes, he did!!

EDDIE: Get out before I slug your teeth apart!

JOE *(jumping to his feet):* Eddie, for God sakes, don't hit him! Let him alone! (EDDIE *immediately desists.* BARKER *stands there, a weeping idiot.*)

MOODY: Accidents can happen.

BARKER: I know . . . I know. . . .

MOODY: Chocolate fouled us twice.

BARKER: I know, I know. . . . (BARKER *stammers, gulps and tries to say something more. Suddenly he dashes out of the room. There is a long silent pause during which* JOE *sits down again.*)

EDDIE: We'll have to wait for an investigation.

TOKIO *(to* JOE): Don't blame yourself for nothing. . . .

JOE: That poor guy . . . with those sleepy little eyes. . . .

ROXY *(solemnly):* It's in the hands of God, a thing like that. (LEWIS, *the sports writer, tries to enter the room.*)

EDDIE *(herding him out):* Stay outside. *(To* MOODY): See what's happening? (MOODY *immediately leaves.*) Everybody out—leave Bonaparte to calm hisself. I'll watch the door.

TOKIO: Don't worry, Joe. *(He exits, followed by* ROXY. EDDIE *turns and looks at* LORNA.)

EDDIE: You too, Miss Moon—this ain't no cocktail lounge.

LORNA: I'll stay here. (EDDIE *looks at her sharply, shifts his glance from her to* JOE *and back again; he exits.*) Joe. . . .

JOE: Gee, that poor boy. . . .

LORNA *(holding herself off):* But it wasn't your fault.

JOE: That's right—it wasn't my fault!

LORNA: You didn't mean it!

JOE: That's right—I didn't mean it! I wouldn't want to do that, would I? Everybody knows I wouldn't want to kill a man. Lorna, you know it!

LORNA: Of course!

JOE: But I *did* it! That's the thing—I *did* it! What will my father say when he hears I murdered a man? Lorna, I see what I did. I murdered myself, too! I've been running around in circles. Now I'm smashed! That's the truth. Yes, I was a real sparrow, and I wanted to be a fake eagle! But now I'm hung up by my finger tips —I'm no good—my feet are off the earth!

LORNA *(in a sudden burst, going to* JOE): Joe, I love you! We love each other. Need each other!

JOE: Lorna darling, I see what's happened!

LORNA: You wanted to conquer the world——

JOE: Yes——

LORNA: But it's not the kings and dictators who do it—it's that kid in the park——

JOE: Yes, that boy who might have said, "I have myself; I am what I want to be!"

LORNA: And now, tonight, here, this minute—finding yourself again —that's what makes you a champ. Don't you see that?

JOE: Yes, Lorna—yes!

LORNA: It isn't too late to tell the world good evening again!

JOE: With what? These fists?

LORNA: Give up the fighting business!

JOE: Tonight!

LORNA: Yes, and go back to your music——

JOE: But my hands are ruined. I'll never play again! What's left, Lorna? Half a man, nothing, useless. . . .

LORNA: No, *we're* left! Two together! We have each other! Somewhere there must be happy boys and girls who can teach us the way of life! We'll find some city where poverty's no shame—where music is no crime!—where there's no war in the streets—where a man is glad to be himself, to live and make his woman herself!

JOE: No more fighting, but where do we go?

LORNA: Tonight? Joe, we ride in your car. We speed through the night, across the park, over the Triboro Bridge——

JOE (*taking* LORNA'S *arms in his trembling hands*): Ride! That's it, we ride—clear my head. We'll drive through the night. When you mow down the night with headlights, nobody gets you! You're on top of the world then—nobody laughs! That's it—speed! We're off the earth—unconnected! We don't have to think!! That's what speed's for, an easy way to live! Lorna darling, we'll burn up the night! (*He turns and as he begins to throw his street clothes out of his locker*)

Medium Fadeout

SCENE III

Late the same night.

In the Bonaparte home sit EDDIE FUSELI, MOODY, ROXY *and* SIGGIE, *drinking homemade wine, already half drunk.* MR. BONAPARTE *stands on the other side of the room, looking out of the window.* FRANK *sits near him, a bandage around his head.*

MOODY *is at the telephone as the lights fade in.*

MOODY (*impatiently*): . . . 'lo? Hello! . . .

SIGGIE: I'll tell you why we need another drink. . . .

ROXY: No, I'll tell you. . . .

MOODY (*turning*): Quiet! For Pete's sake! I can't hear myself think! (*Turning to the phone.*) Hello? . . . This is Moody. Any calls for me? Messages? . . . No sign of Miss Moon? . . . Thanks. Call me if she comes in—the number I gave you before. (*Hanging up and returning to his wine glass; to* MR. BONAPARTE): I thought you said Joe was coming up here!

MR. BONAPARTE: I say maybe. . . .

MOODY (*sitting*): I'll wait another fifteen minutes. (*He drinks.*)

SIGGIE: Here's why we need another drink; it's a night of success! Joe's in those lofty brackets from now on! We're gonna move to a better neighborhood, have a buncha kids! (*To* MR. BONAPARTE): Hey, pop, I wish we had a mortgage so we could pay it off! To the next champ of the world! (SIGGIE *lifts his glass; the others join him.*)

ROXY: Bonaparte.

EDDIE: Don't you drink, Mr. Bonaparte?

SIGGIE: You, too, Frank—it's all in the family. (MR. BONAPARTE *shrugs and comes down, accepting a glass.*)

ROXY: It's in the nature of a celebration!

MR. BONAPARTE: My son'sa kill a man tonight—what'sa celebrate? What'so gonna be, heh?

SIGGIE: Ahh, don't worry—they can't do him nothing for that! An accident!

EDDIE (*coldly, to* MR. BONAPARTE): Listen, it's old news. It's been out on the front page two-three hours.

MR. BONAPARTE: Poor color' boy . . .

MOODY: Nobody's fault. Everybody's sorry—we give the mother a few bucks. But we got the next champ! Bottoms up. (*All drink,* FRANK *included.*)

ROXY (*to* MR. BONAPARTE): You see how a boy can make a success nowadays?

MR. BONAPARTE: Yeah . . . I see.

EDDIE (*resenting* MR. BONAPARTE'S *attitude*): Do we bother you? If I didn't think Joe was here I don't come up. I don't like nobody to gimme a boycott!

MR. BONAPARTE (*going back to the window*): Helpa you'self to more wine.

SIGGIE *(to* EDDIE): Leave him alone—he don't feel social tonight.

MOODY: Don't worry, Mr. Bonaparte. Looka me—take a lesson from me—I'm not worried. I'm getting married tomorrow—*this after-noon!*—I don't know where my girl is, but I'm not worried! What for? We're all in clover up to our necks!

SIGGIE: Shh . . . don't wake up my wife. (MOODY *suddenly sits heavily; jealousy begins to gnaw at him despite his optimism.* ROXY *takes another drink.* EDDIE *asks* FRANK, *apropos of his bandaged head):*

EDDIE: What's that "Spirit of '76" outfit for?

SIGGIE *(grinning to* EDDIE): Didn't you hear what he said before? They gave it to him in a strike——

EDDIE *(to* FRANK): You got a good build—you could be a fighter.

FRANK: I fight. . . .

EDDIE: Yeah? For what?

FRANK: A lotta things I believe in. . . . (EDDIE *looks at* FRANK *and appreciates his quality.)*

EDDIE: Whatta you get for it?

ROXY *(laughing):* Can't you see? A busted head!

FRANK: I'm not fooled by a lotta things Joe's fooled by. I don't get autos and custom-made suits. But I get what Joe don't.

EDDIE: What don't he get? (MR. BONAPARTE *comes in and listens intently.)*

FRANK *(modestly):* The pleasure of acting as you think! The satisfaction of staying where you belong, being what you are . . . at harmony with millions of others!

ROXY *(pricking up his ears):* Harmony? That's music! the family's starting up music again!

FRANK *(smiling):* That's right, that's music——*(Now* MOODY *emphatically stamps his glass down on the table and stands.)*

MOODY: What's the use waiting around! They won't be back. *(Bitterly.)* Lorna's got a helluva lotta nerve, riding around in Long Island with him! Without even asking me!

SIGGIE: Long Island's famous for the best eating ducks.

EDDIE *(to* MOODY): You got the champ—you can't have everything.

MOODY: What's that supposed to mean?

EDDIE *(coldly):* That girl belongs to Bonaparte. They're together now, in some roadhouse . . . and they ain't eating duck!

MOODY *(finally, unsteadily):* You don't know what you're talking about!

EDDIE: Moody, what do you figger your interest is worth in Bonaparte?

MOODY: Why?

EDDIE *(without turning):* Roxy . . . are you listening?

ROXY: Yeah. . . .

EDDIE: 'Cause after tonight I'd like to handle Bonaparte myself.

MOODY: . . . Your gall is gorgeous! But I got a contract. . . .

ROXY: Eddie, have a heart—I'm holding a little twenty percent. . . .
(Out of sheer rage MOODY *drinks more wine;* ROXY *follows his example.)*

FRANK *(to* EDDIE*):* How much does Joe own of himself?

EDDIE: Thirty percent. After tonight I own the rest.

MOODY: Oh, no! No, sir-ee!!

EDDIE: You're drunk tonight! Tomorrow!

MR. BONAPARTE *(coming forward):* Maybe Joe don't gonna fight no more, after tonight. . . .

EDDIE: Listen, you creep! Why don't you change your tune for a minute!

ROXY *(to* MR. BONAPARTE*):* What're YOU worried about?

MR. BONAPARTE: My boy usta coulda be great for all men. Whatta he got now, heh? Pardon me fora nota to feel so confident in Joe'sa future! Pardon me fora to be anxious. . . .

EDDIE *(standing up):* I don't like this talk!

SIGGIE: Sit down, pop—you're rocking the boat! Shh! Shh! *(He slips out of the room.)*

ROXY: Does anyone here know what he's talking about?

FRANK: He's trying to say he's worried for Joe.

ROXY: But why? Why? Don't he realize his kid's worth a fortune from tonight on? *(After giving* EDDIE *a quick glance.)* Ain't he got brains enough to see two feet ahead? Tell him in Italian—he don't understand our language—this is a festive occasion! To Bonaparte, the Monarch of the Masses! *(The telephone rings.)*

MOODY *(triumphantly, to* EDDIE*):* That's my hotel! You see, you were all wrong! That's Lorna! *(Speaking into the telephone.)* Hello? . . . No. . . . *(Turning to* MR. BONAPARTE.*)* It's for you. (MOODY *extends the telephone in* MR. BONAPARTE'S *direction, but the latter stands in his place, unable to move. After a few seconds* FRANK *sees this and briskly moves to the telephone, taking it from* MOODY. *In the meantime* MOODY *has begun to address* EDDIE *with drunken eloquence. Wavering on his feet.)* There's a constitution in this country, Eddie Fuseli. Every man here enjoys life, liberty and the pursuit of happiness!

FRANK *(speaking into the telephone):* Yes? . . . No, this is his son. . . . (MR. BONAPARTE *watches* FRANK *mutely as he listens at the telephone.)*

MOODY: There's laws in this country, Fuseli!—*contracts!* We live in a civilized world—!

FRANK *(loudly, to the others):* Keep quiet! *(Resumes listening.)* Yes . . . yes. . . .

ROXY *(to* EDDIE): And there's a God in heaven—don't forget it!

FRANK *(on the telephone):* Say it again. . . . *(He listens.)* Yes.

MOODY *(to* EDDIE): You're a killer! A man tries to do his best—but you're a killer! (FRANK *lowers the telephone and comes down to the others.)*

FRANK: *You're all killers!* (MR. BONAPARTE *advances a step toward* FRANK.)

MR. BONAPARTE: Frank . . . is it . . . ?

FRANK: I don't know how to tell you, poppa. . . .

MR. BONAPARTE *(hopefully):* Yes? . . .

FRANK: We'll have to go there——

EDDIE: Go where?

FRANK: Both of them . . . they were killed in a crash——

EDDIE: Who?! What?!

FRANK: They're waiting for identification—Long Island, Babylon.

EDDIE *(moving to* FRANK): What are you handing me?! (EDDIE, *suddenly knowing the truth, stops in his tracks. The telephone operator signals for the telephone to be replaced. The mechanical clicks call* FRANK *to attention; he slowly replaces the instrument.)*

MOODY: I don't believe that! Do you hear me? I don't believe it——

FRANK: What waste! . . .

MOODY: It's a goddam lie!!

MR. BONAPARTE: What have-a you expect? . . .

MOODY *(suddenly weeping):* Lorna! . . .

MR. BONAPARTE *(standing, his head high):* Joe. . . . Come, we bring-a him home . . . where he belong. . . .

Slow Fadeout

ROCKET TO THE MOON

A Romance In Three Acts

FOR HAROLD CLURMAN, FRIEND

Rocket to the Moon was first presented by the Group Theatre at the Belasco Theatre on the evening of November 24, 1938, with the following members of the Group Theatre Acting Company:

(In order of speech)

BEN STARK, D.D.S.	*Morris Carnovsky*
BELLE STARK	*Ruth Nelson*
CLEO SINGER	*Eleanor Lynn*
PHIL COOPER, D.D.S.	*Art Smith*
MR. PRINCE	*Luther Adler*
FRENCHY	*Leif Erickson*
WILLY WAX	*Sanford Meisner*
A SALESMAN	*William Challee*

Directed by HAROLD CLURMAN
Settings by MORDECAI GORELIK

SCENES

ACT ONE

Dr. Stark's waiting room. A June afternoon.

ACT TWO

The same.

Scene I. An afternoon in July.
Scene II. Late afternoon, the beginning of August.

ACT THREE

The same. Night. The end of August.

ROCKET TO THE MOON

ACT ONE

TIME: *The Present.*

PLACE: *A dentist's waiting room in a New York office building. A door to the elevators at the left. On the right side is a window. At the back are two doors, one leading to the dentist's office, the other open and showing the dentist's chair and apparatus. There is also a small hall, up right, which leads to another dentist's office.*

The curtain rises on the waiting room during an early hot June afternoon. Present are DR. BEN STARK *and his wife,* BELLE. *At the moment there is a strain and coolness between them, resulting from a family discussion on economics. In the silence* STARK *puffs strongly on his pipe as he looks at a page of a dental magazine in his hand.* BELLE *is depressed but hides it well.*

STARK *(finally):* You've had your last word. There's nothing more to say.

BELLE: No, I want you to make up your own mind, or see that I'm right.

STARK: Aren't you always right, Belle?

BELLE: Ben, dear, such remarks are uncalled for.

STARK: You know I've wanted to specialize all my life. Yesterday your father proposes that I open a new office in a suitable neighborhood. He offers to bear all the expense, new equipment and all that. Look at that outfit—this x-ray unit! All night I didn't sleep thinking about it!

BELLE: Ben, you mustn't over-simplify——

STARK *(breaking in):* Let's forget it, Belle.

BELLE: Poppa would pay the initial cost, but the rent there would be three times what it is here.

STARK: A little over two.

BELLE: A little less than three. You know the people here won't come uptown. It's too far away and that expensive neighborhood would frighten them off. It takes years to develop a practice. We had the experience twice——

STARK *(breaking in):* You win, you win!

BELLE *(earnestly):* It's not that I want to win, Ben. Don't you see that, Ben? Don't you see it?

STARK *(harshly, standing up): I told you let's forget it. It's settled!* *(Moodily, after a pause.)* I was a pioneer with Gladstone in orthodontia, once. Now I'm a dentist, good for sixty dollars a week, while men with half my brains and talents are making their twenty and thirty thousand a year!—I came over to the water cooler and I can't remember what for.

BELLE: To take a drink. . . .

STARK: I wanted to do something . . . what was it? Not a drink. . . . Oh, the flowers! *(He fills a paper cup, puts his pipe between his teeth and tries without success, one hand full, to fill a second cup.)*

BELLE: Try one at a time, dear.

STARK *(coolly):* One at a time is a good idea. *(At the window, right, he pours the water on a window box of drooping petunias. As he turns for more water he faces* BELLE *who has brought him the second cupful.)* Thanks.

BELLE *(smiling):* Any day now I'm expecting to have to powder and diaper you. *(Without an answer,* STARK *turns from the window and sits on the couch. After further silence, to make conversation):*

STARK: I like flowers. . . .

BELLE *(to ease the tension):* You missed your profession, Ben.

STARK *(soberly):* Botany?

BELLE: No, a florist shop.

STARK: I don't think you'd have married a florist.

BELLE: Why not? The way Poppa and Momma were always quarreling?—My nerves mincemeat? The way I felt when I married you, I'd have married a shoemaker almost.

STARK: I have a bunch of answers for that, but I won't give them.

BELLE: But he would have had to be calm and quiet, the way you were. You have such dignity, Ben . . . even when you're angry.

STARK *(annoyed):* I'm not angry, dear.

BELLE *(softly):* I know what it means to you. . . . *(Seductively.)* Don't you think I know?

STARK: I know you know. . . .

BELLE: Tell Poppa what you decided. Is he coming here?

STARK: Some time this afternoon.

BELLE: Is it settled?

STARK: It's settled.

BELLE *(cautiously):* Did Poppa bring up the question of moving in with us again?

STARK: Yes. . . .

BELLE: Don't encourage him.

STARK *(half indignantly):* I don't, but I must say I can't understand how a father and daughter can be on the outs for so many years.

BELLE: If you'd seen the life of hell he gave my mother, you'd understand.

STARK: All right, but your mother's been dead a year. He's an old man, lonely——

BELLE: He'll manage—he's been to school.

STARK: I only mean that he's alone in the world——

BELLE *(seriously):* A man and his wife should live alone, always. Poppa would be an intruder in our house. We wouldn't have a minute to ourselves. And out of sheer respect for my mother's memory——

STARK: Your father isn't a villain——

BELLE: Why do you take his part?

STARK *(again indignantly):* I'm not, but after all, a man wants to spend thousands of dollars putting me in a better practice and you expect me to think he's a villain?

BELLE: Now, Ben, you know he'd be in the way, don't you?

STARK *(reluctantly, after a pause):* I guess so. . . .

BELLE: Don't you know it?

STARK *(with a faint ironic smile):* Yes, ma'm. . . .

BELLE *(moving around the irony):* Then it's settled.

STARK *(nodding his head):* Umm.

BELLE *(crossing for purse):* Where's the girl, your new secretary? My, my, two hours for lunch—a fancy lady, indeed! That girl isn't working out!

STARK: She's new at the job, dear. Give her time.

BELLE: She's taking plenty, two hours for lunch. And then the third week here you raise her salary. I don't understand you, Ben Stark.

STARK: Can a girl live on twelve dollars a week?

BELLE: I could manage if I had to, for the both of us.

STARK: Thank God we don't have to——

BELLE: It's not God who keeps us off the dole.

STARK: It's you, Belle. I don't know what I'd do without you! *(He puts his arms around her.)*

BELLE: Take the pipe out of my face. *(He moves his pipe and they kiss.*) And now your terrible wife is going to give you another push. Did you put the ad in the paper? If we don't sublet the apartment soon, we'll have it on our hands all summer, and we can't afford it.

STARK: That's why Miss Singer's late. I asked her to put the ad in while she was out to lunch.

BELLE: She'll forget.

STARK: I'll eat my hat if she does. (DR. COOPER *enters from up right and crosses to the water cooler, where he drinks.*)

COOPER: Hot day.

BELLE: Yes.

COOPER (*crossing back*): Beer makes you hotter. It's not a hot-weather drink like they think. (*Exits right again.*)

BELLE (*lowering her voice*): I didn't know Dr. Cooper was in his office.

STARK: He's pouring some model or something. He's got his own troubles.

BELLE: How much does he owe us?

STARK (*sotto voce*): Not so loud, Belle.

BELLE (*dropping her voice*): How much?

STARK (*trying to remember*): He hasn't paid his rent for three months.

BELLE: Four. Charity's a fine trait.

STARK: But it begins at home?

BELLE: You think it shouldn't? . . . Move the pipe away. Stop being soft-hearted. Will you be able to take a vacation this summer?

STARK: Why, we're taking a bungalow at the beach.

BELLE: That's a substitute for a vacation. Why can't we do what Jack and Milly Heitner do? Go to the Rockies, or to Europe in the summer? But you're considerate of others. Not of yourself or your wife!

STARK (*slowly*): I never thought of it that way.

BELLE: A woman wants to live *with* a man—not next to him. I see you three or four hours a night—in the morning you're gone before I get up. I'll elope some day. Then you'll cry your blue eyes black.

STARK: Every once in awhile I see something I didn't see before.

BELLE: What vision hit you now?

STARK: That being a dentist's wife is no joke——

BELLE: That's an old story——

STARK (*with sudden buoyancy*): I wish I could change everything. I'd buy Aladdin's lamp for a thousand dollars if I could. We'd rub it up, we'd rub it down—Slam! We'd be in China——!

BELLE: I'll settle for Lake George—*(The door, left, opens. An elderly man walks in, quickly takes in the scene, and hastily exits.* BELLE'S *back is to the door, but she catches* STARK'S *glance.)* Who was that?

STARK: Your father.

BELLE: Where?

STARK *(going to the door):* He looked in and walked right out again.

BELLE: Don't call him. He'll be back in his own sweet time . . . in case you should both want to discuss me.

STARK *(surprised):* Discuss you? Why?

BELLE: I heard him make a remark to you once: "The mother ate sour grapes and the daughter's teeth are set on edge." Ben, don't let Poppa turn you against me. Explain to him why you can't accept his offer——

STARK: Say, I see I've walked into something today.

BELLE: I happen to have been feeling blue all morning.

STARK: Why?

BELLE: Never mind. . . .

STARK: Tell me why.

BELLE: It doesn't matter, Ben . . . if you don't remember it.

STARK: What?

BELLE: Did you really forget, Ben? (STARK *is puzzled and tries to joke away her distressed look.)*

STARK *(with a boyish twinkle):* It's not your birthday and we were married in the winter. Or is it *my* birthday? . . . *(Then suddenly.)* Oh . . .

BELLE: What?

STARK: You're thinking about . . . the boy?

BELLE: Yes. . . .

STARK *(putting his arms around her):* Well . . . it's not as if we had him . . . he died at birth. . . .

BELLE: Three years ago this morning. I had him, I felt I had him. . . .

STARK: Don't think about it, dear.

BELLE: But never to be able to have another one . . . well . . .

STARK: Don't think about it, Belle.

BELLE: We could adopt a boy . . . if you wanted. . . .

STARK: Someone else's?

BELLE: If you wanted. . . .

STARK: We'll talk about it some other time, dear.

BELLE: Ben, you have to love me all the time. I have to know my husband's there, loving me and needing me.

STARK *(wanting to escape further involvement):* Which I do, Belle, you know I do. Come on downstairs and let me buy you an ice cream soda.

BELLE: You know as much about women as the man in the moon!

STARK: I admit it. . . .

BELLE: No wonder your women patients don't like you.

STARK: They like me.

BELLE: Who? (CLEO SINGER *enters the waiting room.* STARK *quickly looks from secretary to wife and back again.)*

STARK *(sternly, for his wife's sake):* You're late, Miss Singer——

CLEO: Late? Good afternoon, Mrs. Stark.

STARK: You're not supposed to take two hours for lunch.

CLEO: The buses take so long. . . . I'm sorry.

BELLE: Are you eating lunch in the Waldorf Astoria these days?

STARK: No, she went down to put the ad in.

CLEO: Ad? . . .

BELLE *(watching her closely):* Eat your hat—she forgot it!

STARK: Did you?

CLEO: I meant to . . . Yes, it seems——

STARK: You're not very efficient, Miss Singer.

CLEO: It's so hot today.

BELLE: But how about the whole week? You had a whole week to clean the instruments and cut some cotton rolls for Dr. Stark.

CLEO *(helplessly):* I'm going to do that right now, Mrs. Stark.

BELLE: No, right now you're going to take the ad to the *Times.*

STARK *(to* BELLE): She'd better stay here now. I'll send the ad down with a messenger boy. *(To* CLEO.) You'd better change into your uniform.

CLEO: Right away, Dr. Stark. (CLEO *escapes into the office and closes the door behind her.)*

STARK *(in a low voice):* Let's not discuss her now.

BELLE: She has to be told——

STARK: Not now, Belle, not in front of her.

BELLE: Why not?

STARK: Belle, don't you think the girl has feelings? You and I are going downstairs. A soda for you, pipe tobacco for me. *(Seeing her face.)* What's the matter, Belle?

BELLE: Go without me. I want to talk to her a minute.

STARK: Belle . . .

BELLE: On your way, Dr. Stark. *(He looks at her, shrugs his shoulders and starts for the door.)* Put your street jacket on—be professional, Ben. (STARK *changes his dentist's gown for a street jacket, looks at his wife again and exits left. Clearing her voice and then calling.)* Miss Singer!

CLEO *(within):* Yes?

BELLE: Are you changing?

CLEO: Yes.

BELLE: I want to have a few words with you.

CLEO *(opening the door but standing behind it):* I'll be out in just a sec', Mrs. Stark.

BELLE: You're dressed to kill, Miss Singer.

CLEO: That's one of my ordinary everyday dresses—angel-skin satin.

BELLE: It looks hot.

CLEO *(coming into the waiting room in her uniform):* It's one of my coolest dresses.

BELLE: Is that why you don't wear stockings?

CLEO: Yes.

BELLE *(disapprovingly):* I thought maybe to save money.

CLEO: I come from a well-to-do family.

BELLE: How well to do?

CLEO: I really don't need this job.

BELLE *(archly):* Nevertheless, as long as you have the job, you should wear stockings in the office.

CLEO: Yes?

BELLE: Yes, it looks sloppy and it makes a very bad impression on the patients. Why do you wear your hair up in the air like that?

CLEO: Don't you like it this way?

BELLE: You're not modeling dresses now, Miss Singer.

CLEO: Oh, did Dr. Stark tell you——

BELLE: Dr. Stark tells me everything. The bills have to be sent out.

CLEO: I know that.

BELLE: Also, the reminder cards——

CLEO: I know that.

BELLE *(overly patient):* If you know so much, why don't you do it?

CLEO *(flustered):* You see, I was . . . (DR. COOPER *enters again from his office off right. He is wearing the usual dentist's gown. He is a big man, hot and troubled at present. He speaks and moves in irregular unexpected rhythms, but his manner is always frank and winning. He is boyish and uncomplex, but worried.)*

COOPER: Did the phone ring just now? Did I hear a phone ring?

BELLE: No, you didn't, Dr. Cooper.

COOPER: I must be imagining things. *(Goes to water cooler to drink.)*

CLEO: Probably.

COOPER: What?

CLEO *(innocently):* I said probably. *(Seeing* BELLE *give her a strong look.)* I'll start on the bills now. *(She exits into the office, closing the door behind her.)*

COOPER *(drinking):* Municipal champagne! *(Sitting heavily.)* Bills!— She thinks people pay bills! I'm expecting a call. What did you say?

BELLE: Nothing. . . .

COOPER: I'm hot—hot hot hot! In my younger days I was inclined to poetry. In my older days I'm inclined to poverty.

BELLE: What are your plans for the summer?

COOPER: What are the plans of a horse?

BELLE: You sound discouraged.

COOPER: My boy fell on his skates yesterday and broke his arm.

BELLE: I'm sorry to hear that.

COOPER: And that's the only break I've had in years! Yes, I went through the whole war and nothing happened to me. They could have left me there——

BELLE: You . . . owe us a few months' rent here.

COOPER: You have my sympathies.

BELLE: I know it's a bad time to remind you——

COOPER: To tell the truth, I'm waiting for a call from the loan company. I'll see what they have to say.

BELLE *(not unkindly):* Why do you drink so much?

COOPER: Who drinks so much?

BELLE: Maybe it's coffee I smell.

COOPER: Yeah, Scotch coffee.

BELLE: Fair is fair, and if you share an office with another dentist, you have to share expenses. You won't do that by letting patients smell liquor on your breath, will you?

COOPER: What're you doing? Bawling me out?

BELLE: I'm telling you what I think.

COOPER: Maybe I'm not interested.

BELLE: My husband lets people walk all over him—Don't you think you're taking advantage of his good nature?

COOPER: That's a real nervy remark!

BELLE *(quietly):* You don't meet your obligations.

COOPER: Sure, but give a man a chance!

BELLE: Dr. Cooper, to drink his practice away?

COOPER *(wrathfully):* Who're you talking to? I'm not some shyster, some drunken bum!

BELLE *(patient, as with a child):* Please don't shout.

COOPER: Is that what I am? A bum? Is that how I look to you?

BELLE: Nothing of the sort——

COOPER *(after a pause):* I don't blame you.

BELLE: For what?

COOPER *(sitting again):* For looking out for your husband's interests. A civilized person can't tolerate me. Business won't pick up till after Labor Day. But if the loan company decides to—*(Within the office the telephone rings.* COOPER *quickly opens the door and takes the telephone from* CLEO'S *hands.)* Hello? . . . Yes, this is your party . . . yes . . . yes . . . yes . . . (COOPER *hangs up the telephone and trails back into the waiting room.* BELLE *sees* CLEO *staring out with curiosity and closes the office door on her.)* No, no dice . . . no shoes for baby. . . . I don't know what I'll do with my boy—Children are not like furniture—You can't put them in storage. If his mother was alive . . .

BELLE *(genuinely touched by his abject attitude):* Stay another month. . . .

COOPER *(slowly):* The summer'll be dead. Excuse me for the rumpus before. When I'm happy I'm a different person. You'd be surprised —everybody likes Phil Cooper. *(He moves to the outer door, left.)*

BELLE: Where are you going?

COOPER: For a drink of coffee, Scotch coffee. (COOPER *exits.* BELLE *goes to the side table for her purse and gloves. From there she reaches up to the electric fan and slows it down a notch. Then she calls to* CLEO.)

BELLE: Miss Singer?

CLEO *(opening the office door):* Yes, Mrs. Stark?

BELLE: I'm going now. Tell Dr. Stark his terrible wife expects him home at seven. Good-bye.

CLEO: Good-bye. *(In crossing the room* BELLE *picks up the dental magazine which* STARK *left on the couch.)*

BELLE: Oh, one more thing. *(Handing over the magazine.)* Put this in the office, like a good girl.

CLEO: Surely.

BELLE: Good-bye. *(As she looks* CLEO *over.)*

CLEO: Good-bye, Mrs. Stark. *(As* BELLE *goes to the door it is opened from the outside.* MR. PRINCE, BELLE'S *father, enters again. He is near sixty, wears an old panama hat, a fine Palm Beach suit of twenty years ago and a malacca cane. There is about him the dignity and elegant portliness of a Jewish actor, a sort of aristocratic air. He is an extremely self-confident man with a strong sense of humor which, however, is often veiled. He is very alive in the eyes and mouth, the rest of him relaxed and heavy.* BELLE *looks at her father, who looks back at her with the same silence. He holds the door open for her as she exits.* MR. PRINCE *slowly crosses and seats himself, leaning on his cane with both hands.)*

PRINCE *(with genuine curiosity):* Who are you?

CLEO *(timidly):* Who are you?

PRINCE *(pointing to the door):* I am the old father of that lady, so called.

CLEO: Mr. Prince?

PRINCE *(with suave gravity):* Yes.

CLEO: I heard of you.

PRINCE: From who?

CLEO: Frenchy.

PRINCE: Who?

CLEO: Frenchy—Dr. Jensen.

PRINCE *(moving restlessly around the room):* You mean the foot doctor down the hall.

CLEO: Yes. Don't you speak to her?

PRINCE: No.

CLEO: Why?

PRINCE *(grandly):* I am the American King Lear. *(Seeing her bewildered look.)* Where is Dr. Stark?

CLEO: He'll be back in a minute.

PRINCE: And who are you?

CLEO: I'm the new secretary.

PRINCE: Hmm . . . what are your opinions?

CLEO: On what?

PRINCE: On anything. *(Taking newspaper from side table.)* Here's the paper. Do you read? What are you? A communist? A fascist? A democrat?

CLEO: I don't know about all these things.

PRINCE: *(glancing at the paper):* Here it says in India a snake swallowed a man. What is your opinion of that, Miss . . . ?

CLEO: Singer.

PRINCE: What is that book in your hand?

CLEO: A dental magazine.

PRINCE: Leave it here—I like to look at pictures. (CLEO *gives him the magazine.)* Are you afraid of me?

CLEO: No. . . .

PRINCE: Then why do you act nervous before me?

CLEO: I'm not nervous.

PRINCE: What's your first name?

CLEO: Cleo. . . .

PRINCE: Yes, Miss Cleo. . . . That's a name for a dancer. Do you dance?

CLEO: Yes.

PRINCE: You don't say!

CLEO: I've been with several shows.

PRINCE: You don't say! A dancer? What is the secret of life? Do you know?

CLEO: The secret?

PRINCE: I don't chew my cabbage twice, Miss Cleo. Let us pass on to my opinion of this *(Indicating the newspaper)* front page. Are you listening?

CLEO: Yes.

PRINCE: In my opinion the universe is governed by a committee; one man couldn't make so many mistakes. *(Seeing* CLEO *laugh heartily.)* Is that funny?

CLEO: Yes.

PRINCE *(smiling):* I like to make people laugh. My daughter calls me a clown. The two of them, my wife included—with their bills they ate holes in me like Swiss cheese, but I was a clown!

CLEO: Mrs. Stark is very observant.

PRINCE: She annoys you?

CLEO *(withdrawing):* I wouldn't say that.

PRINCE: Speak freely, Miss Cleo——

CLEO: Excuse me for being so personal before.

PRINCE: Everything that's healthy is personal.

CLEO: You're a very peculiar man, Mr. Prince.

PRINCE: Because I joke?

CLEO: Are you joking?

PRINCE *(twisting his hand from the wrist):* Yes and no, hot and cold, like a shower. Do you have a gospel?

CLEO *(warily puzzled):* What?

PRINCE: Every woman wants to convert a man to the gospel of herself. Fact? Fact! What is your gospel?

CLEO *(after a pause):* I don't understand a word you're saying, Mr. Prince!

PRINCE: It doesn't matter—I'm only a minor person in life. But I see you're honest.

CLEO *(narrowly):* You're making fun of me!

PRINCE *(raising a hand):* God forbid! You know something? . . . often I wished I was a young girl. I'd get somebody to support me —no worries about money——

CLEO *(flashingly):* Nobody supports me!

PRINCE: A beautiful girl like you? Nobody supports you?

CLEO: No!

PRINCE: My remark makes you angry?

CLEO: Yes! I come from a very good home——

PRINCE: Miss Cleo, I think you need a revision of your philosophy——

CLEO: I heard enough from you! In fact I heard enough all day! I don't need this job. They burn your ears off around here for sixteen dollars a week. That's chicken feed!

PRINCE *(more than agreeing):* Less! *Pigeon* feed!

CLEO *(excited beyond diplomacy):* I don't have to stand in Macy's window and let people throw rocks at me!

PRINCE *(calmly agreeing):* Of course not.

CLEO: Am I the kind of girl who lets anybody make suggestive remarks to her?

PRINCE: No!

CLEO: Your daughter thinks——

PRINCE: Refer to her in the impersonal.

CLEO: Mrs. Stark, she thinks I'm a dummy. Do this, do that!—I'm a person!

PRINCE: One of the nicest I met in many years. Yes, Miss Cleo——

CLEO: And you?—You're an old fool!

PRINCE *(piously):* What is age? A matter of psychology. Am I decrepit in my psychology?

CLEO *(tossing her head):* I can't say!

PRINCE: The answer is no.

CLEO: And I don't care! If nobody cares for me I don't care for them!

PRINCE: Fair enough.

CLEO: I thought Dr. Stark was a nice man when I came here. But his wife just twists him around her little finger, like a spit curl.

PRINCE: Correct! And any woman could do the same.

CLEO: He stands there like a big shepherd dog and she tells him what to do!

PRINCE: Correct!

CLEO: He's afraid of his own shadow!

PRINCE: Correct!

CLEO *(excitedly):* You can't get in my good graces by agreeing with me in everything I say. I see right through you, Mr. Prince, like cellophane.

PRINCE *(calmly):* And when you look through the cellophane, what do you see?

CLEO: Never mind! How dare you say I have no opinions!

PRINCE: Did I say that?

CLEO: You insinuated that I was stupid——

PRINCE: Miss Cleo, I feel I know you for a lifetime.

CLEO *(scornfully):* Thanks for the compliment!

PRINCE: You know something? You're just like me——

CLEO: Oh, no I'm not!

PRINCE: So you're not. Then who are you like?

CLEO: Like myself, like Cleo Singer! And I'm good and mad!

PRINCE *(suddenly snapping out):* Calm down!

CLEO: What?

PRINCE *(sharply):* Calm down. You have expressed yourself enough! You work here in an office—a regular insect society—so don't act like a tiger. Unless you don't want the job.

CLEO *(immediately contrite):* Did I raise my voice?

PRINCE *(calmly):* You don't know the facts of life, Miss Cleo.

CLEO: I'm not thinking of the job, but I'm sorry I hurt your feelings. Please excuse me.

PRINCE: Always address your elders with respect. They could leave you a fortune.

CLEO: I didn't mean to say all those things——

PRINCE: Do you get along well with people?

CLEO: No.

PRINCE: Why?

CLEO *(changing her mind):* I get along with them.

PRINCE: Which is it?

CLEO (*distressed*): I'm sorry I said so much. . . .

PRINCE: Are you going to cry, Miss Cleo?

CLEO: No.

PRINCE: I see dewdrops. . . .

CLEO: Something's in my eye.

PRINCE (*drawing a white silk handkerchief from breast pocket*): Where? Which one?

CLEO: This.

PRINCE: Take your finger away. Look up. I won't hurt you. (*Delicately working on the eye.*) Don't move. . . . (*Unseen by them* DR. STARK *opens the door. He watches the scene with disapproval.*)

PRINCE: Is it out?

CLEO (*blinking*): I . . . think so.

PRINCE (*standing off a little*): Don't rub it.

CLEO (*blinking*): No.

PRINCE: You use nice toilet water. It smells like thousands of flowers——

CLEO: Gardenia.

PRINCE: Pleasant.

CLEO: Forty dollars an ounce.

PRINCE: Unpleasant.

CLEO: That's a beautiful handkerchief.

PRINCE: You like it? Have it.

CLEO: Oh, no——

PRINCE (*spying* STARK): Here is Benny, the shepherd dog. (CLEO *whirls around, guilt written all over her.*)

STARK: Hello, Poppa. . . .

CLEO (*rapidly*): There was something in my eye and Mr. Prince——

STARK: Is it out now?

CLEO: It was nothing——

PRINCE: A glass splinter . . . from my daughter's heart.

STARK (*with a slight frown, to* CLEO): I think you'd better take that ad down to the *Times,* Miss Singer. Just slip your coat on . . . (*In the silence* CLEO *takes her coat and goes to the door, left.*)

CLEO (*lamely*): Mrs. Stark says she expects you home at seven o'clock. She told me to tell you. . . . (*She exits.*)

STARK (*lightly*): What was going on here?

PRINCE (*sitting*): Just like she told you. (STARK *is changing jackets.*)

STARK: You're a great hand with the girls, Poppa.

PRINCE: It's the last thing in my mind.

STARK: But you mustn't talk that way about Belle in front of strangers.

PRINCE: Bad taste?

STARK: It doesn't happen to be true.

PRINCE: How old is Miss Cleo?

STARK *(smiling):* None of your business. Where did you disappear to before?

PRINCE *(sauntering to the window):* I often meant to ask you—What is that over there?

STARK: The back of the Hotel Algiers.

PRINCE: Hmm, I know a bookie in there. What must go on in those rooms at night . . .

STARK: What does it matter?

PRINCE: You got a decrepit psychology, Benny. Sometimes you talk like an old lady. *(Going back to his seat.)* Do they rent out rooms to couples?

STARK: Riffraff.

PRINCE: Some night I'll come and look . . . just as if it interests me!

STARK: Tell me, what interests you, Poppa?

PRINCE: I love to gamble; cards, the races, the market . . .

STARK: Wine, women and song.

PRINCE: In all my life I never took a drink, and I don't sing. Yes, Benny, *I* started from an idealist, too, believe it or not. Now I'm a villain. . . . What does your friend Shakespeare say on this point?

STARK: What point?

PRINCE: The point of all points—happiness! Where is she hiding, happiness? *(After giving* STARK *a quizzical glance.)* So when do you expect to move?

STARK *(nervously):* Move?

PRINCE *(picking up the dental magazine):* I see you turned down the pages—the machinery——

STARK: That Ritter outfit is a beauty. . . .

PRINCE *(seeing the other's hesitation):* But?

STARK: I've decided to stay here for the present, Poppa. Not that your kindness——

PRINCE: Why?

STARK: Belle thought . . . she thinks it won't be wise.

PRINCE *(pursing his lips):* I see. And you, what do you think?

STARK: After all, it's an economic risk. . . . *(He flushes off into silence.)*

PRINCE (*almost vehemently*): Crazy boy, I offer it to you on a silver platter——

STARK (*painfully*): That's how it is, Poppa.

PRINCE: Your nose is just the right shape to fit your wife's hand!

STARK: Is that a right thing to say?

PRINCE: Well, it's your life—yours and Mrs. Belle Stark!

STARK: Why do you insist, Poppa?

PRINCE: Because I like to do some good to a man who needs it! A lovable being!

STARK: Why don't you make it up with Belle?

PRINCE (*with a smile*): How's business?

STARK (*smiling*): Slow. . . .

PRINCE: The summer slump?

STARK: Yes. Why don't you get along with Belle, Poppa?

PRINCE (*wryly*): It's a pleasant June afternoon, Benny.

STARK: It grieves her very much.

PRINCE (*reluctantly*): Benny, my daughter don't like me; she claims I ruined her mother's life. I claim her mother ruined *my* life!

STARK: How?

PRINCE: There are two kinds of marriages, Benny—where the husband quotes the wife, or where the wife quotes the husband. Fact? Fact!

STARK: But you didn't speak to her for ten years.

PRINCE: Because she insulted my soul, me, a first-class man, a lover of his brother man——

STARK: And his sister!

PRINCE: Never! *But never!* Not once did I make a sexual deviation! And what did I ask from my wife? To be a companion, to help me succeed——

STARK: You did—you're worth a fortune.

PRINCE: In spite of her! I shouldn't be ambitious. Go work for somebody else for twenty dollars a week—a man with my brains! Play safe! A housewife's conception of life! In the bargain, she had more respectability under the blankets than you have on Fifth Avenue! A man of my strength, my fire! (*Now masking his feelings again.*) Drip, drip, the matrimonial waters go, and a man wears away. My wife is dead, I'm an old man who missed his boat. Ida Prince had her revenge . . . her husband has disappeared in the corner, with the dust, under the rug.

STARK *(grinning):* Nonsense! You haven't disappeared, Poppa. You're a very dominant person—

PRINCE *(passionately):* Without marriage I would have been one of the greatest actors in the world! . . . You don't believe it?

STARK *(having heard this before):* I believe it. . . .

PRINCE *(suddenly):* All my life I wanted to do something. . . . Pfu! . . . We'll talk of something pleasant.

STARK: After all is said and done, Poppa, Belle is your only child.

PRINCE: I'm her only father.

STARK: She's very lonely since Momma died. I feel sure she wants to bury the axe.

PRINCE *(cynically):* Certainly. . . . Right in my head! I have a certain respectable mania for the truth—we don't like each other.

STARK: And yet you want to live with us.

PRINCE: You I like, Benny. But in my whole life one sensible woman came to my attention—she killed herself. She left a note, "I am a pest."

STARK *(shaking his head):* You're in a bad mood today. . . .

PRINCE *(mopping his brow with the silk handkerchief and looking out at the Hotel Algiers again):* True, true—*(Turning back from the window.)* I made six thousand dollars this morning.

STARK: ! ? !

PRINCE: The more money I make, the more heartache. Who'll I leave all my money to? Mrs. Belle Stark, née Prince?

STARK *(smiling):* I know a certain orphan home in Philadelphia, where I was raised . . . they'd use it.

PRINCE: I don't know . . . maybe I'll leave it to Jascha Heifetz.

STARK: You going to Saratoga this summer?

PRINCE: Why should I drink Saratoga waters?—It only prolongs my life. *(Smiling slyly and winking.)* Am I wrong? . . . Hotel Algiers. A man is a mirror. He tells me his wife is wonderful. . . . I look in his face to see the truth.

STARK *(uncomfortably):* What do you see in my face?

PRINCE: A better liar than I gave you credit for. Is this the life you dreamed for yourself?

STARK: It's not Belle's fault.

PRINCE: One answer at a time. Is it?

STARK *(evasively, after a pause):* I don't know what you mean.

PRINCE: A life where every day is Monday. There used to be a weekend, but now it's always Monday. Awnings up, awnings down, coat on, coat off. Sweat in summer, freeze in winter—a movie, a bridge game, an auto ride to Peekskill. Gas is twenty cents a gallon, worry about the bills, write a budget—the maid is too expensive—you bought a pair of shoes *last* month. You're old, you're getting old—she's old. Yesterday you didn't look in my face. Tomorrow you forgot I'm here. Two aspirin pills are good for headaches. The world is getting . . . so dull, let me sleep, let me sleep! You sneeze, you have a cold. No, that was last month. No, it's now. Which is now and which is then? Benny . . . you used to be a clever boy! *(A silence follows, which* STARK *finally breaks.)*

STARK *(defiantly):* Yes, a certain man once said that in our youth we collect materials to build a bridge to the moon; but in our old age, he says, we use the materials to build a shack.

PRINCE *(looking around the room):* Yes, *this is it!* But you, you graduated first in the class! You played tennis, you were full of life and plans. Look, you don't even resent me now.

STARK *(slowly):* I'm what I am . . . it's not Belle's fault!

PRINCE: What are you?

STARK: Not unhappy. . . .

PRINCE: You fell asleep at the switch. But Belle is worried——

STARK: Is she?

PRINCE: She's intelligent. You don't have children to hold you together. You're almost forty . . . a time for special adventures.

STARK *(stung, with sudden hotness):* You have no right to speak this way! We're happy——

PRINCE *(cutting in):* You're happy? You're sure of your future? You go home with a happy face at night?

STARK: Don't make trouble, Poppa!

PRINCE *(half smiling):* Whose voice do you hear in your ear? Mine or yours? *(And then he smiles.)*

STARK *(slowing down):* Gee, Poppa, I never know when you're serious.

PRINCE: A housewife rules your destiny. You love her?

STARK: Of course!

PRINCE: She's got you where she wants you. . . . Like an iceberg, three-quarters under water. . . . *(Pause.)* I mightn't live forever. I want you to know what I think. *(He starts for the door.)*

STARK: You going home?

PRINCE: To my brokers and watch the board. My electric shares are going up. Your secretary uses too much paint and powder.

STARK: She'll tone it down.

PRINCE (*suddenly turning, hand on door knob, pointing his cane at* STARK *and lowering his voice to a near whisper*): Iceberg, listen . . . why don't you come up and see the world, the sea gulls and the ships to Europe? (*Coming back into the room.*) When did you look at another woman last? The year they put the buffalo nickel on the market? Why don't you suddenly ride away, an airplane, a boat! Take a rocket to the moon! Explode! What holds you back? You don't want to hurt Belle's feelings? You'll die soon enough——

STARK: I'll just have to laugh at that!

PRINCE: Laugh. . . . But make a motto for yourself: "Out of the coffin by Labor Day!" Have an affair with—with—with this girl . . . this Miss Cleo. She'll make you a living man again.

STARK (*laughing*): You're a great joker, Poppa. (PRINCE *follows* STARK'S *laughter; both men laugh together.*)

PRINCE: . . . Never look away from a problem, Benny.

STARK: I never know when you're serious.

PRINCE: When you look away from the problem, it don't disappear. But maybe *you* might disappear! Remember I told you! (PRINCE *abruptly exits.* STARK *is still laughing; now he suddenly stops, mouth half open. He is not feeling humorous and he realizes it in a flash. Rather he is now depressed, even frightened a little. Twice he mutters to himself.*)

STARK: "Sonofagun! . . . Sonofagun! . . ." (*Now* DR. JENSEN, *a chiropodist with office down the hall, commonly called Frenchy, breezes into the waiting room. He is an American of Swedish parents, aged thirty, realistic and alert, fast and practical. He has an active wiry body; wears a white jacket. Now he pins the door back.*)

FRENCHY: Hello, Doc. Pin back the door—it's hot. (*Goes to water cooler.*)

STARK (*abstracted*): Hello, Frenchy.

FRENCHY: Some day, when I can afford it, I'll get a water cooler. You don't mind me running in and out like that, do you? (*He sits.*)

STARK (*depressed*): Of course not, Frenchy.

FRENCHY: The Palm Beach kid was here again.

STARK: Who?

FRENCHY: Mr. Prince. He gave me a gloomy hello in the hall.

STARK: He's a gloomy man.

FRENCHY: Why?

STARK: I can't make out. He disturbs me.

FRENCHY: Why?

STARK: Every time he drops in here I'm depressed for hours after.

FRENCHY: Make a phonograph record—let me listen.

STARK: You wouldn't understand. You have to be married first.

FRENCHY: I see.

STARK: Do you know something about women?

FRENCHY: What?

STARK: No, I mean do you know anything about women?

FRENCHY: I'll be explicit: no!

STARK *(musingly):* A man falls asleep in marriage. And after a time he wants to keep on sleeping, undisturbed. I'm surprised how little I've thought about it. Gee!—What I don't know would fill a book.

FRENCHY *(watching him):* You look like helplessness personified.

STARK: He tries to tell me I'm dissatisfied with my married life——

FRENCHY: Maybe you are. . . .

STARK: He's very persuasive in some things, but I know he's incorrect. *(Suddenly grinning.)* Do I look like an unhappy man?

FRENCHY *(after a pause, soberly):* You'd know that better than me, Doc.

STARK *(shaking his head again):* Sonofagun! . . . Don't all married couples argue and disagree? Even the joke papers tell us that. A man would be a mad idealist to want a honeymoon all his life.

FRENCHY: No, he'd be a woman. A man can't be both lover and banker, enchanter and provider. But the girls want those combined talents. . . . The man who worries for the bucks is not the one to kiss his wife behind the ear.

STARK: Yes. . . . *(But continuing with his own thoughts.)* There's something positively *sinister* about that man!

FRENCHY: Prince? *Cynical.*

STARK: I don't understand human nature, not the off-color things. Suddenly he tells me he wants to be an actor! I like normal people, like you.

FRENCHY: Hell, who's normal nowadays! Take that kid of yours, that Cleo——

STARK: Sometimes people embarrass me. The most ordinary people suddenly become sinister——

FRENCHY: Sinister? They're just sleepy.

STARK: What about Miss Singer? You were saying—(COOPER *enters the waiting room, distracted and brooding.)*

FRENCHY *(with a glad shout):* Here's Coop! Let's hear what he has to say.

COOPER *(sitting heavily):* What?

FRENCHY: What's your opinion of women, Coop?

COOPER: Who's got time to think about women! I'm trying to make a living!

FRENCHY *(turning to* STARK *with a laugh):* You see!

COOPER: Is there a man in our generation with time to think about women? Show me that man and I'll show you a loafer!—*(To* STARK.) Did anybody call me while I was out?

STARK: No.

COOPER: This morning I had a hunch there'd be some business. Nobody called?

STARK: No. *(Notice here* FRENCHY'S *constant activity of watching people, listening and probing them, watching their reactions to things he says and does. It must be confessed: He is a self-educated, amateur student of human nature in all its aspects.)*

COOPER *(after a pause):* It's gonna be a hot summer. . . .

STARK: Nothing on your calendar today?

COOPER *(with a snort):* Yeah! At four o'clock a distant relative is coming in for a free cleaning. *(Mopping his brow.)* I'm dead! *(Pause.)* Your wife made me a proposition, to put up or get out.

STARK: When? !

COOPER: Recently. She almost chewed my head off. Before.

STARK *(embarrassed, trying to explain):* She thinks people take advantage of me. . . .

FRENCHY: You're doing those W.P.A. boys' work for half price—that's advantage.

STARK: I hope she doesn't hear about it.

FRENCHY: It's her business to hear about it: every generous impulse on your part brings her closer to insecurity.

COOPER *(defensively, annoyed):* You're a big busybody, Frenchy!

STARK *(protestingly):* You can't let poor boys like that just walk out.

FRENCHY: I know plenty who let them walk.

COOPER: Walk yourself, please—I have to talk business here.

FRENCHY *(giving* COOPER *a shrewd look):* Excusé moi. . . . I'll go back and take a nap.

STARK: In the middle of the day?

FRENCHY *(going to the door):* Why not? Just had my lunch. A snake eats a rabbit and falls asleep, don't it? Why should I be better than a snake? (FRENCHY *laughs and exits left.*)

COOPER: He's a madman. *(An uncomfortable silence ensues):* Who wears the pants in your family, Stark?

STARK *(indignantly):* Belle had no right to tell you that!

COOPER *(humble in the face of necessity):* Tell her you decided to let me stay in the office till after Labor Day. How is that for a request? *(After waiting for an answer.)* She might object . . . ?

STARK: I'll decide that, Phil!

COOPER: Well, that's my problem in a nutshell. You'll have an empty office on your hands if I leave.

STARK: Where would you go?

COOPER: In the park and eat grass.

STARK *(shocked back to attention):* As bad as that? *(After another uncomfortable pause.)* Can't you pay anything, Phil?

COOPER: No. . . .

STARK: I mean . . . you know . . .

COOPER: Sure. . . .

STARK *(finally):* . . . You'd better stay here till something happens. You can't move now.

COOPER: In July I'll pay a month—I'll get the money.

STARK *(uncomfortably):* You know how it is. . . .

COOPER: So it's settled?

STARK: Yes.

COOPER *(with the joy of relief):* You gave me a new lease on life! You're good, you're kind, you're generous to the nth degree!

STARK *(embarrassed):* No, I'm not. . . .

COOPER: Hail, Ben Stark!

STARK: Stop it, Phil. . . .

COOPER: No, I mean it, every word!

STARK: I hope things pick up for you.

COOPER: You're a pride to me, a pleasure! Now I'll go down for a shave. Again, thanks. *(He offers his hand, which* STARK *takes.)*

STARK: Shhh! *(With a laugh and a wave of his hand,* COOPER *starts for the exit, right.* CLEO SINGER *enters,* COOPER *almost knocking her down.)*

COOPER: Miss Singer, you're a lovely girl. Take any messages for me. *(*COOPER *exits, left.* CLEO *stands in her place a moment, surprised.* STARK *looks at her as if he had never seen her before, secretly examining her throughout the following scene. Because of his* *previous scene with* PRINCE *she now presents a challenge to him which he might never have come to alone.)*

CLEO: Why did he say that?

STARK: He's feeling good.

CLEO *(taking off her coat):* I almost roasted to death in this coat. They call weather like this earthquake weather in California.

STARK: Were you ever there?

CLEO: Surely, several times. *(Hanging up the coat.)* The more expensive kinds of camel hair don't wear well, do they?

STARK: Did you put the ad in?

CLEO: I don't forget my duties twice, Dr. Stark.

STARK *(appeased by her attractive humble air):* I owe you an apology for the way I shouted at you before.

CLEO *(pleasantly):* Into every life a little rain must fall. I don't mind.

STARK *(hesitantly):* You'd be much more attractive . . . if . . . you didn't . . . use so much lipstick.

CLEO: Too much? . . . It's so dark at this mirror here. *(Goes to the wall mirror.)*

STARK: It's only my opinion, Cleo——

CLEO *(turning rapidly):* Do you realize that's the first time you've called me Cleo since I've been here? !

STARK *(taken aback):* Is there any reason why I shouldn't?

CLEO: Oh, no! Certainly not!

STARK: How old are you, Cleo?

CLEO *(coquetting slightly):* Don't you think that's a personal question?

STARK: I have no personal motives. . . .

CLEO *(smiling back):* Mr. Prince asked me the same thing. He's a terrible flirt, isn't he?

STARK *(frowning):* That's his way. He tries to be interesting——

CLEO: Lots of men are trying to be interesting.

STARK: Are they?

CLEO *(she starts for the office door but stops short):* Would you mind if I don't wear stockings in the office in the summer? Mr. Bernstein at Chelsea-Pontiac didn't mind.

STARK: Well . . .

CLEO *(hastily):* If you say not to——

STARK *(ditto):* It's quite all right.

CLEO: Your wife might object.

STARK: Why should she?

CLEO: I may be wrong, but so many wives like to keep an eye on their husband's secretary.

STARK: Mrs. Stark runs my home. I run the office.

CLEO: After all, we must keep cool, mustn't we? May I say this?—I like you, Dr. Stark. Maybe that's too personal, but everything that's healthy is personal, don't you think?

STARK (*ponderously*): Very possible. . . . (CLEO *stops at the side table on her way to the office again.*)

CLEO: Looking at this newspaper makes me think—the universe must be ruled by a committee; one man couldn't be so stupid.

STARK (*smiling*): That's a very witty remark!

CLEO (*pleased*): I'm glad you think so, Dr. Stark.

STARK (*looking at his watch*): Mrs. Nelson will be here any minute. You'd better clean up the instruments, particularly the scalers.

CLEO: The scalers? . . . Which are those, Dr. Stark? I know, but I want to make sure.

STARK (*taking one from his top pocket*): These.

CLEO: I'll cut some cotton rolls, too.

STARK: Always dry an instrument when you remove it from the sterilizer. It'll clean easier.

CLEO: That's a very good hint.

STARK (*dryly*): I wasn't hinting. Patients like clean instruments.

CLEO: Of course. (*Stopping at the operating room door.*) Your wife was very angry with me before.

STARK (*impatiently*): Mrs. Stark is not the terrible person many people think she is!

CLEO (*dismayed*): Oh, I didn't mean anything. . . .

STARK (*almost savagely*): She's one of the most loyal, sincere and helpful persons I've ever met!

CLEO (*in a small voice*): I'm sure she is, I'm sure of that. . . . (CLEO *now disappears into the operating room. For a moment* STARK *stands there, wagging his head. His eye falls on the dental magazine. He picks it up, looks at the ad and then throws the magazine across the room. As he begins to fill his pipe his glance turns to the window, right. He moves over to the window and looks out at the Hotel Algiers.* CLEO'S *voice from the operating-room threshold turns him around with a guilty start. In a small contrite voice.*) Pardon me . . . did I tell you before? Your wife expects you home at seven.

STARK (*annoyed*): Yes, thanks—you told me—thanks!

CLEO *(meekly):* You're welcome, Dr. Stark. (CLEO *disappears into the operating room again.* STARK *looks after her, annoyed. For a moment he stands reflectively. Finally he strikes a match and begins to light his pipe.)*

Slow Curtain

ACT TWO

SCENE I

TIME: *July.*
PLACE: *The same.*

DR. STARK *is standing where we last saw him, now perusing a small volume of Shakespeare and smoking his pipe. He is much calmer than when last seen.* FRENCHY *is lazily turning over the pages of a picture magazine, his attention obliquely on* CLEO. *She sits near the water cooler, hands in lap, frankly watching and examining* DR. STARK. *Above, the electric fan hums busily; the outward door is held back for any possible extra ventilation.*

DR. STARK'S *pipe has gone out—he puffs on it strongly.* CLEO *immediately gives him a paper of matches. Then she crosses to the water cooler and drinks. Next she brings a cup of water to* STARK. FRENCHY *watches all of this.*

CLEO: I thought you'd like some cold water, Dr. Stark. It's so hot.

STARK: Thank you, Cleo.

CLEO: That's all right. . . . *(A quick glance passes between them,* FRENCHY *not missing it. To make conversation.)* Is that Shakespeare which interests you so much?

STARK *(turning the book over in his hand):* This? Yes, this is the very copy Dr. Gladstone gave me fifteen years ago. . . . Fifteen? Can that be right? . . . Yes, it's fifteen years ago. *(Shaking his head.)* Gosh . . .

CLEO: Was he your teacher?

STARK: Yes, and he was best man at my wedding, too. Shakespeare's a companion, he said—Whatever you want to know, look in his plays.

CLEO: Like a Bible?

STARK: Like a Bible. It was a great loss to me when Dr. Gladstone died. A wonderful man. Mrs. Stark didn't like him——

FRENCHY *(suddenly):* Must be hell to sleep two in a bed these nights.

STARK *(to* FRENCHY): What? Did you say something?

FRENCHY: The days and nights are just a congregation of sodden hours. (CLEO *seats herself and crosses her legs.*) Yeah, July is a month for celibacy.

CLEO: What does that mean, celibacy?

FRENCHY *(looking across at her):* Your skirt is up to your neck. *(After* CLEO *hastily adjusts her skirt)* Up at Fire Island yesterday a man collapsed from the heat while clipping a hedge. (CLEO *is and has been annoyed for days by* FRENCHY'S *consistently insolent attitude toward her.*)

CLEO: Dr. Jensen, you may be the world to your mother, but you're no joy to us. We know it's hot——

FRENCHY *(sharply):* Don't be so fresh, Angel Skin!

CLEO *(immediately cowed):* I'm sorry. . . .

FRENCHY: You make me rue the day I picked you out of fifty-three girls for this job.

CLEO *(defiantly):* It seems to me that Dr. Stark could have picked me just as well.

FRENCHY: Except that he was too shy to look them over. You pushed that jingling body in my face and you got the job. It was a moment of aberration for me.

STARK *(protestingly):* Frenchy, what are you saying?

FRENCHY: It's the heat—Do I know what I'm saying?

CLEO: Some people say more than is good for them!

FRENCHY *(warningly):* Some people *do* more!

CLEO *(indignantly):* Sometimes you act as if you're talking to an animal!

FRENCHY: What's in a name? Look at me. They call me Frenchy. Why? Cause I'm a Swede. . . . A little Swede from Utica, New York.

CLEO: Well, I don't like it—you keep picking on me!

FRENCHY *(contemptuously):* You gonna cry?

CLEO *(scoffingly):* What for?

STARK: Frenchy likes you, Cleo.

CLEO: Yes, like poison! God knows why—I never did anything to him.

FRENCHY *(significantly):* And don't do anything to my friends either.

STARK *(puzzled):* What are you talking about?

CLEO: He wouldn't talk about me that way if my brother was here.

FRENCHY: What's your brother, a fireman or a cop?

STARK *(to* CLEO*):* Goodness, he's not talking about you.

CLEO: Well, he's looking me straight in the eye.

FRENCHY (*changing the subject*): How is it you live down the beach and don't look sunburnt, Doc?

STARK: I spend only Sundays and an occasional Saturday in the sun.

FRENCHY: You must be coining money here.

STARK: My wife hasn't made a bank deposit in several weeks.

FRENCHY: I'm very satisfied to live on twenty-thirty bucks a week. They got me all steamed up in school about being president, but this suits me from the ground up.

CLEO (*scornfully*): The ground *down*, you mean.

FRENCHY (*after a glance, ignoring her*): Fire Island's getting awful crowded though. Some show people moved up there last week.

CLEO (*immediately interested, coming forward*): Show people? Who?

FRENCHY (*shrugging*): I should worry who.

CLEO: From the legitimate?

FRENCHY: I should worry. (*Waving the magazine in his hands.*) I sent a snapshot to this picture paper—"Dr. Walter Jensen—Frenchy to his friends—Manicuring Milady's Feet." But they didn't print it. No matter what you do, you can't make people foot-conscious. (FRENCHY *looks at a few more pictures. In the meantime* CLEO *has gone to the wall mirror. Looking into the mirror she lifts her damp hair from the back of her neck. She sees* STARK's *eyes on her and offers the following explanation,* FRENCHY *observant and listening.*)

CLEO: You get so damp under here, right at the neck.

STARK: Why don't you keep it up?

CLEO: Keep the hair up? Mrs. Stark told me not to. . . .

STARK: When was that?

CLEO: Oh, weeks ago. She said I wasn't modeling dresses here.

STARK (*after giving* FRENCHY *a quick look*): She must have been joking.

CLEO: No, she said——

STARK (*quickly*): You wear it any way you like, the most comfortable . . .

FRENCHY (*dryly, intent on the pictures*): My, Doc, we're getting independent.

CLEO (*flashing a haughty look at* FRENCHY): I'll do that, Dr. Stark.

FRENCHY (*rising from his seat*): I'll return this paper after.

STARK: Okay.

FRENCHY: Maybe my office cooled off.

CLEO (*saucily*): You oughta pay rent on two offices, Dr. Jensen.

FRENCHY *(scornfully):* I'm not sure what's going on in your fertile brain, Juicy Fruit. . . . But you stripped your gears with me. *(He drifts out of the office. There is a momentary silence.)*

STARK: Don't mind him—he's peculiar.

CLEO *(with lofty superiority):* Don't worry, I don't. I take the source into account.

STARK *(with sudden unrestrained eloquence):*
> "For slander's mark was ever yet the fair;
> The ornament of beauty is suspect,
> A crow that flies in Heaven's sweetest air.
> So thou be good, slander doth but approve
> Thy worth the greater. . . ."

(With apologetic embarrassment now) Shakespeare. . . .

CLEO: Oh, that's nice. Shakespeare? Do you know something? I can't read Shakespeare—the type is too small.

STARK: That isn't all editions——

CLEO *(hastily):* Oh, of course it isn't. I know it isn't—of course. *(After a pause.)* Dr. Jensen don't seem to have any manners, does he? His personality is really nil, isn't it?

STARK: I wouldn't say that. . . .

CLEO: An interesting personality must have a foundation of good character.

STARK: Who told you that?

CLEO: No one has to tell me such things. Dr. Jensen really offends. He does not know and obey the fundamental rules of etiquette.

STARK: He's a self-educated man——

CLEO: That don't cut no ice——So am I. My parents wanted to send me to a fashionable girl's college, but I went to secretarial school instead—just for the experience. Notwithstanding, I know the correct things to do and say. My husband, when I get married, will find me the perfect hostess.

STARK *(not knowing what to say):* Do you intend to marry?

CLEO: I don't know—marriage is so sordid. I'd never marry for money. *(Abruptly.)* Do you love your wife?

STARK *(torn between her foolishness and attractiveness):* Yes. . . .

CLEO: That was a ridiculous thing to ask, wasn't it?

STARK: No.

CLEO: She must be an ideal wife.

STARK: You think so?

CLEO: I've often admired her for the way she manages and takes care of herself.

STARK: Do you like her?

CLEO: She has very good manners. God knows, there's not much courtesy left in the world! . . . May I be frank, Dr. Stark?

STARK: Yes.

CLEO: I've often resented the way she speaks to you.

STARK: How?

CLEO: Perhaps I better not mention it. . . .

STARK: You can. . . .

CLEO: Well, she seems angry with you, Dr. Stark.

STARK *(half smiling):* Isn't that permissible?

CLEO: Permanently? I may be wrong. . . .

STARK: That's just your impression.

CLEO: It must be. . . . *(Seeing him smile.)* Everything amuses you, Dr. Stark.

STARK *(very close to her):* Why?

CLEO: You're smiling.

STARK: It just seems that way. It's a habit. . . . When I can't meet a situation, I smile as if it amuses me. I don't mean to, but it comes out that way.

CLEO: Don't you feel foolish sometimes?

STARK: To tell the truth, yes. . . .

CLEO: I think you're not a happy man. You have so much to live for—I can't see why. Have you got troubles?

STARK: No.

CLEO: Do you mind my saying this?

STARK: No.

CLEO: I think happiness is everything. You can have a castle, and what have you got if you're not happy? An important person once told me Mr. Rockerfeller—you know, that one, his father—he had a silver windpipe. With all that money! It goes to show you.

STARK: True. . . . Are you?—Happy?

CLEO: Oh, yes! Life is so full of a number of things! Parties, dances—— But I do resent having to change so often——

STARK: Change?

CLEO: You know, clothes—it irks me. Cruises are pleasant. I've taken several of those, but not recently. A girl makes a mistake to go alone on a cruise; it makes you so conspicuous.

STARK (*quietly, but completely aware of her*): Life must be very pleasant for you.

CLEO: Yes, it is. That's why I didn't mind in the least when you said we'd have to work late tonight. Most of my friends are away for the summer—the city's dead. (*After a pause.*) Summer is beautiful, I think. All the people have such an unbuttoned mood, don't they? People can be so kind and good when they're relaxed, can't they?

STARK (*touched by her genuine lyric mood*): Yes. . . .

CLEO: Not many people are as happy as I am, not many!

STARK: Your friend, Willy Wax, is back from the coast. I saw it in the papers——

CLEO: Willy Wax, the dance director?

STARK: He's back from the coast.

CLEO: I saw his name in the files——

STARK: I do most of his work.

CLEO: What kind of teeth does he have?

STARK (*laughing*): Teeth? Ordinary teeth.

CLEO: I mean he must be a nice man. He must have a beautiful mind to put on all those artistic ballet numbers. I saw that Sea Grotto number in his last picture. And then to travel by air, back and forth, here a show, there a film. . . . He must be a wonderful man, Mr. Wax!

STARK: Well, he's your friend—you ought to know.

CLEO (*surprised*): Mine? I don't know Mr. Wax.

STARK: You said you knew him.

CLEO: *I* said so?

STARK: The first day? You said you'd come into the building to see him?

CLEO: You must be mistaken, Doctor.

STARK (*slowly, looking at her keenly*): Yes . . . I must be.

CLEO: I'd never go out with a man the first time I met him. Not even Mr. Wax, as much as I admire that type of man.

STARK: Why not?

CLEO: They lose their respect for you. Didn't you know that?

STARK: No.

CLEO: You have to be very careful with most men. Not you—you're different.

STARK: Am I?

CLEO: Supremely! Men must drink too much nowadays, the things they do and say. I used to laugh when my mother told me.

STARK: What kind of woman is your mother?

CLEO: Mother . . . ? Opera singer. Was, used to be . . .

STARK *(measuring her):* That's interesting. Where?

CLEO *(flustered):* Where? In Europe. . . . *(Uneasily.)* Didn't I ever tell you that before?

STARK: No.

CLEO: I come from a very interesting family. Don't you believe me?

STARK: I believe everything you want me to believe, Cleo . . . Cleo . . .

CLEO: Yes?

STARK *(slowly):* That's a curious name . . . for a curious girl.

CLEO: May I ask you something?

STARK: Please.

CLEO: Why do you stare at me? Really, Doctor, all during the past weeks you kept looking at me as if I belong in a museum.

STARK *(in a low voice):* Perhaps . . . it's admiration.

CLEO: You're just saying that to make me feel good.

STARK: No. . . .

CLEO: You mean it?

STARK: Yes.

CLEO: Why?

STARK *(lamely):* You've become very efficient. . . . Do you like it here?

CLEO: Very much. . . .

STARK *(after a pause):* You must excuse me if I annoyed you . . . by looking at you.

CLEO: Oh, I know it don't mean anything. Does it, Doctor?

STARK: No.

CLEO: I think you need me here. That's why I enjoy it so much. That's why I stay here. Don't you need me here?

STARK: Yes.

CLEO: Then I'll keep on staying here, Doctor, and you'll have to put me on a pension.

STARK: I'm older—I'll go first.

CLEO: There's not so much difference in our age, is there?

STARK: Some. . . .

CLEO: What does it matter? *(After a pause.)* Dr. Stark, do you like me?

STARK *(dropping her hand):* What?

CLEO: Do you?

STARK: Like you? *(The telephone in the office rings and startles them.* CLEO *answers it.)*

CLEO *(on the telephone):* Dr. Stark's office. . . . One moment please. *(To* STARK.*)* Mrs. Stark. (CLEO *proffers the telephone to* STARK *who takes it without looking at her.)*

STARK: Hello, dear. . . . No, he hasn't come in yet—he's due any minute. . . . We can think about that later, dear. . . . I can't charge him—he's your father. . . . Yes. . . . Yes. . . .Yes, dear. . . . About ten—I won't finish with Mrs. Harris till after eight. . . . Yes. . . . Good-bye, dear. (STARK *returns to the waiting room, looking at his pocket watch.)* I forgot about it: my father-in-law's a half hour late for his appointment. (CLEO *has just been hastily adjusting her undergarments.)*

CLEO *(wiggling a shoulder):* I never adjust my shoulder straps or girdle in public, as some women do. God knows, it's so warm I'm practically naked underneath.

STARK *(with surprising asperity):* You mustn't say things like that!

CLEO *(with quick genuine humility):* I'm sorry if I offended.

STARK *(immediately softer):* For your own good, Cleo, I mean. Naïveness goes just so far.

CLEO *(sulkily):* I'm not naïve.

STARK *(after an uncomfortable pause):* May I tell you something?

CLEO: You have a right to tell me anything. I work here; you pay——

STARK: That would be terrible, if you really thought that——

CLEO *(aloof):* Tell me whatever you want. I don't care.

STARK: Not if you feel——(STARK *quickly breaks off.* MR. PRINCE *has walked into the waiting room.* CLEO *does not change her tired sulky attitude.)*

PRINCE: My children, good afternoon. *(Getting no response.)* How am I feeling? Very secondary today.

CLEO: So am I. . . .

PRINCE *(sitting):* I'm piling up a fortune. Why? To be the richest man in the cemetery! Who's coming to a stadium concert with me tonight? What nice little girl?

CLEO: Don't look at me.

STARK: You're late, Poppa. . . .

PRINCE *(smiling):* By whose clock?

STARK: What's the joke?

PRINCE: You't can't be in your right brains if you think someone can come early in such weather. Nicht wahr?

STARK: I can't give you another appointment today.

PRINCE: So another day! *(Turning to* CLEO.*)* How is Miss Cleo? Grumpy?

CLEO *(shortly):* No.

PRINCE: A teenchy-weenchy bit? *(After a pause.)* I'm talking in a sea shell. Nobody answers. All because I came ten minutes late.

STARK *(very annoyed):* Forty. I can't do anything in twenty——

PRINCE: I told you—another day. And how is your little affair going, between you two? (STARK *stares at* PRINCE *and turns away.)*

CLEO: It's too hot for such things.

PRINCE: That's right. If it was colder you'd be right in his arms. That's the beauty of cold weather: comfort.

CLEO: Nobody ever knows what you're talking about, Mr. Prince. *(Answering a look from* STARK.*)* Well, they don't. Do you?

PRINCE: I invite you to come and listen to Jascha Heifetz tonight. Don't you understand that?

STARK: She's right . . . nobody ever knows when you're serious.

PRINCE *(to* STARK*)*: You go take a walk around the block and she'll soon find out how serious I am. *(Then he laughs his remark away.)*

STARK *(to* CLEO*)*: Put Mr. Prince down for another appointment, tomorrow, the same time. (CLEO *goes into the office to do so.)*

PRINCE: Did Belle puts bugs into your ear?

STARK: About what?

PRINCE: I thought maybe she wanted payment in advance, to put in two gold inlays.

STARK: Belle didn't say a word.

PRINCE *(looking down at a newspaper):* They expect trouble—they'll get it.

CLEO *(entering):* Who?

PRINCE: Those Japs. *(Looking up at* STARK *keenly.)* Belle didn't tell you not to work on my teeth without pay?

STARK *(irritably):* Belle has other things to think about, Poppa!

PRINCE *(turning to* CLEO*)*: Learn an object lesson from life. You want to irritate a man?—Tell him the truth. Remember this for the time you get married.

CLEO: I don't intend to get married. It's too sordid.

PRINCE: Not with an older man. *(Winking.)* Why don't you marry me, Miss Cleo? *(To* STARK *who goes to the office door.)* Where are you going, Benny? Humilified by my remarks?

STARK *(taking the lavatory key from a hook):* No. (STARK *gives him a look of irritation and exits, left.)*

PRINCE: Hmm . . . humilified.

CLEO: No wonder. You say such foolish things to him.

PRINCE *(glancing out at the Hotel Algiers):* You like him?

CLEO *(defiantly):* He's a very nice man.

PRINCE: But he lost his enterprise, years ago. He's no more resourceful. I offered to put him in a swell office—he could become a big specialist—but he likes it here.

CLEO: Why?

PRINCE: Afraid, no courage. My good daughter made him like that—afraid to take a chance. Keep what you got—"A half a loaf is better . . ." In life, my child, you must go forward. And if you don't go forward, where are you? Backward!

CLEO: You're trying to impress me. But I think you should help everybody you can. You don't have long to live—you're an old man.

PRINCE *(with a grand flourish):* Miss Cleo, you're talking to a man with a body like silk. Every year he takes the waters at Saratoga. He possesses the original teeth, every one! *(As* CLEO *laughs.)* In all the multitudes of your acquaintanceship you won't find a man with younger ideas than your present speaker. How old are you, my child?

CLEO: How old do I look?

PRINCE *(ignoring her interpolation):* I am speaking to you from wisdom, with a voice of velvet, as a past master of a Masonic Lodge: consort with an older man. In short, use your brains!

CLEO: It's lucky for me I don't take you serious. You're the biggest kidder on earth.

PRINCE *(smiling):* Don't my young ideas reach out to your young ideas?

CLEO *(emphatically):* I think you're flirting with me, that's all.

PRINCE *(winking):* You see, you understand me to perfection! Tonight Heifetz is playing a piece by a famous author——

CLEO: I don't care for that.

PRINCE: Tomorrow night . . .

CLEO: Where?

PRINCE: You say where.

CLEO: Do you like me?

PRINCE: Truth is stranger than fiction: yes!

CLEO *(studying him):* Where would you take me?

PRINCE: Anywhere. You're a girl like candy, a honeydew melon—a delicious girl. Yes, I like you. *(After a pause, the veins suddenly standing out on his face.)* I'm serious . . . do you understand that? I'm very serious, Miss Cleo. I'm talking to you from the roots up!

CLEO *(hesitantly):* I'd have to tell Dr. Stark.

PRINCE: What would I have against that? Yes, you give me pleasure, Miss Cleo—just to talk.

CLEO: I'm glad you appreciate talk.

PRINCE: Why?

CLEO: Because you won't get more, Mr. Prince.

PRINCE: My child, it suits me to a T. (STARK *enters, his manner restrained, hangs up the key.)*

PRINCE: Look at her, Benny! Isn't she beautiful? Womanhood is fermenting through her veins. Am I wrong? *(Getting a blank look from* STARK.) Don't look so humilified.

CLEO *(with sudden discovery):* Why do you wear high heels?!

PRINCE: I don't like to be so small. Now I go, I go, but to return. Until tomorrow . . . to both of you. Good-bye.

CLEO: Good-bye, Mr. Prince. (PRINCE *exits. Silence.)*

STARK: What did he mean by that?

CLEO *(defiantly):* He dated me up—we're going out tomorrow night.

STARK *(coldly):* That doesn't seem very wise to me.

CLEO *(as coldly):* It's my personal life.

STARK *(not knowing what else to say):* Did you call the lab about the porcelain jackets for Mrs. Harris?

CLEO *(righteously):* They're on the way over, Dr. Stark.

STARK *(starting for the office):* I suppose you know what you're doing.

CLEO: You can be sure that I do.

STARK: Perhaps you'd better go out and eat an early supper before Mrs. Harris gets here.

CLEO: I'm not hungry.

STARK: Why are you so perverse? Otherwise you'll have to wait——

CLEO: Who's perverse, Dr. Stark?

STARK: Sometimes you irritate me.

CLEO: I suppose I have to listen to you——

STARK: No, go out and eat.

CLEO: I won't. You're blaming me for something I didn't do.

STARK: Blaming you?

CLEO: Aren't you? You have thoughts in your head and then you blame me because you have them.

STARK: What thoughts?

CLEO *(in a defiant outburst):* You're jealous! *(This statement momentarily paralyzes* STARK. *In that moment* FRENCHY *abruptly pokes his head in at the door, left.)*

FRENCHY: Pisst! I got a customer. *(He ducks out again.* STARK *goes to the door, quickly closes it and turns back to* CLEO, *lowering his voice.)*

STARK *(angrily):* I'm . . . you're making it very difficult for me, Cleo. I'm trying to keep you on here. You're not the most efficient girl in the world——

CLEO *(breaking in):* I'll leave any time you say!

STARK: I didn't say that——

CLEO *(at bay):* I don't have to work. My family has more money than we know what to do with. One of my brothers is at West Point——

STARK: And I suppose your father's a senator!

CLEO: What?

STARK: Why do you lie! After all, we're not all nitwits around here!

CLEO: What? . . . (STARK *falls off into angry silence, wagging his head. And* CLEO *is stopped, completely. Silence.)*

STARK *(finally seeing her flushed desperate face):* I'm sorry I said that.

CLEO *(desperately):* You don't believe me!

STARK *(gruffly, but apologetically, going to her):* Yes, I do. Listen, Cleo, you're an unhappy lonely girl——

CLEO *(moving away):* No!

STARK: But after all——

CLEO: No, you don't! Keep your hands off!

STARK *(genuinely contrite):* I'm sorry if I hurt your feelings.

CLEO: I'll change my clothes and get right out!

STARK: No, you mustn't——

CLEO: Please stand out of my way.

STARK: Just a minute——

CLEO: I can't listen to you.

STARK *(holding her and shaking her despite himself):* You know you tell stories, Cleo.

CLEO *(trying to loosen herself):* You're stronger than I am.

STARK: Calm down a moment.

CLEO: I won't! Let me go! Please—you'd better do it——! (STARK *suddenly releases her. She starts away from him but stumbles and falls. She begins to get up but starts to cry instead, remaining on the floor.)*

STARK *(melted):* Oh, my dear girl . . . !

CLEO: No! *(Weeping.)* Keep away. . . . (CLEO *weeps bitterly.* STARK *stands off balance, not knowing what to do. He walks to the outer door, stands there, comes back.* CLEO *slowly gets up and sits on a chair. Finally, quietly):* I'll change my uniform and go.

STARK: You know you need the job. . . .

CLEO *(tearfully):* You never show anyone they're wrong by showing them you're right. Don't you know that? Don't you? Does it make you a great man to tell me I'm a liar? I know I'm a liar!

STARK *(gently, going to her):* Cleo, I'm your friend . . . please believe me. *(She permits him to take one of her hands.)* Everyone tells little fables, Cleo. Sometimes to themselves, sometimes to others. Life is so full of brutal facts . . . we all try to soften them by making believe.

CLEO *(tearfully):* You're talking of somebody else.

STARK: We all like to have good opinions of ourselves. That's why we squirm around and tell stories and adjust ourselves. It's a way to go on living proudly——

CLEO: I don't care to talk about it!

STARK: Why, I lie, myself, a dozen times a day. You can tell me anything, Cleo. *(After a silent pause.)* Where do you come from?

CLEO *(defiantly):* Madison Avenue! No more! I don't care to think. Sometimes I wish I didn't have a head. Last night I didn't have a wink of sleep. *(With sudden vehemence.)* Nobody loves me! Millions of people moving around the city and nobody cares if you live or die. Go up a high building and see them down below. Some day I'll fall down on them all!

STARK *(gently):* Is that a right thing to say?

CLEO: My home life is fearful—eight in one apartment. My father had a very hard life; he ran the store. He, my father, he shrinked— shrank?—what is it?

STARK *(not sure):* Shrunk or shrank.

CLEO: My father got littler and littler . . . and one morning he died right in bed while everyone was sleeping. Mom and Gert and two married sisters and their husbands and babies—eight in one apartment! I tell them I want to be a dancer—everybody laughs. I make believe they're not my sisters. They don't know anything—they're washed out, bleached . . . everybody forgets how to dream. . . .

STARK: I understand. . . .

CLEO: That's the biggest joke around the house: "Cleo, the dancer—the Queen of Sheba!" My sister Gert's a garment worker. We share one room. She's keeping company—she comes in late. I never sleep. I have all the inconvenience of love with none of the pleasure.

STARK: Yes. . . . You're tired. Go home. I won't need you tonight.

CLEO *(wanly):* I never go home if there's another place—here, the office, I mean. Where can you go? Sit in the park till it's time to go to bed?

STARK: The park is nice, cool——

CLEO: Don't you know they molest you there? You're naïve. Even policemen. *(With sudden fresh strength.)* Would you laugh if I told you I want to be a dancer? Would you? Or an actress?

STARK: I certainly wouldn't!

CLEO: I like you very much!

STARK: Do you?

CLEO: Now don't smile!

STARK *(earnestly):* I'm not.

CLEO: You're kind and you're good. But you're not resourceful or enterprising . . . don't smile.

STARK: No. . . .

CLEO: You're too used to this life—you lost your ambition. *(Insistently.)* I must ask you not to smile and seem foolish! *(After waiting.)* You don't go *out* to things any more. You move away instead of going to it. It's your wife's fault.

STARK: Is it?

CLEO: Don't you see it is? You're evasive and sideways. Where's your courage, Dr. Stark?

STARK: Courage for what?

CLEO: To go out to things, to new experiences. *(Rapidly.)* My mother's always trying to hold me back, not to have all the experiences I can. Those people think you can live on good advice. Don't you think life is to live all you can and experience everything? Isn't that the only way you can develop to be a real human being? Shouldn't a wife help a man do that? *(Excited by her own flow.)* They won't hold me back. Their idea is to get married and have babies right away. I want babies, three or four——!

STARK: Do you?

CLEO: Sure. I'm healthy enough to have a dozen!

STARK: Are you?

CLEO: Sure, but there's time for them. Must they come the first year? Is that refined? *(Pausing to catch her breath.)* Well, as I was saying, no good comes out of good advice, even if it's good. And that's how your wife broke up your courage——

STARK *(breaking in):* Don't you think you're going too far?

CLEO *(not to be stopped now):* If you expect to find out about me, you must expect me to find out about you.

STARK: Okay, but don't you think you have arbitrary opinions?

CLEO *(emphatically):* No. *(Then.)* What does that mean, arbitrary?

STARK: You're hungry for expression, Cleo. That makes you talk sometimes without thinking too much about what you're saying. But don't ever hesitate to say what's on your mind. . . . I like to hear it.

CLEO: Yes? . . . Well, I don't like your wife.

STARK: Why?

CLEO *(after a pause, shyly):* I love you!

STARK *(after a pause, in a low voice):* You're a fanciful girl. . . .

CLEO: Did you hear what I said?

STARK: No. . . .

CLEO *(in a low voice):* Do you want me to say it again?

STARK: No.

CLEO: And now you smile again. . . . *(They suddenly stop their conversation.* COOPER *has entered the waiting room, seeing nothing, his mind completely on his own troubles and the heat. He is too hot and discomfited to sit, prowling around instead.)*

COOPER: They're frying eggs on the sidewalk. The public is staggering around. *(At the water cooler.)* Municipal champagne . . . ah-cha-cha!

CLEO *(making conversation):* People in the city have a sweet kind of dizziness in the summer time, don't they?

COOPER: Maybe you, Cleo, not me. *(Flopping down heavily.)* God was smart. He promised no more floods——He knew fire was a worse way. *(Getting up and prowling to the window, right.)* How are your petunias doing here?

STARK *(over-casual):* I forgot to water them today.

CLEO *(quickly, with veiled pride):* I did it before, Dr. Stark.

STARK *(as above):* Did you? Thank you, Cleo.

CLEO *(with a glance in* COOPER'S *direction):* You're welcome, Dr. Stark.

STARK *(as above):* They don't seem to do so well there.

CLEO: They look just like orphan babies. I feel so sorry for them.

COOPER *(mopping his brow):* Fire, fire—fire in the church. *(He sits again and picks up a newspaper. Indicating the newspaper.)* According to this man, the katydids began to sing this week, across the Hudson. *(Bitterly.)* Everybody should rejoice . . . it means an early frost, he says.

CLEO: With all this heat, I don't see how anyone could have the nerve to predict that.

COOPER *(heavily, throwing the paper aside):* What does it cost him to predict . . .

STARK *(sympathetically):* Rest, Phil, take it easy.

COOPER *(snorting):* Rest! Who rests in the front-line trench? I suddenly realized life is a war . . . for forty years it never entered my mind.

CLEO: What kind of war?

COOPER: You expect me to explain forty-one years in a minute?

CLEO *(naïvely):* Take more than a minute. . . .

COOPER: Cleo, take a number from one to ten. You got it? Add three, divide by four. You got it . . . throw it away! Ah—cha-cha! *(There is a pause of silence which comes from both STARK and CLEO being frightened and discomfited by COOPER'S mood. Finally COOPER stops fanning himself with the newspaper and starts across to the water cooler for another drink. STARK catches CLEO looking at him earnestly. CLEO covers up by shifting her glance to the water cooler.)*

CLEO: It's nice how a cooler keeps giving water. You press a button——

COOPER: If only they invented hydrants in the streets which give out milk and honey! . . . we'd be happier people. *(Turning to them with new belligerence.)* Don't I try? Can anyone accuse me of indifference to my work? Why can't I make a living? I'm falling apart by inches. *(Suddenly sobbing.)* Where can I sail away? To where? I'm ashamed to live! An ostrich can hide his head. Diphtheria gets more respect than me! They coddle germs in laboratories —they feed the white mice twice a day. . . . Why don't somebody coddle *me? (Controlling himself now.)* What did I do to my fellow man? Why am I punished like this? *(Trembling again on the brink of sobs, but holding them back.)* Where is the God they told me about? Why should an innocent boy and an old lady suffer? I ask you to tell me, what is the Congress doing? Where are they in the hour of the needs of the people? *(Appealing to* STARK *personally.)* Did you ever see such times? Where will it end if they can't use millions of Coopers? Why can't they fit me in, a man of my talents? The sick ones walk the streets, the doctors sit at home. Where, where is it? What is it? . . . what, what, what? . . . (COOPER *trickles off into silence.* CLEO *and* STARK *can be only helplessly silent in the face of this emotional speech. After* COOPER *blows his nose and wipes his eyes, a little ashamed of his feeling, he says with a faint bitter smile, mocking himself.)* Gaze on the Columbia University lunatic! The warrior of Ypres and Verdun! . . . *(He moves his trembling hand across his brow, at the same time taking a card from his pocket and handing it to* STARK.*)*

STARK *(of the card):* What is this, Phil?

COOPER: I came just now from being registered. I'm classified— you're talking to type four.

STARK *(puzzled, turning the card over):* I don't see what——

COOPER: Blood.

CLEO *(moving forward):* What?

COOPER *(with self-mockery):* I decided to become a blood donor on the side.

CLEO *(horrified):* Oh, no!

COOPER: They pay well, thirty dollars a pint.

CLEO *(in a low voice):* A pint's a lot of blood, Dr. Cooper. . . .

COOPER: A boy there gave fifteen times last year: a young fortune. He told me he lives on a plain diet, onions and bread, no meats or anything.

STARK *(after a pause):* Phil . . . you mean it?

COOPER *(bitterly):* They didn't want me at first. But it seems I'm a type everybody needs . . . I'm a very common type.

STARK: Phil, you don't mean that!

COOPER: Why not? It's a legitimate business, like pressing pants or cleaning fish.

CLEO *(trying to be helpful):* I think he's joking, Dr. Stark. *(Now* COOPER *turns and unleashes the wrath of many weeks on* CLEO'S *head.)*

COOPER: Why don't you mind your business! Who do you think you are? Keep your mouth shut around here, Miss Smarty! Learn to mind your lousy business! (COOPER *abruptly starts right, as if to his office.* CLEO *and* STARK *sit, frozen. Just as abruptly* COOPER *now returns. He walks right up to* CLEO, *tears in eyes, wrathfully shaking his fist in her face again. She stands motionless, pale, tragic.* STARK *scrambles to his feet, about to get between the other two. But now* COOPER *suddenly drops his fist and throws his arms around* CLEO. *She, crying, does likewise.* COOPER *kisses her and breaks away.)*

CLEO *(crying):* Stay here, Dr. Cooper. Sit down. Don't go out, Doct——*(But* COOPER *is gone, plunged off through the door, left. There is a further silence.* STARK *has no words.* CLEO *slowly sits, crying a little.* STARK *crosses and sits by her side, stroking her hair.)*

STARK *(softly):* Don't cry, dear. . . .

CLEO *(shaking her head):* No. . . . *(Now no longer crying, head up.)* I feel so sorry for Dr. Cooper. . . .

STARK: You mustn't mind what he said.

CLEO: He'll hurt himself.

STARK: A man with that sense of responsibility for his family? No. . . .

CLEO: Are you sure?

STARK: Yes. . . .

CLEO: I understand his feelings. . . . He's all alone in the world. Nobody wants him . . . like an orphan.

STARK: I wish I could give you an idea of his talent.

CLEO: Better than you?

STARK: He always was.

CLEO *(quickly):* Don't say that. *(She draws her hand away from his.)*

STARK: Well, some people don't agree with me.

CLEO: Who don't?

STARK: You don't. My wife, she——

CLEO *(starting up, fresh and indestructible):* Don't mention her to me! And let Dr. Cooper be better than you, but don't tell me. I never want to hear those things.

STARK *(slowly standing):* Why? . . .

CLEO: You're asking me why again? I told you why before. . . . *(They look at each other in silence. Finally:)*

STARK: We both must forget what was said before. . . .

CLEO *(coolly, intently):* You don't love your wife. . . .

STARK: You mustn't say that!

CLEO *(as above):* If you did . . . would you let me talk this way?

STARK *(flustered):* Forget it, Cleo!

CLEO *(defiantly):* I won't forget it.

STARK (*hardly audible*): This is an office. I'm a married man. . . . You know I'm a married man, don't you?

CLEO: Just because you're sad you can't make me sad. No one can. I have too much in me!

STARK: You're wonderful. . . .

CLEO (*almost dancing*): Talent!—I'm talented. I don't know for what, but it makes me want to dance in my bones! Don't want to be lonely, never left alone! Why should I cry? I have a throat to sing with, a heart to love with! Why don't you love me, Dr. Stark? I was ten, then fifteen—I'm almost twenty now. Everything is in a hurry and you ought to love me.

STARK: Cleo, please. . . .

CLEO: You're good, you're kind, you're like a father. Do you love your wife? I'm intuitive—I know you don't!

STARK (*making a last effort to stop her*): Cleo!

CLEO: We're *both* alone, so alone. You might be like Cooper in a year or two. Maybe I lie. You know why. Because I'm alone—nobody loves me. But I won't have it that way. I'll change life.

STARK: You're wonderful. . . .

CLEO: You don't deserve me. Not you or any other man I ever met.

STARK (*in an agony of indecision*): Cleo, dear. . . .

CLEO (*shyly*): I'll call you Benny in a minute! (*After a throb of hesitation.*) Ben! Benny! . . . (*They are standing off from each other, poised on needles.*) Don't be afraid. . . .

STARK: . . . No? . . .

CLEO: Love me. . . . Love me, Ben.

STARK: . . . Can't do that. . . .

CLEO (*moving forward a step*): Put your arms up and around me.

STARK: Cleo. . . . (*Now they move in on each other. Everything else gone, they are together in a full, fierce embrace, together in a swelter of heat, misunderstanding, loneliness and simple sex.*)

Curtain

SCENE II

TIME: *The beginning of August.*

PLACE: *The same.*

The waiting room is empty. The electric fan buzzes monotonously, matching the sound of the dentist's drill within STARK'S *operating room. Through his glass door we see moving shadows. A newspaper rattles on the chair every time the fan moves that way. It is late afternoon; soon the brazen day will cool off into quiet evening. The telephone rings.* CLEO *comes out of the operating room to answer it. She is hurriedly and tensely followed by* STARK. *He speaks in a low voice, not wanting to be heard by his patient.*

STARK: If that's my wife, I'll speak to her.

CLEO *(stopping and shrugging her shoulders):* Speak to her . . . what do I care?

STARK *(in a low voice):* Cleo. . . . *(She turns away from him. The telephone rings again.* STARK *hastens to it.)* Hello? . . . Oh, yes . . . yes. . . . *(Returning to* CLEO.) My father-in-law. For you.

CLEO: For me?

STARK: He wants to speak to you.

CLEO *(staring at him):* To me?

STARK: Yes. *(They look at each other a moment, she crossly. Then she starts for the telephone, but he stops her timidly, awkwardly, almost nervously.)*

STARK: Don't be angry, Cleo.

CLEO *(impatiently):* I'm not.

STARK: Yesterday, when she called, you told her I was busy. It's all I heard from her last night.

CLEO: Oh, your wife.

PATIENT *(from within):* Can I smoke a cigar?

STARK *(calling out to the patient):* Just let that dry a minute, Mr. Wax. *(To* CLEO.) After all, we don't want her to——

CLEO *(in a final burst):* You must think that's all I have to do, think about your wife. *(CLEO pulls away from him, going to the telephone. For a moment* STARK *watches her and then returns to his patient, closing the door behind him.)*

CLEO *(on the telephone):* This is Cleo. *(After a pause.)* That's very nice, but I can't go. *(Listens.)* Because. . . . Because why? I don't like that kind of music. . . . I don't care if it's the best seats, Mr. Prince. *(Listens.)* No. . . . Maybe some other time. . . . I think once a week is enough to go out with an old man. Anyway, I have a date. *(Listens.)* Yes, next week . . . yes. 'Bye. *(CLEO indolently comes out into the waiting room. She has been making a display of temper with* STARK, *but she is really enjoying her life in the office,* PRINCE *is pursuing her,* WILLY WAX *is inside—she is busy and excited. Now she adjusts her damp underclothing. She catches sight of herself in the wall mirror to which she draws closer. She waves her hands, poises herself in a dancing position, shakes out her hair. Suddenly she turns with a start.* FRENCHY *has been standing at the door for a few seconds.)* You frightened me!

FRENCHY: I'm a boogey man. *(He drinks from the cooler.)* You were getting quite enthusiastic about yourself, there in the mirror.

CLEO *(sarcastically):* I like myself, Dr. Jensen.

FRENCHY: So it seems, Goldilocks.

CLEO: Anyone can see I'm not a blonde.

FRENCHY *(looking her over frankly):* All the girls are Goldilocks to me. Is the Doc busy?

CLEO: Yes.

FRENCHY: Any picture magazines in there? *(Without waiting for an answer* FRENCHY *goes into the office, where he rummages around.* CLEO *goes to the water cooler for a drink.* STARK *opens his door and looks out. Seeing she is alone he crosses the waiting room and speaks to her in a low voice.)*

STARK: Cleo. . . . Wax is leaving the chair. Don't go out with him. . . .

CLEO: I'd better wait till I'm asked.

STARK: Don't, for my sake. . . . (FRENCHY *is standing in the office doorway, taking in this little private drama.* CLEO *signals to* STARK *that* FRENCHY *is there.* STARK *turns and sees they are not alone.)*

STARK *(hurriedly):* Oh, you, Frenchy. Be with you in five minutes. (FRENCHY *waves to the retreating* STARK, *who exits, closing the operating-room door behind him.* FRENCHY *comes down into the waiting room, perusing the magazine in his hands.)*

FRENCHY *(softly):* You oughta be careful . . . there's a soft shoulder ahead.

CLEO: I don't know what that means.

FRENCHY *(with a smoothing-out gesture):* You might go off the road——*(Without another word* CLEO *starts for the operating room.)*

FRENCHY *(blocking her way):* Wait a minute, don't give me that flight-of-the-bumble-bee stuff!

CLEO *(haughtily):* I beg your pardon?

FRENCHY: Who's in there?

CLEO *(coldly):* A very distinguished gentleman . . . which you are not.

FRENCHY: Who?

CLEO: Mr. Wax, Mr. Willy Wax, the dance director.

FRENCHY: He ain't even distinguished to his mother!

CLEO (loftily): A man who gets his name in the paper so often must be important to some people.

FRENCHY (warningly): You got a lot to learn, Cleo. What's between you?

CLEO: "Between you?" Who?

FRENCHY: Or don't you speak without your lawyer? (Coming up closer to her and dropping his voice.) Listen, don't twist Stark's head. He's foolish, but he's good and we like him. Don't get him in trouble. (Taking her arm.) Come on over to my office.

CLEO (pulling away): I'll do nothing of the sort.

FRENCHY (after a silent penetrating look): Are you honest?

CLEO: What?

FRENCHY: Do you like him?

CLEO (indignantly): Who do you think you are? A government agent?

FRENCHY: Weave, weave patiently, thou gentle spider . . . one of these days you might get hurt.

CLEO: I would like to see you touch me. I would just like to see it!

FRENCHY: Don't forget, I see what you're up to.

CLEO: You don't see anything!

FRENCHY: Quoth the raven! Look, Cleo, for him there is sleep and day and work again. He's not a happy man. He spends his days trying to exhaust himself so he can fall asleep quick. Not that he told me this. . . . I seen it with my two good eyes. Don't make trouble for him, Cleo. Don't take him over the coals. Unless you're serious, unless you love him. . . .

CLEO: And if I do?

FRENCHY (appraisingly): Do you? See if you can understand this: through unhappy marriage he's lost power for accomplishment— he don't get much personal satisfaction out of his work; and the man who don't get that is a lost man. Lots of things he longs for he'll never take. And like millions of others he constantly feels worried, depressed and inadequate. But!——His unhappiness is a dangerous habit of which he is not fully aware—it may make him bust loose in some curious way . . . can you be it?

CLEO: You must have read all that in a book.

FRENCHY (disgusted): What goes on in the head of a moth?—Nothing! *(He reaches out and smacks an imaginary moth between his palms. Emphatically.)* That was you, in effigy and promise!

CLEO *(her mood abruptly changing):* Why don't you like me? Did I ever harm you or anyone else?

FRENCHY: Cleo, I work like an antitoxin—*before* the complications come. And I know the difference between love and pound cake. . . . *(The operating-room door opens and out comes* WILLY WAX, *followed by* STARK. WAX *is a small dark man with shrewd roving eyes and a glib tongue, plus a definite tired sense of his own importance. Success has given him an unpleasant easiness. Now he is shuffling a thin panatela in his soft hands.)*

WAX *(twisting his face):* Can I smoke with this materia medica in my mouth?

STARK *(smiling uneasily):* Better wait ten minutes, Mr. Wax.

(Note: One attractive woman is an entire grandstand for WAX. *Now he plays charmingly, eruditely for* CLEO. *As for* CLEO, WAX *present, even her breasts stand at attention. Alas, she is not yet wise in the ways of the world and the creatures therein.)*

WAX *(affably, of* FRENCHY): Who's this? Haven't I met you somewhere? Don't you work in the cafeteria downstairs? I'm Willy Wax.

FRENCHY: I'm Dr. Jensen.

WAX *(knowing who he was all the time):* Certainly! To be sure! You did that excellent foot work for me last year. *(Appealingly.)* No?

FRENCHY *(smiling faintly):* Now you placed me. . . .

WAX *(shuffling his cigar):* Well, I suppose I'll have to chew this cigar. I'd like to look at the x-rays, too.

STARK *(promptly):* Miss Singer, please show Mr. Wax the x-rays.

CLEO *(all attention):* This way, please, Mr. Wax.

WAX: Peculiar how I never remember names, but *never!* That comes from living alone. I have to admit I'm a lone wolf——

FRENCHY *(involuntarily):* Bow wow! (WAX *gives* FRENCHY *a quick stabbing look and then follows* CLEO *into the office.* FRENCHY *smiles faintly.* STARK'S *worried eye goes after* CLEO.)

FRENCHY *(sotto voce):* That boy, he'd better be a genius!

STARK: I'll look at that tooth now, Frenchy. (FRENCHY *and* STARK *exit to the operating room, closing the door.* WAX *comes to the office door, holding up a small strip of x-ray film, but first making sure the others are gone. Now he is alone with his prey, but gently, gently, winningly.)*

WAX *(the tired, appealing boy):* One needs a code for these things. No?

CLEO *(made nervous by his proximity):* You see, if you hold it this way——

WAX *(abruptly hands them back):* No, put them back. I'll live without them. *(Coming into the waiting room.)* I'd like to smoke and I can't smoke.

CLEO *(sympathetically, following him out):* It'll go away, Mr. Wax.

WAX: I'm nervous.

CLEO: Why?

WAX: Overworked, but definitely! Talent's a responsibility——

CLEO: Is it?

WAX: You have to work hard . . . and lead a lonely life. What's your name? First name, I mean.

CLEO *(shyly):* Cleo Singer.

WAX: You're a strange girl to find in this office. No?

CLEO: Why? I'm a very efficient dental assistant——

WAX: I mean that sort of mazda glow in your eyes. *(Suddenly.)* There's a fever in you! You're talented! For what?

CLEO: I don't want to spend the rest of my life in an office.

WAX: I've seen you somewhere.

CLEO: I don't think so, Mr. Wax.

WAX *(winningly):* Don't be shy with me, Cleo.

CLEO: I'm not, but you have so much on your mind. The late hours and all that, putting on shows one after another—you're different than the other men I know——

WAX: No, my texture is just as coarse.

CLEO: I don't know *coarse* men. . . .

WAX: Most men are. You're living in the city of the dreadful night: a man is coarse or he doesn't survive.

CLEO: Are you married, if you don't mind my asking?

WAX *(sadly):* An artist hasn't time for that, dear. Not that he wouldn't want a home and children. Are you sure I haven't seen you somewhere?

CLEO: Last week, in the elevator? I was in the back when you——

WAX: Not on a choo-choo train? Never out to the coast?

CLEO: No, I wasn't. . . .

WAX *(groaning):* Movies! They're what started me off on my path of painless perversion.

CLEO *(sadly):* You must be a very lonely man.

WAX: I'm nourished by my sensitivity, such as is left. *(Looking at her open eyes.)* Do I glisten with arrogance, Cleo?

CLEO *(stoutly):* I think you're one of the nicest men I ever met.

WAX *(sotto voce):* Your eyes are beautiful, Cleo—fresh and alive. Where do you eat your dinner?

CLEO: When?

WAX: Tonight, for example.

CLEO *(dismayed):* Oh, I have a date tonight.

WAX: I have a better idea than that.

CLEO: What?

WAX: Have you had your lunch?

CLEO: No.

WAX: Have it with me, down my office, in twenty minutes. I won't have time to go out, but they send up sandwiches and milk.

CLEO *(hesitantly, looking at* STARK'S *door):* Well, I don't . . .

WAX *(quickly):* Have you seen the new method of charting dances on a board? You'd like to see that . . . and then we can talk. . . .

CLEO: I'll be there, Mr. Wax. Twenty minutes?

WAX: Good. I'll tell my secretary you're coming. Do you know what I see about you, Cleo? You're looking for a Columbus to discover you ——It's in your eyes. *(Going to the door.)* Stewed fruit, do you like that?

CLEO: Whatever you eat, Mr. Wax.

WAX *(with great charm):* Come down soon. . . .

CLEO: Yes. . . . Good-bye.

WAX: Good-bye.

CLEO *(suddenly):* Can I tell you something?

WAX *(smiling):* A thousand volumes full.

CLEO: Any dance routine—if I watch it once, I can do it.

WAX: So . . . you're interested in dancing!

CLEO: Yes.

WAX: Well, we'll see if you have any talent. Good-bye for now. (WAX *exits.* CLEO *stands stock still, thrilling all over. Suddenly she flings her arms out, stretching on her toes. She is embracing the world!* FRENCHY *and* STARK *come out of the operating room.* CLEO *sits and demurely fans herself with a magazine.)*

STARK: I can't fix it till the swelling goes down.

FRENCHY: Yeah, but when the swelling goes down it won't hurt.

STARK *(his eyes on* CLEO*):* That's the time to fix it.

FRENCHY *(agreeing):* You're the doctor. *(Turning to leave; to* CLEO.) So long, Angel Skin.

CLEO: Don't say good-bye; you'll be back in five minutes.

FRENCHY: Yeah, Cleo, you're like a magnet!

CLEO: You're wild, Dr. Jensen—just like a sea-bird. (FRENCHY *chortles at that and exits, right.* CLEO *and* STARK *are now alone for the first time in hours. She begins to peruse the magazine, waiting for his advances. He watches her for a moment.)*

STARK *(softly, despite his several anxieties):* "How green you are and fresh in this old world." . . . Shakespeare. *(Going to her.)* Are you mad, Cleo?

CLEO *(pertly):* Only dogs are mad. *(He sits down beside her and suddenly kisses her shyly.)*

CLEO *(coquetting):* When I was a little girl a fortune teller told me I'd meet a man like you. *(He kisses her again.)* You're a regular kissing bug.

STARK: Yes, perhaps I oughtn't to do that.

CLEO: I didn't say not to.

STARK *(holding her hand):* I like to hold your hand.

CLEO: Where will we go tonight?

STARK: After the lecture? Well . . .

CLEO *(archly):* I suppose you have to go home. Mr. Prince takes me to interesting places. You're not doing me a favor when you take me out.

STARK: The favor's all on your side, Cleo.

CLEO: Palisades Park is not my idea of heaven.

STARK: I don't know any places, Cleo. I'm not the kind of man who goes out much. You can help me find places to go. We'll go to a Eugene O'Neill play in the winter——

CLEO: You're ashamed of me.

STARK *(surprised):* Why do you say that?

CLEO: You take me to out-of-the-way places—a movie on 14th Street! You don't want people to see us together; isn't that true?

STARK: It's not shame. . . .

CLEO: You're very cautious then.

STARK: Yes. . . .

CLEO: Why are you cautious? We didn't do anything. *(After waiting for an answer.)* You think about your wife all the time.

STARK: I have to, Cleo.

CLEO: Why? She doesn't think about you.

STARK: That isn't true. Maybe we could go to the Planetarium to-night. You said you wanted to see it.

CLEO: Mr. Wax was very attracted to me.

STARK: What did he say?

CLEO: Are you jealous?

STARK *(smiling):* No.

CLEO: Then why should I tell you? Do you love me?
(Note: CLEO, *in her contact with those she thinks "superior people," is often afraid of repudiation on one score or another. This is so in her relationship with* STARK. *For this reason she seldom fully extends the power she feels over him. This gives most of her impulses and gestures a contained tentative quality; an impulse is seldom fully released.)*

STARK *(uneasily):* Do you want to go to the Planetarium——

CLEO: Are you listening to me?

STARK: Yes. *(He tries to take her hand.)*

CLEO: No, I won't let you hold my hand. *(Moving across the room.)* I feel discouraged. I'd like to leave this place.

STARK: Why?

CLEO: You don't need me here. I don't make much difference in your life.

STARK: It's not fair to say that. I can't do everything I'd like to do, Cleo. *(Suddenly.)* But you make me very happy, very happy!

CLEO: Do I?

STARK: Gee, yes! *(He crosses to her as if to embrace her, but* CLEO *eludes him with a laugh.)*

CLEO: Here comes that kissing bug!

STARK: You make me very happy! Let me put my arms around you.

CLEO: Nope.

STARK: Please.

CLEO: You can't creep up on me like that. You never think of me.

STARK: I thought of you all last night. I was walking on the boardwalk and I thought of you. Do you know what the waves are saying?

CLEO: What?

STARK: Your name . . .

CLEO: Well, were you walking alone?

STARK: No.

CLEO: With your wife?

STARK: Yes. . . . *(There is a pause;* CLEO *walks to the water cooler.)*

CLEO: I have some bad news temporarily.

STARK *(strained)*: What?

CLEO: I'm having lunch with Mr. Wax, down his office.

STARK: When?

CLEO: Now. Do you mind?

STARK *(in a low voice)*: No.

CLEO: Are you jealous?

STARK: Yes.

CLEO: He's a very interesting man—I want to hear what he has to say. I can learn from him. He's interested in my dancing.

STARK *(miserably)*: Wax makes propaganda for Willy Wax, dear. He's interested in two things—himself and girls for himself. I know him —he's been in this building for years.

CLEO *(touched by his misery, softly)*: You act as if I was leaving. I'm not leaving you, Ben.

STARK *(pleadingly)*: Don't go down there.

CLEO *(earnestly)*: Don't you know you're my best friend? My *only* friend?

STARK: Being a friend is one thing. . . . *(Taking her hand.)* Cleo . . . we don't belong to each other. . . . I mean I don't have the right . . . this is like living in a subway and never getting off the train. . . .

CLEO *(softly)*: Is it fair for you to question my motives? Is it?

STARK: Cleo. . . . *(Suddenly he kisses her hand.)*

CLEO: That's right—kiss it. And kiss the fingers, every one. *(He does so.)* And you do that of your own free will. *(With sudden anxiety.)* Did I offend?

STARK: No, dear, no. . . .

CLEO: You have to always remember that you belong to me! Let me pull your nose. *(She does.)* Your ears. *(She does.)* No, you can't kiss me. *(She eludes him.)* For another week, no kissing. . . . Now I have to go.

STARK: Don't go. . . .

CLEO: I have to, Ben. Don't worry. I'll be back soon. (STARK *releases her hand. She goes to the door.)* Don't worry, Ben. . . . *(The door is opened by* BELLE STARK *just in time to hear the name being uttered by* CLEO. *To* BELLE.) Ooh, you frightened me! Excuse me, I'm going to lunch. . . . *(The two women look at each other briefly, and* CLEO *exits.)*

BELLE: She uses a very heavy perfume.

STARK *(over-brightly)*: Belle, I'm surprised to see you in town!

BELLE *(quizzically):* But pleased?

STARK: Very pleased.

BELLE *(sitting):* The beach is boring.

STARK: It must be cool down there. I wish I didn't have to stick in the office——

BELLE *(wanly):* I feel like a poached egg.

STARK: Why don't you stay down there, dear? It's cool, you can rest——

BELLE *(wearily):* Don't be funny, Ben! A place is not a place. A place is who you're with!

STARK *(meekly, wondering what she knows):* Unfortunately, I have this lecture tonight, at the Clinic. But I'll be down early in the afternoon, tomorrow . . . tomorrow? . . . Yes, Saturday, and we'll have the whole week-end together.

BELLE: A week-end starts on Friday in the summer. If you saw the other husbands at the beach today you'd know it. *(Suddenly she almost sobs, but immediately catches herself. STARK is immediately at her side, his arm around her shoulder. He is both touched and uneasy, a little sick at heart.)*

STARK *(gently):* Is that why you came to town, dear? You felt alone?

BELLE *(dry-eyed):* Yes.

STARK: Why don't you have Milly Heitner down till I get there? They can use the other room—I'll move the table out——

BELLE: Milly and Jack are in San Diego, California.

STARK: I forgot that. . . . *(After a pause.)* Would you want to stay in town tonight? . . .

BELLE: Do you want me to?

STARK: I wouldn't ask if I didn't. *(Seeing her distressed face.)* What's the matter, Belle?

BELLE: Your heart is so faint, the way you ask. Am I being a pest?

STARK: You're not a pest, Belle.

BELLE: For God's sake, tell me if I am. I'll go back to the beach and bury myself in the sand up to the chin!

STARK *(meekly):* I was only thinking——I have that lecture tonight, . . . *(Now BELLE begins to flirt with her husband, an activity which does not become her. But she is desperate. The flirting comes out thin, pitiful, dry and nervous. To both of them it is an extremely painful interlude.)*

BELLE: Aren't you afraid I'll leave you, Ben? Down there at the beach, alone? All day long? Suppose an interesting man came along? Don't you care?

STARK (*smiling uneasily*): You won't run away, dear. . . .

BELLE (*half smiling*): I might . . . or don't you think I'm attractive enough for a man——

STARK: You're as attractive as you ever were, Belle.

BELLE: Confess to your wife—aren't you ever afraid to leave her alone as much as you do?

STARK (*shaking a finger at her*): Send me a wire before you elope. (*They both laugh weakly.*)

BELLE (*fishing for affirmations*): You'd *like* to get rid of me.

STARK: Never, never!

BELLE: Admit it——

STARK: Never, dear, not for a day. . . . And I don't want you to talk that way, even in a joke.

BELLE (*suddenly*): I'll make you an offer, Ben. Why don't I take this job?

STARK: This . . .

BELLE (*quickly*): I'd get my typing back in no time. In one week I'd have this office on an efficient working basis. . . .

STARK: You don't mean it.

BELLE: Yes, I do.

STARK (*dubiously*): You wouldn't want this job.

BELLE: Why not? I'm loyal, honest—you'd get me cheap——

STARK: A wife in her husband's office? I need a girl here who can take orders. She has to clean instruments, be yelled at, be impersonal——

BELLE: I can be impersonal.

STARK: Why do you bring up a thing like that, after all these years?

BELLE: Why are you so outraged?

STARK (*angrily*): Who's outraged?

BELLE: Isn't your tone unreasonable?

STARK: Isn't your request? In all fairness . . . Well, I see your point, Belle, but I give in to you on many things. Gee, I know it's no bed of roses for you, but a man's office is his castle——

BELLE: I can be as impersonal as some snip of a girl with vaseline on her eyelids. I want you to fire her and let me——

STARK: Yes? Well, I won't do it!

BELLE: Why does she call you Ben, that little papoose?

STARK: What?

BELLE: I heard her call you Ben when I came in. Is that a habit of hers?

STARK: I didn't notice that.

BELLE: Ask her to call you Dr. Stark—do me the favor. Or would that be straining relationships too much?

STARK *(quickly):* What relationships?

BELLE *(acidly):* Any which might exist. Secondly, I intend to go to that lecture tonight.

STARK: That doesn't frighten me.

BELLE: Will she be there?

STARK: She takes notes.

BELLE: Notes? Will they be printed in a book, "Confessions of a Dentist"?

STARK: Belle, I deplore these suspicions!

BELLE: Let her go or you'll confirm them!

STARK *(going to her after a pause):* Belle, can you stand there and seriously tell me . . .

BELLE *(eluding him):* Off . . . the scrawny shoulders, my dental friend. Now make up your mind, Ben. . . .

STARK *(blazing out):* Will you stop that stuff for a change! It's about time you began to realize there are two ends to a rope. *I* have needs, too! This one-way street has to end! I'm not going to stay under water like an iceberg the rest of my life. You've got me licked—I must admit it. All right, I'm sleeping, I don't love you enough. But what do *you* give? What do you know about *my* needs?

BELLE: Don't you dare speak that way to me!

STARK: You've been speaking like that for ten years!

BELLE: You won't throw me away for that dirty rag of a girl!

STARK: The hell with the girl! I'm talking of us. . . .

BELLE *(wildly):* I gave you too much of my life for that. You've used me up. . . .

STARK: Belle, for Pete's sake . . . !

BELLE: And now you want to throw me off. But you're a man, not an animal—you can't do that!

STARK: If you can't talk facts, keep quiet!

BELLE *(weeping):* My mother sat crying by the window for twenty years——

STARK: Every word is nonsense!

BELLE: But you can't do that to me. I wasn't born in Europe——I'm a modern woman——I don't weep, not me. . . . *(She trails off into silence.* STARK *gruffly hands her a handkerchief, which she uses.)*

STARK *(bitterly):* Sonofagun. . . .

BELLE: Not weep, not weep. . . . (BELLE *turns scornfully and enters the office, slamming the door in* STARK'S *following face.)*

STARK *(at the door):* No, open the door, Belle. Open it. *(Rattling and turning the knob.)* Unlock the door, Belle. *(Twisting the knob again.)* Belle? . . . Belle? . . . Let me in. . . . *(*DR. COOPER *now enters the waiting room.* STARK *quickly walks away from the door.)*

COOPER: Just the man I'm looking for.

STARK: Hello, Phil.

COOPER: I came in today for one express purpose. *(He sees* BELLE'S *shadow moving on the glass of the closed office door.)* What is that shadow in there, moving?

STARK *(gloomily):* My wife. . . .

COOPER *(calling jovially):* Come out of hiding, Mrs. Stark. Phil Cooper's got a surprise. *(Draws a check from his pocket, followed by fountain pen.)* See Phil Cooper create a historical moment, like the signing of the Declaration of Independence. *(Signing the check on the back.)* A check for thirty dollars and I now sign it over to you. *(Calling over his shoulder.)* Come out, Mrs. Stark, and see history in the making.

STARK: She has a little headache.

COOPER: What can take it away easier? *(Handing it over to* STARK.) There it is. . . . A first payment, on account. (BELLE *now stands in the doorway, outwardly calm and collected.)* Look what I gave your spouse, Mrs. Stark. *(Laughingly.)* Blood money!

STARK *(to* BELLE): You can bank that, dear. *(He extends the check to her, a peace offering, but she rejects it, saying with a coolness which* COOPER *doesn't notice.)*

BELLE: Bank it yourself. *(Rebuked and hurt,* STARK *silently folds the check and puts it in his wallet.* BELLE *goes for her purse and gloves.)*

STARK *(sullenly):* Where are you going?

BELLE *(coldly):* Home, to my palace on the beach.

STARK *(trying to stop her):* Belle, listen——

BELLE: You're such an actor, Ben. Good-bye, Dr. Cooper.

COOPER: Good-bye. (BELLE *exits, leaving* STARK *feeling foolish and angry. Joyfully.)* I'm hot, but who can blame me for that? *(Drinking at the water cooler.)* Nature makes the heat and the heat eats me up. What am I to Nature?—A hot dog on a roll! Say, a few more transfusions and I'll dream it's better days. *(Turning to face* STARK.) Stark?

STARK: What? (COOPER'S *answer is to look at* STARK, *then step forward and kiss him on the cheek.)*

COOPER: Imagine what a kiss you would get if I paid the *whole* debt! *(And* COOPER *has exited happily through the door, left.* STARK *stands there angrily thoughtful. He wags his head angrily, strides around the room several times. Finally he looks out of the window, examining the Hotel Algiers. A sense of resolution grows into his appearance. Suddenly he puts his hand to his heart, not having noticed before how strongly it is beating. Now* CLEO *enters, defiantly pushing open the door,* WAX *behind her.* STARK *turns on them, momentarily unnerved.)*

WAX *(gayly):* Stark, what kind of hold have you got on this girl? Couldn't keep her down my office—said she had to be back——

CLEO *(breaking in):* Dr. Stark has no hold on me. I have some work to do.

WAX *(to* STARK): I call Cleo the Radium Girl—gives off heat and light.

STARK *(foolishly):* Yes. . . .

WAX: Take back the precious capsule, Stark.

CLEO *(annoyed):* I wish you wouldn't say that!

WAX: Say what?

CLEO: Hinting—as if I belong to him. (WAX *looks from one to the other, understanding their relationship in a flash.)*

WAX: I beg your pardon, Cleo; that never crossed my mind.

STARK *(darkly):* What never crossed your mind?

WAX: We're getting mixed up here, aren't we?

STARK: Not at all.

WAX: Come to see me again, Cleo. Or I'll call you.

CLEO: Yes.

WAX: Why are your brows bulging, Stark?

STARK: What?

WAX *(pleasantly):* See you soon. *(He exits. After a momentary silence* CLEO *goes to the door, beginning to pin it back.)*

STARK: Close the door.

CLEO *(fretfully):* It's hot.

STARK: I know, but close it. . . . (CLEO *closes the door, struck by* STARK'S *resolute manner. Her outing to* WAX'S *office has been a dismal failure. Her mind has been up here with* STARK *and* BELLE *all the time. She is nervous and defiant now, even feeling un-wanted, a feeling which motivates much that she does.)*

CLEO *(defiantly):* I suppose you want me to melt into a little pool of water. Why're you looking at me like that?

STARK: I don't want him calling you Cleo. Who is he?

CLEO *(sitting):* Oh, you! . . .

STARK *(angrily):* I didn't call you Cleo till I knew you for weeks. Why should he?

CLEO: What's the matter with you anyway?

STARK: Nothing, Cleo.

CLEO: This whole thing has to end!

STARK *(staring at her):* Does it?

CLEO: It can't go on like this. I'll go out with other men.

STARK *(crossing to her):* No, you won't.

CLEO: I was thinking about you and your wife in Mr. Wax's office——

STARK: After the lecture we're going to the Planetarium——

CLEO: What did she say?

STARK: I don't care what she said.

CLEO: But I do——

STARK: After we visit the Planetarium——

CLEO: You don't think of me, don't care for me. . . .

STARK: We're going to leave early and have a cool supper. . . .

CLEO: Have a party by yourself!——

STARK: Listen to me. . . .

CLEO: I used to think you cared for me. . . .

STARK: But I do, Cleo. . . .

CLEO: Since when?

STARK: Since now. Tu amo, Cleo. . . . That means "I love you." You're right, darling. The stars are useless. I'll take you to a different place tonight.

CLEO: Where?

STARK: They won't know us from Adam there.

CLEO: But you don't love me.

STARK: Only you. Tonight we'll be together, Cleo. . . . Alone, alone together. . . .

CLEO: I don't trust you.

STARK: You're more important to me than anything I know, Cleo, dear. . . .

CLEO: What happened?

STARK: Nothing. I only know I love you, Cleo.

CLEO *(after a pause, suddenly):* Then hold me tight, Ben. Kiss me, love me—kiss me till I can't be kissed no more. Hold me. Don't let me be alone in the world, Ben. . . . Don't let me be alone. . . . (STARK *moves to her and they embrace passionately.)*

Curtain

ACT THREE

TIME: *Three weeks later, the end of August.*
PLACE: *The same.*

BELLE *and* STARK *are present, he sitting motionlessly, a newspaper sprawled in his lap. She is sitting on the couch, looking over canceled checks. There is a dead awful silence between them, each one revolving in his own tight little world.*

The office is only partly lighted. A spill of light comes from the hallway left. Far off in the Hotel Algiers a radio crooner is heard. A faint blue light is burning in the operating room. The electric fan hums busily. After a moment, BELLE *looking up obliquely,* STARK *goes to the fan, hoists its speed and returns to his seat. Outside the waiting room the air is hot and still, as before a storm.*

STARK *(finally):* That fan must eat up juice a mile a minute. . . . *(After further silence.)* One of these days I'd like to get air conditioning. Those small units aren't expensive. . . .

BELLE *(suddenly):* Why can't we drop this farce? Don't you owe me that much courtesy?

STARK *(stubbornly):* Belle, I've told you the truth.

BELLE: You really stayed here to look over these vouchers?

STARK: I've told you so several times.

BELLE: You're looking for an eighteen-dollar error?

STARK: Since when do we sneeze at eighteen dollars?

BELLE: And that kept you here till nine at night?

STARK *(challengingly):* Yes.

BELLE *(triumphantly):* There's no mistake in these vouchers!

STARK: No? . . . Then *I've* made a mistake. But if I *didn't* check them over, you'd say I was careless. *(Shaking his head.)* You can't win with a woman!

BELLE: Not my type.

STARK: I found that out years ago. *(Getting a sarcastically baleful glare from her.)* I know, you've still got the girl on your mind.

BELLE: You're not waiting here for her?

STARK: No. *(He goes to the water cooler and drinks.)*

BELLE: You don't think you owe me certain common courtesies?

STARK: And what may those be?

BELLE: The truth! The truth! The truth! *(Before* STARK *can answer, the office telephone rings.)*

STARK *(hurrying to the office door):* I'll answer that.

BELLE *(blocking his way):* No, I'll take it. *(They look at each other a moment.* STARK *finally steps to one side.* BELLE *picks up the telephone, looking out at* STARK.*)*

BELLE: Hello. . . . No, this isn't Miss Singer. Who is——? (BELLE *clips her words short. She proffers the phone to* STARK, *saying):* Your esteemed father-in-law. (STARK *takes the telephone nervously.)*

STARK: Yes, Poppa. . . . No, she isn't. . . . I don't know. . . . Tonight? . . . Well, don't come too late; I'll wait a half hour. Goodbye. *(He hangs up the telephone and comes into the waiting room.)* Poppa's coming over. He wants to see me.

BELLE: What about?

STARK: He didn't say.

BELLE: You might have told him we're going home.

STARK: I'll call him back and tell him.

BELLE: But you don't want to go home.

STARK *(over-patient):* I'll call him back and tell him.

BELLE *(insistently):* Do you . . . ? (STARK *slowly turns and looks at her with a twisted face. Finally he says in a twisted voice.)*

STARK: No, Belle, I don't. That's a shack on the beach, and this is a shack. Don't be angry . . . it won't do us no good to quarrel again. I know you're my wife, but it's like we're enemies. We're like two exposed nerves!

BELLE *(bitterly):* It's *my* fault!

STARK *(quietly):* Much more mine. I don't know what happened. I thought about these things a lot these past few months. You expect many things from marriage, but I can't give them. I feel a moral obligation but I don't know what to do. These scenes go on. We're always worried . . . we're two machines counting up the petty cash. Something about me cheats you—I'm not the man to help you be the best woman it's in you to be. So your attitude's justified. I know I owe you a lot, Belle——

BELLE *(bitterly):* Hallelujah!

STARK *(anger mounting despite himself):* Now I realize I've had a guilty feeling for years. "Marriage is the only adventure open to the coward," a certain man says. He made a mistake; you have to be a hero to face the pains and disappointments. *(As she tries to speak.)* No, let me finish. Because now I'm really guilty. . . . I mean with this girl——

BELLE *(quickly):* That's enough!

STARK: I can't lie any more——

BELLE: *That's enough! Do you hear me? Enough!*

STARK *(insistently):* I have to tell you——

BELLE *(jumping up):* But you don't love her! You had an affair, all right, but you don't *love* her! (STARK *sits, head in hands,* BELLE *continues with fearful agitation.)* The girl was here all day. You were close together and you fell into that thing. I can forget it, I can forget it, Ben. I'm your wife. It doesn't involve our whole relationship. We can have many happy years together. I'll do anything you want. We're young—we have our life together in common, our ten years. We can talk it out—we're civilized beings—I'll never mention it. We'll both forget it! We need each other, Ben. We . . . (BELLE *stands there, wavering, a spout of water.* STARK *goes to her, embracing her. She is bloodless, stunned.)*

STARK: Belle, dear, dear, dear, dear. . . .

BELLE *(moving away and staring at him):* It was only a thing of the moment, wasn't it? Wasn't it? Do you hear me—wasn't it?

STARK *(anything to blot out this pale ghost before him):* Yes, yes! *(A pause, she wavers again, has to hold on to furniture to steady herself. Finally.)*

BELLE *(wildly):* I'll wait for her. When is she coming back?

STARK *(frightened):* I'll take you home, Belle. We'll go home.

BELLE: When is she coming back here?

STARK: I don't know.

BELLE *(wildly):* You don't know? Did you tell me you don't know? *(Sitting.)* I'll sit and wait for her.

STARK *(after a pause):* Belle, you can't do that. . . . We'll talk about it tomorrow—we'll be more sensible——

BELLE: Do you love her?

STARK *(twisting):* . . . It can't be settled in a minute, Belle.

BELLE *(white to the lips):* What can't be settled?

STARK: I don't know what. . . . I have a responsibility. . . .

BELLE: Your first responsibility's to me! You hear that?

STARK: I have to know what to do, Belle, and . . .

BELLE: To do? . . . You don't know what to do? You're in doubts? You have the slightest doubt?

STARK *(writhingly):* I don't know what. . . .

BELLE *(instantly):* Give me the key to the car!

STARK: I'll go down with you.

BELLE: Give me the key.

STARK *(giving her the key):* It's across the street—I'll take you down. . . .

BELLE: Stay here.

STARK: Downstairs to the car. . . . *(She slaps him strongly across the face. He is silent.)*

BELLE: When you know what to do . . . I'll be at Milly Heitner's apartment. *(A blazing fury—but watery in the legs—she exits in silence.* STARK *stands in his place, literally shivering. Then he turns out a light. After a moment he sits, unable to stand. The newspaper has slipped to the floor; he picks it up and puts it in his lap. A knock sounds at the door—it is repeated—*STARK *pays no attention. Then the door knob is rattled.)*

FRENCHY *(without):* Nobody home?

STARK *(clearing his throat):* Who is it?

FRENCHY: Me, Doc—Frenchy. *(After* STARK *opens the door.)* I knew I didn't see you leave. *(*STARK *has resumed his seat, newspaper in lap.)* In the dark? Getting to be a poet in your old age, Doc?

STARK *(clearing his throat again):* Cooler in the dark. . . .

FRENCHY *(sitting):* The days are getting shorter . . . you notice that?

STARK: Yes. . . .

FRENCHY: It starts early.

STARK: What starts early?

FRENCHY: Night starts early. . . . I got a headache—some carbon knocking around in the dome. . . .

STARK *(abstracted):* What?

FRENCHY *(giving him a shrewd glance):* Who you sticking around for?

STARK *(after a pause):* . . . Cleo.

FRENCHY: Where is she?

STARK *(after a pause):* What? Out with Wax. . . .

FRENCHY: Again? *(Silence.)*

STARK: In a few weeks I'll be forty. . . .

FRENCHY *(giving him a sharp glance):* Yeah? . . .

STARK: I feel like a boy. *(After a pause.)* Did you ever wish to have some children?

FRENCHY: They break too easy. . . . (FRENCHY *waits for another question, which finally comes.)*

STARK: What do *you* get out of life?

FRENCHY *(blinking):* I just woke up. I was reading a book before, and then I thought about it and then I fell asleep. What I get out of life? —Lemme think about it. Well . . . small change, I guess, but I like it. I tinker with my motors, the little boat and the jalopy. The jalopy cost me ninety bucks. Three times I took her apart and put it together again. Does General Motors himself get more fun?

STARK: But you're a man!——

FRENCHY: With all the accoutrements of man, I can't deny that.

STARK: Don't you want to get married?

FRENCHY: When it's time, Doc.

STARK: When you fall in love, you mean?

FRENCHY *(with extreme seriousness):* Love? Depends on what you mean by love. Love, for most people, is a curious sensation below the equator. Love—as they call it—is easy—even the rabbits do it! The girl I want . . . she'd have to be made in heaven. That's why I wait——

STARK: You're that good, you think?

FRENCHY *(correcting him):* That *bad,* Doc! *She'll* have to be the good one. This is why: Love is a beginning, a jumping-off place. It's like what heat is at the forge—makes the metal easy to handle and shape. *But love and the grace to use it!*—To develop, expand it, variate it!—Oh, dearie me, that's the problem, as the poet said!

STARK: Yes, I see your point. . . .

FRENCHY: Who can do that today? Who's got time and place for "love and the grace to use it"? Is it something apart, love? A good book you go to in a spare hour? An entertainment? Christ, no! It's a synthesis of good and bad, economics, work, play, all contacts . . . it's not a Sunday suit for special occasions. That's why Broadway songs are phony, Doc!—Love is no solution of life! Au contraire, as the Frenchman says—the opposite. You have to bring a whole balanced normal life to love if you want it to go!

STARK: Yes, I see your point.

FRENCHY: In this day of stresses I don't see much normal life, myself included. The woman's not a wife. She's the dependent of a salesman who can't make sales and is ashamed to tell her so, of a federal project worker . . . or a Cooper, a dentist . . . the free exercise of love, I figure, gets harder every day.

STARK: I see your point.

FRENCHY: We live in a nervous time. How can I marry? With what? . . . Unless the girl is with me, up to the minute on all these things. Otherwise they get a dirty deal, the girls.

STARK *(abstracted)*: Yes, I see. . . .

FRENCHY: You're not listening. . . .

STARK *(pale and strained)*: I heard most . . . of what you said.

FRENCHY *(after a pause)*: I hope you excuse me, Doc; you and your wife woke me up before. . . .

STARK: Yes? . . .

FRENCHY *(starting hesitantly)*: Suppose . . . do you mind if I say this?

STARK: What? . . .

FRENCHY *(plunging in)*: Do you know what I'd ask myself? . . . What can I do for the girl, for Cleo? What will she be in ten years, with my help?

STARK *(with a burning face)*: You talk as if a happy marriage isn't possible——

FRENCHY: No, I don't. But they're rare, like the dodo bird, mostly extinct. You know it yourself, Doc.

STARK *(suddenly bursting out)*: Frenchy, I love her, I love her! . . . I love that girl! I'm half out of my mind. I don't know what to do. *(Striding to the light switch.)* Look at me. My face is so twisted. It feels twisted—is it twisted? . . .

FRENCHY *(quietly)*: Sit down, Doc.

STARK: I'm sick to my stomach. Where's my wife? Where did she go? Where's Cleo? She said she'd be back at seven. It's way past nine.

FRENCHY: No, sit down, Doc. Let's sit and talk. Let's be practical.

STARK *(out of control)*: Practical? Huh! What's practical about this slow exhaustion, this shame—not knowing what to do—I told my wife—I'm ready for the nut house——

FRENCHY: Leave the morals out. Sit down. Never mind the shame and guilt.

STARK: All my life I've been afraid to do something wrong and now I've done it.

FRENCHY: Leave the Scriptures out, Doc. Let's separate the problems. (STARK *stares at* FRENCHY *a moment, wags his head and sits, assisted by* FRENCHY.)

STARK *(in a low voice, smiling faintly):* I'm not sick. . . .

FRENCHY *(after a pause):* Leaving Scriptures out. . . . Do you want the girl or your wife? That's problem number one.

STARK *(mopping his head):* I don't know where I stand. . . .

FRENCHY: Can you answer that tonight? *(The outer door knob is rattled from the outside.* FRENCHY *opens the door.* MR. PRINCE *steps in, rolled umbrella in hand, the handle a fancily carved dog's head of ivory.)*

PRINCE: Look, the gathering of the clans. What's here, a pinochle game? *(Sitting.)* Where's Belle?—I heard her on the phone.

STARK: She went home.

FRENCHY *(looking from one to the other):* And so will I. . . . *(Pointedly.)* If no one minds? Doc?

STARK: I'll see you in the morning, Frenchy.

FRENCHY: That's a nice umbrella head you got there, Mr. Prince. Does he bite?

PRINCE *(smiling smoothly):* A quiet dog always bites.

FRENCHY *(at the door):* Au revoir, gentry.

PRINCE: Gute nacht, mein Herr. (FRENCHY *exits.)*

STARK: Why so late, Poppa? It's nearly ten.

PRINCE: The logic is on your side. . . . *(Watching* STARK *wind his watch.)* I seen Mrs. Heitner on the street today.

STARK: I hate that woman! *(Then masking his vehemence.)* It's cooling off outside, isn't it?

PRINCE: Rain can be expected any minute. The good Lord keeps a balance, dry and wet. . . . Yes, we face serious problems before us.

STARK: What problems?

PRINCE: I feel again the shudder of humility, Benny.

STARK: What? Why? *(Incredulously.)* What?

PRINCE: The good Lord sees all, knows all. . . .

STARK *(impatiently):* Don't be so circular, Poppa! What're you driving at?

PRINCE: Last night I fell asleep and dreamed the secret of the world. It is not good for Man to live alone. You hear?

STARK: I hear.

PRINCE: Where's Miss Cleo?

STARK *(briefly):* Gone for the night.

PRINCE: You're not waiting for her?

STARK: No. Why?

PRINCE *(solemnly):* Belle is getting suspicious.

STARK *(dry in the mouth):* . . . Of what?

PRINCE: You have to get up like a morning glory to bamboozle me.

STARK *(angrily):* What the hell are you trying to say?

PRINCE *(raising his voice):* That a great thought occurred in my mind. To be frank, I like your taste.

STARK: I don't like these insinuations!

PRINCE *(suddenly standing up):* Then come out in the open.

STARK: Poppa!——

PRINCE: Yes?

STARK *(wildly):* Leave the office!

PRINCE *(solemnly):* That's how you speak to King Midas? *(The two men stare at each other,* STARK *slowly turning away and getting himself in hand. Finally.)*

STARK *(in a low voice):* You're a wretched man, Mr. Prince.

PRINCE *(down to business):* A desperate man, Dr. Benny. A man in love.

STARK: With whom?

PRINCE: Miss Cleo.

STARK *(incredulously):* Miss? . . . Miss? . . .

PRINCE: Let us chew some brass tacks. You're having an affair with her. . . .

STARK: No!

PRINCE: I have experience—let *me* be the liar. *(Holding* STARK *with his eye.)* It is my intention to renovate my life. Miss Cleo was elected on the first count: I want her in marriage.

STARK: Poppa!

PRINCE: She pleases my eye and ear—in every way a constant pleasure.

STARK: You must be out of your mind! Crazy! She won't have you!

PRINCE *(the men standing face to face):* You like to choke me? Do it . . . put your two hands on my old guzzle and squeeze! That's the only way you'll stop me!

STARK *(after momentary consideration, shaking his head):* No, you can't be sane!

PRINCE: Are you? What can you offer her? Did it ever enter your befuddled mind?

STARK: I won't discuss this! And leave the office!

PRINCE: She's coming back here tonight?

STARK: If I could only see your true face just once!

PRINCE: Is she?

STARK *(bitingly):* Maybe!

PRINCE: Good!

STARK *(scornfully):* You're very confident.

PRINCE *(quietly):* I know human nature.

STARK: And you dare to think you'll buy that girl? You're a damned smiling villain! Go home, get out! *(A slow flush creeps up* PRINCE'S *face. He tries to hold back his anger, but it comes out warmly.)*

PRINCE: Listen, a man in the fullness of his life speaks to you. I didn't come here to make you unhappy. I came here to make *myself happy!* You don't like it—I can understand that. Circumstances insulted me enough in my life. But *your* insults I don't need! And I don't apologize to no man because I try to take happiness by the throat! Remember, Dr. Benny, I want what I want! There are seven fundamental words in life, and one of these is love, and I didn't have it! And another one is love, and I don't have it! *And the third of these is love, and I shall have it! (Beating the furniture with his umbrella.)* De corpso you think! I'm dead and buried you think! I'll sit in the long winter night with a shawl on my shoulders? Now you see my face, Dr. Benny. Now you know your father-in-law, that damned smiling villain! I'll fight you to the last ditch—you'll get mowed down like a train. I want that girl. I'll wait downstairs. When she returns I'll come right up, in five minutes. I'll test *your* sanity!—*You,* you Nobel prize winner! *(He stops, exhausted, wipes his face with a large silk handkerchief, does the same to the umbrella head and then slowly exits.* STARK *stands motionlessly a moment, licking his lips nervously. He looks at his watch again, putting it to his ear. He hears a sound outside the window, rain. He goes to the window, right, putting his hand out to feel the rain. He puts the cool hand to his fevered face. With a handkerchief he mops his face and neck nervously. The door knob rattles;* STARK *immediately opens the door.* WILLY WAX *enters.)*

WAX: Hello, Dr. Stark-sky.

STARK: Oh, you. . . .

WAX: Mopping up your brain sweat?

STARK: It's hot enough. . . .

WAX: Raining out.

STARK: I can hear it.

WAX *(listening with over-intentness):* That's right; you can hear it. Well, Stark-sky, your little Neon light spluttered right in my face.

That's a curious girl, that one. Was she ever an ice skater in the Olympics? She said she was.

STARK (*impatiently*): Where is she?

WAX: Somewhere in the last century, where she belongs.

STARK: I beg your pardon?

WAX: I mean she's old-fashioned, romantic—she believes in love!

STARK (*coldly*): I find her quite modern.

WAX: Because you're old-fashioned yourself.

STARK: Where is Miss Singer?

WAX (*chuckling*): Sent her home. She thinks I'm a wolf.

STARK: So do I.

WAX (*with a laugh*): Got some business down my office. That's why I returned. (*He starts for the door.*)

STARK: Business with whom?

WAX (*suddenly dropping his mask of affability*): None of your goddam business!

STARK: Is Miss Singer down there?

WAX: I told you she spluttered in my face, you idiot! Where do you think I got these scratches?

STARK: Where is she?

WAX: What's giving you cancer?

STARK: I want you to keep away from her.

WAX: You want *what?*

STARK: You have no interest in her, not the slightest. You have lots of girls, Wax—all you want and . . .

WAX (*jeeringly*): This prosecuting-attorney role becomes you not.

STARK (*earnestly*): Cleo's young, extremely naïve in some ways. You might warp her for life——(WAX *laughs.*) Please, Wax, seriously——I must ask you to leave her alone. She's a mere mechanism to you, for a night——

WAX: Certainly, I'm a mechanical man in a mechanical era!

STARK: Please listen to me. . . .

WAX: You're making a clown of yourself. And secondly, since when does a stinker dentist, a prime pinhead, have the right to dictate the morals and manners of a Willy Wax!

STARK: You keep away from her!

WAX (*vehemently*): You mind your goddam business!

STARK: Wax, for God's sake——!

WAX: Understand this for once and all: any white woman who pleases me——(STARK *abruptly plunges forward and seizes* WAX *by the*

throat. WAX *is frightened out of his wits.)* Stark! Stop it! Stop . . .
that! Are you . . . (STARK *releasing him.)* nuts? . . . Are you
nuts? *(Both men are breathing heavily, very pale, watching each
other narrowly.* WAX, *a physical coward, immediately puts on a
bold front.)* That's how you act over a little pony who can't stand
on her own legs? You're walking around in the shadow of the noose,
Stark-sky. *(Making his clothing orderly.)* Don't I know your type?
——A bourgeois balcony climber—married, prates of purity—
gives temperance lectures, but drinks and plays around——
STARK: Leave the office, please.
WAX: You're lucky I didn't eviscerate you!
STARK: Please, please. . . .
WAX: You want that girl yourself.
STARK: I'm asking you to——
WAX *(emphatically):* No further commerce between us! *(Going to
the door.)* Years of dentistry have gone to your head. *(Before* WAX
can open the door CLEO *has done so from the other side. She
removes the key from the lock.* WAX *stiffly stands his ground.* CLEO
enters, soberly moving past him.) Well, it's not in my nature to hold
a grudge. . . .
CLEO *(flashing on him):* Mr. Wax, we don't want you around this
office. You make love very small and dirty. I understand your type
very well now. No man can take a bite out of me, like an apple and
throw it away. Now go away, and we won't miss you.
WAX *(angrily):* Yeah, I'm forming a Society for the Extermination of
the Superfluous. You two are charter members! (WAX *exits, slamming the door behind him.* STARK *looks at* CLEO; *she is wearing a
new colorful raincoat.)*
CLEO: It's raining like the devil.
STARK: I almost killed that man. . . . *(He looks down at his hands.
Then he moves to the operating room and we see his back as he
bends over the wash basin.)*
CLEO *(frightened):* What're you doing?
STARK: Washing my hands.
CLEO *(glibly, making conversation):* I went home for my new raincoat. That's why I'm late—aside from Mr. Wax. Don't you think this
is a beautiful coat? (STARK *silently appears in the doorway, towel-
ing his hands. Finally he flings the towel away and begins to prowl
around the room.* CLEO *watches him, not knowing what to do or
say. Finally* STARK *confronts her.)*

STARK: Cleo dear, we have to come to an understanding.

CLEO *(frightened):* I think we do. . . .

STARK *(after a pause):* I feel so helpless . . . no judgment left. I don't know what I'm doing or saying. I almost want to cry. . . .

CLEO: Why, Ben? You have me—I didn't run away or do anything bad.

STARK: Do you love me very much?

CLEO *(simply):* Yes.

STARK: Try to understand my problems, darling.

CLEO: At the moment the words "problem" and "darling" don't go together. You have to be honest with me, Ben. *(Taking his hand.)* You must tell me what you're thinking. . . .

STARK *(hesitantly):* Cleo, if I could . . . I don't know how to put it. . . . If . . .

CLEO *(trying to help him):* What do you want to say? . . .

STARK: Help me. . . .

CLEO: How? *(Suddenly they embrace swiftly,* STARK *shaking all over.* PRINCE *now enters, finding them in this position. They do not see him until he speaks.* PRINCE *comes into the room.* CLEO *moves away from* STARK *and stares at* PRINCE.*)*

PRINCE: Excuse me—intrusion is not my purpose. *(To* STARK*):* Did you tell her? *(Receiving no answer from* STARK.*)* I told Dr. Stark I love you——

CLEO *(looking from one to the other):* You must be joking. . . .

PRINCE: No. . . . *(There is a silence during which the three persons look at one another.* CLEO *is annoyed and puzzled;* STARK *is sullen, nervous and angry, even a little hang-dog in attitude.* PRINCE *is determined and passionately desperate, but* CLEO'S *attitude adds a certain wariness to his demeanor. Finally.)* I think we are ready for a preliminary analysis, as my friend Mr. Sugarman used to say.

STARK *(with a curt laugh):* Your aberration grows by the minute!

PRINCE: Look at him—the pebble sneers at the ocean!

CLEO *(warningly):* Don't act high and mighty, Mr. Prince!

PRINCE *(warily):* I come in all humility to propose marriage.

CLEO: You pick a bad time to joke.

PRINCE: No, Miss Cleo——Is this a comedian's face?

STARK: I think so.

PRINCE *(restraining his anger):* I'm speaking to an intelligent young woman who'll understand my points.

CLEO: What points?

PRINCE: One by one, allow me to ask: why don't he *(pointing to* STARK) stand by your side? He's across the room, caving in. With what? Fear and worry. Why? He might lose you.

CLEO *(stoutly):* He won't lose me!

PRINCE: Then *you* might lose *him.*

CLEO *(warningly):* You'd better mind your business.

PRINCE: My love for you is my business. In the whole world I have no other business.

CLEO: Tell him to go home, Ben. It's your office—chase him out!

PRINCE: I admire your loyalty, Miss Cleo; but not Dr. Stark's. Give up a vain delusion—this man won't divorce his wife.

STARK: How can you . . . how do you dare! . . .

PRINCE: What, what? Tell us what, Benny! We want to hear your mind. What? *(But* STARK *doesn't know what to say and lapses into fuming knotted silence.* PRINCE *and* CLEO *both stare at him.)*

CLEO *(to* PRINCE): I don't want to hear another word from you. Do I have to slap your face to make you stop? Because you're an old man and I wouldn't like to do that! And you can take your present back. *(She tears off the coat and flings it at* PRINCE *who tosses it to one side with the end of his umbrella.)* Ben, what're you waiting for? Why don't you say something?

STARK *(writhing with indecision):* Cleo. . . .

PRINCE: Give this girl a logical answer.

STARK *(bursting out):* Cleo and I'll talk in private!

PRINCE: If I leave now, you'll give an answer?

CLEO *(turning on* STARK): Are you going to let him go on like that? *(*STARK'S *answer is again knotted writhing silence.)*

PRINCE: You are clay, Miss Cleo, on the way to great womanhood. *(*CLEO *has been staring at* STARK, *who is unable to meet her eyes. Now she turns back to* PRINCE.)*

CLEO: What did you say?

PRINCE: What can he offer you? He loves you—his memoirs are written on his face. But I see a big chapter heading: "No Divorce." Why not? Ten years they're married. She runs his life like a credit manager. They lost a child together . . . they're attached underground by a hundred different roots. But if he left her—as he knows—could he leave his practice? Never! Then *you'd* be a credit manager. . . . But why go on? He won't leave her. That needs courage, strength, and he's not strong.

CLEO *(to* STARK): Why don't you answer him? *(There is a momentary silence.* CLEO *is looking from one to the other, realizing that* STARK *has no case.)*

PRINCE *(finally):* My girl, I studied you like a scientist. I understand your needs.

CLEO *(not knowing what to do or say):* What are they?

PRINCE: A man to help you learn and grow. A man of maturity and experience in everything—love, what to eat, where, what to wear and where to buy it—money to buy it—an eye turned out to the world! You need a man who is proud to serve you and has the means to do it. He knows how to speak to the head waiter and the captain on the ship. He don't look foolish before authority. He is a missionary in life with one mission, to serve and love you.

STARK *(laughing desperately):* How absolute the knave is!

PRINCE: Now let us come down to terra firma. You're a brilliant girl. . . . I'm old enough to be your father.

CLEO: Well?

PRINCE: But notice! Every president of this great country is my age. Because this is the time he's at his best. . . . He has learned how to serve. And there is a simple worldly consideration—it has its importance. In twenty years you'll still be young, a beautiful woman of the world. Cremate me, burn me up and throw me away, and what have you got? A fortune! And so you go, a great woman, scattering good as you go. . . .

CLEO *(after a pause):* What do you say, Ben? *(After waiting.)* Don't stand there like a dead man. . . .

PRINCE: What can he say? He's as mixed up as the twentieth century!

STARK *(turning wrathfully on* PRINCE*):* You come here with this lust!

CLEO *(shaking* STARK *by the arm):* Don't fight with him. Talk to *me*, Ben.

PRINCE: Time is of the essence.

CLEO *(almost crying):* Don't discuss him, Ben. Tell me what *our* plans are. What'll you do with me?

STARK: Cleo, I can't talk now. . . . This man standing here . . .

CLEO: No, you have to tell me now. Where do I stand? . . .

STARK *(evasively):* Stand? . . .

PRINCE *(harshly):* In short, will you leave your wife? (STARK *is silent, unable to make an answer.* CLEO *looks at him appealingly.* PRINCE *stands in the background, unwilling to provoke* CLEO'S *wrath.)*

CLEO: What do you say, Ben . . . ?

STARK *(lost):* Nothing. . . . I can't say . . . Nothing. . . .

CLEO: You'll let me go away? *(She gets no reply from him. Half stunned, she seats herself. Finally.)*

CLEO: I'd like to hold my breath and die.

PRINCE *(softly):* He'd let you do that, too.

STARK *(to* PRINCE): You're a dog, the lowest dog I ever met! *(To* CLEO): Do you know what this man is trying to do?

CLEO *(crushed):* I don't care.

STARK *(gently):* Listen, Cleo . . . think. What can I give you? All I can offer you is a second-hand life, dedicated to trifles and troubles . . . and they go on forever. This isn't self-justification . . . but facts are stubborn things, Cleo; I've wrestled with myself for weeks. This is how it must end. *(His voice trembling.)* Try to understand . . . I can't say more. . . . *(He turns away. There is a momentary silence, which is broken by* PRINCE.)

PRINCE *(approaching her from the other side):* And I offer you a vitalizing relationship: a father, counselor, lover, a friend!

CLEO *(wearily):* Why don't you stop it, Mr. Prince?

PRINCE: Because I mean it.

CLEO: I see you mean it. But you forget one thing—I don't love you.

PRINCE *(insistently):* Put yourself in my hands. . . .

CLEO *(wanly):* I think I have to leave now.

PRINCE: Wear this . . . it's wet outside. (PRINCE *picks up the raincoat and spreads it for her.)*

CLEO *(smiling faintly):* Would it make you happy if I kept it? *(He nods soberly. She goes to him and slips into the coat. Suddenly, from behind, he grips her two arms.)*

PRINCE: Miss Cleo, believe me, life is lonely, life is empty. Love isn't everything. A dear true friend is more than love—the serge outlasts the silk. Give me a chance. I know your needs. I *love* your needs. . . . What do you have to lose?

CLEO *(immobile):* Everything that's me.

PRINCE: What is you? You haven't arrived yet. You're only on the way to being you.

CLEO: I don't want you, Mr. Prince. I'm sorry.

PRINCE *(passionately):* You can't refuse me! What do you want?

CLEO: I don't know. . . .

PRINCE *(as above):* By what you don't know, you can't live! You'll never get what you're looking for! You want a life like Heifetz's music—up from the roots, perfect, clean, every note in place. But that, my girl, is music!

CLEO: I'm looking for love. . . .

PRINCE: From a book of stories!

CLEO: Don't say that. I know what's real. *(Of* STARK): Is his love real?

PRINCE: But *mine!* . . .

CLEO: It's real for *you.* If I can't find love here, I'll find it there.

PRINCE *(insistently):* Where?

CLEO: Somewhere. . . . How can I tell you what I mean? . . .

PRINCE: You'll go down the road alone—like Charlie Chaplin?

CLEO *(to both men):* Yes, if there's roads, I'll take them. I'll go up all those roads till I find what I want. I want a love that uses me, that needs me. Don't you think there's a world of joyful men and women? Must all men live afraid to laugh and sing? Can't we sing at work and love our work? It's getting late to play at life; I want to *live* it. Something has to feel real for me, more than both of you. You see? I don't ask for much. . . .

PRINCE: She's an artist.

CLEO: I'm a girl, and I want to be a woman, and the man I love must help me be a woman! Ben isn't free. He's a citizen of another country. And you, Mr. Prince, don't let me hurt your feelings; you've lived your life. I think you're good, but you're too old for me. And Mr. Wax, his type loves himself. None of you can give me what I'm looking for: a whole full world, with all the trimmings! *(There is a silence.* PRINCE *sees he is licked. Finally he sighs and says softly.)*

PRINCE: Silence is better than rubies. . . .

CLEO: Experience gives more confidence, you know. I have more confidence than when I came here. Button my coat, Ben.

STARK *(coming right to her):* Yes. . . . *(He quickly buttons the front of her coat with fumbling nervous hands. Then suddenly he embraces her strongly, tears in his eyes.)* How your heart beats, Cleo . . . how it beats. . . .

CLEO *(finally, as they separate):* I understand you, Ben. . . . Good night. (STARK *is silent.* PRINCE *shakes his head and says.)*

PRINCE: I'll drive you home.

CLEO: No, I'll go alone. Don't follow me—stay here. Count a hundred till I'm gone. . . .

PRINCE: Good-bye, Miss Cleo.

CLEO *(as they gravely shake hands):* Good-bye, Mr. Prince. If you close your eyes, you'd never know I'd been here. Count a hundred——

PRINCE *(closing his eyes):* One, two, three . . . four, five . . . (CLEO *has left the room.* PRINCE *slowly opens his eyes.)* . . . fifteen, thirty-seven, eighty-nine . . . *(Then in a whisper)* one hundred. . . . Lebewohl! I'm a judge of human nature. She means it; why don't we walk with shut eyes around in the world? . . . *(Looking at his watch.)* It's very late. . . .

STARK *(who has been listening intently):* There! . . . The elevator took her down. . . .

PRINCE: Yes, you love her. But now, my iceberg boy, we both have disappeared.

STARK *(tremblingly):* I don't believe that. This isn't disappearance, when you're living, feeling what you never felt before.

PRINCE *(heavily):* Yes. . . .

STARK *(eyes flooding with tears):* I insist this is a beginning. Do you hear?—I insist.

PRINCE: I hear. . . . *(He slowly moves to the door.)* My mind is blank. Next week I'll buy myself a dog. . . .

STARK: You going home, Poppa?

PRINCE: It's Labor Day on Monday. In the morning I'm going to the mountains. I excuse you for the names you called me . . . as you excuse me.

STARK: Yes. . . .

PRINCE *(smiling faintly):* You'll permit me to come around and disturb you, as usual. Good-bye, Benny.

STARK: Good-bye, Poppa. *(They smile at each other.* PRINCE *goes to the door.)*

PRINCE *(at the door):* Go home, to my daughter. . . .

STARK *(slowly rises from his seat; calls* PRINCE *back):* Poppa, wait a minute. . . . *(Gropingly.)* For years I sat here, taking things for granted, my wife, everything. Then just for an hour my life was in a spotlight. . . . I saw myself clearly, realized who and what I was. Isn't that a beginning? Isn't it? . . .

PRINCE: Yes. . . .

STARK: And this is strange! . . . For the first time in years I don't feel guilty. . . . But I'll never take things for granted again. You see? Do you see, Poppa?

PRINCE: Go home, Benny. . . . *(He turns out the lamp.)*

STARK *(turning out the other lamp):* Yes, I, who sat here in this prison-office, closed off from the world . . . for the first time in years I looked out on the world and saw things as they really are. . . .

PRINCE *(wearily):* It's getting late. . . .

STARK *(almost laughing):* Sonofagun! . . . What I don't know would fill a book! (PRINCE *exits heavily.* STARK *turns out the last light, then exits, closing the door behind him. The room is dark, except for red neon lights of the Hotel Algiers and a spill of light from the hall.)*

Slow curtain